Spain in America

Hispanisms

Series Editor

Anne J. Cruz

*A list of books in the series
appears at the back of this book.*

Spain in America

The Origins of Hispanism in the United States

Edited by Richard L. Kagan

University of Illinois Press

Urbana and Chicago

Publication of this book was supported by a grant from the
Program for Cultural Cooperation between Spain's Ministry
of Education, Culture, and Sports and United States Universities.

Library of Congress Cataloging-in-Publication Data
Spain in America : the origins of hispanism in the United States /
edited by Richard L. Kagan.
p.   cm. — (Hispanisms)
Includes bibliographical references and index.
ISBN 0-252-02724-8 (alk. paper)
1. Spain—Civilization—Study and teaching—United States.
2. Spain—Foreign public opinion, American—History.
3. Public opinion—United States—History.
I. Kagan, Richard L., 1943– . II. Series.
DP48.S6118   2002
306'.0917'561—dc21   2001004253

To our friends and colleagues in Spain

Contents

The Image of Spain in the United States

Jonathan Brown

I have long been an avowed enemy of bullfighting and flamenco. It is not that these activities have come to typify Spain in the minds of my compatriots. Both spectacles require great skill and can be exciting to watch, assuming that one can stand the slaughter of the bull ring. And both have venerable histories. No, it is not the intrinsic worth of bullfighting and flamenco that perturbs me but rather the way in which they reduce the rich history and culture of Spain to the level of exotic folklore.

The question of how these two secondary manifestations of Spanish life came to assume such prominence in the image of Spain in the United States is worth pondering. Many answers appear in this admirable book, which, despite the multiplicity of authors and perspectives, has an undeniable unity. This unity is manifested above all in the tension between a genuine admiration for Spanish culture and the need to frame that culture by contrasting it to that of the United States. And this unity is enhanced by the chronological, geographical, and social matrix in which the North American image of Spain was formed.

As the reader will discover, our image of Spain was created by a Protestant intellectual and social elite centered in Boston and New York in the first half of the nineteenth century. United by time, place, and outlook, the creators of the American image of Spain—William H. Prescott, George Ticknor, Washington Irving, Henry Wadsworth Longfellow—largely agreed that Spain had been frozen in time by its slow pace of modernization. Spain continued to live in the past even as the United States was moving at full speed into the future. This American future, whatever its advantages, was also a frightening place; progress was threatening to compromise, even if it did not destroy the ideals in which these New Englanders and New Yorkers had a huge moral investment. Spain, where the past seemed alive and the present mostly absent (especially in the rural areas), provided an escape where romantic fantasies could be brought to life.

In viewing Spain through the lens of romantic nostalgia, Americans were hardly alone. This vision of Spain had been created in France early in the nineteenth century by writers and travelers such as Théophile Gautier. The French, like the Americans, wrote from the vantage point of powerful nation-states and imposed their interpretations on Spain and the Spanish, often shaping one-dimensional images that satisfied American and French needs at the cost of oversimplifying the complexities of the Spanish situation. Eventually, Spanish writers attempted to wrest control of their history from the foreign interpreters. This was one of the missions of the Generation of '98, the name given to a cluster of intellectuals who pondered Spain's past and future after their country's defeat in the Spanish-American War. However, this attempt, for all its brilliance, had an equivocal outcome. One set of topics, in effect, replaced another. Furthermore, it is safe to say that the writings of the Generation of '98 were little read in the United States, with the possible exception of the essays of José Ortega y Gasset, whose adherence to phenomenology situated his works within an international intellectual current.

The Generation of '98, in any case, was soon upstaged by the Lost Generation, the intellectual, pleasure-seeking nomads from the United States immortalized in Hemingway's novel, *The Sun Also Rises* (1926), which had more influence on the U.S. perception of Spain than any literary endeavor since Prescott's *History of the Reign of Ferdinand and Isabella* (1837). Yet just beneath Hemingway's steely prose lurk the old American verities about Spain; its quaint, picturesque image was shifted from Andalucian pueblos, redolent of the Moorish past, to the contemporary plaza de toros and the *tablao flamenco*. Every year, as the bulls thunder down the narrow streets of Pamplona, the ghost of Hemingway smiles with satisfaction and Washington Irving, standing in the background, nods approvingly.

The importance of Hemingway's novels for our story is surpassed only by the Spanish Civil War and the ensuing interminable years of the Franco dictatorship. Having entered the modern epoch during the tumultuous period of the Republic, Spain suddenly found itself in a netherworld of despotism that would last thirty-six years. These events made a deep, enduring impression on the U.S. intelligentsia, an impression that was constantly being reinforced by the Republican exiles who came to hold professorships in our universities.

My parents' friends, some of whom had fought in the Spanish Civil War, thought me treacherous when, in the early 1960s, I decided to study the history of Spanish art and consequently to spend long periods of time in what they disparagingly called "Franco's Spain." Since 1975, the year of Franco's death, Spain has undergone a widely admired transition to democracy and transformed itself into a vibrant, modern state. It is surely time for citizens of the United States to cast off the ideas initially formed by the writers and scholars of the nineteenth and early twentieth centuries. Indeed, only by understanding how that image was invented can we begin to change it. Toros and flamenco will occupy a small segment of the new picture, which will teem with the complex history and culture of Spain and the vitality and diversity that characterize it today.

Acknowledgments

This volume had its origins in a conference, "Spain and the United States: The Origins of American Hispanism," which was held at the Spanish Institute in New York City in October 1996. I am grateful to Inmaculada de Habsburgo, the Institute's director, for making that gathering possible and, in addition, for planting the seeds from which this volume eventually grew. Additional support came from Anne J. Cruz, of the University of Illinois at Chicago, and Willis G. Regier, director of the University of Illinois Press, whose foresight and encouragement made possible the publication of this book. I would also like to acknowledge the assistance provided by Theresa L. Sears, managing editor of the University of Illinois Press; our copy editor, Polly Kummel; and our indexer, Nancy Wolff. I especially want to thank all the contributors to this volume: their knowledge, and wisdom, helped make what once seemed a dream into reality.

—Richard L. Kagan

ferred also to that branch of Spanish studies practiced by individuals foreign to Spain itself.[6]

That *hispanismo* acquired this additional meaning at the start of the last century is best explained with reference to the spread, institutionalization, and professionalization of Hispanic studies in countries other than Spain itself. In France, a country where Spanish studies began in the eighteenth century, this development was reflected in the more or less simultaneous appearance of several journals exclusively devoted to Spanish subjects. The oldest was the *Revue hispanique,* founded in 1894 and published in Paris by the noted *hispaniste* Raymond Foulché-Delbosc (1864–1929). Its rival, printed in Bordeaux, was the *Bulletin hispanique,* started in 1899 under the direction of two historians, Alfred Morel-Fatio and Georges Cirot. Other landmarks in French *hispanisme* included the creation of the Institut des Études Hispaniques in 1912 and the publication of Ernesto Martinenche's *Les études hispaniques* (1916), a small book outlining the contributions of French scholars to Spanish studies.[7]

Similar developments were occurring elsewhere. Germany, like France, had a tradition of Spanish studies that dated to the eighteenth century and to the interest of Gotthold E. Lessing (1729–1781) in playwrights of Spain's Golden Age. Furthermore, by the end of that century the University of Göttingen had emerged as one of Europe's major centers for the study of the Spanish language and literature, attracting students from as far away as the United States. Göttingen's reputation in the area owed much to the presence there of several important scholars who engaged Spanish subjects, notably Friedrich Bouterwek (1766–1828), who helped to popularize the idea of a "national" literature in his massive *Geschichte der Poesie und Beredsamkeit . . .* (1801–19), one volume of which was dedicated to Spain.[8] Later in the nineteenth century Göttingen lost some of its prestige in the Hispanic field, but other universities— Berlin, Bonn, Munich, Weimar—took up the slack, especially in studies relating to Pedro Calderón de la Barca (1600–1681), the Spanish playwright preferred by German scholars. Such was this fascination that in 1906 a group of enthusiasts in Munich founded the Calderón Society for the Encouragement of Christian Theatrical Art. By this time, moreover, German scholars had emerged as pioneers in other areas of Spanish studies, especially the history of art, a field in which Karl Justi (1832–1912), a professor at Bonn and author of an important book on Velázquez, achieved particular distinction.[9]

The onset of the twentieth century also lent new impetus to Hispanic studies in Great Britain. Here too the study of Spanish history and literature had eighteenth-century roots, but it found an institutional base only in 1828 when the University of London created a professorship in Spanish literature for the exiled Spanish scholar Antonio Alcalá Galiano. Even then, most nineteenth-

3

century Britons who wrote about Spain—Lord Holland, Robert Southey, Richard Ford, George Borrow, and William Stirling-Maxwell—were independent scholars rather than university lecturers. In 1908, however, Cambridge created a lectureship in Spanish literature—it first went to James Fitzmaurice-Kelley (1858–1923), author of a new history of Spanish literature—and in 1909 the University of Liverpool created the Gilmour Chair in Spanish Language and Literature and used it to lure Fitzmaurice-Kelley away from Cambridge.[10] Other universities followed suit. In 1916 King's College, London, marked the three-hundredth anniversary of the death of Miguel de Cervantes Saavedra by creating the Cervantes Professorship of the Spanish Language and Literature.[11] Ten years later it was Oxford's turn. Thanks to a gift from Sir Robert Bedford, in 1926 the ancient university inaugurated the King Alfonso XIII Professorship of Spanish Studies. The creation of these chairs, part of a broader upturn in Spanish studies outside Spain, helps to explain why *hispanismo* adjusted its meaning when it did.[12]

Crucial to this etymological shift were the contributions of Hispanists in the United States. As in Europe, U.S. Hispanism had eighteenth-century roots. Garrat Noel, for example, published a textbook for the study of the Spanish language in 1751, and in 1766 a certain Paul Fooks was reported to have offered lessons in Spanish at the University of Pennsylvania.[13] In comparison to Europe, however, the colonies made no made independent contributions to Spanish scholarship, and indeed what little they knew about Spain came mainly from Continental authors. The only available English translation of *Don Quixote,* for example, was that completed in 1742 by the British scholar Charles Jarvis. Similarly, any colonists who wanted to read about Spanish history in English had to turn to the work of such Scottish historians as John Campbell, William Robertson, and Robert Watson.[14] Around 1800, however, a mixture of hemispheric politics and history not only increased American awareness of Spain but also led, rather more slowly, to the birth of Hispanism in the United States.

History came first, in the guise of the American Revolution (1775–1783), a conflict in which France and Spain, England's European enemies, quickly became embroiled. French support for the rebels was substantial, and most schoolchildren in the United States still learn something about the assistance provided by General Lafayette. In comparison, few learn about Bernardo de Gálvez, the Spanish governor of Louisiana whose troops seriously damaged British naval power in the Caribbean and the Gulf of Mexico and thus provided indirect aid for the rebel cause. Compared to France, however, Spain did relatively little to help the rebels, and for the most part its reigning Bourbon monarch, Charles III (1759–1788), only supported the Americans in the hope that a British defeat would enable him to recover those parts of Spanish America—Jamaica, Honduras, portions of west Florida—that the British, taking advantage of Spanish weakness, had occupied. As a result, relations between the Americans and the Spanish were often strained, as John Jay, the first American representative to Spain, discovered shortly after his arrival in Madrid in October 1780 on a mission to enlist Spanish aid. Jay was in a hurry; Charles was not and kept Jay waiting for almost two years. Furthermore, in marked contrast to the experiences of Carlos Martínez de Yrujo and other Spanish diplomats—who not only befriended George Washington but also married into American families and integrated quickly into American society—Jay complained about the lack of "sufficient opportunities of mixing with, and personally knowing many of them" (i.e., Spaniards).[15] Jay attributed his isolation to the monarch's personal reluctance to deal with the Americans, but it was also linked to such territorial issues as control of the Mississippi River, the Gulf Coast, and Florida, all of which remained sore points between the two countries for nearly forty years. Nevertheless, in the course of the early nineteenth century the two governments did manage to negotiate a series of bilateral agreements, notably the Transcontinental Treaty (1819) in which the United States obtained Florida, while Spain, in exchange for a vague U.S. promise to stay out of Mexico, recognized the validity of the Louisiana Purchase, a sale arranged by Thomas Jefferson with Napoleon in 1803. This treaty, however, symbolized the lopsided relationship between the two countries. Spain, weakened at home by an unpopular monarch and abroad by colonial revolt, was not in a position to bargain. Nor could the Spanish government do anything to prevent the United States from helping Spanish colonies in the Americas to achieve independence. Meanwhile, the United States used both its money and its muscle to pry open new markets in Cuba and, as articulated in the Monroe Doctrine (1823), to announce that America, both North and South, was for the Americans. According to this new policy of hemispheric politics, Spain (and the rest of Europe) had no business in the New World.

Despite these divergent interests, these efforts by the U.S. government to promote hemispheric politics worked, somewhat paradoxically but in accordance with what James D. Fernández calls "Longfellow's law," to foster the study of both the culture and language of Spain in the United States.[16] Here Thomas Jefferson played a crucial if not necessarily decisive role. Jefferson himself could read Spanish, although when he read *Don Quixote,* he apparently did so in translation. Before he became president, Jefferson was also in correspondence with a number of Spanish scientists, and his library—the core of today's Library of Congress—contained many Spanish books.[17] In 1779, moreover, Jefferson introduced modern languages, Spanish apparently among them, into the curriculum of the College of William and Mary and in 1818 made certain that instruction in the language would be offered at the soon-to-be-established University of Virginia.[18] Yet Jefferson's interest in Spanish was something other than academic, as a letter written to his nephew John Rutledge Jr. in 1788 seems to suggest. At the time Rutledge was traveling in Europe, and Jefferson, thinking about the future of the United States, urged him to visit both Lisbon and Madrid, specifically noting that "I should think the knowledge of their language, manners, and situation, might eventually and even probably become more useful to yourself and country than that of any other place you will have seen. The womb of time is big with events to take place between us and them, and a little knowledge of them will give you great advantage over those who have none at all."[19]

In this instance Jefferson did not define what he meant by "useful" or "advantage," but commerce, particularly with Spain's American colonies, was clearly on his mind. So too was the day when Spain's American colonies, independent and democratic, would enter into close association with the United States. More specifically, "useful" and "advantage" seem also to have referred to the acquisition of Florida and Louisiana by the United States, a process of expansion that Jefferson initiated when he negotiated the Louisiana Purchase, and opened preliminary discussions with the Spanish monarchy about buying "east" Florida for the United States. Jefferson, who was otherwise an ardent Francophile, seemingly promoted knowledge of Spanish less on account of its intrinsic merits or scientific importance but rather because he conceived of it as a "useful" diplomatic tool that ultimately could work to the "advantage" of his new country. In other words, self-interest in the guise of hemispheric politics and trade helped kindle U.S. interest in both Spain and its language.

This development did not occur overnight. For one thing, the United States had far greater commercial interest in Cuba—a source of sugar, molasses, lumber, and slaves—than in Spain itself. Nevertheless, trade between the two countries increased steadily and by the end of the eighteenth century reached the point at which a number of U.S. merchant houses found it useful to maintain permanent trade representatives (or factors) in Cádiz and other Spanish ports. As in the case of George Loring, a Massachusetts merchant in Málaga during the 1790s, some of these factors married into Spanish families; others learned the Spanish language, became "Hispaneolized," and served as cultural bridges between the two nations.[20] Notable in this regard was Obadiah Rich (1783–1850), another Massachusetts merchant, who arrived in Spain in 1807 and remained there until 1828. In 1818 Rich entered diplomatic service as the U.S. consul in Valencia and in 1823 moved to Madrid as secretary of the U.S. legation there. A lifelong bibliophile, Rich was a charter member of the Boston Atheneum and collected Spanish books and manuscripts, portions of which wound up in the Atheneum as well as in the New York Public Library.[21] While in Madrid, Rich also made friends with such scholars as Martín Fernández de Navarrete, the academician then in the process of editing an important collection of documents pertaining to the discovery of the Americas, and the important Arabist José Antonio Conde (1765–1820). Rich in turn introduced his Spanish friends to visiting Americans, among them Washington Irving and Henry Wadsworth Longfellow, two of the first U.S. writers ever to engage Spanish themes. Rich's Madrid library became Irving's most important resource during the two and a half years he spent in Spain. Following his return to the United States, Rich also made his collection of books and manuscripts available to George Ticknor, William H. Prescott, and other scholars with interests in Spain. In so doing, this merchant-turned-diplomat was instrumental in the birth of Hispanism in the United States.

Rich's example speaks to the importance of diplomats in fostering the initial interest of the United States in Spain and understanding its culture. In the beginning, as Jay's experience demonstrates, U.S. ministers in Madrid had a difficult time getting established, and few ever spent more than a year or two in the Spanish capital until after the end of the Peninsular War and the restoration of the Bourbon monarchy in 1814. These developments allowed for the establishment of a permanent U.S. diplomatic legation in Madrid and the arrival there of diplomats who managed to integrate into Spanish society, some to the point of acquiring a certain interest in and sympathy for Spanish culture. One of the first was George W. Erving (1771–1850), a diplomat who had first arrived in Madrid in 1805, was subsequently in and out of the country for reasons associated with the war against the French, and finally returned in 1816 as the permanent U.S. chargé d'affaires.[22] Erving's attitude toward Spain was somewhat ambivalent. As a Protestant, he complained that Spain was "a land ruled by priests." Yet Erving, a devoted man of letters, also acquired a particular interest in the Basque language and culture. This fascination led to his *Alphabet of the Primitive Language of Spain, and Philosophical Examination of the Antiquity and Civilization of the Basque People* (1829), a book based on a previous study by a Basque philologist who believed that Euskera was an antediluvian language, spoken by Noah and perhaps by Adam as well.[23]

Spanish culture also had a special appeal for Mordecai M. Noah, a Jewish Philadelphian who was sent on a diplomatic mission aimed at freeing American sailors taken prisoner by pirates stationed along the Barbary Coast. En route to North Africa in 1813, Noah spent several months in Spain, talking with American merchants in several of the ports that he visited and keeping a detailed travel journal in which he noted his impressions of the country and various reflections upon its history. These subsequently appeared in his *Trav-*

els in England, France, and Spain and the Barbary States in the Years 1813–4 and 1815 (1819), a volume that offered the first detailed description of Spain ever written by a citizen of the United States.[24] Other U.S. diplomats to write about Spain included Alexander Everett, minister plenipotentiary in Madrid from 1824 to 1828 and the official responsible for Washington Irving's invitation to Spain in 1826, and Caleb Cushing, who first visited Spain in 1829 and soon published *Reminiscences of Spain* (1833), another book that helped introduce Americans to the diversity of Spanish culture.

Beginning with these initial contacts, nineteenth-century U.S. Hispanism moved along two parallel tracks. One was literary and initially was epitomized in the work of Washington Irving, especially his enormously popular *Life and Voyages of Christopher Columbus* (1828), which was adopted for use in U.S. schools and universities throughout most of the nineteenth century. As Rolena Adorno observes, Irving tailored this romantic biography to appeal to a U.S. audience. He also provided the spark that fired what became the ongoing interest of the United States in Spain and its culture.[25] Irving's equally successful *The Alhambra* (1831) had much the same effect. In fact, the book's evocative tales of Moorish Spain and romanticized descriptions of Andalucia proved so popular that other authors—and their publishers—sought to imitate it, generally in the guise of imaginative travel books highlighting those aspects of Spain—gypsies, fandangos, bullfights, pícaros, and the like—thought to be picturesque. The first such book, written by a friend of Irving's, was Alexander Slidell Mackenzie's *A Year in Spain* (1829). Following it were others by Caroline Cushing, her husband, Caleb, and Longfellow, all of which bore the romantic imprint that Irving had helped to create.[26] Dissenters existed, among them the Baltimore author Severn Teackle Wallis, whose own contribution to this genre, *Glimpses of Spain* (1847), attempted to persuade Americans that Spain was less romantic than modern. Yet the romantic view had such broad and lasting appeal that those Americans who wrote about Spain later in the nineteenth century—they included John Hay, Kate Field, H. C. Chatfield-Taylor, and James Russell Lowell—did so in ways that reinforced the popular image of Spaniards as a pleasing but backward people who were caught in a time warp that prevented them from embracing modernity of any sort.[27] Admittedly, such an image failed to embrace the reality of a country that, especially at the end of the nineteenth century, was experiencing dramatic change: new industries and railroads, the creation of a modern banking system, and, starting with the Constitution of 1876, the beginnings of democratic government. On the other hand, gypsies sold books, and in general the romantic view of Spain, whatever its defects, carved out a niche for Spain in the U.S. literary imagination while also serving to promote broader U.S. interest in Spanish history, language, and art.

U.S. Hispanism's other track followed the scholarly path originally blazed in Europe by Bouterwek, his Swiss disciple, J. C. L. Sismonde di Sismondi (1773–1842), and other scholars interested in the influence of national character upon history and literature.[28] One of the first to take this particular route was George Ticknor (1791–1881), a Bostonian who, after having abandoned the law for a career in letters, traveled to Göttingen in 1815 to study literature with Bouterwek. While Ticknor was there, Harvard College appointed him to its newly established Smith Professorship of the French and Spanish Languages, a position that Ticknor assumed in 1819 after short visits to both France and Spain. At this point Ticknor decided that his scholarly future lay with Spain, and as Smith Professor he delivered lectures on Spanish literature and drama that culminated in his massive *History of Spanish Literature* (1849). This book, a triumph on both sides of the Atlantic, represents one of the crowning achievements of early Hispanism in the United States.

Ticknor's counterpart in history was his friend and fellow Bostonian William Hickling Prescott (1796–1859), a gentleman scholar who became one of the most respected historians of his generation. Like Edward Gibbon before him, Prescott conceived of history on an epic scale: the discovery and conquest of continents, the dynamics of territorial expansion, the rise and fall of nations—these and other grandly conceived subjects all fell within his ken. Prescott sought also to infuse history with philosophical insights about issues that he considered transcendental: political liberty, religious freedom, the role of Providence in human affairs. Initially, he conceived of writing this kind of history with reference to such established themes as the Roman Republic or the Italian Renaissance, but by the mid-1820s, influenced in part by Ticknor, Prescott became interested in Spain because it offered an example of an expansive people who discovered and then conquered America but whose energy and enterprise were seemingly cut short by a pernicious combination of religious bigotry and royal absolutism. Spain's turning point, Prescott concluded, occurred during the reign of the Catholic Monarchs Ferdinand and Isabella (1474–1516), and this eventually became the subject of his masterful *History of the Reign of Ferdinand and Isabella* (1837), a narrative whose powerful character portraits, painterly prose, and wealth of historical detail appealed to a wide audience. Prescott's histories of the conquest of Mexico (1843) and Peru (1847), and his later biography of Philip II (1855), further whetted the U.S. appetite for Spanish history, even though it did so, somewhat paradoxically, in an openly negative way. Prescott's portrayal of Spain as a failed nation that had allowed progress to slip through its hands helped forge what, in a previous essay (see the appendix), I called "Prescott's paradigm" and defined "as an understanding of Spain as America's antithesis." Spain was "everything that the United

States was not. America was the future—republican, enterprising, rational; while Spain—monarchical, indolent, fanatic—represented the past."[29] As it developed, Prescott's paradigm was less a clear analytical model of analysis than a series of assumptions and presuppositions about the inherent backwardness of Spanish culture and the progressiveness and superiority of that of the United States. Combined with the pervasive belief in national character engendered by the rise of nineteenth-century nationalism, Prescott's ideas managed to exert a powerful influence on the way that later generations of U.S. historians thought and wrote about Spain. His influence, for example, was clearly evident in John S. C. Abbott's overtly critical *The Romance of Spanish History* (1869) as well as in the history of Spain by Edward Everett Hale that appeared in the popular *History of Nations* series in 1886. Other historians who wrote well within the confines of Prescott's paradigm included John Lothrop Motley, famous for his history of the Dutch Republic, and Hubert Howe Bancroft, one of the first U.S. historians to chronicle the history of the American Southwest.

After Ticknor and Prescott little remains to be said about either the importance or originality of nineteenth-century U.S. Hispanism. The histories published by Abbott and Hale were popular works and could not begin to compare with those published by Leopold von Ranke (1795–1886) or Louis-Prosper Gachard (1800–1885), pioneers in the new kind of "scientific" history grounded in original documents and archival research that emerged in Europe in the middle years of the nineteenth century.[30] After Ticknor, in fact, U.S. scholarship on Spanish literature went into the doldrums even as the number of U.S. colleges offering instruction in the Spanish language began to increase. Yale added the language in 1826, and in 1830 Mariano Velázquez de la Cadena, compiler of what became a standard Spanish-English dictionary, became Columbia's first professor of the Spanish language and literature.[31] Yet professors in this era were generally teachers first, scholars second, and most lacked the resources and the inclination to pursue original research. What happened at Harvard is typical. Longfellow succeeded Ticknor as Smith Professor in 1836 and remained in this position until 1854. While at Bowdoin, his previous teaching position, Longfellow had published several articles on Spanish poetry and one on the history of the Spanish language. He also had prepared an English translation of Jorge Manrique's *Coplas por la muerte de su padre* in addition to completing *Outre-Mer,* a "European sketch book" that included several poetic passages about Spain. At Harvard, Longfellow's fascination with Spain continued, and he once acknowledged that inspiration for his play *The Spanish Student,* which dates to around 1840, came from the "exquisite" Spanish dances of a woman whose movements not only reminded him "of days gone by" but also stirred his romantic imagination (and, possibly, something else).[32]

Longfellow's teaching at Harvard even included a course on the history of Spanish drama, and his general survey of European poetry touched briefly upon Spanish authors. On the other hand, except for a few translations of Spanish poems, Longfellow's tenure as Smith Professor did not result in much original writing about Spanish subjects.[33] The same can be said of his successor, James Russell Lowell, Smith Professor from 1854 until 1891. Although "drawn," as he put it, to both Cervantes and Calderón, Lowell knew relatively little about Spain or its literature until 1877, when he was named U.S. minister in Madrid. Once there Lowell perfected his Spanish but his letters—published posthumously in the form of a travel book, *Impressions of Spain* (1899)—reveal his ambivalence about Spanish culture and his tendency to view Spaniards as a "semioriental people" ill equipped to enter the modern world.[34] Otherwise, Lowell wrote—and apparently taught—little either about Spain or its literature. Strictly speaking, a Hispanist he was not.

Yet for all his fame as a preeminent man of letters, Lowell was something of an anachronism by the time he retired from Harvard in 1891. By then the scholarly climate of the United States had changed. Starting with the establishment of Johns Hopkins in 1872, major universities expected their faculty to combine teaching with research, generally in some specialized area or field. In history this new emphasis led to the rise of subspecialties in specific geographical regions or subdisciplines—economics, political institutions, social change—that eventually coalesced into separate social sciences. Specialization also facilitated the spread of positivism, the rejection of Prescott's brand of epic history, and its replacement by the new species of fact-driven "scientific" history associated with von Ranke. This evolution, moreover, occurred just as Americans developed new interests in Latin America as well as those portions of their own country—the Southwest and so-called borderlands—that were formerly under Spanish rule. Thus in keeping with Longfellow's law, scholars who worked in these areas—two pioneers were Frank Blackmar of Kansas State and Bernard Moses of Berkeley—were necessarily obliged to learn more about Spain itself.[35]

In literature specialization took a somewhat different tack, although this discipline, in keeping with the times, also looked to positivism as way of escaping from the canon of "national" literature earlier espoused by Bouterwek and Ticknor. Positivism, with its emphasis on "facts" as opposed to "interpretation," implied a historical approach to literature that placed a premium on documenting the lives of individual authors and the publication of new editions of previously neglected authors and texts. At the end of the nineteenth century U.S. universities stood at the forefront of this new trend, and it was this, probably more than anything else, that contributed to the rise of U.S. Hispanism and elicited the favorable comments from Unamuno and Hume cited at the beginning of this introduction. Another sign of the times was the appointment in 1907 of J. D. M. Ford to the Smith chair at Harvard. As noted earlier, James Russell Lowell, Ford's predecessor, was a distinguished man of letters who, although drawn to Spanish literature, did not do much research in this (or any other) literary field. In contrast, Ford had already published two monographs—one on the eighteenth-century Venetian dramatist Carlo Goldoni, another, *The Old Spanish Sibilants,* on Spanish phonetics—before assuming the chair, and he continued to make important scholarly contributions thereafter. Finally, the Spanish-American War of 1898 and the U.S. acquisition of Cuba, Puerto Rico, and the Philippines, together with the prospects of increased trade with Spanish America, sparked new interest in the Spanish language. In 1885 the United States had only about ten Spanish professorships. By 1900 scarcely a major U.S. institution of higher learning failed to offer its students opportunities to learn Spanish and something about Spanish literature as well.[36]

In order to appreciate the full extent of U.S. contributions to the birth of *hispanismo* as a recognized field, there is no better place to begin than Miguel Romera-Navarro's *El hispanismo en Norte América* (1917). Romera-Navarro (1888–1954), a Spanish émigré then teaching at the University of Pennsylvania, apparently wrote this book in an effort to boost his countrymen's pride after their disastrous defeat by the United States in the war of 1898.[37] He especially wanted Spaniards to understand that the United States still respected their language, literature, and culture, and in the preface he announced, quite correctly, that "the history and exposition of literary hispanism in the United States remains to be written." What followed was an attempt to provide his readers with a broad sampling of what Americans were writing about Spain.

The opening section, dedicated to the "precursors" of U.S. Hispanism, examined the contributions of Irving, Ticknor, Prescott, Longfellow, and Lowell. He also singled out for discussion The Hispanic Society of America, founded in 1904. The rest of the book divided the contributions of U.S. Hispanists into a series of loosely defined genres: "contemporaries," "expositors and critics," "biographers and historians," "collectors and commentators," "travelers," and so on. Each section offered a detailed bibliography and examined in detail those whom Romera-Navarro especially admired. This pantheon included Archer M. Huntington, lauded both for his work at The Hispanic Society and for his edition and translation of *El Cid.* Romera-Navarro also accorded special attention to Hugo Rennert and his disciple, J. P. Wickersham Crawford, a scholar best known for his 1907 biography of the seventeenth-century author Cristóbal Suárez de Figueroa; Carlos Upson Clark, a Yale historian who wrote bout Visigothic Spain; Frank W. Chandler, a specialist in the picaresque novel; Chandler Rathfon Post, the Harvard professor who had published a book on medieval Spanish allegory and was soon to embark on a major study of Spanish art; the historian Henry Charles Lea; and Edward G. Bourne, a historian whose *Spain and America* (1907) offered a sympathetic account of Spanish activities in the New World. Yet for all its usefulness as a bio-bibliography, Romera-Navarro's survey did not attempt to explain the U.S. interest in Hispanic culture, nor did it offer any conjectures about the future of Hispanism in the United States. It was simply a celebration of the ongoing U.S. engagement with Spain.

The next major—one might almost say, definitive—account of U.S. Hispanism was that of Stanley T. Williams, *The Spanish Background of American Literature,* published in 1955. Williams, a professor of U.S. literature at Yale, came to this subject through his earlier research on Washington Irving. Through this writer he became interested in what he called the Spanish influence on U.S. literature as well as "the diverse channels by which Spanish culture has become part of our own."[38] Like Romera-Navarro before him, he approached his subject historically and via such generic categories as travelers, writers for periodicals, teachers, and scholars. Ultimately, he compiled a comprehensive list of U.S. writers who, starting in the early nineteenth century, developed a fascination for Spain and Spanish America. All this, however, was but a prelude (a mere 443 pages!) to eight writers whom Williams considered "the major interpreters in American literature of Spanish and Spanish-American culture." This group included many of the same figures—Irving, Ticknor, Prescott, Longfellow, Lowell—highlighted by Romera-Navarro, but it also embraced William Cullen Bryant, a poet who dabbled in Spanish subjects; the California novelist Bret Harte; and William Dean Howells, an essayist who, despite a lifelong passion for Spain, never managed to visit the country until he was seventy-four. In this sense Williams was less interested in Hispanism per se than in the influence of Spanish (and to a much lesser degree, Spanish-American) culture upon the literary imagination of the United States.

Of almost equal importance was Williams's concern with the way his writers interpreted what he alternately defined as the "soul" of Spain, the "Spanish mind," the "Spanish whole," and the *personalismo* that he equated with the "Spanish passion for the separate man [that] creates individuals, each inviolate, each in himself a walled city, yet each a part of Spain."[39] This preoccupation with the Spanish "essence" can be traced to Bouterwek and the generalized nineteenth-century belief in national character. More directly, it derived from attempts by Spanish writers who belonged to the famous Generation of '98 to define *Spanishness* and, along with it, their nation's relationship with modernity. Of particular importance here was the work of two philosophers, Unamuno, the most senior member of the Generation of '98 (Unamuno was actually born in 1846), and José Ortega y Gasset (1883–1955), both of whom devoted important works to outlining the major features of the Spanish character.[40] Williams's fascination with the definitions of *Spanishness* also came from Salvador de Madariaga, an influential and prolific Spanish émigré scholar whose interpretation of "the genius of Spain" was distinctly Unamuno-esque—it was quasi-biological, fundamentally immutable, and uniform to the extent that it tended to ignore cultural and linguistic differences within Spain itself.[41]

To be fair, Williams was not alone in applying this essentialist approach to Spanish culture. Rather, it was part and parcel of a generation of scholars who, still working under the influence of Prescott's paradigm and having confronted both the horrors of Spain's civil war (1936–39) and the misery and repression that accompanied the start of General Franco's fascist regime, questioned the ability of Spaniards to cope with modern, Western-style democratic politics. In the process many tended to compartmentalize Spaniards, almost to the point of considering them a race apart. Some, like Claudio Sánchez-Albornoz (1893–1982), a noted medievalist and civil war exile, argued powerfully in favor of the notion of "eternal Spain" in his *Spain: A Historical Enigma,* first published in 1956.[42] Others, like Américo Castro (1885–1972), another exile who spent part of his distinguished scholarly career in the United States, adopted a more historicist approach to Spanish history, notably in his *Structure of Spanish History* (1954), a book that enjoyed remarkable popularity, particularly among U.S. Hispanists, during the 1950s and 1960s.[43] In this and other books Castro argued that the Spanish character had less to do with racial than with various historical factors, the most important of which was the intermingling of Christians, Jews, and Moors during the Middle Ages. Yet even avowed historicists like Castro were reluctant to surrender the idea of Spanish difference, and his ideas concerning the peculiar characteristics of "Spanishness" inspired other scholars—historians, literary critics, political scientists—to explore the various racial and historical elements that allegedly rendered Spaniards unique. In 1964, for example, Donald E. Worcester, in a controversial article, cited Castro directly in an effort to explain that the Spanish (and, by extension, the Spanish-American) temperament disposed it to "orthodoxy and absolutism" as opposed to democratic political regimes.[44] Similar arguments can be found in John Crow's *The Root and the Flower* (1963), a popular history that argued that Spaniards belonged to an "Afro-Semitic race" whose exaggerated sense of individualism was incompatible with "the primary values of the west."[45]

In this respect Williams's search for the Spanish "essence" was simply part of the times, and basically it represents a moment in U.S. history when, as a result of Francoism, both scholarly and popular interest in all things Spanish seemed to erode. On the other hand, the death of Franco in 1975 and Spain's subsequent rapid and remarkably successful transition to democracy quickly put an end to this situation. These events also triggered the beginnings of a new, and much more positive, moment in the history of Hispanism in the United States, one in which the last vestiges of Prescott's paradigm began to erode.[46]

Viewed from this perspective, Williams's book is a period piece, one that still conceived of Spain as a nation far removed from the modern world. Despite these prejudices, it remains a gold mine of information about U.S. writers who cultivated Spanish subjects. On the other hand, it does not specifically address the origins of U.S. Hispanism, nor does it fully explain the circumstances surrounding the study of Spanish history, literature, music, and art in the United States. This is the lacuna that this volume proposes to fill.

Notes

1. Martin Hume, "The United States and Spain," *International Conciliation* 23 (October 1909): 3–9, quote on 5.

2. Hugo Rennert's books included *The Life of Lope de Vega, 1562–1635* (Glasgow: Gowans and Gray, 1904) and *The Spanish Stage in the Time of Lope de Vega* (New York: Hispanic Society of America, 1909). As for Henry Charles Lea, I refer to his *History of the Inquisition of Spain*, 4 vols. (New York: Macmillan, 1906–7). Samuel Parsons Scott also translated and published *The Visigothic Code (Forum Judicum)* (Boston: Boston Book Co., 1910).

3. Miguel de Unamuno, "Los hispanistas norteaméricanos" (Salamanca, agosto de 1906), in Miguel de Unamuno, *De Patriotismo espiritual: Artículos de "La Nación" de Buenos Aires, 1901–1914*, ed. Victor Ouimette (Salamanca: Universidad de Salamanca, 1997), 58.

4. *Diccionario de literatura española*, 3d ed. (Madrid: Revista de Occidente, 1964), 387.

5. For a recent examination of some English and American Hispanophiles, Ernest Hemmingway and Gerald Brennan among them, see Tomás Burns Marañón, *Hispanomania* (Barcelona: Plaza and James, 2000).

6. Ramón Menéndez Pidal's lecture, "El hispanismo en Alemania, los Estados Unidos, Inglaterra, Francia e Italia, en sus tres aspectos, literario, lingüístico, y utilitario," was delivered at Madrid's Centro de Estudios Históricos and is mentioned in *Diccionario de la literatura española*, 387. Note that during the twentieth century *Hispanismo* acquired other, more cultural, even racial, meanings. See, for example, Frederick B. Pike, *Hispanismo, 1898–1936: Spanish Conservatives and Liberals and Their Relations with Spanish America* (Notre Dame, Ind.: University of Notre Dame Press, 1971), 1–9, where *hispanismo* becomes an antecedent to *hispanidad*, a term used by the regime of General Franco to connect Spain with Spanish America. I am grateful to James Fernández for this reference.

7. The history of French Hispanism is examined in Antonio Niño, *Cultura y diplomacia: Los hispanistas franceses y España de 1875–1931* (Madrid: C.S.I.C., 1988).

8. See Friedrich Bouterwek, *Geschichte der Poesie und Beredsamkeit seit dem Ende des dreizehnten Jahrhunderts,* 12 vols. (Göttingen: J. F. Röwer, 1801–19), the third volume of which, published in 1803, dealt with Spain. This volume was translated into French as *L'Histoire de la littérature espagnole* (Paris: Renard, 1812) and into English as the *History of Spanish Literature* (London: David Bogne, 1847).

9. Karl Justi's masterpiece is *Diego Velázquez und sein Jahrhundert* (Berlin: Bonn, Cohen and Sohn, 1888). It appeared in English translation in 1889. My information on German Hispanism derives principally from Henry W. Sullivan, *Calderón in the German Lands and the Low Countries: His Reception and Influence, 1654–1980* (Cambridge: Cambridge University Press, 1983).

10. I refer to James Fitzmaurice-Kelley, *A History of Spanish Literature* (London: William Heinemann, 1898).

11. The Cervantes chair first went to Fitzmaurice-Kelley. For details on this famous Hispanist's career see John D. Fitz-Gerald, "James Fitzmaurice-Kelley," *Bulletin of Spanish Studies* 7 (1930): 129–35.

12. The history of British Hispanism is briefly examined in Antonio Pastor, "Breve historia del hispanismo inglés," *Arbor* 28, no. 9 (1948): 549–66.

13. Garrat Noel, *A Short Introduction to the Spanish Language* (New York: N.p., 1751). Paul Fooks is mentioned in Henry Grattan Doyle, "Spanish Studies in the United States," *Bulletin of Spanish Studies* 2 (1924–25): 163–73. For the teaching of Spanish in the colonies see Stanley T. Williams, *The Spanish Background of American Literature,* 2 vols. (New Haven, Conn.: Yale University Press, 1955), 1:3–47. Other studies include Harry Bernstein, "Las primeras relaciones intelectuales entre New England y el mundo hispánico, 1700–1815," *Revista hispánica moderna* 5 (1939): 1–17, and Edith F. Helman, "Early Interest in Spanish in New England (1815–1835)," *Hispania* 29 (1946): 326–51.

14. John Campbell wrote about Spain in *A Concise History of the Spanish America* (London: N.p., 1741), *The Present State of Europe* (London: T. Longman and C. Hitch, 1753), 304–56, and in volumes 20–22 of *An Universal History,* 65 vols. (London: N.p., 1747–66). William Robertson was known both for his *History of the Reign of Charles the Fifth,* 3 vols. (London: W. and W. Strahan, 1769) and his *History of America,* 2 vols. (London: Printed for Messrs. Whitestone, 1777), Robert Watson for his *History of the Reign of Philip II,* 2 vols. (London: W. Strahan, 1777).

15. John Jay to Robert Morris, April 25, 1782, *Correspondence and Public Papers of John Jay,* 4 vols. (New York: G. P. Putnam's Sons, 1890–93), 2:198. For an introduction to Spanish-American relations in the eighteenth century, see Darío Fernández Flórez, *The Spanish Heritage in the United States* (Madrid: Publicaciones Españolas, 1965); Carlos M. Fernández-Shaw, *Presencia española en los Estados Unidos* (Madrid: Cultura Hispánica, 1972); and James W. Cortada, *Two Nations over Time: Spain and the United States, 1776–1977* (Westport, Conn.: Greenwood, 1978), 3–19. Jay's embassy is the subject of Rafael Sánchez Mantero's "La misión de John Jay en España (1779–1782)," *Anuario de Estudios Americanos* 24 (1967): 1389–1431. Diplomatic haggling between the two countries during the American Revolution is explored in Enrique Fernández y Fernán-

dez, "Spain's Contribution to the Independence of the United States," *Revista/Review Interamericana* 10 (Fall 1980): 290–304.

16. See James D. Fernández's essay in this volume.

17. For Jefferson and Spain see Williams, *Spanish Background*, 1:24–26. Jefferson's contacts with Spanish scientists, among them Juan Bautista Bru de Ramón, director of Madrid's Real Gabinete de Historia Natural, are discussed in José María López Piñero and Thomas F. Glick, *El Megatorio de Bru y el Presidente Jefferson* (Valencia: Universidad de Valnecia/C.S.I.C., 1993).

18. For Jefferson's interest in the teaching of Spanish see Rolena Adorno's essay in this volume, especially note 10.

19. *The Papers of Thomas Jefferson*, vol. 13: *March to 7 October 1788*, ed. Julian P. Boyd (Princeton, N.J.: Princeton University Press, 1956), 358. Note that Jefferson promoted the study of language as early as 1787 in a letter to T. M. Randolph Jr.: "With respect to modern languages, French, as I have observed, is indispensable. Next to this, the Spanish is the most important to an American. . . . Besides this, the ancient part of American history is written chiefly in Spanish" (*Papers of Thomas Jefferson*, vol. 11: *1 January to 6 August 1787*, ed. Julian P. Boyd [Princeton, N.J.: Princeton University Press, 1955], 558).

20. For Loring see Williams, *Spanish Background*, 1:327.

21. For Rich see Norman P. Tucker, *Americans in Spain: Patriots, Expatriots, and Early American Hispanists, 1780–1850* (Boston: Athenaeum, 1980). I have not been able to consult his "Obadiah Rich, 1783–1850: Early American Hispanist" (Ph.D. diss., Harvard University, 1973).

22. On Erving and other diplomats of this generation, see French E. Chadwick, *The Relations of the United States and Spain: Diplomacy* (New York: Charles Scribner's Sons, 1909).

23. Erving's work was based on Juan Bautista de Erro y Azpiroz, *Alfabeto de la lengua primitiva de España, y explicación de sus más antiguos monumentos de inscripciones y medallas* (Madrid: Imprenta de Repullés, 1806).

24. For Noah see Jonathan D. Sarna, *Jacksonian Jew: The Two Worlds of Mordecai Noah* (New York: Holmes and Meier, 1981), and *The Selected Writings of Mordecai Noah*, ed. Michael Schuldiner and Daniel J. Kleinfeld (Westport, Conn.: Greenwood, 1999).

25. See Adorno's essay in this volume.

26. For nineteenth-century U.S. travelers in Spain, see Williams, *Spanish Background*, 1:51–101. See also C. Evangeline Farnham, "American Travelers in Spain (1777–1867)," *Romanic Review* (1922): 44–64, 252–330, and Tucker, *Americans in Spain*.

27. I refer here to John Hay, *Castilian Days* (Boston: James R. Osgood and Co., 1871), Kate Field, *Ten Days in Spain* (Boston: James R. Osgood and Co., 1875), H. C. Chatfield-Taylor, *Land of the Castinet* (Chicago: Herbert S. Stone, 1896), and James Russell Lowell, *Impressions of Spain* (Boston: Houghton Mifflin, 1898). One Spanish reviewer, insulted by the title of Chatfield-Taylor's book, suggested that it was the equivalent of calling the United States "*la tierra del bacón*" (the land of bacon). See Rafael Sánchez Mantero, "La imagen de España en los Estados Unidos," in *La imagen de España en*

América, 1898–1931, ed. Rafael Sánchez Mantero, José Manuel Macarro Vera, and Leandro Alverez Rey (Sevilla: Escuela de Estudios Hispano-Americanos, 1994), 38–39.

28. Bouterwek and his school are best approached through Thomas R. Hart Jr., "Friedrich Bouterwek: A Pioneer Historian of Spanish Literature," *Comparative Literature* 5 (1953): 351–61.

29. See the appendix, p. 253.

30. Leopold von Ranke's *The Ottoman and the Spanish Empires in the Sixteenth and Seventeenth Centuries* first appeared in English in 1843. Louis-Prosper Gachard, a Belgian historian who was among the first scholars to use documents from Spain's Archivo General de Simancas, was the author of *Correspondance de Philippe II et les Pas-Bays, 1558–1577* (1848) and studies that dealt with both Spain and the Low Countries in the sixteenth century.

31. Initially published as *A Dictionary of the Spanish and English Languages* (New York: N.p., 1855), what became known as the Velázquez dictionary appeared in many revised editions.

32. Cited in Williams, *Spanish Imagination,* 2:162. The dancer was Fanny Essler.

33. See Carl L. Johnson, *Professor Longfellow at Harvard* (Eugene: University of Oregon Press, 1944), and Dwight C. Marshall, "Professor Longfellow at Harvard," *Bulletin of Spanish Studies* 21 (1944): 227–30.

34. James Russell Lowell, letter dated May 4, 1879, Madrid, cited in Williams, *Spanish Background,* 1:197.

35. For a discussion of these scholars see my essay (chapter 1) in this volume.

36. For the evolution of the teaching of Spanish in U.S. higher education, see Charles H. Handschin, *Modern Language Teaching* (Yonkers-on-Hudson, N.Y.: World Book Co., 1940), and Madaline Wallis Nichols, "The History of Spanish and Portuguese Teaching in the United States," in *A Handbook on the Teaching of Spanish and Portuguese,* ed. Henry Grattan Doyle (Boston: D. C. Heath, 1945), 97–146.

37. In 1927 Romera-Navarro became a naturalized citizen of the United States and moved to the University of Texas at Austin, where he published extensively on Golden Age literature. For U.S. attitudes toward Spain during and after the Spanish-American War, see Rafael Sánchez Mantero, "La imagen de Espana en los Estados Unidos," 17–60.

38. Williams, *Spanish Background,* 1:xxi.

39. Ibid., 2:288–89.

40. Miguel de Unamuno's interest in the peculiar characteristics of Spanishness was manifested in his essay "En torno al casticismo," first published in 1902, whereas José Ortega y Gasset dealt with this subject in his influential *España invertebrada* (Madrid: Calpe, 1921).

41. Salvador de Madariaga was the first Alfonso XIII Professor at Oxford. His books touching on the issue of the Spanish temperament include *Englishmen, Frenchmen, Spaniards: An Essay in Comparative Psychology* (London: Oxford University Press, 1928) and *The Genius of Spain and Other Essays on Spanish Contemporary Literature* (Oxford: Clarendon Press, 1923).

42. This thesis is elaborated in Claudio Sánchez-Albornoz, *España, un enigma histórico*, 2 vols. (Buenos Aires: Editorial Sudamericana, 1956). This appeared in English as *Spain, a Historical Enigma*, trans. Colette Joly Dees and David Sven Reher, 2 vols. (Madrid: Fundación Universitaria Española, 1975). This book was essentially written to refute the ideas of another Spanish exile, Américo Castro, whose work is cited in note 43.

43. This book is a translation of Américo Castro's *España en su historia: Cristianos, moros y judíos* (Buenos Aires: Editorial Losada, 1948), in which he argues for the importance of the Middle Ages in the development of the Spanish character. Castro also addressed the issue of the Spanish character in *The Spaniards: An Introduction to Their History*, trans. Willard F. King and Selma Margaretten (Berkeley: University of California Press, 1971), a later work in which he wrote that "the Spaniards created for themselves a very unique civilization, one of whose most outstanding aspects was to affirm man's absolute or combative worth and self-reliance against his environment" (568). See also his *La realidad histórica de España* (México: Editorial Porrúa, 1954). For Castro's influence see Ronald E. Surtz, Jaime Ferrán, and Daniel P. Testa, eds., *Américo Castro: The Impact of His Thought* (Madison, Wis.: Hispanic Seminary of Medieval Studies, 1988).

44. Donald E. Worcester, "Historical and Cultural Sources of Spanish Resistence to Change," *Journal of Interamerican Studies* 6 (1964): 173–80.

45. John Crow, *The Root and the Flower* (New York: Harper and Row, 1963), 12. The book was re-edited in 1985.

46. For a current look at the state of U.S. Hispanism, with particular emphasis on literary criticism, see José M. del Pino and Francisco La Rubia Prado, eds., *El hispanismo en los Estados Unidos* (Madrid: Visor, 1999).

~~ 1

From Noah to Moses: The Genesis of Historical Scholarship on Spain in the United States
Richard L. Kagan

"Spain never changes." So wrote the British missionary George Borrow in 1843.[1] In this pithy phrase, Borrow summarized the romantic view of a nation so backward that it actually became "picturesque," a word that evoked the singular kind of beauty nineteenth-century travelers equated with rural areas or those so backward to be regarded as quaint. Borrow's notion of timeless Spain also reflected the growing importance accorded to the concept of national character as a key factor in history. As formulated by the eighteenth-century German philosopher Johann Gottfried von Herder, national character was a biological, almost racial, construct that manifested itself early in the history of every people, or *volk,* and subsequently charted the course of their future accomplishments, their culture, even the kind of governing institutions that they evolved.[2] National character was also held responsible for the particular "genius," best manifested in literature and art, that rendered every nation, Spain among them, both exceptional and unique.

Spain, the United States, and the "Picturesque"

Similar notions of national character quickly took root in the young United States. As David Tyack has demonstrated, the start of what later became known as "American exceptionalism" and the attendant idea of a distinctive Anglo-Saxon, soon to be labeled "American," race can be traced to the colonial era.[3] This movement surged after the U.S. victory over Britain in the War of 1812, when it found literary expression in the work of Joseph Cogswell, Edward Everett, and other conservative Whig writers, all of whom tended to conceive of the United States as the embodiment of progress and enlightened thought and regarded race as one of the factors that had contributed to the country's success.[4] For these and other proponents of American exceptionalism, the citizens of the United States represented a distinctive people endowed with such hereditary characteristics as a propensity for republican forms of government, a penchant for hard work, and a capacity to embrace various forms of technological innovation and change. Europeans, the British in particular, were thought to exhibit some if not all of these traits, but other peoples—blacks, Native Americans, Arabs, and Asians—did not and were consequently labeled "inferior." As for Spaniards, their country's Muslim heritage linked them to the Orient and thus assigned them retrograde status, a prejudice confirmed by their seeming inability at the start of the nineteenth century to embrace democratic forms of government, to industrialize, or even to defend their empire. Initially, racialized discourses of this kind applied only to economic and political issues; but owing to the growing influence of Herder and other European writers who postulated a direct link between national character and all forms of artistic expression, what is now referred to as "cultural racialism" allowed U.S. scholars to explain what they perceived as the distinctive, and from their perspective backward, qualities of Spanish culture in racial or quasi-racial terms.

Compounding this perception of Spain as an inferior "other" was the Black Legend, the centuries-old cluster of Protestant beliefs that the United States inherited from the British and, to a certain degree, from the Dutch.[5] The Black Legend equated Spain with the Inquisition, religious bigotry, and the bloody persecution of Protestants and Jews. It also conjured up images of despotic monarchs who denied their subjects access to any semblance of economic and political freedom and who had consequently set Spain onto the road to economic weakness and political decline. Such a reading of Spanish history was overly simplistic, but early nineteenth-century promoters of American exceptionalism found it useful to see Spain as an example of what would happen to a country whose fundamental values were antithetical to those of the United States. If the latter embodied democracy, liberty, and enlightenment, then Spain was the opposite. This formulation helps to explain why U.S. scholars, especially those with Whiggish inclinations, developed a particular fascination with Spanish history and culture.[6] For these scholars the United States was the future and Spain represented the past. They wanted to know why Spain, as compared with the United States, had failed to progress.

To be sure, most Americans at the start of the nineteenth century knew relatively little about Spain and probably cared less, even though libraries of the period contained a relatively large selection of books relating to Spain and to Spanish America.[7] During the colonial era knowledge of Spain derived primarily from English and Scottish writers such as John Campbell, William Robertson, and Adam Smith and from sermons—those of Cotton Mather and Samuel Sewall regularly bashed Spain—that were inspired by the Black Legend and represented the dark side of Spain and its people. By the nineteenth century, however, these old prejudices had combined with the emergent, racially based notions of national character associated with American exceptionalism. It was therefore relatively easy to characterize Spaniards, as one popular textbook put it, as a bunch of "bigotted Catholics" prone to "the practice of every vice" or, more generally, as a "a poor, lazy, idle, dirty, ignorant race of semi-savages."[8] These stereotypes, replicated in articles posing such questions as "Are they [i.e., Spaniards] thinking men? No. . . . Are they active men? No," also allowed Americans at the start of the nineteenth century to attribute Spain's political and economic problems to the character of the Spanish themselves.[9]

Starting in the 1820s, this negative image of Spaniards merged with another, more romantic vision of the country and is commonly associated with Washington Irving. This vision portrayed Spaniards as picturesque, a people more quaint than cruel. Thus Irving, in a letter written shortly after his arrival in Madrid in February 1826, could write: "The Spaniards seem to surpass even the Italians in picturesqueness."[10] Two months later he added a bit more detail: "The countenance, figure, air, attitude, walk, dress of a Spaniard, all have a peculiar character. The common people are wonderfully picturesque in all their attitudes, groups, and customs."[11] Subsequently, in a letter dated May 7, 1827, Irving provided additional information about the Spaniards he had met: "I have never known finer people than the common people of Spain. Shrewd, sententious, proud, courteous (and disinterested), and full of fire and courage."[12]

Irving's vision of Spain, as Rolena Adorno argues, was colored by a romantic sensibility that he developed in boyhood, perhaps from English sources.[13] Yet Irving shared this vision with Henry Wadsworth Longfellow, who, in an 1828 visit to Madrid, sensed a certain timelessness about Spaniards. So too did George Ticknor, Harvard's first professor of modern languages and the author of *The History of Spanish Literature* (1849). Ticknor, fresh from his studies in Göttingen, arrived in Spain on April 30, 1818. Two weeks later, having visited only Catalonia, he was already formulating "some general notions of their [that is, the Spanish] character."[14] Initially impressed by Spain's religious "fanaticism," by the time Ticknor reached Zaragoza he also detected a fierce "spirit of independence," specifically noting that the spirit exhibited by the Spaniards who had defended Zaragoza against the French in 1808 was the same as that exhibited by their ancestors against the Romans. This "spirit," he wrote, "has always existed in Spain and never existed anywhere else."[15] This particular observation resembles one previously made by the French antiquary Alexandre de Laborde in his influential *Voyage pittoresque et historique de l'Espagne* (1806–20), yet it also suggests that Ticknor was already well acquainted with Herder's ideas about national character.[16] Furthermore, having already been influenced by Friedrich Bouterwek (1766–1828) and J. C. L. Sismonde di Sismondi (1773–1842), two scholars (the first German, the second Swiss) who had applied Herder's ideas about national character to the study of literature, Ticknor argued that the spirit that accounted for the peculiar trajectory of a nation's literature also explained the character of its governing institutions.[17] Applying this theory to Spain, Ticknor remarked that the country's apparent timelessness derived in large measure from Spaniards' innate sense of loyalty toward their leaders. Such loyalty was a virtue in ancient times, but it had more recently degenerated into "blind submission" to both despotism and bigotry. It follows that Ticknor regarded Spain's national character as the modal force behind the Inquisition, along with the despotic monarchy created by the Habsburgs.[18] People, in short, got the kinds of institutions that they deserved.

As with Ticknor, national character appealed to other nineteenth-century U.S. historians who, in keeping with the new fascination with Spain, found themselves drawn to the study of the Spanish past.[19] This certainly applies to Ticknor's friend and fellow Bostonian William H. Prescott (figure 1.1), whose best-selling *The History of Ferdinand and Isabella* (1837) provided a case study of the manner in which Spain, a nation once capable of greatness, had sunk into stagnation and decay. Similar notions underscored the work of Prescott's disciple, John Lothrop Motley, whose *Rise of the Dutch Republic* (1856) villain-

Figure 1.1. William H. Prescott (1796–1859), late in life. Engraving by D. H. Pound after a photograph by Whipple and Black. (MHS #2722; courtesy of the Massachusetts Historical Society)

ized Philip II with one curt phrase: "He was a Spaniard."[20] The idea of Spaniards as a retrograde people also influenced John S. C. Abbott (1805–77), one of the most prolific and widely read U.S. historians during the middle years of the nineteenth century. Abbott, a Congregational minister living in New Haven, Connecticut, wrote primarily about the United States, but Spain also interested him, and his one work on the subject, *The Romance of Spanish History* (1869), represents the first complete history of the country ever written by a U.S. author. Writing within the familiar vein of national character, Abbott linked Spain's "melancholic temperament" with the "ignorance" and "superstition" that left the country with "little hope" for progress.[21]

The short but decisive Spanish-American War of 1898 evoked similar comments from scholars and journalists alike. This conflict persuaded James Fernald, a noted lexicologist, to write *The Spaniard in History* (1898), a book that argued that the "cruelty," "ferocious spirit," and "intolerance" integral to the "Spanish race" were incompatible with empire.[22] Similar cant filled the pages of the popular, mostly yellow, press, but even the more sober *New York Times*, in an article devoted to "The Spanish Character" published on April 4, 1898, explained: "Spain is situated between two continents, the most advanced and most backward, the most illumed and the darkest—Europe and Africa. The institutions of Spain naturally enough respond to the influences of each. . . . There are, then, in the Spanish national character, dwelling side by side, and most of the time blended into one, these two forces—civilization and barbarism."[23]

Yet for all its influence on nineteenth-century American perceptions of Spain, romanticism, with its penchant for national character, did not go uncontested. Rather, it had to compete with another, albeit lesser-known, view of the country, which, while it did not altogether refute the romantic view, attributed Spain's problems less to its people than to its governing institutions, both secular and spiritual. The first proponents of this more pragmatic—dare I say "modern"—view of Spain were diplomats such as Mordecai Noah, ambassadors sent to Spain either to negotiate the purchase of Spanish Florida (a sale that, after almost two decades of negotiations, was eventually effected in 1819) or later to deal with negotiations pertaining to the status of Cuba. Many were also lawyers, and this too may explain why their view of Spain was somewhat less fanciful than that of literati like Irving and Longfellow. And toward the end of the century the group also included professional historians, notably Bernard Moses, a scholar whose interest in Latin American politics led him to develop an image of Spain quite different from that formulated earlier by writers of the romantic school. To be sure, none of these individuals, not even Moses, could entirely resist the lure of national character, but for the most part their inspiration came less from Herder and Bouterwek than from a desire to explain the underlying conditions that seemingly had deprived Spaniards of democracy and freedom. In other words, as they saw it, Spaniards were not a people apart, nor was Spain decidedly different or exceptional. Rather, it constituted a nation whose fundamental values, especially where liberty was concerned, were roughly similar to those of the United States.

"Spain Is Not a *Dead* but Sleeping Lion"

One place to begin this inquiry into this alternative view of Spain is to return to a somewhat unusual banquet held in Boston on the evening of January 24, 1809. On this occasion a group of about three hundred Bostonians, among them the aging ex-revolutionary Paul Revere, gathered in the coffeehouse of Boston's Exchange Hall for a dinner in honor of "the patriots of Spain."[24] Worried by news of Napoleon's recent invasion of the country yet heartened by the resistance offered to the French troops in Zaragoza and other cities, the citizens of Boston—the evening's guest list was not published, but it apparently included many merchants with commercial interests in Spain—rallied to the Spanish cause. For those in Exchange Hall, Napoleon and his armies represented a grave threat to liberty, a concept that the Bostonians, leaders in the American War of Independence against British rule, championed as their own. For these party goers, Napoleon was little more than another George III, a tyrannical despot out to squash the forces of democracy and freedom, and indeed the banner of freedom was what led this particular group to make common cause with the Spanish people as a whole.

As the banquet wore on—unfortunately, nothing is known about the menu—the speeches and songs rallying the Spaniards to victory grew in number and intensity. The Reverend Joseph Eckley (1750–1811), a local Presbyterian minister, set the tone for the evening in his benediction: a prayer for the Spanish nation. A certain Mr. Core then spoke about the "political condition of Spain," pointedly referring to the "treacherous acts" that Napoleon was using to "subdue" Spain and to destroy the independence of a nation that had "never been conquered," a possible reference to the failure of the Muslims in the eighth century to conquer the whole of Visigothic Spain. In the cause of "universal nature" Core also called upon all Americans, as lovers of both independence and liberty, to espouse the Spanish cause. He then continued with references to the "horrors" committed by the French troops—rape, pillage, destruction of property. Even worse were reports that "the altars of religion [were] profaned and robbed." These were crimes were so evil, Core averred, that "they made angels weep."

After the speeches came the toasts, but the message was the same:

[To] the Patriots of Spain. May they establish such liberty as will make Government just.—and such a government as will make liberty immortal.

[To] the Spanish Peoples. Led to slavery by the Prince of the Peace, may they be led to freedom by the God of War.

[To] the Nation that discovered our country. As they were the first that openly favored our independence, may we not be the last openly to favor theirs.

Next came such songs as "Spain, Commerce, Freedom" and "Spanish Patriots," all of which evoked causes with which the Bostonians in Exchange Hall could readily identify. The evening ended with a rousing "Address to the Spanish Nation." It began:

Noble Spaniards, fam'd in story.
To your king and country true.
Gallant warriors, on to glory,
Freedom lives or dies with you.

As impoverished as this kind of patriotic doggerel may strike a modern reader, it was integral to a gathering that was not only unprecedented—never before, to my knowledge, had a group of Americans gathered to honor Spain—but unusual to the extent that the evening's activities contained no traces of the Black Legend: not one reference to the horrors of the Inquisition or the pernicious effects of Catholicism, topics that colored most early U.S. writing about Spain. Rather, the Bostonians in Exchange Hall seemed to view Spaniards in wholly positive terms, referring to their "heroism," "the constancy and the elevation of the Spanish character," their "resolution to act." True, the anonymous author who compiled the pamphlet recounting that evening's activities would refer to the "decline" of Iberian "glory" in the seventeenth century, attributing this development to a "government" that had lost its "firmness" and "doubled" its "despotism." Yet whereas writers of the romantic school seemingly believed that absolute monarchy had irreparably damaged the Spanish spirit, the author of this pamphlet, striking a more optimistic chord, noted that "a great people can never be debased by weak government." As I argue here, this notion of a great people, and a strong national spirit, characterized an important but little known strain in nineteenth-century U.S. writing about Spain.

Mordecai M. Noah

One of the first writers to articulate this particular approach to the Spanish past was Mordecai M. Noah (1785–1851), a U.S. diplomat who visited Spain in 1813 in conjunction with his work as the new consul in Tunis (figure 1.2). As

Figure 1.2. Mordecai M. Noah (1785–1851).
(Courtesy of the Jewish Archives of America)

consul, Noah's main responsibility was to secure the freedom of U.S. sailors taken captive by the notorious pirates who then plagued North Africa's Barbary Coast. For Noah, Spain served initially as a base from which he might negotiate the sailors' release, but as an Ashkenazi Jew whose father had pretended to be of Sephardic origin in an effort to obtain the prestige then attached to Jews of Spanish origin, he also proved to have a special interest in the country, especially with respect to its history during the Middle Ages and its treatment of both Muslims and Jews. Mordecai Noah's observations concerning these and related matters soon found their way into his *Travels in England, France, and Spain and the Barbary States in the Years 1813–4 and 1815* (1819), a two-volume travelogue-cum-history that included the first detailed description of Spain ever written by a citizen of the United States.[25]

Mordecai Noah belonged to a prominent, well-connected Ashkenazi family of German origin. Noah was born in Philadelphia and as a young man lived an itinerant life, shuttling between New York, Philadelphia, and Charleston, and working variously in commerce, journalism, and politics. More than anything, however, Noah was a patriot, proud that his father, an émigré from Mannheim, had fought in the Revolutionary War against Britain. Like his father, Noah was also eager to serve his country, partly, it seems, to prove that his new democracy both provided opportunities for and welcomed the services of Jews such as himself. These ambitions explain why, starting in 1811, he used his family's connections to help him obtain a diplomatic post such as the consulship in Tunis to which he was appointed in 1813. It turns out, however, that Noah was neither an accomplished or skillful diplomat, and in 1815 he was recalled, only to enter a career in New York politics and later to distinguish himself by his innovative but ill-fated Ararat Project, which aimed at creating a Jewish homeland on a island in the Niagara River. In the end, therefore, Noah's visit to Spain was relatively short, lasting only a few months in 1813–14. It was also essentially limited to its ports, Cádiz in particular, but also Málaga, Valencia, and Barcelona. In these cities Noah made contact with local U.S. consuls and merchants, and it appears that much of what he learned about Spain from these informants later wound up in his book. Yet Noah himself was a keen observer. He was also well versed in Spanish history, and this is what makes his impressions of Spain both original and important.[26]

At first glance Noah's account of the country offers few surprises. As later nineteenth-century travelers would regularly do, he offered his readers a mixture of amusing anecdotes about his encounters with bandits and gypsies, comments on the beauty of Spanish women, descriptions of bullfights and folk dances, and reflections on the Spanish character. Yet Noah also fancied himself a historian, and he endeavored to include in his account philosophical reflections concerning Spain's past, present, and future. Furthermore, and in keeping with his compatriots' impression of Spain as a retrograde nation, Noah had a particular interest in what he perceived as the nation's failure to develop its resources, both human and material. In this respect Noah's book was less of a travelogue than a treatise that endeavored to explain why Spain had fallen so far behind the United States.

It follows that Noah's book, derived in part from a travel diary, is filled with reflections on the "decline of Spain." Arriving in Cádiz, for example, in a comment probably inspired by that earlier critic of Spanish imperialism, Adam Smith, Noah wrote about Spain's overreliance on empire and its consequent failure to develop its natural resources. "Dazzled by a false splendor, they [Spaniards] lost sight of that maxim, which nations never should forget, that industry, science, and the arts are the only true sources of wealth and national character."[27] The dream of El Dorado, the embrace of overseas colonies as a source of wealth, had so corrupted Spain that its naturally fertile soil was "greatly neglected," its manufacturing industry permitted to languish.

Given his personal interest in the history and suffering of Spanish Jews during the Middle Ages, and notwithstanding his interest in Spain's failure to promote industry and agriculture, Noah zeroed in on the corrosive effects of Roman Catholicism and consequently peppered his book with comments reminiscent of the Black Legend. "Religion in Spain," he wrote, "is a combination of ceremonies, grandly enforced by priests"; the Inquisition "a curse to humanity, and to that country," an institution that "still shackled" the country's mind;

and clerical schoolmasters wholly responsible for having weakened the nation's "manly spirit."[28] To illustrate this last point Noah offered an account of the manner in which priests in Cádiz accompanied boys to their homes instead of allowing them to find their own way home after school. "They [the boys] are led like sheep, their spirit is crushed, the inquiring disposition is checked, and, in their infancy, they are taught to be slaves, and led by some in authority. Here, the origin of that humble spirit, and obedience to ecclesiastical power, are first traced."[29] Following this line of argument, Noah called for the secularization of Spanish education. Otherwise, "Spain will never alter; she will ever be internally weak and puerile"; this, in turn, would inhibit the growth of what he called an "effective national character," a quality he regarded as essential for modernization and progress.

To be fair, Noah's view of Spain was not wholly negative. For one thing, he developed a fondness for the freshly fried fish that he first tasted in Cádiz, as well as for dry sherry, Spanish lamb, and chocolate. For another, he commented favorably on the "conmixture" of architectural styles that he encountered in Seville. Further, with reference to the glories of Spain during the Middle Ages and at the time of Columbus, he affirmed that the Spaniards were fully capable of momentous achievement. Yet Noah, an ardent proponent of religious tolerance, could not free himself of the notion that the "undue and dangerous influence" of priests had so weakened the country that Spain, if not released from their yoke, "will remain poor in spirit and resources—its energy confined, and its independence destroyed."[30] Consequently, he offered a clarion call, one that, in effect, echoed the sentiments of the Spanish liberal reformers who, only two years before Noah's visit, had gathered in Cádiz to draft their country's first constitution:

> Spain, Spain, raze your inquisitions to the ground; turn your monasteries into seminaries of learning; place your priests between the handles of a plough; tolerate all religions; call back the Moors and the Jews, who gave you character and wealth; declare your provinces in South America sovereign and independent; and establish a profitable commerce with them, founded on equal and exact justice; invite to your court the learned of every clime; let industry, science and good faith prevail; and you may yet obtain a distinguished rank among the governments of the earth![31]

Noah's criticisms of Spain thus left room for improvement. The idea of national character formed part of this thought, but Noah did not use it to account for the many problems that Spain as a nation had to confront. In other words, he recognized that what he saw as the country's backwardness had less to do with any inherent weakness in the Spanish people than in the shortcomings of the nation's governing institutions, notably the monarchy and the church. Change these and Spain could improve, or to quote him directly: "Everything in Spain must be reversed." Indeed, Noah saw a distinct possibility of progress, once the necessary reforms had been instituted: "There is still left for her [Spain] a road to prosperity and character."[32]

Alexander H. Everett

Noah's conception of Spain as something of a genie waiting to be released from a bottle was by no means unique. Similar ideas can be found in the work of Alexander H. Everett (1790–1847), a diplomat-lawyer who served as the U.S. chargé d'affaires in Madrid from 1825 to 1829. A native of Boston and a graduate of Harvard (class of 1806), Everett began his diplomatic career by studying law in the offices of John Quincy Adams, who later helped Everett secure a series of important diplomatic posts, first in the Hague and subsequently in Madrid. Once in the Spanish capital, Everett, a supporter of the Monroe Doctrine, actively promoted the acquisition of Cuba by the United States. He was also a man of letters, author of several books on contemporary politics, and, after 1830, editor of the prestigious *North American Review,* the nation's leading outlet for Whig thought. History was another of Everett's interests, and it was he who invited Washington Irving to Spain in the hope of persuading him to translate into English the documents about Columbus and the discovery of America that Martín Fernández de Navarrete had recently published.[33]

What we know about Everett's view of Spain derives principally from his *Europe; or, A General Survey of the Present Situation of the Principal Powers, with Conjectures of Their Future Prospects* (1822) and, to a lesser degree, his companion volume, *America* (1827), two books that expounded his Whig views on history, government, and the superiority of the United States within the "great political system of Christendom."[34] The two volumes also analyzed the "age of revolutions," that moment in which society, in a search for the "happiness" that comes from "the progress of civilization," showed itself determined to increase agriculture, industry, commerce, and knowledge as well as to institute a general improvement, both public and political. In keeping with this proposition, Everett's *Europe,* a skillful comparative account of European politics circa 1820, outlined the extent to which the principal powers of Europe measured up. England and France stood highest on Everett's chart, Turkey the lowest inasmuch as it had entered a "retrograde course" leading in the direction of "utter desolation and complete physical ruin."[35]

Where did Spain figure on Everett's scale? Not nearly as a low as might be expected, and in many ways his analysis of the country's political situation was surprisingly current. "Spain," he noted, "is not, as generally supposed, constantly declining," inasmuch as the moment of its "greatest weakness and degradation," which he calculated had occurred around 1700, had long since passed. Thanks to the Bourbons, moreover, Spain's eighteenth century was one in which "industry and wealth" were "regularly and rapidly advancing." He further remarked that the "spirit of improvement" had taken deep root in the country, so much so that, when Napoleon invaded, there already existed "a mass of population, intelligence and character, competent to resist this aggression."[36]

Yet all was not rosy. Everett worried about the failure of Spain's ruling monarch, Ferdinand VII, to embrace "improvement." The king rather presented himself as "a disgusting spectacle of imbecility and iniquity" whose rule had led to the "separation" of the nation from the monarchy. Yet Everett, like Noah before him, remained optimistic; he believed that Spaniards were fully capable of creating "political institutions founded in political liberty," that is, democracy.[37] Everett also saw a glimmer of hope in the Spanish constitution adopted in Cádiz in 1812, as well as in the new representative assembly known as the Cortes. Everett also echoed Noah on Spain's need to offer its American colonies, if not total independence, some degree of local autonomy. If Spain did this, he argued, "she will find, as England did, the emancipation of her colonies more profitable than their possession. In exchange for the vain name of ruling the Indies, she will find the wealth of the Indies pouring into her territory in fertilizing streams, instead of merely rolling through it, as it does now, like a mountain torrent, and leaving no marks of its passage, but barrenness and desolation."[38]

In offering this assessment, Everett, writing at a time when "romantic nationalism" was in full bloom, made no reference to national character. Spain's problems resulted from the imperfections of government, not from any inherent flaws in its people. In this respect Everett's approach to Spain had little in common with that of Longfellow, who, in a letter commenting on the religious ceremonies he had seen in Madrid, offered the somewhat facile observation that "Spaniards are the most obedient people in the world; they will believe everything a priest tells them to, without asking why or wherefore."[39] In comparison Everett credited the monarchy with "the notorious decrepitude and wretched imbecility of Spain."[40]

The Cushings: Caleb and Caroline

The analysis offered by Caleb Cushing, another U.S. diplomat who visited Spain during the decade of the 1820s, differed only in detail. Like Everett before him, Cushing (1800–1879) was both a Bostonian and a Whig. He too attended Harvard (class of 1817) and mixed the study of law with the pursuit of letters. A frequent contributor to the *North American Review,* Cushing wrote essays on subjects as diverse as Columbus and Sir Edward Coke. In 1826 he published *A Summary of the Practical Principles of Political Economy,* a textbook that touted the advantages of democracy, industry, and free trade. Subsequently, after a failed bid for political office, Cushing, accompanied by his wife, Caroline, traveled to Europe in 1829 and embarked on a tour of Spain, a country to which he would later be named ambassador.[41]

Cushing's first visit to Spain resulted in a book: *Reminscences of Spain, the Country, Its People, History, and Monuments,* first published in 1833. It led also to Caroline Cushing's *Letters Descriptive of Public Monuments, Scenery, and Manners in France and Spain,* a posthumous work based on her letters (she died toward the end of their journey, shortly after leaving Barcelona) and privately published in 1832. In this travelogue Caroline Cushing—the first U.S. woman to write about Spain—recorded her impressions of both town and country, generally filtering her accounts of the bullfight and other Spanish pastimes through a romantic lens. In addition, she ventured observations on Spanish art and, following a visit to the recently opened Prado Museum, commented on the "great superiority" of the Spanish school of painting over the French.[42] A visit to Córdoba allowed her an opportunity to comment on current affairs. In this Andalucian city she observed "wandering groups of men reclining listlessly against some building, smoking their cigars, and warming themselves in the sun." To explain this "idleness" she referred to what were already the standard topoi in foreigners' accounts of Spain, notably, "the habitual want of industry" and the "absence" of an "enterprising spirit." On the other hand, she sounded more like a social scientist when she noted that this "idleness" had its roots in the difficulty that these men had in finding suitable employment to sustain themselves and their families. In the end, however, after weighing both factors, Caroline Cushing opted for a romantic interpretation, with the statement that Córdoba's underemployment was due "less to the necessity of the case, than to settled, constitutional indolence."[43]

A similar romantic quality pervaded her husband's impressions of the country. Caleb Cushing's letters referred repeatedly to the "oddities" that made Spanish culture unique: "They do not drink their chocolate but eat it"; "they bury their dead above the ground instead of under it."[44] Romantic leanings also help to explain why Spain affected him, as it did Irving, particularly in the Alhambra, as if it were some sort of powerful hallucinogen capable of producing fanciful reveries that instantly carried him back to the Middle Ages and to the time of the Moors. The simple act of crossing the Bidassoa, the river that marks the border between southwestern France and Spain, created for Caleb Cushing "the most inspiring associations of the days of knighthood." Mountains appeared "towering and romantic," the whole of the country "picturesque."[45] His visit to the Alhambra was equally magical and culminated in a "moving phantasmagoria" of the city's Islamic past in which a series of caliphs and qadis made cameo appearances.[46]

These reveries aside—and he may well have used them as a marketing technique[47]—Cushing's main interest was politics, and, together with other Whig writers, he seemed determined to understand the differences between Spain and the United States. He thus larded his *Reminscences of Spain* with philosophical observations intended to shed light on Spain's present as well as its past and then combined these to comment on the extent to which bad government was responsible for Spain's multiple ills. Taking his cue from Robert Watson and other Enlightenment historians who had written about Spain, Cushing took aim at the "ruinous" policies of Philip II and a legacy of Habsburg despotism that created "a country, a nation, a people, which affords a standing monument of the public degradation and private misery, to which vicious political institutions can reduce a country the richest in its natural resources among the states of Europe, a nation once the most powerful in all of the elements of political greatness, and a people surpassed by none, even at the present day, in genius, courage, and every moral capability."[48]

As this passage suggests, Cushing's prose could be convoluted, his ideas none too original, but, together with Noah and Everett, he was arguing that Spain's ills as a country had less to do with the character of its people than with the defects of its ruling institutions, the monarchy in particular. Toward this end Caleb Cushing included a detailed account of the prosperity of the agriculture he found in the gardens surrounding Valencia. Reflecting upon the region's "appearance of thrift and populousness combined," he took issue with those who believed that Spain's problems were inextricably connected to its national character. "It is so common," he wrote, "to think and speak of the Spaniards as a thriftless or at least idle people,—the manners of particular provinces are so frequently taken as characteristic of the whole nation,—that I have entered, thus at length, into a description of the country [i.e., Valencia] as it met my eye, in order to correct some of the prevailing errors in regard to Spain."[49]

Cushing summarized his observations about Spain in a closing chapter inspired by a visit to Bellegarde (Bellesguard), a promontory that afforded him a prospect of Barcelona and its port. From this lookout he reflected upon the course of Spanish history and the nation's loss of pride and splendor. Spain's empire, he noted, was ebbing away, "the enterprise of her people . . . consumed and eaten in the rust." Yet unlike Caroline Cushing, who attributed these developments to inherited indolence, Caleb Cushing saw the root cause in the "retrogressive or stationary spirit of her [i.e., Spain's] clergy" and a series of maladroit kings (i.e., the Habsburgs) who together constituted the "the weakest of all the dynasties of Christendom." Making things worse were mercantilist policies that had precipitated three centuries of "decay and of decline. . . . The narrow commercial policy of her rulers, instead of enabling the people to derive advantage from her transatlantic dominions, erected a system of ruinous monopolies, which impoverished the colonies, without adding any permanent or available wealth to the metropolis." Spain, in brief, had succumbed to a series of "imbecile kings," as well as a tyrannical Inquisition. As a result, "the land of Cervantes, Lope de Vega, and Calderón, of Ercilla, Garcilaso and Mariana, became a kind of patrimony of monks and nuns, a Dead Sea of superstition, while the sciences and the arts were flourishing with all the luxuriance of successful culture in the rest of Western Europe."[50]

In the end Cushing perceived a profound contradiction in nineteenth-century Spain. On the one hand, he saw "a people proverbially brave, chivalrous, and noble, capable of the most elevated actions, and approved in many of the most trying emergencies." On the other, a people "deadened by the conspiring influence of bigotry and servitude;—and a kingdom, which contained the elemental parts of greatness without any principle of union to cement them together, which possessed the sinews of manly strength, wanting only a spirit of liberty to rouse, awaken, animate and inform its slumbering energies." But where was Spain going? Here, commenting upon Spain's remaining a monarchy, he offered these closing, somewhat sobering, remarks:

> I fear there is none, among the adult members of the royal family, who is likely to realize the idea of Plato. But a firm and able prince might do much for that unfortunate country. If such a Bourbon should by possibility appear in Spain, or even a wise and popular minister capable of rightly using the royal power;—and if such a prince or minister should succeed to abridge the exorbitant power of the priesthood by the only sure means, the revival of the Cortes;—if the rulers of the country would encourage liberality of sentiment, re-open the sources of internal prosperity in which the kingdom so richly abounds, and abolish the odious seignorial rights of the nobles and great landed proprietors;—and if by repealing the absurd restrictions on commerce, they should afford countenance to a more enlightened system of political economy than that on which the present mercantile laws are predicated;—and if they could bring their minds to the generous resolve of making a full recognition of the actual independence of their colonies:—if a government, of whatever form, will do this, we may live to see Spain restored to equal prosperity, if not equal power, with that which she could boast when she was the rival of England, the terror of France, and the mistress of Italy.[51]

Caleb Cushing, in short, recognized that Spaniards were, on the whole, capable of progress. Their problem was a corrupt and inefficient system of government that prevented them from reaching their full potential.

Severn T. Wallis

Another diplomat-lawyer to write about nineteenth-century Spain was Severn Teackle Wallis (1816–94), a Baltimore resident who first visited the country in 1847 (figure 1.3). When he did so, Wallis carried with him intellectual baggage quite different from that of other authors discussed here. Just as Ticknor was taken with Herder and Bouterwek, Wallis's particular muse was Alexis de Tocqueville, especially his *Democracy in America* (1835), a book famous for what many considered its balanced, relatively objective analysis of the customs and institutions of the United States.

It is not certain when Wallis first read *Democracy in America*, but the book's influence was such that Wallis, in writing about Spain, set out to do for that country what the Frenchman had done for the United States. As I noted earlier, Wallis visited Spain for the first time in 1847 on a private visit. He was there again—in an official capacity—in 1850–51—to negotiate certain land claims arising from the annexation of Florida. From the start, however, Wallis was "Hispaneolized," the nineteenth-century term for people who were favorably disposed toward Spain and its culture. To begin with, he knew Spanish, having been tutored in the subject at St. Mary's Seminary in Baltimore by José Antonio Pizarro, then the Spanish vice consul in the city and someone who, in addition to language, taught the young Wallis something about Spain's history and culture. For another, before his initial visit Wallis had already published a

Figure 1.3. Severn T. Wallis (1816–94).
(Courtesy of the Gilman Collection, Johns Hopkins University)

series of essays about Spain in the *Southern Literary Messenger,* an important literary journal published in Richmond, Virginia. Wallis wrote several of these essays simply to criticize Washington Irving, claiming that he had failed to give adequate credit to Manuel Fernández de Navarrete, the Spanish scholar who had unearthed the documents to which Irving had access when he wrote his biography of Columbus.[52] Other Wallis articles defended the Spanish character as well as Spanish contributions to learning and the arts. These articles, at least one of which was reprinted in Madrid, brought Wallis the honor of an appointment as corresponding member of Madrid's Royal Academy of History in 1844, three years before the Baltimorean had ever set foot in Spain itself.[53]

Two subsequent books brought further recognition. The first, *Glimpses of Spain* (1849), was a travelogue studded with philosophical reflections of various sorts, including a protracted and, for its time, unusual defense of the bullfight. The second was *Spain: Her Institutions, Politics, and Public Men* (1853)—a fascinating but nowadays little-known analysis of life, culture, and politics in mid-nineteenth-century Madrid. In both Wallis offered a spirited defense of Spanish culture, primarily by attempting, much as Tocqueville had done, to explain it on its own terms rather than in light of ideas and attitudes imported from abroad. On this score Wallis criticized virtually every foreigner who had written about Spain. His targets included Théophile Gautier, Alexandre Dumas, and other Frenchmen who arrived in Spain with their own "idées" and national "préscriptions."[54] Wallis accused these authors of creating a totally romanticized Spain, transforming it into a tableau vivant comprised of Figaro, Almavivá, and other characters drawn from the *Barbier de Seville* (1775), the Beaumarchais comedy that Rossini transformed into the light opera *Il barbarie di Siviglia* in 1816. Wallis was no less critical of British travelers such as Richard Ford, author of the influential *Handbook for Travellers in Spain* (1845), who saw everything in Spain "through an exclusively English medium," along with those Americans—probably Cushing and most definitely Alexander Slidell Mackenzie—who arrived in the country without any knowledge of Spanish and armed with a preconceived notion of Spaniards as standing halfway between "a bloody-minded grand inquisitor and an illustrious hidalgo." Wallis was especially upset by the American habit of equating Spaniards with what he termed the "the half-breed Indians and negroes in Mexico and South America."[55]

In his own work Wallis endeavored to correct these misconceptions and stereotypes. To begin with, whereas writers of the romantic school tended to view Spain monolithically, a single people with a shared national trait, Wallis saw it as a country of countries, a people of peoples, each with characteristics and customs uniquely their own. He thus made a sharp distinction between Castilians, Catalans, and Basques. In addition, Wallis, despite an Episcopalian background, or perhaps because of it, took pains to separate himself from what he called "ultra-Protestant opinion," namely, the tendency of Anglo-Americans to exaggerate both the influence of the Catholic clergy in Spain (he detested the term *priest-ridden*) and to attribute to the Church problems—economic underdevelopment, for example—that were really the work of other forces, among them incompetent monarchs, foreign invasion and war, and Mother Nature herself. In Wallis's words:

> All of the errors and follies and abominations of the many despots who have reigned over her, all the evils that have been entailed on her by foreign invasion and domestic broil,—all the obstacles by which nature and circumstances have interrupted the march of her civilization, have, in turn, been set down to the influence of the clergy, and the pernicious doctrines they have taught. When public, or literary, or religious opinion has once begun to run in a particular channel, observation generally takes the same direction. The foregone conclusion is a sort of mould for the facts which come after it. Men explain the phenomena by the theory, instead of correcting the theory by the phenomena.[56]

In this context Wallis singled out Slidell Mackenzie's *A Year in Spain* (1829), a travelogue that offered the portrait of a stagnant nation rendered prostrate by monarchical absolutism and religious fanaticism.[57] Wallis disagreed, observing that Slidell MacKenzie and other U.S. travelers repeated such absurdities because of the influence of publishers: "Such things," Wallis wrote, "make a lively and picturesque book. . . . They [the travelers] have discovered that nothing sells so well as a little piquant uncharitableness."[58] Wallis seems also to have understood that the majority of foreigners who visited Spain wore eyeglasses fitted with special lenses that allowed them to see poverty, backwardness, and everything that smacked of the picturesque—bandits, bullfights, gypsies, pícaros, and the like—but that filtered out smoke, industry, commerce, and other indicators of progress and change.

Wallis wore spectacles of a different sort. Just as Tocqueville had done for the United States, Wallis did not hesitate to underscore Spain's shortcomings. These ranged from a bloated army, top heavy with generals who exerted too much political influence, to the "want of proper and complete indexes" in the National Library in Madrid.[59] He also recognized Spain's poverty, as well as the extent to which it lagged behind other European nations with respect to industrial growth and international trade. But whereas the other Americans who wrote about Spain tended to keep well within the comfortable confines of national stereotypes, Wallis struck out of his own. Where they saw shade, he saw light; where they saw decadence, he detected signs of progress and change, among them the iron foundry that he encountered in Málaga, along with the railroad line running between Barcelona and Mataró. As for national character, Wallis avoided this subject entirely and, more like a modern economist, attributed Spain's economic difficulties to such structural factors as the lack of foreign investment capital and a protective tariff—imposed at the insistence of Catalan industrialists—that served in his view to dampen the nation's international trade. In a similar vein Wallis maintained that peace, good government—Spain, he asserted, would benefit from a federal system—and stable democratic institutions would soon bring to Spain the prosperity enjoyed by other countries. Indeed, after a year of closely observing the political scene in Madrid, he confidently wrote: "The popular element is fully at work in the Peninsula."[60]

Finally, as part of his effort to correct the notion that Spain was a country whose problems stemmed directly from the privileged position of the Catholic Church, he asserted by way of comparison that the influence of the clergy on the press and public opinion was probably far less in Spain than in the United States. Indeed, in this as well as in other matters, including the extent to which municipal governments invested in public walkways and parks, Wallis claimed that Spain was a nation from which the United States had much to learn.

Wallis, in brief, turned the romantic view of Spain inside out and in doing so rejected some of its central tenets, among them the notion of Spain as the antithesis of the United States and the representation of Spaniards as a picturesque, quasi-Oriental people resistant to change. For Wallis, Spain and the United States were not polar opposites, one modern and progressive, the other backward and retrograde. Rather, he positioned the two countries at two different points on the same track—the road to modernity. The United States was moving faster, but Spain was accelerating, and Wallis sincerely believed that, with a few changes, Spain was fully capable of catching up.

Bernard Moses

Following his second (and last) sojourn in Spain, in 1856 Severn T. Wallis returned to his native Baltimore, where he dabbled in local politics, got involved (on the losing side) in the Civil War, collected books on Spanish literature, delivered lectures on Spanish culture, and generally promoted the Spanish cause when and wherever he could. Yet outside Baltimore, Wallis's voice was scarcely heard. For the most part his books went unread, and his effort to represent Spain as something other than "backward" and "timeless" was essentially a failure. Wallis received some support from the poet William Cullen Bryant, whose travel letters, published in New York's *Evening Standard* dur-

Richard L. Kagan

ing the fall of 1857, informed readers that Spain was changing to the extent that it not only possessed mills and forges but also the "electric telegraph" and railroads. Despite these signs of technological progress, Bryant still represented Spain as a "backward" country and Spaniards as a people whose national character prevented them from doing anything except cling to what he called "old customs, old prejudices, old roads."[61]

This romanticized image of a backward Spain did not change very much in the decades following the American Civil War. Periodicals of this era held to the aging yet popular (and presumably profitable) "land of romance and superstition" formula.[62] Publishers of travel books did the same, the result being that Americans who wanted to learn about Spain had little to read except for John Hay's *Castilian Days* (1871), Kate Field's *Ten Days in Spain* (1875), and, toward the end of the century, H. C. Chatfield-Taylor's *Land of the Castinet* (1896), all of which adhered to the view that Spain's national character impeded both progress and change.[63] As the number of travel writers increased during the 1880s and early 1890s, this view of Spain proliferated. Still, indirect support for Wallis's structural approach to Spain could be found in U.S. universities, especially among a handful of professional historians dedicated to the history of Latin America. Notable in this regard was Bernard Moses (1846–1930), professor of history and political economy at the University of California at Berkeley (figure 1.4).

A Connecticut native, Moses studied law at the University of Michigan before traveling to Heidelberg to earn his doctoral degree in 1873.[64] Back in the

Figure 1.4. Bernard Moses (1846–1930).
(#3:3489; courtesy of the Bancroft Library,
University of California at Berkeley)

40

United States, Moses started teaching history at Berkeley in 1876 and soon became an advocate of that mixture of history, law, and politics that Dorothy Ross has called "historico-politics." This particular field of study, new in the 1880s and the forerunner of what later evolved into the social sciences, concerned itself with various issues of social and political development. As the term *historico-politics* suggests, adherents of this particular school—the most famous are Woodrow Wilson and Frederick Jackson Turner—were avowed historicists, scholars who believed that a full understanding of politics and society could be achieved only by means of a thorough historical examination of the fundamental social, economic, and institutional forces.[65] Accordingly, they questioned the work of those whose approach to these issues often relied on such vague notions as national character.

Such was the methodology that Moses, starting in the late 1880s, brought to the study of Spanish America. In doing so, he was reacting against the work of Hubert H. Bancroft, the wealthy California publisher and book collector whose grand narrative (and team-written) histories of California, Mexico, and the American Southwest tended to privilege the influence of both national character and race. In contrast, Moses, while he did not entirely dismiss the role of national character in history, relegated it to a secondary or even tertiary role, a method he may have learned from Frank Blackmar (1854–1931), a professor at Kansas State University who published two pioneering books on the Southwest.[66] Moses's own research had been initially directed toward an understanding of U.S. politics, both national and local, but by the late 1880s he was drawn to the study of Latin America, especially the problem of why the new nations comprising that region were finding it so difficult to establish stable democracies. In keeping, moreover, with historico-politics, Moses turned to history, especially that of Spain, in the hope that the answers he was seeking might be found in the political inheritance that Spain had imparted to its former colonies.

Moses's first publication in this area was "The Economic Condition of Spain in the Sixteenth Century," an article that appeared in the inaugural issue of the *Journal of Political Economy* (1893), one of the flagship journals of historico-politics. In this study Moses argued that Spain's seventeenth-century decline had less to do with national character than with a variety of economic and institutional factors. He subsequently elaborated this thesis in his teaching—his course on the history of Spanish America, first offered in 1894, represented one of the first on this subject offered in a U.S. university—and then in his *Establishment of the Spanish Rule in America* (1898), a study designed to explain "the origins and character of the political and economic institutions constructed for the government of Spanish America."[67] This book brought

Moses national attention and soon landed him a position on the federal commission created to transform the Philippines from a Spanish colony into one whose governing institutions matched those of the United States. After returning to Berkeley in 1903, Moses helped to establish that university's Department of Political Science and then embarked on a series of books devoted to later periods in the history of Spanish America. Among them was his magisterial two-volume work, *The Spanish Dependencies in South America* (1914).

What distinguishes Moses as a historian is a comparative framework that makes him a pioneer of "hemispheric history," that is, the comparative history of the Americas, north and south, a field later popularized by his disciple, Herbert Bolton.[68] This particular framework enabled Moses to broaden his field of vision and thus to compare the factors that contributed to the formation of stable democracy in North America and those that apparently inhibited it in nations south of the Rio Grande. This comparison centered on legal and institutional issues and emphasized the differences between Spain's highly centralized imperial system and the looser system that prevailed in British America. Crucial to this comparison is what Moses called "local control." England had exported this particular ingredient to its colonies, and this in turn enabled the United States to develop responsible self-government. Spain, in contrast, did not, and for Moses the absence of local control explained the subsequent failure of Spanish America to develop a stable democratic mode of government.

In making this comparison, Moses raised the issue of "national or race character." On the one hand, he accepted the idea that different peoples possess "an inherited bias, aptitude, or propensity, which makes certain ideas acceptable, and others repugnant." Differences in these biases helped to explain in his mind why Spanish America, as the direct heir of Spain, developed as it did. On the other hand, Moses gave greater weight in this process to inherited traditions of government, ultimately concluding that "in the difference between Spain's system of centralized administration and England's strong local government may be discovered the difference between the institutions which England and Spain planted in the New World."[69] As for Spain itself, Moses recognized that it had evolved from an era of "enterprise and daring" to one of "weakness and degeneracy." In offering this analysis, Moses differed markedly from Hubert Bancroft, one of whose articles suggested that "self-conceit and laziness" rendered Spain "too unreliable for imperial undertakings."[70] It also separated Moses from his contemporaries, the majority of whom, especially at the time of the Spanish-American War, would have been likely to credit this transition to flaws in the Spanish national character. Moses, in contrast, credited it to those institutions, notably the monarchy and the church, that had failed to embrace policies—free trade, local autonomy, freedom of worship—that might have forestalled Spain's imperial decline.

⌒⌒⌒

The image of Spain in America in the nineteenth century was clearly far more complex than those U.S. scholars who have written about the history of the Black Legend often maintain.[71] That image, tinged heavily with romanticism—derived partly from Irving, partly from Prescott, as well as the travel writers about whom Wallis complained—presented Spain as if it were a nation caught in a time warp that seemingly rendered it incapable of both progress and change. So pervasive was this image that it persuaded me, some years ago, to coin the phrase "Prescott's paradigm" in an effort to describe the traditional ways in which Americans both thought and wrote about Spain. Further research, however, has convinced me that this paradigm, for all its vitality, did not begin to encompass the full range of nineteenth-century U.S. attitudes about both Spain and its people. As this essay has endeavored to demonstrate, other voices existed, together with alternative points of view, although in the long run the cluster of ideas associated with Prescott's paradigm, including that of Spain as the antithesis of the United States, won the day. The views of the country offered by Noah, Everett, Wallis, and Moses were clearly more balanced, as well as more optimistic, but none ever enjoyed the same imaginative weight as that of a picturesque Spain peopled by idlers and dominated by priests. In a word, the alternative image of Spain never sold, especially when compared to that served up by Irving and Prescott, authors whose books were always best-sellers, reprinted in multiple editions, and still widely available today. In comparison, the books of the diplomat-lawyers and professors who wrote about Spain never reached a broad popular audience, a difference that probably explains why, compared to Irving and Prescott, the individuals examined in this essay are all but forgotten. So too, I am afraid, is their vision of Spain as a nation with more in common with the United States than many Hispanists, even today, are likely to acknowledge.

Notes

1. George H. Borrow, *The Bible in Spain* (Philadelphia: J. M. Campbell, 1843), 10.

2. For Herder's ideas on national character, I have used Johann Gottfried von Herder, *On World History,* ed. Hans Adler and Ernest A. Menze, trans. Ernest A. Menze and Michael Palma (New York: M. E. Sharpe, 1997), and Herder, *Reflections on the History of Mankind,* ed. and trans. Frank E. Manuel (Chicago: University of Chicago Press, 1968).

3. David Tyack, "Forming the National Character: Paradox in Educational Thought of the Revolutionary Generation," *Harvard Educational Review* 36 (Winter 1966): 29–41.

4. On national character in the early United States, see Malcolm Kelsall, *Jefferson and the Iconography of Romanticism* (London: Macmillan, 1999). Whigs in the nineteenth century constituted a conservative cultural and political movement that advocated the nation's development along coherent, somewhat centralized, and rational lines. Toward this end they favored economic development, industrialization, and the creation of a national university and a national bank. They also believed in limiting democracy to property holders and thus opposed efforts to broaden the electoral franchise. For a succinct summary of Whig and other conservative movements in antebellum America, see George Fredrickson, *The Inner Civil War: Northern Intellectuals and the Crisis of the Union* (New York: Harper and Row, 1965).

5. The term *Black Legend* was coined by the Spanish scholar Julián Juderías in *La leyenda negra: Estudios acerca del concepto de España en el extranjero* (Madrid: Tip. de la Revista de Archivos, Bibliotecas y Museos, 1914). English-language books on the subject include Charles Gibson, ed., *The Black Legend: Anti-Spanish Attitudes in the Old World and the New* (New York: Alfred E. Knopf, 1971), and William S. Maltby, *The Black Legend in England: The Development of Anti-Spanish Sentiment, 1558–1660* (Durham, N.C.: Duke University Press, 1971). The most authoritative survey of Black Legend history is Ricardo García Carcel, *La leyenda negra: Historia y opinion* (Madrid: Alianza Editorial, 1992).

6. For the Whig fascination with Spain see Daniel Walker Howe, *The Political Culture of American Whigs* (Chicago: University of Chicago Press, 1979), 74.

7. In "Las primeras relaciones intelectuales entre New England y el mundo hispánico, 1700–1815," *Revista Hispánica Moderna* 5 (1939): 1–17, Harry Bernstein challenges the notion that North American interest in Spain only began in the 1820s. See also Edith F. Helman, "Early Interest in Spanish in New England (1815–1835)," *Hispania* 29 (1946): 326–51.

8. Jedadiah Morse, *The American Universal Geography,* 6th ed., 2 vols. (Boston: Isaiah Thomas and Ebenezer T. Andrews, 1812), 2:349; Samuel Whelpley, *A Compend of History,* quoted in Sr. Marie Leonore Fell, *The Foundations of Nativism in American Textbooks, 1783–1860* (Washington, D.C.: Catholic University of America Press, 1941), 37. For the persistence of such ideas in later nineteenth-century textbooks, see Ruth Miller Elson, *Guardians of Tradition: American Schoolbooks in the Nineteenth Century* (Lincoln: University of Nebraska Press, 1964), 150–56.

9. "Trait of Spanish Character," *North American Review* 7 (May 1816): 56. The article was adapted from a speech delivered in 1813 before the Spanish Cortes by Antonio Joseph Ruiz de Padrón, but the *NAR* published it anonymously.

10. Washington Irving to Charles R. Leslie, February 23, 1826, *Letters,* ed. Ralph M. Aderman, Herbert L. Kleinfield, and Jenifer S. Banks, 3 vols. (Boston: Twayne, 1979), 2:179. Language similar to Irving's can be found in "Amusements in Spain," *North American Review* 21 (July 1825): 52–78, esp. 58.

11. Irving to Leslie, April 21, 1826, *Letters,* 2:196.

12. Irving to Lady Granard, May 7, 1827, *Letters*, 2:236.

13. See Rolena Adorno's essay in this volume.

14. *George Ticknor's Travels in Spain*, ed. George T. Northrup (New York: George T. Northrup, 1913), 15. See also *Life, Letters, and Journals of George Ticknor*, 2 vols. (Boston: J. R. Osgood and Co., 1876).

15. *George Ticknor's Travels*, 21.

16. Laborde's comments came in response to the suggestion by another French writer that Spain's national character was subject to change. Laborde wrote: "This is a mistake, the Spaniard has always been the same. The Spaniards are brave: they have always been so" (*A View of Spain*, 5 vols. [London: Longman, Hurst, Rees and Orme, 1809], 5:274).

17. Friedrich Bouterwek's ideas about the linkage between literature and nationality were to be found in the introduction to his massive *Geschichte der Poesie und Beredsamkeit seit dem Ende des dreizehnten Jahrhunderts*, 12 vols. (Göttingen: J. F. Röwer, 1801–19), the third volume of which was published in 1803 and dealt with Spain. This volume was translated into English as the *History of Spanish Literature* (London: D. Bogne, 1847). My understanding of Bouterwek's contribution to Spanish literature rests largely on Thomas R. Hart Jr., "Friedrich Bouterwek: A Pioneer Historian of Spanish Literature," *Comparative Literature* 5 (1953): 351–61. Ideas similar to those of Bouterwek were found in J. C. L. Sismonde di Sismondi, *Littératures du midi de l'Europe*, 4 vols. (Paris: Treutell et Würtz, 1813).

18. George Ticknor, *History of Spanish Literature*, 6th ed., 3 vols. (New York: Gordian Press, 1965), 1:470.

19. The French, albeit for different reasons, were also drawn to the study of Spanish history and literature during the 1820s and 1830s. For an introduction to the work of early *hispanisants*, see the opening chapters of Antonio Niño, *Cultura y diplomacia: Los hispanistas franceses y España, 1875–1931* (Madrid: C.S.I.C., 1988).

20. John Lothrop Motley, *Rise of the Dutch Republic*, 3 vols. (New York: Thomas Y. Crowell, 1901), 1:118.

21. John S. C. Abbott, *The Romance of Spanish History* (New York: Harper and Bros., 1869), 338, 462. For more on Abbott see Stanley T. Williams, *The Spanish Background of American Literature*, 2 vols. (New Haven, Conn.: Yale University Press, 1955), 1:148.

22. James C. Fernald, *The Spaniard in History* (New York: Funk and Wagnalls, 1898), 3, 35, 54. The noted medievalist Henry Charles Lea had similar ideas. See his article "The Decadence of Spain," *Atlantic Monthly* 82 (1898): 32–46, in which he argued that Spain was condemned to be a colonial failure because a "blind and impenetrable pride" fostered a "spirit of conservatism which rejected all innovation in a world of incessant change" (37).

23. "The Spanish Character," *New York Times*, April 4, 1898, 3. I am grateful to Bonnie Goldenberg, a graduate student in history at Johns Hopkins University, for this reference, which appeared in her paper "'Remember the Alamo' to 'Remember the Maine': A Comparative Study of Visual Propaganda during the Mexican and Spanish-American Wars."

24. What follows is extracted from the pamphlet *Spain: An Account of the Public Festival Given by the Citizens of Boston, at the Exchange Coffee House, January 24, 1809, in Honor of Spanish Valour and Patriotism . . . in Which Is Also Introduced a Brief Sketch of Spain . . .* (Boston: Russell and Cutler, 1809). I have used the Library of Congress's copy, cataloged as Thorndike Pamphlets, no. 41. My section heading is a quote from the title page of this pamphlet.

25. I am indebted to Don Jaime Ojeda, former ambassador of Spain to the United States, for introducing me to the writings of Noah.

26. For Noah's biography I have relied on Jonathan D. Sarna, *Jacksonian Jew: The Two Worlds of Mordecai Noah* (New York: Holmes and Meier, 1981).

27. Mordecai M. Noah, *Travels in England, France, and Spain and the Barbary States in the Years 1813–4 and 1815* (New York: Kirk and Mercein, 1819), 67.

28. Ibid., 57.

29. Ibid.

30. Ibid., 92.

31. Ibid., 119.

32. Ibid., 193.

33. The only complete biography of Everett is Elizabeth Evans, "Alexander Hill Everett: Man of Letters" (Ph.D. diss., University of North Carolina at Chapel Hill, 1970).

34. Alexander H. Everett, *America* (Philadelphia: H. C. Carey and I. Lea, 1827), 11.

35. Alexander H. Everett, *Europe; or, A General Survey of the Present Situation of the Principal Powers, with Conjectures of Their Future Prospects* (Boston: O. Everett, 1822), 120.

36. Ibid., 122.

37. Ibid., 131.

38. Ibid., 138.

39. Longfellow to Stephen Longfellow, July 16, 1827, Madrid, *Letters of Henry Wadsworth Longfellow,* ed. Andrew Hilen, 6 vols. (Cambridge, Mass.: Belknap Press of Harvard University Press), 1:235.

40. Everett, *America,* 172.

41. For Caleb Cushing's biography see Claude M. Fuess, *The Life of Caleb Cushing,* 2 vols. (New York: Harcourt, Brace, 1923). Cushing was named ambassador to Spain in 1860.

42. Quoted in Fuess, *Life of Caleb Cushing,* 1:107.

43. Caroline Cushing, *Letters Descriptive of Public Monuments, Scenery, and Manners in France and Spain,* 2 vols. (Newburyport, Mass.: Allen and Co., 1832), 2:201–2.

44. Fuess, *Life of Caleb Cushing,* 1:110.

45. Caleb Cushing, *Reminiscences of Spain, the Country, Its People, History, and Monuments,* 2 vols. (Boston: Carter, Hendee, Allen and Ticknor, 1833), 1:4–5.

46. Ibid., 1:21.

47. Alexander Everett, in a review published in the *North American Review* 37 (July 1833): 84–115, notes that Caleb Cushing, with an eye toward commercial success, modeled his *Reminiscences of Spain* upon Washington Irving's *Sketch Book.*

48. Caleb Cushing, *Reminiscences of Spain* 1:46.

49. Ibid., 2:123.

50. Ibid., 2:297.

51. Ibid., 2:299–300.

52. Severn T. Wallis's essays, published anonymously, include "Navarrete on Spain," *Southern Literary Messenger* 7 (1841): 230–39; "Mr. Washington Irving, Mr. Navarrete, and the *Knickerbocker*," *Southern Literary Messenger* 8 (1842): 725–35; and "The *Knickerbocker*, Mr. Irving, and Mr. Navarrete," *Southern Literary Messenger* 9 (1843): 14–16, in which Wallis indicates that he was the author of the two earlier essays. For the controversy generated by Wallis against Irving's *Columbus*, see Adorno's essay in this volume.

53. These essays by Severn T. Wallis, also published anonymously, included "Spain: Her History, Character, and Literature: Vulgar Errors—Their Extent and Sources," *Southern Literary Messenger* 7 (1841): 441–51, and "Spain, Popular Errors—Their Causes—Travellers," *Southern Literary Messenger* 8 (1842): 305–31. In this last article Wallis wrote that his "Navarrete on Spain" was translated and reprinted in the Madrid newspaper *Espectador* (306n.1).

54. Severn T. Wallis, *Glimpses of Spain: Notes of an Unfinished Tour in 1847* (New York: Harper and Bros., 1849), 363. The French authors mentioned were Théophile Gautier, Alexandre Dumas, and François Guizot. In making these comments, Wallis anticipated by more than fifty years those of Royall Tyler, an English author who, with reference to the same authors whom Wallis was criticizing, wrote, "All of them ran riot in a Spain of their own imagining." See Royall Tyler, *Spain: A Study of Her Life and Arts* (London: G. Richards, 1909), 19.

55. Wallis, *Glimpses of Spain*, 365.

56. Severn T. Wallis, *Spain: Her Institutions, Politics, and Public Men* (Boston: Ticknor, Reed and Fields, 1853), reprinted in *The Writings of Severn Teackle Wallis*, 4 vols. (Baltimore: J. Murphy, 1896), 4:250–51. All citations to this book are from the later edition.

57. Alexander Slidell (1803–47) was a naval lieutenant whose first visit to Spain in 1826 led to *A Year in Spain*, published in 1829 and followed by three later editions. Half travelogue, half political commentary, the book sharply criticized Ferdinand VII—it alleged that Fernando "el absoluto" brought "fury and fanaticism to Spain"—and when the monarch learned about it, he prohibited its sale in Spain and ordered the author's arrest should he ever return to the country. But return he did. Slidell, who later added MacKenzie to his name, sneaked back into Spain in 1834 and spent almost a year there, skillfully eluding the police, and subsequently published *Spain Revisited* in 1836.

58. Wallis, *Spain*, 249.

59. Ibid., 335.

60. Ibid., 171.

61. See James Watson, "Bernard Moses: Pioneer in Latin American Scholarship," *Hispanic American Historical Review* 42 (1962): 212–16.

62. *Letters of William Cullen Bryant*, ed. William Cullen Bryant II and Thomas G. Voss, 3 vols. (New York: Fordham University Press, 1981), 3:451, 465, 484.

63. These articles include Junius Henri Brown, "Jottings and Journeyings in Spain," *New Harper's Monthly Magazine* 41 (June 1870): 1–21, esp. 19; and Charles D. Warner, "Random Spanish Notes," *Atlantic Monthly* 52 (November 1883): 647–58, where the author wrote, "Spain is for all the world the land of Romance" (647).

64. Note that British travel writers of this era dished up similar fare. Typical was William George Clark's *Gazapcho: Summer Months in Spain* (London: J. W. Parker, 1850). Other than Wallis's publications, the first U.S. travel book to portray a somewhat different Spain was Edward E. Hale's *Seven Spanish Cities and the Way to them* (Boston: Little, Brown, 1899), in which the author, a historian, admitted that he found the country quite different from the one described by romantic writers (143). He even expressed praise for the Spanish road engineering (144).

65. My understanding of "historico-politics" is based upon Dorothy Ross, *The Origins of American Social Science* (Cambridge: Cambridge University Press, 1991), 257–300.

66. Frank Blackmar was a Johns Hopkins graduate whose books included *Spanish Colonization in the Southwest* (Baltimore: Johns Hopkins University Press, 1890) and *Spanish Institutions of the Southwest* (Baltimore: Johns Hopkins University Press, 1891).

67. Bernard Moses, preface to *Establishment of the Spanish Rule in America* (New York: G. P. Putnam's Sons, 1898), iii.

68. For Herbert Bolton see Russell M. Magnaghi, *Herbert E. Bolton and the Historiography of the Americas* (Westport, Conn.: Greenwood, 1998).

69. Moses, *Establishment of the Spanish Rule*, 295–96.

70. Hubert H. Bancroft, "Social Analysis," in his *Works*, 39 vols. (San Francisco: A. L. Bancroft and Co., 1890), 38:199.

71. See Philip W. Powell, *Tree of Hate: Power, Propaganda, and Prejudices Affecting the United States Relations with the Hispanic World* (New York: Basic Books, 1971), and Joseph P. Sánchez, *The Spanish Black Legend: Origins of Anti-Hispanic Stereotypes* (Albuquerque, N.Mex.: National Park Service, Spanish Colonial Research Center, 1990).

~~~ 2

Washington Irving's Romantic Hispanism and Its Columbian Legacies
Rolena Adorno

> It appeared to me that a history, faithfully digested from these various materials,
> was a desideratum in literature, and would be a more satisfactory occupation to myself,
> and a more acceptable work to my country, than the translation I had contemplated.
> —Washington Irving, *A History of the Life and Voyages of Christopher Columbus*

> What is biography? Unadorned romance. What is romance? Adorned biography.
> —Mark Twain, *Mark Twain's Notebooks and Journals*

Washington Irving's Romance with Spain

Any consideration of the origins of Anglo–North American Hispanism must take into account the United States' first man of letters, Washington Irving (1783–1859). Irving's lifelong interest in Spanish culture can be summed up by the literary production of his first long stay in Spain: *A History of the Life and Voyages of Christopher Columbus* (1828), *The Conquest of Granada* (1829), and the always-in-print *Alhambra* (1832), better known today as *Legends of the Alhambra.* Whether working in the private library of the U.S. consul and bibliophile Obadiah Rich in Madrid, living in apartments of the Alhambra in Granada, or recalling his Alhambra days while carrying out diplomatic chores in London, Washington Irving represented a triangulation of interests and influences that embraced Spain, England, and the United States. Born of English parents and ever grateful, he said, to have been born on the banks of the Hudson River, Irving had a love affair with Spain that extended from the time of his boyhood readings through the end of his life. Irving's literary and diplomatic work in Spain is best remembered in *The Alhambra,* which has been called "the most distinguished book written on Spain before 1850." It remains in print in the United States and Spain today.[1]

The role of Washington Irving in the history of U.S. literature at large is viewed with ambivalence. On one hand, he is acknowledged as a foundational figure of U.S. letters.[2] On the other, he is seen as a romantic narrator whose sentimentality and superficiality hardly merit a hallowed place in U.S. literary history. Irving's fate has been that he was viewed in his own century as a source of national pride and in the twentieth century as a source of critical embarrassment.[3] Yet his enormous popular editorial success demands another look at his literary production and the reception that it enjoyed in the nineteenth century. This book invites a fresh examination of his work and the place it occupied in early North American letters.

In depicting Spain, Washington Irving was at his best when writing what he called his "traveling sketches."[4] Plainness, ruin, or squalor never disturbed Irving because he painted scenes based on their colors, which he then overlaid with his own iridescent palette. Irving celebrated the glories of the past, whether epitomized in the austere simplicity of a Spanish convent or the opulent halls and gardens of the Alhambra. His saving grace as a writer was that he could swing between the sublime and the prosaic in a movement that kept the willing reader enthralled. A highly engaging example of this effect is found in his *Alhambra* sketch, "The Author's Chamber." There he brings to life the recollection of his first night's stay in the apartments of the Alhambra, while the ghosts of the past and the chimeras of the present commingled in his senses.[5] The account is noticeably reminiscent of the eerie prelude to Ichabod Crane's disappearance as described by Irving in "The Legend of Sleepy Hollow" in *The Sketch Book* of 1819–20.

In like manner Irving's travel account of his visit to Palos, scene of Columbus's departure for the New World, is more engaging (by today's standards) than his historical account of Columbus's sojourn there. Irving's narration of his personal journey does not escape sentimentality, but its literary construction rests on a more profound principle: the ironic, intimate linking of past and present. Thus, while the evidence of a remarkable past was in full view in the form of its landscapes and architectural ruins, history was utterly lost on its heirs. The Pinzones and the residents of Palos, Irving wrote ironically, were indifferent to their forebears' role in Spanish and world history. Irving the sentimentalist knew well how to convey the indifference of unsentimental loss.

Spain gave Washington Irving an unlimited opportunity to elaborate this fundamental dynamic. Spain's multiple heritages—Muslim and Christian, African and European, Mediterranean and Atlantic—were his ongoing sources of fascination. Five of his major books are on Spanish themes, and they stand in sharp contrast to the undistinguished work he did afterward for John Jacob Astor.[6] With Spain as his subject, Irving tirelessly explored the contrast between history's eternal absence and the abiding presence of the past. Irving characterized Granada and Palos by the irretrievable data of their histories and the survival and transformation of their legends and traditions. This tension creates a seductive appeal that helps to explain his extraordinary popularity at the time. In true romantic fashion Irving rendered desolation agreeable and made it habitable for the human imagination. He did so by placing the process of decline and decay far enough back in time that it would not evoke the human suffering that constituted it. Although the unrestored Alhambra of 1829 was the habitat of vagrants, criminals, and poachers, and its imminent demise was prophesied by distinguished travelers, Irving saw beyond its decay to its past splendors and made enormous contributions to the preservation of its timeless lore.[7]

Irving was also committed to the recreation of early modern history in the form of Spain's earliest triumphs in the Americas. The ultimate failure of Spanish imperialism provided the United States with ample room to maneuver as it pursued its own "manifest" national destiny.[8] In that context Irving conceived the history of Columbus's life and voyages to be a topic of remarkable relevance to the United States. His first "Spanish" work, *A History of the Life and Voyages of Christopher Columbus* (1828), earned him a reputation as a serious writer of nonfiction, and its influence and legacy grant him a permanent place in the history of literary cultural relations among Spain, the United States, and Latin America. That history includes the brief but intense regional and transatlantic polemics that *Columbus* spawned.

Irving's extraordinarily influential biography gave Columbus to the United States and made the admiral a staple of nineteenth-century U.S. culture that filters into the teaching of basic U.S. history to this day. Even the most recent approaches in today's school textbooks—featuring Columbus as a Renaissance Darth Vader—are but the latest transformation of Irving's cultural enterprise.[9] When the author of the *Sketch Book* set foot on Spanish soil for the first time in 1826, he immediately turned his attention to the tale of the Admiral of the Ocean Sea. Spain sharpened Irving's sensibilities to the themes of heroism, adventure, and romance, which he in turn poured into every line of *Columbus*. As I will show, Irving's images of nineteenth-century Spain (and the United States) are diffused throughout his biography of the Genoese mariner.

Irving's turn to Spain and Columbus did not come out of nowhere. Colonial times in British North America, particularly the eighteenth century, brought the development of a widening consciousness about Spanish culture as exemplified by the study of the Spanish language, the collection of Spanish materials for libraries, and the introduction of Spanish themes in the literary and historical arts. Thomas Jefferson's establishment of Spanish-language study as part of the modern language curricula he instituted at the College of William and Mary and later at the University of Virginia was especially significant.[10] Although his motives were pragmatic, he was fully aware of the potential scholarly value of Spanish. He acknowledged it as the language in which "the greater part of the earlier history of America" was written.[11] Irving was the first, a decade later, to make use of Spanish as a tool of humanistic learning and research. The trend that Irving started, namely, to move beyond English-language perspectives on the Americas' history, was summed up many years later in a reviewer's reference to the writings of William Hickling Prescott: While "England, our good mother, with a common language, has indoctrinated us after her own fashion," U.S. writers now embarked upon a "new path that let in . . . a new light." This new light came from "the sources of truth, common to all," which meant, in part, the use of Spanish sources in their original language.[12]

During the first four decades of the nineteenth century, travelers, writers for magazines, historians, scholars, fiction writers, and artists turned their attention to Spain. Readings of Cervantes continued to have the direct and powerful influence first evidenced in the eighteenth century. The period from 1830 to 1860 was particularly productive for the growth of Hispanism in literature, and if the best of the representative travelers and early writers was found in Washington Irving, the honors went to Prescott in history, to George Ticknor in literary scholarship, and to William Cullen Bryant and Herman Melville in the fields of poetry and fiction, respectively.[13]

U.S. literary and historical interest in Spain and Latin America paralleled U.S. economic and political expansionism and growing literary independence. To be sure, the ultimate roots of early U.S. folklore were English, not American, and early U.S. writers faithfully maintained the British cultural heritage. Other influences also came into play. U.S. interest focused on Spain because of hemispheric political motives. Political intervention and economic ventures in the Americas made the United States the self-styled heir to Spain's failed efforts, taking up where Spain's Columbian legacy left off.[14] Jefferson's promotion of the study of Spanish was, after all, an act of political foresight based on his judgment about the importance of the use of Spanish by "so great a portion of the inhabitants of our continents, with whom we shall probably have great intercourse ere long."

Interest in Christopher Columbus as historical figure and cultural icon had been developing in the decades after the Tammany Society and Columbian

Order were established in New York in 1789 and the first Columbian observances were held during the third centenary of 1790–92.[15] Dr. Jeremy Belknap's 1792 commemorative discourse before the Massachusetts Historical Society in Boston, later augmented in his *American Biography* (1794), offered the first notable recounting, in the United States, of the admiral's life. Columbus served the purpose of popular public history in an ideal fashion. The figure of a solitary genius and entrepreneur carrying European civilization over new frontiers to uncharted lands resonated well with the aspirations of a young country. Irving's Columbus was to dramatize, in short, the model of the North American "self-made man" who could do good for others by doing well for himself.

Irving's *Columbus* anticipates the expression "self-made man" made famous in Henry Clay's February 1832 speech before the U.S. Senate. As analyzed by John G. Cawelti, the underlying convictions that produced Clay's self-made man can apply equally to Irving's creation of his Columbus, namely, (1) a conviction that social mobility depends completely on the will and action of the individual; (2) a belief in the essentially benevolent character of economic power, however heavily concentrated; and (3) the conviction that the central arena of action is business enterprise. In other words, the United States was a land of opportunity, and any individual willing to work could tap those opportunities. The pursuit of economic advancement by the individual was also viewed as the best way to help others.[16] It is in this light that the adventures of Christopher Columbus are best understood as a topic of historical investigation and popular appeal in nineteenth-century North America.

Irving's Columbian Encounter

Washington Irving was forty-two, living in London, and tending none too successfully to the family hardware business when Martín Fernández de Navarrete (1765–1844) brought out the first systematic collection of Columbian documentation ever assembled. Published under the royal imprimatur of Spain, the first two volumes of Navarrete's *Colección de los viages y descubrimientos que hicieron por mar los españoles desde fines del siglo XV* appeared in 1825.[17] When in 1826 Irving faced near-bankruptcy because of his brothers' failed investments in South American mining interests, he sought a position in the U.S. ministry in Madrid. Alexander H. Everett, the U.S. minister plenipotentiary, responded with a suitable offer and suggested that Irving come to Spain and translate Navarrete's newly published Columbian corpus into English. Irving was apparently already competent in Spanish, having begun his study of the language in December 1824 in Paris.[18]

Irving's arrival in Madrid in early 1826 marked the beginning of his lifelong relationship with the Iberian Peninsula. He lived in Spain for two periods, totaling more than seven years. During his first stay (1826–29) he devoted himself to literary pursuits while holding an all-but-honorary diplomatic post (figure 2.1).[19] At the invitation of the governor of the Alhambra, Irving lived in the fabled Alhambra palace for three brief months in 1829 (May 12 through the first days of August). His stay was cut short by his acceptance of a diplomatic post in London.[20] During Irving's second sojourn (1842–46) he served as envoy extraordinary and minister plenipotentiary to the Court of Spain. His acquaintance with the country and knowledge of its principal language had been persuasive arguments in favor of his appointment by Secretary of State Daniel Webster. Overall, Washington Irving's literary career reached the peak of its prestige, and his career in public service was culminated, on the shores of the Iberian Peninsula. As the Irving biographer Stanley T. Williams observed, "No other major American writer of the nineteenth century became through residence and use of materials so deeply identified with any one continental nation."[21]

What literary sensibilities and aspirations did the *Sketch Book* author of "Rip Van Winkle" and "The Legend of Sleepy Hollow" take to Spain in 1826? We might expect that his self-described "conjurings of the imagination" and commonly remarked propensity for "the legendary, the bygone, and the remote" would have led him immediately to the pursuit of Moorish and ancient Spanish legends. In fact, he would later remark in *The Alhambra:* "From earliest boyhood, when, on the banks of the Hudson, I first pored over the pages of

Figure 2.1. Portrait of Washington Irving (1783–1859) by H. B. Hall, after a drawing by David Wilkie, in Seville, 1828. (Washington Irving Papers, Manuscripts and Archives Division, New York Public Library, Astor, Lenox, and Tilden Foundations)

an old Spanish story about the wars of Granada, that city has ever been a subject of my waking dreams, and often have I trod in fancy the romantic halls of the Alhambra."[22] Yet Irving arrived in Spain with the suggestion already planted by Alexander Everett that he devote himself to Columbus and the Spanish role in the age of discovery.

If the diplomat Alexander Everett suggested that Irving translate the freshly minted volumes of Columbus documents, Obadiah Rich claimed credit for suggesting to Irving the project of a narrative history of the life of the admiral.[23] Irving was quickly persuaded for a number of reasons that writing a history of the life of Columbus was a more prudent course than translating the enormous collection of Columbian documents. He immediately gave himself over to the task that produced, twenty-one months later (in October 1827), *A History of the Life and Voyages of Christopher Columbus.* It was published in 1828, first in London and then in New York.[24] Although Richard Hakluyt and Samuel Purchas had given Columbus's career a cursory glance and William Robertson's 1777 *History of America* had treated the topic more fully, Washington Irving was now the author of the first great biography of Columbus in the English language.[25]

The success of *Columbus* provides compelling evidence of the prominent role that Hispanist/Americanist themes played in the foundational literary and pedagogical culture of the United States. Irving's biography of Columbus was received in the United States as the standard life of Columbus in English long after its 1828 publication. It enjoyed immense editorial success: 116 editions and reprintings in its first eight decades.[26] More important, his abridged version of 1829—a single volume—was used in schools and universities abroad as well as in the United States. Irving's work was not rapidly superseded because successive works were too scholarly in apparatus, too limited in scope, or too focused on the cruelties of conquest to inspire trust.[27] For erudite audiences the shift away from Irving's *Columbus* began only in the 1880s with such works as Henry Harrisse's *Christophe Colomb* (1884) and Sir Clements R. Markham's *Life of Christopher Columbus* (1892).[28] Irving's work nevertheless continued to be reissued in editions throughout the 1890s, and it appeared at slightly less frequent but still regular intervals through the 1920s.

Irving's *Columbus* was known early to Spanish audiences, thanks to the 1834 translation by José García de Villalta. This version was reprinted fourteen times by 1893. It was joined by other Spanish translations, plus a number of translations to other European languages, which appeared with remarkable frequency through the 1890s.[29] In 1892 Marcelino Menéndez y Pelayo assessed Irving's *Columbus* as still current and recommendable to the general public ("hombres de mundo y aficionados," i.e., men of the world and amateur enthusiasts).

Recognizing that it is a work of art notable for the beauty of its descriptive and narrative style, Menéndez y Pelayo lamented that such books were no longer being written. He judged as a "tacit expression of their own impotence" the criticisms by contemporary writers who disdained Irving's type of picturesque and dramatic historical narrative.[30]

Irving's (Transatlantic) Literary and Historical Romanticism

Washington Irving stands at the head of several nineteenth-century romantic trends in U.S. history, and he is the primary exemplar of popular history writing on Spanish themes. Three strains of nineteenth-century U.S. Hispanist interest stand out: an emphasis on Spain's Roman and Muslim antiquities, its modern and contemporary societies and cultures, and its potential as a "magic carpet" for the free flight of the romantic narrative imagination.[31] Although the tendencies of the antiquarian, the realist, and the romantic commonly overlapped in the writings of any single author, the romantic approach predominates for the period in question and for Washington Irving in particular. David Levin's classic study of the great U.S. romantic historians (George Bancroft, William Hickling Prescott, John Lothrop Motley, and Francis Parkman) sums up the tendencies that can also be applied to Irving as their predecessor.[32] Enthusiasm for the past, admiration for its great heroes, and devotion to nature and "the natural" characterized the romantic historians who strove to give meaning and immediacy to history and its major figures. They considered themselves "painters." That is, they conceived their subjects pictorially, dealt in character types, exploited readers' familiarity with convention, and used landscape to convey notions that they considered especially significant. These writers commonly offered detailed anecdotes to create an episodic quality and give the reader the illusion of participation. They frequently relied on well-known stories that had the power to captivate the reader's attention.[33]

Insofar as the romantic historians considered themselves judges of nations and men, they operated on a theory of history that included the intervention of a divine and dynamic Providence whose wisdom established the laws of the moral world and controlled the direction of history. This notion of progress in turn was based on an assumption of advancement in human affairs. Progress was viewed as a trajectory of political and religious change that ran its full course from the fifteenth century through the American Revolution. It began in the Spain of Ferdinand and Isabella, was further developed in the Netherlands, and reached its apogee with the Puritans of New England. If Castilian and Leonese Spain occupied the vanguard of political and territorial progress, opening the way to the New World and setting new standards of national unity, royal justice, and efficiency, Spain's ultimate heir was Puritan New England. Francis Parkman's statement about nineteenth-century American puritanism applies to Irving's Christopher Columbus: "An uncommon vigor, joined to the hardy virtues of a masculine race, marked the New England type. The sinews, it is true, were hardened at the expense of blood and flesh,—and this literally as well as figuratively; but the staple of character was a steady conscientiousness, an undespairing courage, patriotism, public spirit, sagacity, and a strong good sense."[34]

The values celebrated by Parkman implicitly reveal his peers' (and Irving's earlier) disdain for theological argument and metaphysical speculation. Active experience was the predominant feature: spirituality came from the heart and conscience, civil and religious freedoms from the creative powers of action. Consisting of courage, self-reliance, self-denial, endurance, candor, and vigorous activity, these masculine and chivalric values were considered "natural" virtues. That is, they stood in contrast to "artificial" materialist impulses with their selfish search to preserve their own power and sophisticated vices. The materialist tendency was considered to be effeminate insofar as it was self-indulgent, prone to the use of subtlety and deceit, and given over to "languor" or moral torpor.[35] These natural virtues and materialist vices epitomize Irving's portrayal of Columbus and his enemies, respectively.

The romantic historians were also distinguished by their choice of topics. Their deep interest in human character led to the selection of grand themes such as the origins of a nation (preferably, in some way, the United States), the progress of liberty in its struggle against absolutism, or the conquest of a continent (by the colonists and conquistadors of North and South America, respectively). In each, "a varied group of remarkable, vigorous characters acted heroically on the largest possible stage."[36] Irving's *Columbus* led the way. He pronounced the subject to be "of so interesting and national a kind" that he could not willingly abandon it.[37] Irving planted the seeds of the progressive view of history that would be fully realized by the U.S. romantic historians of the next generation. His Christopher Columbus grafted the values of the hardy frontiersman onto the project of Castilian/Leonese nationalism.

As Irving worked on *Columbus,* his romantic penchant for the Mediterranean and peninsular Spanish past carried him away from the task of writing Atlantic exploration history and into the realm of Moorish romance amid the tales of Isabella and Ferdinand's 1492 conquest of the exotic and opulent Granada. When in August 1826 *Columbus* was "merely a rough outline," Irving yielded to the temptation to turn to the conquest of Granada. Working in Obadiah Rich's private library in Madrid (the significance of which I will address later), Irving found himself torn between two lines of reading, the Columbian and the Moorish Granadine. As he struggled with "many petty points to be adjusted and disputed facts to be settled" regarding Columbus, he became enthralled with the exploits of Granada's Muslim cavaliers.[38] Much later (in 1843) he recalled this quixotic struggle between love and duty: "While writing the history of Columbus I was obliged to consult several records relating to the Conquest of Granada, and got so deeply interested in the subject that I wrote out the heads of chapters for the whole work and then laid it [to] one side until I had finished the History of Columbus, when I took it up and in less than six months had completed it."[39]

Around that time in Puerto de Santa María (Cádiz), Irving made the acquaintance of the Continental romantic and German man of letters Johann Nikolaus Böhl von Faber.[40] Böhl had married a Spanish woman, Doña Francisca Larrea, and settled in southern Spain, where he devoted himself to the study of Spanish literature.[41] The friendship between Irving and Böhl flourished. It included Böhl's married daughter, Cecilia Böhl von Faber de Arrom, marchioness of Arco Hermoso, who would become known to the world of Spanish letters as the novelist Fernán Caballero.[42]

Böhl played a crucial role in the development of Spanish romanticism. He was a powerful advocate of the aesthetic ideas of his compatriots August and Frederick Schlegel, and he convened in Cádiz an impressive circle of Spanish writers. Like the Schlegels, Böhl devoted himself to the recovery of medieval oral traditions of Castilian balladry (the *Romancero*) and sixteenth- and seventeenth-century Spanish drama. He published in Germany an important, three-volume compilation of traditional Spanish verse, *Floresta de rimas antiguas castellanas* (1821–25), and a monograph on the Spanish national theater, *Teatro español anterior a Lope de Vega* (1832). At the same time he produced on stage in Cádiz the dramatic works of Pedro Calderón de la Barca. The Böhls and Irving shared a devotion to "a renewal of the ancient literary glory of Spain" and were disappointed by Spanish subservience to French models.[43] The importance of this enduring Böhl-Irving relationship, which transcended the latter's 1832 return to the United States, can hardly be overestimated. Irving temporarily gave up English society in Spain as the Böhls brought him into greater contact with Spanish authors and Spanish literature, which allowed him to confirm his romantic views about Spanish themes.

At the same time neither Irving's close contact with German and Spanish romanticism through Böhl nor his sojourn in Spain can be said to have generated Irving's romantic Hispanism. By his own account even *The Alhambra* derived first from his early bookish acquaintance with Spanish lore and only secondarily from his personal experience in Spain.[44] Irving's contact with Spanish medieval history and contemporary German romanticism merely intensified and emboldened his natural proclivities toward romance. Irving's youthful reading experiences offer the fullest glimpses of his early fascination with the topics of "romantic Spain."

Washington Irving's Anglo-American Christopher Columbus

Irving's encounter with the Columbian corpus published by Martín Fernández de Navarrete is best accessed through the evidence of Irving's exchanges with that distinguished Spanish historian. In telegraphic entries in his journals from 1826 and 1827, Irving offers brief remarks. Freshly arrived in Spain, he was received at the Minister Plenipotentiary Everett's residence on February 16, 1826, and he was at Navarrete's door less than a week later. His diary entry for February 21 reads simply: "Called this morning on Sigr. Navarrete, Secretary to the Academy of History. Showed me the work concerning Columbus voyage, etc." In a letter to T. W. Storrow of April 14, 1826, Irving remarked: "I have access to the manuscripts, from which Navarette [*sic*] has compiled his work just published, and many of which it would be almost impossible to procure out of Madrid."[45] A year later a few more brief references appear; he apparently called five times on Navarrete in January and February 1827, and he mentioned obtaining manuscripts from him on one of these occasions.[46] He was more eloquent in the published preface to his *Columbus:* "From Don Martín Fernández de Navarrete, who communicated various valuable and curious pieces of information, discovered in the course of his researches, I received the most obliging assistance: nor can I refrain from testifying my admiration of the self-sustained zeal of that estimable man, one of the last veterans of Spanish literature, who is almost alone, yet indefatigable in his labours, in a country where, at present, literary exertion meets with but little excitement."[47] By contrasting Navarrete with his countrymen, Irving's expression of deep respect for the great naval historian may have unwittingly helped provoke a polemic that would emerge about thirteen years later and reflect negatively on Irving.

Irving's prefatory statement about receiving from Navarrete "various valuable and curious pieces of information" has been viewed as too miserly an acknowledgment of a far greater debt. However, Irving acknowledged other Spanish scholars and collectors who were also important to his endeavors. He lauded the liberality of Columbus's descendant, the duke of Veragua, for opening the Columbus family archives for his inspection.[48] He also gave special thanks to Don Antonio de Uguina, a member of the Spanish court whom he admired for his many contributions to early colonial history. Uguina made available to Irving the papers, left in Uguina's possession, of Don Juan Bautista Muñoz, the great historian, bibliophile, and founder of the Archivo General de Indias.[49]

Another factor that mitigated Irving's indebtedness to Navarrete was Irving's dependence on Obadiah Rich's collection of imprints. Irving expressed this indebtedness privately, in letters to friends written as he began and completed his work, and publicly, in a long commentary in his 1828 preface to *Columbus:* "In his [Rich's] extensive and curious library, I found one of the best collections extant of Spanish colonial history, containing many documents for which I might search elsewhere in vain. This he put at my absolute command, with a frankness and unreserve seldom to be met with among the possessors of such rare and valuable books; *and his library has been my main resource throughout the whole of my labors.*"[50] Irving's most important source was a printed one: the biography of Columbus by his son Don Hernando Colón (1488–1539).

From Navarrete's side, the only record that seems to survive regarding his association with Irving pertains to the American's election to the Real Academia de la Historia in December 1828, when Navarrete was the academy's president. Also, the Navarrete family papers contain a notice about the presentation copy of *Columbus* that Irving gave to Don Martín.[51] The relationship between the two men can be deduced only from what each said about the other in print. Although their remarks are brief, their intellectual relationship had an implicit diplomatic dimension that corresponded to the cultural politics that they respectively represented.

Navarrete's work inaugurated an altogether new era in Columbian studies when he discovered and published accounts of Columbus's first and third voyages. These had been exclusively preserved in transcriptions and compilations of Columbus's original records made by Bartolomé de Las Casas in preparation for his *Historia de las Indias* (1527–59). Navarrete labored for thirty-five years to assemble the Columbian corpus. Unstopped in his work even by the Napoleonic invasion and French occupation of Spain, he published the *Colección de los viages y descubrimientos* in three installments: Columbus's voyages and related documents concerning early settlements (volumes 1 and 2 [1825]); the "minor voyages" of Amerigo Vespucci, Pedro Arias Dávila, and Vasco Núñez de Balboa (volume 3 [1829]); and the expeditions to the Moluccas (volumes 4 and 5 [1837]).

With access to Navarrete's first two volumes at the time he wrote his biography, Irving was the first historical writer in any language to take advantage of the Columbus–Las Casas accounts of the first and third voyages. How did Irving handle these extraordinary materials? Even Irving's biographer Stanley Williams referred to him as "an American poacher," and Irving's *Colum-*

bus is often criticized today for near plagiarism, sentimentality, and a lack of historical and critical judgment.[52] A fresh investigation, however, leads to more judicious and productive conclusions about the character of Irving's work, particularly in regard to its status as a landmark in Anglo–North American Hispanism.

Irving's stated intentions were clear from the outset. He aimed to "form his narrative" by comparing the works of Las Casas and Hernando Colón:

> I shall form my narrative from a careful comparison and collation of the works of Las Casas and Columbus' son Fernando [Hernando], both founded on Columbus [*sic*] Journal—and shall at the same time make use of Oviedo, who lived in Columbus [*sic*] time and in fact all the old Spanish writers. I have the various works relative to the subject in Italian, French, etc. I am in fact surrounded by works of the kind. I shall endeavour to make it the most complete and authentic account of Columbus and his voyages extant and, by diligent investigation of the materials around me, to settle various points in dispute.[53]

Because the principal sources of Las Casas and Hernando Colón included Columbus's journal, that text and others collected by Navarrete served only as secondary or tertiary sources for Irving. Irving planned also to use all the compendia available in various languages to construct his history. In other words, he aimed to create not a work of original scholarship but rather the best possible synthesis of what was known and available. His preface to the finished work suggests his satisfaction at having reached that goal.[54]

Washington Irving, as Prescott and others would do after him, turned the Spanish adventure in the New World into a remarkable Anglo-American story. He created a nineteenth-century Columbus on the verge of discovery—and opportunity. Irving smoothly grafted the accounts of Hernando Colón and Bartolomé de Las Casas—the Columbus sources he used with greatest frequency—onto a North American conceptualization of New World Columbian history based on personal entrepreneurship, private enterprise, and the "spirit of commerce." Irving referred to Columbus's goal ("the design of seeking a western route to India") as his "grand project of discovery." He commonly spoke of the admiral's "enterprise," thus underscoring, in typical nineteenth-century language, the progressive economic goals that he attributed to Columbus.[55]

Irving's major contribution to Columbian historiography was to initiate the modern view of the discovery of America as an accident, albeit a glorious one. This crucial point marked his most significant divergence from the model provided by Hernando Colón, who claimed that his father had discovered unknown lands that he had knowingly sought. Irving emphasized the expansion of known navigational routes and the advancement of geographical knowledge of the world at large. Some North American readers criticized him for diminishing the emphasis on Columbus's Christian mission and his hope to rescue the holy sepulcher at Jerusalem.[56] Yet Columbus himself devoted very little ink to his evangelizing goal in the accounts of his four voyages. Irving's account reveals, interestingly, the divergence he found between Columbus's professed aims and the contents of his narrative accounts.[57] At the same time Irving did not shrink from, or take lightly, Columbus's goal of recovering the holy sepulcher.[58] Nevertheless, Irving's narrative emphasis throughout his account is focused, as were his sixteenth-century sources, on the discovery of new navigational routes and the development of ultramarine settlement and trade.

Irving's *Columbus* thus anticipates the manner in which the later romantic historians merged their celebration of honor and masculine vigor with their bourgeois admiration for industry. For the U.S. romantics materialism and commerce were opposing goals, the former representing greed and the latter the spirit of trade that had the power to civilize nations. Via the "natural" economic principles of free trade, "enterprise" or industry, and self-reliance, the merchant's commercial endeavors were not viewed as materialist but rather as the agency of the "spirit of commerce." This view held that the non-Western peoples of the world would inevitably be bettered by contact with commodities, technologies, and values superior to their own.[59] Irving's Christopher Columbus, decidedly not a materialist, was conceived as such an "agent of commerce."[60]

Irving drew a clear line between the "grand enterprises" that Columbus sought to put into effect and the greedy goals of "desperate and grasping adventurers" and "avaricious conquerors." For Columbus "pecuniary calculations and cares . . . gave feasibility to his schemes" but never corrupted his soul's aspirations: "The gains that promised to arise from his discoveries, he intended to appropriate to the same princely and pious spirit in which they were demanded," and Columbus contemplated "works and achievements of benevolence and religion" that included "conciliating and civilizing the natives, building cities, introducing the useful arts, subjecting every thing to the control of law, order, and religion; and thus of founding regular and prosperous empires."[61]

This Columbus suffered from one fatal fault: "He evidently concurred in the opinion that all nations which did not acknowledge the Christian faith were destitute of natural rights; that the sternest measures might be used for their conversion, and the severest punishments inflicted upon their obstinacy in unbelief." In this spirit of bigotry, Irving remarked, Columbus considered himself justified in making captives of the natives, transporting them to Spain to have them taught the doctrines of Christianity, and selling them as slaves.

Irving was quick to point out that the crown itself sanctioned the slavery until "the humanity of Isabella" put a stop to it. He argued that if Columbus erred in this matter, it was because he was "goaded on by the mercenary impatience of the crown [read "Ferdinand"] and by the sneers of his enemies at the unprofitable result of his enterprises."[62] In other words, Irving made economic exploitation and greed the prerogatives of others, never Columbus.

Hence, the right course was inherent to this Columbus. In true romantic style Columbus developed this habit not from the study of law or philosophy but from his natural impulses. If he sinned on the matter of the natives' treatment and the denial of their natural rights, it was not a sin against God but against the godly part of his temperament: "In so doing he sinned against the natural goodness of his character, and against the feelings which he had originally entertained and expressed towards this gentle and hospitable people." Irving's reluctance to cite Columbus for this shortcoming is revealed in his statement that the "bigotry of the age" and the "errors of the times" should be remembered so that the reader would understand that these shortcomings were not solely Columbus's. Irving is nevertheless duty bound to avoid justifying Columbus "on a point where it is inexcusable to err." Hence he attempts to shield the admiral from culpability for the natives' mistreatment by limply referring to the moral lessons that the recounting of history can offer: "Let it remain a blot on his illustrious name, and let others derive a lesson from it."[63]

Irving moves Columbus's responsibility for injustice toward the natives from the arena of his personal integrity to his duties in command of others. He portrays Columbus's subordinates in order to exonerate the admiral, who was "continually outraged in his dignity, and braved in the exercise of his command; . . . foiled in his plans, and endangered in his person by the seditions of turbulent and worthless men." The masculine, chivalric virtues of Columbus's nature prevail; the "benevolence and generosity of his heart" and "the strong powers of his mind" brought him to forbear, to reason, to supplicate, and never to seek revenge but to forgive and forget at the least sign of repentance: "He has been extolled for his skill in controlling others; but far greater praise is due to him for his firmness in governing himself."[64] This is a perfect romantic hero, utterly alone, relying only on the high-minded impulses of his noble heart.

Irving's Columbus was a man of deep emotion, heightened sensibilities, and great piety. Above all, he possessed a great imagination—that "ardent and enthusiastic imagination which threw a magnificence over his whole course of thought." This "poetical temperament," that is, Columbus's imagination, spread around him "a golden and glorious world" that "tinged every thing with its own gorgeous colors." His imagination betrayed him into visionary speculations of

Asia and the terrestrial paradise. It mingled with his religion, filling his mind "with solemn and visionary meditations on mystic passages of the Scriptures, and the shadowy portents of prophecies." At the same time Irving argued that Columbus's ardent imagination and mercurial nature were controlled by a powerful judgment and directed by an acute sagacity. Thus governed, his imagination, "instead of exhausting itself in idle flights, lent aid to his judgment, and enabled him to form conclusions at which common minds could never have arrived, nay, which they could not perceive when pointed out."[65]

Irving fashioned a Columbus whose intended didactic and/or inspirational value can be summed up as follows: To control the imagination through the exercise of judgment in order to reach conclusions not commonly conceived, to trace in the conjectures and reveries of past ages the patterns that should gird and guide the future, and to teach all citizens to practice the virtues of self-restraint in governing themselves.

Irving's Columbus was that variety of self-reliant, courageous, commonsensical New Englander who could oppose the will of a ruler whose personal indifference and greed made him arbitrary and oppressive. The last chapter of Irving's Columbus story portrays his losing contest against Ferdinand after the death of Isabella. Irving noted that with her illness, Columbus's interests languished. Irving remarked, with no small amount of irony: "And when she died, he was left to the justice and generosity of Ferdinand." Irving makes the point that the courageous Columbus of "loyal and generous heart" was pitted against the all-powerful "cold and calculating Ferdinand," "the selfish Ferdinand" who offered many professions of kindness but whose "cold ineffectual smiles, which pass like wintry sunshine over the countenance . . . convey no warmth to the heart."[66] In Irving's narration the disembodied "courtly smile" becomes a trope of high intrigue and hypocrisy at court.[67]

Irving declared himself to be carrying out the historian's duty to impartiality by asserting that attempts had been made "by loyal Spanish writers, to vindicate the conduct of Ferdinand towards Columbus" but that such efforts had been futile and their failure was not to be regretted. Citing Ferdinand's "debt of gratitude due to the discoverer, which the monarch had so faithlessly neglected to discharge," Irving declared that "to screen such injustice in so eminent a character from the reprobation of mankind, is to deprive history of one of its most important uses." The "dark shadow" that Ferdinand's ingratitude cast on Columbus's "brilliant renown, will be a lesson to all rulers, teaching them what is important to their own fame in their treatment of illustrious men."[68]

This Columbus now seems extravagantly optimistic, not to mention anachronistic. Yet Irving was a man rich in imagination who was born two years after the successful conclusion of the American Revolution and wrote his biography of Columbus before the threat of the U.S. Civil War. To Irving, Columbus's entrepreneurial spirit must have seemed not only historically plausible but in fact possible to recreate. With his history of the life of the admiral, Irving indirectly succeeded in creating a historical foundation for the United States that extended further back than the 1609 settlement at Jamestown and the 1620 arrival of the pilgrims at Plymouth. With this purpose in mind Irving consolidated the popular impulses of enthusiasm for Columbus as national forefather and founder that had been given form about forty years earlier with the creation of such institutions as New York's Tammany Society.

Early Anglo-American Responses: Columbus and the Call for a National Literature

The reaction to Irving's work at home was immediate. The earliest reviews of the *Life and Voyages of Columbus* in the United States were overwhelmingly positive. Some reviewers remarked on the impressive and unexpected shift from his customary light satirical literature to serious historical writing.[69] Most of these enthusiastic reviews appeared in the first half of 1828; Irving's own satisfaction with the results is registered in the December 31, 1828, entry in his journal: "Thus ends the year—tranquilly. It has been one of much literary application, and generally speaking one of the most tranquil in spirit of my whole life, the literary success of the Hist[ory] of Columb[us] has been greater than I anticipated and gives me hopes that I have executed something which may have greater duration than I anticipate for my works of mere imagination."[70]

Although almost two centuries later his works of "mere imagination" have fared far better than his works of historical investigation, his forecast was not far off the mark for the nineteenth century. Irving's biography of Columbus made him a steadily productive professional writer. By the end of 1830 he had earned important honors from the civic and learned institutions of Spain and Great Britain. With Navarrete's blessing as its president, Spain's Real Academia de la Historia elected Irving corresponding member on December 12, 1828. In the name of King George IV he was awarded a gold medal from England's Royal Society of Literature in 1830. Oxford University granted him an honorary doctor in civil law (D.C.L.). Significantly, U.S. institutions followed suit only after honors from abroad started to flow in. Columbia University awarded him an honorary doctor of laws (L.L.D.) in 1829, and Harvard University did the same in 1831.[71]

Irving's *Columbus* stirred the civic interests of many U.S. public institutions and the artists who hoped to serve them.[72] The case of Irving's good friend, the artist Washington Allston (1779–1843), serves as a pertinent example. Hoping to receive a commission to create a mural-sized painting of "The First Interview of Columbus with Ferdinand and Isabella" in the U.S. Capitol, Allston banked on the new biography as a catalyst when he proposed his mural project to the chairman of the committee of the House of Representatives, Gulian C. Verplanck, another Irving acquaintance. Allston wrote to Verplanck that he found in Irving's book "magnificence, emotion, and everything, the very triumph of 'matter' to task a painter's powers. The announcement and the proof of the birth of a New World." Allston could think of no subject that more emphatically "belonged to America and her history than the triumph of her discoverer. We, who now enjoy the blessings of his discovery, cannot place him too high in that history which without him would never have been." In Allston's opinion "the beautiful work of Irving has placed him as the presiding Genius over the yet fresh, and, we will hope, immortal fountain of our national literature."[73]

Allston, like others, thus proposed Irving's *Columbus* as the cornerstone of a national U.S. literature and Columbus himself as the model of patriotic duty. Upon Irving's death in 1859 the mayor of New York, Daniel F. Tiemann, expressed similar sentiments in a eulogy that proclaimed that Irving's biographies of Columbus and George Washington would "fire the youthful mind to emulate those examples of heroic duty and heroic patriotism."[74]

Irving's *Columbus* was thought capable of building the national reputation in the field of letters. His benefactor Alexander H. Everett sounded the call in his January 1829 encomium to Irving's new work in the *North American Review*. Everett virtually proclaimed the birth of a national literature whose effect would be to end the decades-long European dismissal of the new country's feeble literary and scientific pursuits. While it was true, he acknowledged, that the "active life" had in previous decades absorbed "the whole talent of the country," the period had now arrived "when the calls of business no longer absorbed all the cultivated intellect existing in the country." In the face of the "continual sneers of a set of heartless and senseless foreigners upon our want of literary talent," a host of literary aspirants had now risen up to occupy "the front rank of what is commonly called a school of polite literature." Everett exulted: "To set this example was the brilliant part reserved, in the course of our literary history, for Mr. Washington Irving."[75] In this manner Washington Irving came to be anointed the first man of American letters.

Everett's use of the U.S. romantic idiom of the active life, progress, and chivalry underscored the colorful character of U.S. public discourse shared by diplomats, politicians, and the authors of "polite literature." The role played by Irving in defending the national honor justified, in Everett's words, Irving's "pretension to be viewed as the valorous knight, who was called, in the order of destiny, to break the spell, which appeared, at least to our good natured European brethren, to be thrown over us in this respect; to achieve the great and hitherto unaccomplished adventure of establishing a purely American literary reputation of the first order; and demonstrate the capacity of his countrymen to excel in the elegant, as they had before done in all the useful and solid branches of learning."[76]

Such a solid branch of learning was history, specifically philosophical history, whose goal was "to set forth, by a record of real events, the general principles, which regulate the march of political affairs." Philosophical history was superior, in Everett's view, to narrative history, which was, "when properly written, substantially poetry." Narrative history had as its goal to "give a correct and lively picture of the same events, as they pass before the eye of the world, but with little or no reference to their causes or effects." He assigned Irving's work on Columbus to the latter category, noting that this "lower species of history" corresponded to the natural bent of Irving's genius, "which does not incline him, as we have repeatedly observed, to philosophical researches."[77]

In contrast to Everett's view Irving had taken the approach that narrative history was superior to the philosophical. He argued that to engage in "mere speculations or general reflections" would be simple indulgence. Irving preferred instead "to give a minute and circumstantial narrative, omitting no particular that appeared characteristic of the persons, the events, or the times; and endeavoring to place every fact under such a point of view, that the reader might perceive its merits, and *draw his own maxims and conclusions.*"[78] This is the U.S. romantic historians' emphasis on active experience. Causality is dramatized, not explained, through the historical protagonist's actions. Everett noted that in the absence of general political speculation, Irving's limited reflections pertained to matters of ordinary private morality. He was right. Irving had interpreted even Columbus's blindness to the natives' natural rights and to Ferdinand's deviousness toward him as personal moral failings. This was the subset of history that corresponded to biography: In Everett's view, for the kind of historical writing of which Irving was capable, the life of Columbus provided one of the best, if not "the very best subject afforded by the annals of the world."[79] Irving's was less a history of Columbian and Caribbean exploration than the life story of a man engaged in personal moral combat.

With respect to biography Everett made clear that no satisfactory account of Columbus's life existed in any language. He considered Hernando Colón's work "merely a brief and imperfect sketch" and judged that even William Robertson's important work in English "did not allow a detailed and accurate investigation of the events" of Columbus's life. Yet "the singular splendor and prodigious permanent importance of his actions, as well as the moral gran-

deur and sublimity of his character, entitled him fully to the honor of a separate and detailed biography." Everett's ardor led him to predict that the career
of Columbus would thereafter be read only in Irving, and Everett considered
it a beautiful coincidence that celebrating "the achievements of the discoverer of our continent, should have been reserved for one of its inhabitants, and
that the earliest professed author of first-rate talent, who appeared among us,
should have devoted one of his most important and finished works to this
pious purpose." Everett insisted that the authorship of the biography of Columbus by the first distinguished U.S. writer signaled the coming of age of U.S.
letters and that this contribution to Columbian biography would stand alone
on the field of universal letters. "We would go even further than this," Everett
enthused, "and express the opinion, that Mr. Irving's production may be justly
ranked with the fine narrative or epic poems of the highest reputation."[80] In
the final analysis Everett located Irving's achievement in the arena of biography and poetry (recall here Mark Twain's definition of romance as "adorned
biography"). Everett's disappointment at Irving's failure to write philosophical history anticipated the views of others. The same critique would be echoed, from a Spanish perspective, by Martín Fernández de Navarrete.

Navarrete's Response: King Ferdinand, *Don Quixote*, and the Demands of Writing History

Navarrete's assessment of Washington Irving's account of Spanish exploration
history allows us to see how American it really was. The extensive commentary that Navarrete offered in his prologue to the third volume of the *Colección* (1829) took the measure of Irving's contribution. Referring to the statement that he had made in his prologue to the first volume (1825), Navarrete
reminded his readers in 1829 that it had not been his intention to write Columbus's personal history. It had thus been impossible for him to examine all
the events of the admiral's life or to combat the calumnies with which modern writers attempted to devalue the achievements of the Spanish in their
overseas discoveries and conquests. This reference to his earlier remarks is
significant, because it reveals that he valued Irving's biographical focus on
Columbus and applauded the U.S. writer's celebration of Columbian exploration as an emphatically Spanish achievement. In this light, Navarrete acknowledged with pleasure Irving's freedom "from the rivalries that have held
sway among European nations regarding Columbus and his discoveries."[81]

It is significant, however, that Navarrete appreciated Irving as a writer of "polite literature" rather than as a historian. He made the point that Irving was a
man of letters, of learning and judgment ("literato juicioso y erudito"), whose

work was a notable proof ("insigne prueba") that the Columbian documentary collection would be of no small use in the "republic of letters." Navarrete informed his readers that Irving, being stationed in Madrid, had availed himself of the opportunity to use "excellent books and precious manuscripts" and to consult scholars learned in the relevant matters, all the while having readily at hand "the authentic documents which we have just published." Thanks to these advantages, Navarrete continued, Irving's work demonstrated the "fullness, impartiality, and precision" that made it superior to those of the writers who had preceded him.[82] Navarrete lauded Irving's "pure, elegant, and animated style," his consideration of various important (often overlooked) personages, and the examination of various difficult questions in which prevailed "the most sound critical evaluation, erudition, and good taste." His only reservation concerned Irving's interpretation of "certain matters" that Navarrete left unspecified. He closed his assessment with the hope that the newly published documents would allow Irving to correct certain statements or opinions that still lacked "the certitude and exactness required to achieve perfection."[83]

Navarrete's reservation about certain of Irving's judgments almost assuredly concerned the latter's treatment of King Ferdinand, particularly the portrayal of the monarch's indifference to Columbus after the death of Isabella. This had long been a sensitive issue to the Spanish, and Navarrete had earlier made it his priority to defend Ferdinand's actions. Refuting the work of Luigi Bossi (*Vita de Cristoforo Colombo*, 1818) in its claim that Spain belatedly provided Columbus with minimum support and later rewarded his success with persecutions, Navarrete summarized with succinctness and force the forms of support that the monarchs had given Columbus throughout his career. He blamed the slights against Columbus on Francisco de Bobadilla, inspector general of Hispaniola. Navarrete argued that although Bobadilla's actions had been justified by circumstances, his abuses of authority could not be imputed to the monarchs, their government, or the Castilian nation. Furthermore, Navarrete emphasized, the monarchs ultimately recognized Bobadilla's criminal excesses and restored Columbus's honors and titles.[84]

Navarrete's mention of the "less pure sources" on which Irving had relied turn out to be various assertions made by Hernando Colón in his biography of his father. It is clear that Navarrete quickly recognized that Irving had relied on Hernando Colón to interpret the life of the admiral in his interactions with the Spanish, from the great personages of the royal court (in particular, King Ferdinand) to the common sailors from Palos who formed the crew of Columbus's first expedition. Irving's portrayals of a heroic, solitary Columbus juxtaposed to an arbitrary, evil Ferdinand and surrounded by Spanish sailors who were fearful, superstitious, and lacking in professional competence came directly from Hernando's biography. Irving had not hidden his admiration for the admiral's son. He proclaimed Hernando's work to be "the corner stone of the history of the American continent."[85]

What Irving did not say (and what I assert here) is that he conceptualized his entire work according to the interpretive model of Hernando Colón. Colón's work provided Irving with the major events of the admiral's life, a ready-made narrative outline for his biography, and an overtly sympathetic point of view toward the devoted, heroic vassal in the service of a foreign monarch. Irving's single significant exception to Hernando's paradigm concerns their divergent conceptualizations of the discovery. Colón attributed his father's discoveries directly to the work of Divine Providence and, in human terms, to information gleaned from mariners' experience (Columbus's and that of others) and classical authorities. Hernando denied altogether that the lands of America had previously been discovered by others. Following Hernando, Irving rejected the "anonymous pilot" theory by which Columbus was alleged to have received prior information about the lands he then only pretended to discover. Yet Irving emphasized human error and accident over any divine plan: "It is singular how much the success of this great undertaking depended upon two happy errors, the imaginary extent of Asia to the east, and the supposed smallness of the earth; both, errors of the most learned and profound philosophers, but without which Columbus would hardly have ventured upon his enterprise."[86]

From Navarrete's perspective Hernando Colón's narrative representation placed Spain's honor—and especially that of its monarchy—under an excessively harsh light. Navarrete expressed these concerns in pointed reference to Irving's conceptualization, thus shedding light on the peculiarly North American character of Washington Irving's life of Columbus. Irving's *Columbus* was not acceptable to Navarrete to the degree that it was detrimental to the historical reputation of King Ferdinand. I surmise this by reading backward: In 1825 Navarrete had concluded the introduction to his first volume with the admonition to his readers that their first obligation as citizens of Spain was to demonstrate a profound respect for their monarch. He did so by citing a letter from the admiral to his son Diego Colón that Navarrete reproduced in the same volume. Columbus wrote that the vassal's greatest obligation was to exceed his own best efforts in service to the king and to strive to remove obstacles from the monarch's path. He reminded Diego that the duty of all good Christians was to pray for the king's long life and health and that those like himself who labored in the royal service were obliged to support him with great diligence.[87] The citation makes patent Navarrete's concern for the political future of the Spanish state and his desire to see the national dignity restored in the aftermath of the Napoleonic invasion, the wars of Latin American independence, and the reestablishment of Fernando VII's absolutist rule.[88]

Whereas Navarrete emphasized that national dignity and honor were earned by the crown's loyal subjects' performance of heroic historic deeds, Irving interpreted those same deeds to signal the values that should guide U.S. citizens in the development of the new nation. Although Irving, like Navarrete, lamented the calumnies suffered by history's greatest heroes, he oriented his characterization of the exemplary value of history somewhat differently.[89] For Irving too history should provide models to emulate, but these were not the models proposed by Navarrete for vassals' loyalty to their monarch but rather the virtues of the self-made man, advancing secular civilization and making economic progress.

Despite the contrast between them, it is unfair to ascribe to Navarrete an exclusive concern for royal service rendered in the past or to Irving a single-minded emphasis on entrepreneurial achievement in the new republic's future. Theirs are differences of degree, not kind, and they arise from their antithetical views on the subject of the monarchy. To be antimonarchical was integral to Irving's republican Americanist vision.[90] Patriotic citizens were loyal to the flag of their country, but they were not subservient to its malevolent ruler. This American Columbus was loyal to Castile in the way that the American colonists of the late eighteenth century had been loyal to their new land while suffering the abuses of its British ruler, King George III. From Irving's Americanist perspective, painting Ferdinand in an unflattering light was not a negative consequence but rather an edifying one. It strengthened the analogy between Columbus and the early American patriots as well as that between the admiral and the new American immigrants.

Navarrete's objections to Irving's work are as clear as Irving's independence of historical and moral didactic criteria. They understood one another very well; they knew how and why they disagreed. Each had clearly announced the patriotic character of his enterprise at the outset of his work. Both understood the necessity of articulating civic and cultural objectives in the fields of statecraft and letters, respectively. Both gave priority to this double objective. Nevertheless, Navarrete made note of the need to correct the assertions of Hernando Colón's interested biography. He also insisted on the imperative to keep separate the prerogatives of history and poetry. On both counts the Spanish scholar succeeded not only in issuing a public warning to future writers but also in letting his readers know that Irving's highly interpretive treatment of a solitary, heroic Columbus somewhat missed the mark and should be read with caution.

As the focus of Navarrete's reservations about Irving's work, the interpretation of Ferdinand's actions reflected broader tensions between Spanish and U.S. viewpoints on Spanish New World history. Irving was not the only U.S. writer critical of Ferdinand. Other U.S. writers also directed their antimonarchical fervor against Ferdinand as though he were King George III of England anachronistically reincarnate. The *North American Review*'s April 1827 essay reviewing Navarrete's first two volumes had taken explicit and outraged exception to Navarrete's defense of Ferdinand and saw the latter as Columbus's intractable enemy. The *Review* writer could not "suffer Ferdinand's apologist to arrogate to him any praise for simple justice, and for justice displayed upon parchment only," nor could he tolerate Navarrete's "zeal to vindicate the character of a Spanish king." By its passion this declaration reveals not only how Ferdinand was characterized but, more interestingly, how Christopher Columbus was imagined by historically minded Americans in the 1820s. As with Irving, Ferdinand was the foil against which to configure the proto-American hero, Christopher Columbus, and "the truly monstrous injuries" that he was "doomed to suffer."[91] By bringing into focus the profile of an American Columbus, the *Review*'s assessment of Navarrete's work anticipated the friendly reception that Irving's work would enjoy among literate Americans when published the following year.

The 1827 American review of Navarrete suggests that the exalted character of Columbus and "his connexion with our own hemisphere" should inspire deep sympathy for his fortunes as were "demand[ed] of us as Americans and as admirers of the noblest qualities of human genius."[92] Royalty might be mediocre in its understanding and narrow-minded in its policies, but the memory of the alien and untitled commoner Columbus would live on and be defended throughout successive ages. Columbus was the model of citizenship for the U.S. romantic era; his modest nobility of spirit rose out of his actions, unbowed and uncorrupted by those lesser than he. Here was a man who felt no sympathy for his corrupt peers, "who would not wink at their misconduct, who preferred the permanent good of the settlement to the gratification of their cruelty and avarice, whose manners were simple, temper austere, discipline exact, and who was a foreigner elevated by his virtues from humble condition to be a Spanish cavalier and viceroy of the Indies."[93] He was an early modern version of the nineteenth-century self-made man.

Whether by Irving or others, this idealization of the foreign Columbus, to the detriment of the portrayals of the monarch and nation he served, was a hallmark of the Americanist viewpoint and a source of consternation for Navarrete. It reveals another dimension of the tension between North American and Spanish outlooks at the time. No doubt implicitly remarking on the tendencies that he perceived to be at work in Irving's just-published *Colum-*

bus, Navarrete addressed the dangers of creating narratives out of history's documents. In a masterful discourse on the proper character of history, sagaciously inserted in his 1829 prologue and motivated by his ongoing consideration of Hernando Colón's biography, Navarrete brought to mind the problems created when interested parties—friends, relatives, or protectors, out of love or vituperation—abandoned the impartiality demanded by history.[94]

Such highly inflected writing, Navarrete argued, was found in panegyrics and novels, which he faulted for "obscuring the truth of history" and "corrupting the development of moral customs." He cited the books of chivalry to exemplify such effects in earlier times, and he added that the historical novel of his own day presented a similar threat by confusing deeds and altering the character of their protagonists in an effort to appeal to "the heart rather than the head."[95] In particular, Navarrete feared that this novelistic spirit would permeate and pervert the narration of Spanish overseas history "because the deeds of Columbus, Cortés, Pizarro and others in lands so distant and fertile, so new and picturesque," would give writers an irresistible opportunity to "compose a poem while pretending to construct a history."[96] He went on to outline the historian's responsibilities to the pursuit of truth, citing Cervantes' immortal dialogue between Don Quixote and the bachelor Sansón Carrasco on the Aristotelian distinction between poetry and history, with the respective obligations of the poet to sing or tell matters as they should have been and the historian to narrate them as they were, "without adding or removing a single thing."[97]

The reference to *Don Quixote* may have been a lingua franca between Navarrete, who had published his own biography of Cervantes in 1819, and Irving, whose mastery of *Don Quixote* had been a visible force in his satirical *History of New York* of 1809.[98] Navarrete's citation of Don Quixote's remark that Aeneas was not as pious as Virgil had painted him, nor Ulysses as prudent as set out in Homer's description, reflected a Cervantine spirit of playful seriousness. It might have been intended as a gentle criticism of Irving, whose work Navarrete discussed after observing that the imagination had no role in the writing of history and that it was incumbent upon the historian to provide the proof and testimony required to establish public confidence in him.

The trickiness of the terrain being traveled in this international realm of literary diplomacy and scholarship is by now self-evident. In 1831 in London Irving published his Columbus biography's complement, *The Voyages of the Companions of Columbus.* Navarrete acknowledged its receipt from Irving in a letter of April 1, 1831, in which he praised the account of the minor voyages for the "good method and graceful coloring" with which Irving described them ("el buen método y gracioso colorido con que sabe describirlos"; see figure 2.2). He also commented on Irving's work in general, noting with pleasure that the doc-

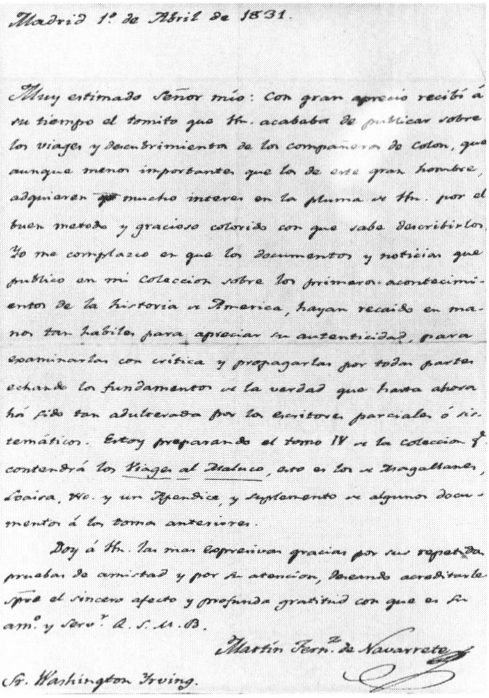

Madrid 1.º de Abril de 1831.

Muy estimado Señor mío: Con gran aprecio recibí á su tiempo el tomito que Vm. acababa de publicar sobre los viages y descubrimientos de los compañeros de Colon, que aunque menos importantes que los de este gran hombre, adquiriran mucho interes en la pluma de Vm. por el buen metodo y gracioso colorido con que sabe describirlos. Yo me complazco en que los documentos y noticias que publico en mi Coleccion sobre los primeros acontecimientos de la historia de America, hayan recaido en manos tan habiles para apreciar su autenticidad, para examinarlas con critica y propagarlas por todas partes echando los fundamentos de la verdad que hasta ahora ha sido tan adulterada por los escritores parciales ó sistemáticos. Estoy preparando el tomo IV de la coleccion q.e contendrá los Viages al Maluco, esto es los de Magallanes, Loaisa, &c. y un Apendice, y suplemento de algunos documentos á los tomos anteriores.

Doy á Vm. las mas expresivas gracias por sus repetidas pruebas de amistad y por su atencion, deseando acreditarle siempre el sincero afecto y profunda gratitud con que es su am.º y serv.r Q. S. M. B.

Martin Fern.z de Navarrete

Sr. Washington Irving.

Figure 2.2. Letter from Martín Fernández de Navarrete to Washington Irving, Madrid, April 1, 1831. (Washington Irving Papers, Manuscripts and Archives Division, New York Public Library, Astor, Lenox, and Tilden Foundations)

uments that he had published had "fallen into hands so able to appreciate their authenticity, to examine them critically, and to circulate them in all directions; establishing fundamental truths which hitherto have been adulterated by partial or systematic writers."[99] The first translation of Irving's biography of Columbus by the novelist José García de Villalta soon appeared under the title *Historia de la vida y los viajes de Cristóbal Colón* (1833–34). Irving's success was unchallenged until the beginning of the 1840s when his indebtedness to Navarrete—and his acknowledgment of it—were suddenly questioned.

Scholarly Integrity, Cultural Diplomacy, and Public Education

Irving's work was attacked for the first time about thirteen years after its initial publication. Although commonly repeated whenever Irving's *Columbus* is mentioned, the charges of plagiarism and inadequate acknowledgment are without substance. I rehearse and refute them here because they reveal elements of Spain's image abroad and the stereotypes of Spain that some of its North American friends strove to correct.

In early 1841 Severn Teackle Wallis (1816–94), an influential Baltimore lawyer who was a devoted Hispanist and author of the 1849 *Glimpses of Spain*, harshly criticized Irving's *Columbus* in an unsigned article in the prestigious *Southern Literary Messenger*.[100] With a circulation of ten thousand, according to its founding editor, Thomas Willis White, the *Messenger* was published monthly at Richmond, Virginia.[101] The journal's interest in the literary and cultural relations of Spain and the United States was matched by its concern for the integrity of public education at home. Wallis's polemical critique was carried out over two years and had its one-time Spanish counterpart in the journalistic writings of Enrique Gil y Carrasco in *El Pensamiento* in Madrid.[102] Appearing almost a decade and a half after Irving's 1828 publication, these critical commentaries were apparently motivated by the work's enormous popularity and its influence in public education.

The *Southern Literary Messenger* devoted a March 1841 review article, "Navarrete on Spain," to the *Colección de los viages y descubrimientos* and the relation of Irving's biography to it. Citing Irving's 1828 preface to the effect that he had "collated all the works" that he could find "in print and manuscript, comparing them with original documents," Wallis faulted Irving with regard to the latter: "With the industry we have been able to exercise in the examination of his references, we can discover no allusion to any manuscript work, which Navarrete had not previously cited."[103] In fact, Wallis continued, Irving cited a total of only three manuscript documents: Las Casas's *Historia de las Indias,* the unpublished portions of Oviedo, and the chronicle of Andrés Bernáldez, "El cura de los palacios." Even these, he added, had been available to Irving through Juan Bautista Muñoz's extracts and Navarrete's published transcriptions. The nub of the issue, Wallis insisted, was Irving's failure to acknowledge that Navarrete was the *principium et fons* (foundation and fountain) of his facts and proofs. Irving's acknowledgment of having received from Navarrete "the most obliging assistance" and the communication of "various valuable and curious pieces of information," Wallis declared, failed to "convey to our minds any just idea" of Irving's great obligation to Navarrete and his documentary corpus, "which a comparison of the two works demonstrates he owes." Wallis concluded: "It leads the mind of the American reader to a notion of independence and originality [of Irving's scholarship] which do not exist." Wallis said he lodged this criticism against Irving "because we take pride in his contributions to our literature, and in this, the most permanent among them, . . . we would have him secure, without cavil, his own meed [*sic*] of praise from posterity, by fully and frankly yielding to others, their share."[104] His deeper concern, however, was for the model of scholarly investigation that Irving's work conveyed to teachers and students as well as the stereotypical views of Spain and Spaniards that Wallis perceived Irving's work to convey.

In order to demonstrate that he should not be suspected "of an inclination 'to swell small things to great,'" Wallis justified the inferences he made from reading Irving's preface "by shewing [*sic*] the conclusions to which it has led others of our countrymen." The issue was public education and the adoption of Irving's 1829 abridgement of *Columbus* for classroom use by the Superintendent of Common Schools of New York and the New York state legislature. A legislative committee made the claims that "some years of the life of the author were devoted to the preparation of the work; and, by a most assiduous study of original and unpublished documents, which, by his personal researches, he discovered in the libraries of Spain, he has been enabled to correct the errors, and supply the defects of preceding writers." Wallis acknowledged no surprise that a legislative committee, "generally (with all due deference) better versed in politics than literature, and especially that of foreign nations, should, in the ardor of State enthusiasm, have resorted to imagination for facts, in regard to a favorite and truly distinguished fellow-citizen." He added, however, that the attachment of the committee's report and circular, along with more than a half-dozen newspaper notices regarding the publication of Irving's 1829 abridgment was, at worst, unconscionable on Irving's part or, at best, utterly careless of him if the business had been merely a bit of "bookmaker's diplomacy."[105]

Wallis was indignant that Navarrete's great labors should be repaid with "the cheap tribute of a well-turned sentence" and that ignorant biases against Spain as a "despotic and bigoted enemy of knowledge" should be perpetrated by one of the leading citizens of the United States. On the contrary, the "liberality of her [Spain's] government" and the labors it "fostered, stimulated, and fed" should be duly celebrated. Lacking the old, bitter rivalries that plagued the nations of Europe, the United States, "standing thus high and aloof, probably, in future times, to be selected as the historical and critical umpires of disputed fact and opinion," should avoid any position that could be perceived as unjust to the literature of other lands: "Like another Bradamont with a new lance and steed, she [Spain] may do battle for her own right" while the United States "ride[s] down the lists by her side." (Today's reader is struck by the juxtaposition of these metaphors from medieval chivalry and modern sports, which seem to respond to contradictory impulses of archaic solemnity and contemporary informality.) Wallis appealed explicitly to the notion of being like Bacon's "citizens of the world" who would do right by Spain. Adamant that Spain should not be seen as though "covered with the crusted lava of ignorance and time," Wallis concluded: "Any one who is familiar with the literature of Spain, must know how deep is the injustice done to it, by the opinion of the day, and how ignorant are many, otherwise well informed, of the true character of the nation, and of its intellectual existence, except as a creature of the past."[106]

Upon scrutinizing Irving's 1828 preface through Wallis's lens, it seems that Irving's remark praising Navarrete inadvertently provoked Wallis's wrath. To distinguish the efforts of "that estimable man, one of the last veterans of Spanish literature," Irving observed that Navarrete had worked alone and indefatigably "in a country where, at present, literary exertion meets with but little excitement or reward."[107]

Four months later (July 1841), in a *Messenger* article entitled "Spain: Her History, Character, and Literature: Vulgar Errors—Their Extent and Sources," Severn T. Wallis again led the charge, again anonymously. Regarding Spain's character, he cited the "living, existing nation, modern, civilized, and Christian" that had not been degraded but merely temporarily exhausted by Napoleon; it now governed itself triumphantly with a free constitution. If Spain was cursed, it was only by its "fatal gift of beauty," which made the country desirable to all, from ancient Phoenicians to contemporary Frenchmen. It was wrong, Wallis proclaimed, to characterize Spain stereotypically by the Inquisition and the bullfight and also to assume that Spanish treatment of the aboriginal inhabitants of the Americas had been worse than that carried out under the flags of England or the United States. Equally misguided was the belief that Spanish greed for gold had been greater than that of the English, who, not content with rival discoveries, engaged in seaborne piracy against Spain under the cover of law.[108]

The source of these errors, Wallis insisted, was England itself and the prejudices that English literature wove into its histories of its rivals, "most especially of Catholic countries since the reformation." Meanwhile, he continued, the English portrayed their own actions as if they had "sought no wealth but a field for industry," characterizing themselves "as enlightened colonists whose only care was to carry into the bosom of the wilderness, agriculture, plenty, and peace." He concluded, with no small amount of irony: "So much for our mother country and ourselves—enlightened, liberal, wise, and free."[109]

Again, the implications are for public education and, from this Americanist perspective, for human progress: "Poison the sources of knowledge, stamp on the susceptible mind of childhood errors and prejudices so disgraceful, in regard to any people, and it is easy to follow the steps, by which their history may be falsified, their name be made a by-word of reproach and scorn." The ultimate implications of these biases affected the exercise of citizenship. Thus the selection of books for elementary instruction had important consequences: "By widening the sphere of our observation," such aids give "breadth to our reasoning and liberality to our sentiments—strengthening our respect for other countries, without weakening our affection for our own. In a degree, this same effect is wrought by judicious education, by the calm inculcation of unprejudiced truth, from childhood upwards. It is by this only, that men can be made better, as well as wiser."[110]

Before the next issue of the *Southern Literary Messenger* to include an article on Spain appeared, Enrique Gil y Carrasco published in *El Pensamiento* of Madrid a review essay entitled "De la literatura y de los literatos de los Estados Unidos de América." The subject was Eugene A. Vail's 1841 *De la Litterature et des hommes de lettres*, which assessed the level and merits of North American literary and intellectual culture. Acknowledging that the United States had risen sufficiently in power and wealth to equal the countries of Europe since gaining its independence less than a century earlier, Gil y Carrasco called the growth of the country "truly miraculous." Its economic forces, he observed, were being devoted almost exclusively to the conquest of the material world and the infinite increase of production. He took as his central data the statistics for U.S. book publication for 1834, observing that of 251 works published, 216 were devoted to "useful and practical matters." In his view higher learning was not cultivated in the United States, and works in political theory, political economy, history, philosophy ("its inferiority on this point is abundantly apparent"), and fictional literature were utterly lacking. Meanwhile, writings on education and journalism flourished.[111] Gil y Carrasco considered that the background of the country's inhabitants was too heterogeneous, and the country itself too dedicated to industry and economic production, to devote any effort to the cultivation of the spirit.

In the field of letters, Gil y Carrasco asserted, Americans should be able to excel in the discipline of history. They could pursue the truth in its purity because they suffered no rancorous rivalries with other nations, and they had no injustices to hide. Yet in this area too, he argued, North Americans fell far short of Europeans.[112] Singling out Irving and Prescott, Gil y Carrasco cited the former for his work as an "able colorist" of the great enterprise of Columbus and the latter for his dispassionate and exacting history of Ferdinand and Isabella. In a pithy footnote to his use of the word *colorist*, Gil y Carrasco discreetly noted that he used the term intentionally, because any readers of the *Colección* of Navarrete would "be convinced that in the account of Washington Irving there is nothing that belongs to him except the high color of his handsome style."[113]

The *Southern Literary Messenger* was delighted to translate and repeat Gil y Carrasco's remarks for the benefit of its U.S. audience. Yet another anonymous Wallis article of May 1842 entitled "Spain: Popular Errors—Their Causes—Travellers," began by noting that, in the fifteen months since the *Messenger's* publication of "Navarrete on Spain," neither Irving nor any of his friends had offered a rejoinder. In the interim, Wallis noted, the piece had been translated and published in Madrid and Havana. He cited Gil y Carrasco's article as well as a speech by Francisco Martínez de la Rosa, the romantic writer, statesman, and director of the Real Academia de la Lengua, to demonstrate the negative Spanish reaction to Irving's work. In Wallis's view Irving's recent appointment as minister plenipotentiary to the Court of Madrid gave "proofs of the fact which we have hitherto alleged—*that the preface to the History of Columbus has created* an almost universal impression, that the whole work was the result of its author's individual labor and research."[114]

Although Wallis attributed Irving's ambassadorial appointment exclusively to *Columbus,* a Spanish diplomatic observer explained it more broadly. The Spanish minister to Washington, Don Pedro Alcántara Argáiz, informed his government that Irving was "well known in the country for his literary productions" and that his knowledge of the Spanish language had "served him to advantage in taking notes and translating Spanish works, in order to offer them in his own country as originals." Alcántara concluded: "Nevertheless, this little blemish does not lessen his great reputation as a man of letters."[115] Here was the answer feared by Irving's critics such as Wallis. Even though they regarded him as an author of light literature and a mere synthesizer of materials, if not a plagiarist, they had to acknowledge that Irving's patriotic, nationalistic appeal—verified here by a source hostile to his renown—seemed to remain untouchable. Irving's *Columbus,* perhaps his *Conquest of Granada,* and certainly his *Alhambra* had earned him considerable prestige in U.S. diplomatic and cultural circles. On balance Alexander Everett's 1829 passionate proclamation of a thriving U.S. literary and intellectual life, as well as Enrique Gil y Carrasco's cool disparagement of the same a dozen years later, speaks eloquently to the issue of a nation struggling to establish its literary and intellectual traditions—and to Washington Irving's central place in that endeavor.

At last, in July and August 1842 the *Knickerbocker* magazine—a well-known Irving vehicle—published in its editorial column rebuttals to the *Southern Literary Messenger.* Despite the public's general indifference to the charges against Irving, the *Knickerbocker*'s editor noted, Irving would speak out on the matter only because the *Messenger*'s "anonymous writer" (that is, Wallis) asserted that silence implied the concession of truth to the claims that Irving had "taken another man's commodities and sold them as his own." Arguing that the *Messenger* willfully distorted the meaning of Irving's 1828 preface, the *Knickerbocker* cited Irving's own words outlining the materials and procedures he had used and quoted at length Navarrete's 1829 published praise for Irving's work's "extension, impartiality, and correctness, which renders it far superior to the narratives of any who have gone before him." The magazine also mentioned that Prescott and George Bancroft had praised *Columbus* and went on to cite the introduction to the 1828 Paris edition of Navarrete, which characterized the relationship between Navarrete's documentary collection and Irving's history as one of complementarity. "Composed upon entirely different plans," the former effectively served as a necessary adjunct to the latter. Most interestingly, the *Knickerbocker* asserted—and here it becomes clear that the editor had consulted with Irving—that all the facts that Irving derived exclusively from Navarrete's collection would not fill even "six of the twelve hundred pages" of Irving's work.[116]

In the November 1842 issue of the *Messenger* the still anonymous Wallis reiterated his criticism of Irving, not for his indebtedness to Navarrete but rather his unwillingness to acknowledge it. Wallis furthermore presented an argument to refute the *Knickerbocker*'s claims that Navarrete himself was satisfied and did not feel wronged by Irving. Expressions of Navarrete's satisfaction, "even if distinctly made," would not be "at all conclusive of the controversy" because "the question is not, whether Navarrete is satisfied, but whether Irving is original and fair." Here is the *Messenger*'s final argument: "In matters that concern the public, the rights of the injured party are merged in the claims of universal justice. It is no defence [*sic*] where the commonwealth prosecutes, to say that the individual pardons."[117]

The *Knickerbocker* published a subsequent rejoinder in December 1842, repeating its claims about Irving's extremely limited reliance on materials exclusive to Navarrete and attacking the *Messenger*'s "intemperate language" and "coarse manner." (To back up the second claim the *Knickerbocker* cited nearly two dozen examples of the *Messenger* article's prose.) The New York journal ridiculed the *Messenger*'s dismissal of Navarrete's praise for Irving, characterizing as absurd the claims that the Spanish historian might have been misled by Irving in private or that he might have been too ignorant of English to be able to take the measure of Irving's work or his published acknowledgment. The *Knickerbocker* announced its withdrawal from the battlefield and its refusal to permit "farther [*sic*] reference to this self-discomfited hypercritic" in the pages of its own "unanimously and universally popular magazine." In its January 1843 number the *Messenger* called its own halt to hostilities but not without lobbing one last volley: "Epithets are a seed easily sown, but they bear no fruit. . . . We shall therefore take present leave of the subject, trusting soon again to meet our readers with more pleasant topics, *and in better company.*[118]

Overall, the *Knickerbocker*'s assertion about the general public indifference to the *Messenger*'s criticisms was correct. Wallis's charges affected neither Irving's editorial success nor his public reputation, as his 1842 appointment as minister to Spain testified. Book sales continued to be sufficiently strong to ensure the publication of the 1849 edition of *Columbus*, which was the last one that Irving personally supervised. The *Knickerbocker*'s claim that Irving's debt to Navarrete was limited was accurate. The Paris review summed it up best: The relationship between Navarrete and Irving was one of complementarity, as any reader of both works quickly perceives. Wallis's unrelenting attack, meanwhile, seems to have been based almost exclusively on a reading of Irving's preface and the summary perusal of his footnoted documentary references. If Irving erred, it was to have singled out Navarrete as a great intellectual force—which he was—while characterizing his country's intellectual production at the time as limited.

On balance Wallis's attack on Irving's *Columbus* seems to be aimed less at the work itself than at the influential reputation that Irving enjoyed. Irving was a well-connected northerner, positioned at the heart of New York's and New England's cultural circles as well as within the governmental and diplomatic elite of Washington, D.C., which at the time many viewed as a southern city. Irving had long stood out, as Richard Henry Dana had observed as early as 1819, as the first U.S. writer who attempted to support himself exclusively by his literary endeavors.[119] Wallis's reservations therefore might be likened to those of an academic writer today who criticizes the mass-market appeal of a nonacademic writer. That is, the object of concern would not be the popularity of the works produced but rather the broad notoriety they brought to their author, propelling him into other spheres of recognition and influence.

Although Irving did not speak out against the criticisms lodged against him by Wallis, he was clearly wearied by them. He acknowledged their toll in his preface to the 1849 *Life and Voyages of Christopher Columbus Together with the Voyages of His Companions,* which joined together for the first time his 1828 and 1831 histories of the Columbus voyages and their sequels, respectively. He reproduced his original 1828 preface, in which he had stated explicitly that his "main source throughout the whole" of his labors had been Obadiah Rich's personal library. He also excerpted and translated Navarrete's published praise for the *Columbus* from the third volume of the *Colección,* and Irving quoted as well Navarrete's 1831 letter of congratulations for his work on the minor voyages. Irving concluded his new introduction by stating: "I had thought I had sufficiently shown, in the preceding preface, which appeared with my first edition, that his [Navarrete's] collection first prompted my work and subsequently furnished its principal materials; and that I had illustrated this by citations at the foot of almost every page. In preparing this revised edition, I have carefully and conscientiously examined into the matter, but find nothing to add to the acknowledgments already made."[120]

Irving had neither claimed for himself the discovery of new documents nor the achievement of historiographical originality. He recognized explicitly his debts to the historians whom he consulted, and his critical treatment of his sources is impressive. Navarrete himself applauded this dimension of Irving's work, with the single (significant) exception of the latter's reliance on Hernando Colón. Only those who knew Hernando Colón's work intimately would recognize Irving's use of its narrative structure, its affective interpretation, and its reliance on the judgment of the admiral's son. Curiously, none of these issues was mentioned by Wallis, who seemed interested only in Irving's use of Navarrete but not his other sources. The abiding targets of Wallis's criticism (and the source of his frustration) were the exaggerations of those, like the New York state legislative committee, who misrepresented the content of Irving's work as pathbreaking and original. Such hyperbolic enthusiasms helped make Irving's *Columbus* as influential as it was. As to original and extensive scholarship, Irving himself never made such claims. He did, however, illuminate the earliest and most pertinent sources of his historiographical enterprise.

Juvenile Readings: *The World Displayed* to Washington Irving

Near the end of book 1 of *Columbus,* Irving characterized "one of the salutary purposes of history" as "furnishing examples of what human genius and laudable enterprise may accomplish." He expressed suspicion of the "meddlesome spirit" that, decked out in the "garb of learned research, goes prying about the traces of history, casting down its monuments and marring and mutilating its fairest trophies." Care should be taken, he admonished, "to vindicate great names from such pernicious erudition."[121] This is an important key to his thinking about history, and it makes available his views on what historical narrative should accomplish and whom it should serve. Here his 1829 abridgment of *Columbus* in a single volume gains significance because of its adoption by public schools and universities. Irving had produced this tome of 440 pages in less than three weeks in late 1828 when he learned that "some paltry fellow" was pirating the work for his own abridgment.[122] Irving rushed into print with the one-volume abridgment not only to protect his intellectual property but also almost certainly to facilitate access to his work by youthful readers.

The importance of this pedagogical interest is apparent from a sentiment Irving expressed late in life. In 1852, when Irving was sixty-nine, he wrote a letter of thanks (figure 2.3) to Philip J. Forbes for sending him a volume of a collection of the narratives of voyages that he had read as a boy. Irving remembered that Forbes's father had given him the entire series,

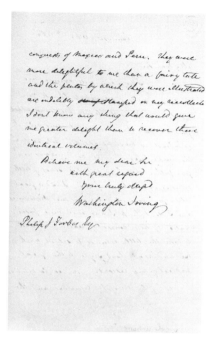

Figure 2.3. Letter from Washington Irving to Philip J. Forbes, Sunnyside, October 25, 1852. (Miscellaneous Manuscripts, neg. 74150 and 74151; © Collection of the New-York Historical Society)

sensing I had a great relish for accounts of voyages and discoveries, and I don't think I was ever more fascinated by any course of reading. I used to take the little volumes to school with me and read them slyly to the great neglect of my lessons. The early volumes treated of the voyages of Columbus and the conquests of Mexico and Peru. They were more delightful to me than a fairy tale and the plates by which they were illustrated are indelibly stamped in my recollection. I don't know any thing that would give me greater delight than to recover these identical volumes.[123]

The work in question was entitled *The World Displayed; or, A Curious Collection of Voyages and Travels, Selected from the Writers of All Nations, in Which the Conjectures and Interpolations of Several Vain Editors and Translators Are Expunged.*[124] With a prologue by Samuel Johnson this compendium in twenty duodecimo volumes narrated the world's great voyages, emphasizing the development of navigation and commerce in the West. Volume 1 begins with Johnson's prologue, which summarizes fifteenth-century Portuguese maritime achievements up to the time of Columbus's first voyage. Volume 20 ends with the French physicist Pierre-Louis Moreau de Maupertuis's 1736–37 expedition to Lapland, which measured the length of a degree along the meridian and settled the dispute regarding the earth's shape as a sphere flattened at the poles. *The World Displayed* was published in London in 1759 and reedited many times in the subsequent decades. It was one among many English-language compendia of voyages and travels that came into print in the eighteenth century, following the English translations of Hernando Colón's biography (1704) and Antonio de Herrera y Tordesillas's history of Castilian discovery and conquest in America (1725).[125]

In Irving's youthful reading of *The World Displayed* the cultural spheres of Spain, England, and the United States came together. As the 1840s writings in the literary magazines of Richmond and Madrid have revealed, cultural relations between Spain and the United States always implied England too. If the U.S. popular imagination suffered negative biases regarding Spain's history, it was due in large measure to England's historical political rivalry with Spain and to English literature's Protestant outlook on Roman Catholic culture. Washington Irving's interest in Spain was made possible and substantially shaped by the powerful, pervasive cultural lens that England provided. Although the passage in *The Alhambra* regarding Irving's dreams of Granada is often cited as significantly autobiographical, it pales beside the genuine delight expressed in Irving's private letter two decades later regarding the accounts of the voyages of discovery and conquests. Never had he been "more fascinated by any other course of reading," and he could still see in his mind's eye their memorable engravings (figure 2.4).

The mediation of Columbian history through the powerful and ubiquitous English lens as provided by *The World Displayed* also leads to the most important of Irving's principal Spanish sources. The scrutiny of the first volume of *The World Displayed,* dedicated to Columbus's four voyages, reveals that one of its principal sources (although without attribution) was Hernando Colón. Colón's anti-Ferdinand perspective coincided with the interests of the anti-Spanish British outlook; one can readily see how Irving's view of the relationship between Columbus and King Ferdinand could later be read as anti-Spanish because Irving too relied on Don Hernando.

Just as Irving would later close his account of Columbus's life with a chapter called "Observations on the Character of Columbus," *The World Displayed* had summed up Columbus's achievements with gusto: "Thus died this truly great man; . . . by his abilities only he raised himself and his family to nobility, but rendered himself by his discoveries the greatest man of the age in which he lived. He was however in many respects treated with ingratitude both by the king and those who were under his own command, and it is no small blemish to king Ferdinand's character, that he did not do justice to his merit, but always meanly endeavoured to falsify his engagements with him."[126]

Figure 2.4. "Columbus describing the lands he had discovered." (*The World Displayed; or, A Curious Collection of Voyages and Travels*, 20 vols. [Dublin: James Williams, 1779], frontispiece to vol. 1)

This English Columbus, a clear antecedent of Irving's North American version, was alone in his integrity, solitary in his achievements, ignored by an indifferent, jealous king, and surrounded by sailors and adventurers "who were too fond of an idle and voluptuous life."[127] Furthermore, this Columbus provided for Irving a model whose muted piety and religious fervor gave way to aims of Spanish settlement and European commerce, not native conversion. In short, this eighteenth-century English Columbus was a leader and navigator, not a mystic who sought the recovery of the Holy Land—the trait that the U.S. reviewer Everett later found wanting in Irving's admiral. Irving's North American Columbus was heir not only to the sixteenth-century interpretation by Hernando Colón but also to its subsequent reinterpretations from an eighteenth-century English perspective.

The discovery of Irving's fondness for *The World Displayed* also reveals that its genre, recalled with such affection by Irving in his later years, would have presented itself to him as an attractive model to emulate. It is easy to imagine that Irving would have hoped that one of his works—particularly *Columbus,* which he hoped would keep him "current with his countrymen"—would be of utility in the great patriotic project of public education in the young nation. The irony here is that upon serving his editorial and scholastic interests, Irving probably irrevocably damaged the reputation for scholarship that he deserved on the basis of the work's full publication. By reducing four volumes to one, the abridged work seems to have confirmed the view of Irving's London publisher, John Murray, that his client's forte was the short popular book.[128] It no doubt convinced the discriminating members of Irving's broad audience of the same. Overall, the popularization and abbreviation of *Columbus,* which necessarily resulted in the reduction of its critical apparatus and citation of sources, no doubt did more to undermine the reputation of Irving's excellent romantic history of Columbus than the harshest words of any critic on either side of the Atlantic. The extraordinary editorial success of the abridgment seems to have ended Alexander Everett's quixotic dream about Washington Irving's contribution to the nobility of American letters, at least as far as the *Columbus* was concerned.

At the same time the abridgment accomplished something quite remarkable in another direction. It consolidated the figure of Christopher Columbus as the entrepreneurial Adam of North America. The staggering number of the work's editions, and the fact that the tale of Columbus continues to be fundamental to North American lore, speaks to the remarkable influence of Irving's *Columbus.* Thanks in large measure to Irving's success, the feats of Columbus were identified with early North American history and the account of Columbus's deeds with the foundation of North American letters. The Americanism of Washington Irving was thus expressed through his Hispanism and his Hispanism through his Americanist goals. For this reason his personal and literary encounter with Navarrete and the eventual criticism it briefly engendered are significant. From their opposite vantage points in the Old World and the New, Navarrete's and Irving's mutual transatlantic gaze reveals their complementary desire to discover or reveal in history the foundations of a glorious past and mobilize them as harbingers of the national future. The overlapping prerogatives that the writers and scholars of Spain and North America in this period shared—emblematized in the figures of Martín Fernández de Navarrete and Washington Irving—give the nineteenth-century "Columbian encounter" and nascent Anglo–North American Hispanism their remarkable strength and vigor.

From Authority to Influence

For Irving the drama and suspense attending human affairs—not "mere" speculation as to their causes—conceptualized and ordered his Columbian narrative. The assessment of his work in this broader context reveals that even a seemingly direct relationship between North American and Spanish history and culture was already mediated by the English cultural heritage and literary traditions of the United States. The Anglo-American Columbus of Washington Irving was not merely the product of twenty-one months in Madrid. It was the result of a lifelong effort to distill romantic themes of adventure that began with his youthful readings of English writers, developed through his contact with European romantics, and bore fruit in his historical and literary works.

If the building blocks of Irving's Columbus story were more commonplace than original, his contribution to U.S. culture was nevertheless unique. Even those critics who found nothing new in his work failed to carry the day.[129] An 1847 journalistic notice about the abridged *Columbus* recommended that Irving's book be read by "every American young man and woman," observing that "for most of them, this is probably the best form in which it can reach them." In 1883, almost four decades later, a critical review of Irving's work as a historian placed him among "the first of American historical scholars" and described *Columbus* as a "comprehensive and useful product of historical research."[130]

The best insights in explaining this longevity come from Irving's contemporaries. Prescott's comments in his *History of the Reign of Ferdinand and Isabella* (1837) are particularly helpful. Although he lamented that the discovery of America and the fall of Granada—"two of the most brilliant portions" of his subjects' reign—already had been treated by Irving, he lauded his countryman's work for executing the task of writing the history of Columbus "in a manner which must secure to the historian a share in the imperishable renown of his subject." Unlike Severn T. Wallis, Prescott recognized Irving's contribution for exactly what it was: the results of Navarrete's researches read "in connexion with whatever had been before known of Columbus, in the lucid and attractive form, which engages the interest of every reader."[131] In his memorial oration for Irving, delivered for the New-York Historical Society on April 3, 1860, William Cullen Bryant also characterized Irving as a historian in his *Columbus,* noting that it "was at once in everybody's hands and eagerly read."[132] From the testimony of Prescott and Bryant it is clear that *Columbus* had reached the broad reading audience that Irving had in mind. If the Columbus biography suffered from any shortcoming, Bryant said, it was Irving's overwriting, "an elaborate uniformity of style—a certain prismatic coloring in passages where absolute simplicity would have satisfied us better."[133]

At the end of Irving's life Bryant was among the first to speak of the endurance of Irving's work, predicting "a deathless renown" and analyzing succinctly the centrality of Irving's work during "half a century in this most changeful of centuries." Bryant enumerated the changes that had taken place in politics, economic life, science and technology, the arts, and travel during the more than fifty years of Irving's literary career, from the 1807–8 *Salmagundi* to the 1855–59 *Life of George Washington*.[134] This was the period bounded at its extremes by Thomas Jefferson's 1803 Louisiana Purchase and Abraham Lincoln's 1860 election to the presidency and interrupted by the War of 1812 and the U.S.-Mexican War of 1846–48. It was characterized by Jacksonian democracy, westward expansion, European immigration, and Indian removal. Throughout, the Americanism of Irving's writings had in fact been a constant. Bryant described Irving's abiding literary presence in a changing world as reassuring. In doing so, he implicitly defined the elements of Irving's brand of nineteenth-century romance:

> The earth seems to reel under our feet, and we turn to those who write like Irving, for some assurance that we are still in the same world into which we were born; we read, and are quieted and consoled. In his pages we see that the language of the heart never becomes obsolete; that Truth and Good and Beauty, the offspring of God, are not subject to the changes which beset the inventions of men. We become satisfied that he whose works were the delight of our fathers, and are still ours, will be read with the same pleasure by those who come after us.[135]

If in Bryant's vocabulary the changeless was defined as the true, the good, and the beautiful, today we might call those same values, as realized in Irving's works, by the names of humor, human frailty, and heroism. The humor and heroism with which Irving endowed his respective works were as timeless as the settings he created for them: the folk village, the ancient palace, the boundless ocean. The world as it should have been—both lost in fact and ever present in the imagination—was the world of romance that Irving created in his biography of Columbus. It is hardly necessary, at this moment in time, to excuse it from the obligations of history, which meant something quite different to Irving than it means to us. "History for whom?" is the question to ask, and in Irving's experience, the answer was the general public and, perhaps more important, the schoolage audience. The emphasis placed by Irving's peers on the breadth of his audience because of his writing's appeal to "every reader" reminds us that writers in the new nation during his lifetime strove to create broader readerships and extend the range of the current reading public. These were significant cultural goals for the United States to 1850.

"What kind of history?" we must ask, not from our perspective but from Irving's. As I have shown, the most critical nineteenth-century U.S. commentators stopped short of denying him identification as a historian with regard to *Columbus*. Wallis and Harrisse in detraction of Irving, like Prescott and Bryant in his praise, quibbled only about *how* he carried out his duties as a historian in *Columbus*, not whether he wrote as a historian or a romancer. Significantly, it was the Spanish scholar Navarrete who denied Irving the title of historian that Americans of his day more freely gave him. To Navarrete romance (we think again of Twain's definition as "adorned biography") should have disappeared with Hernando Colón's interested work. It should not have reappeared centuries later in Irving's four tomes, which made their debut subsequent to the publication of the Columbian documentary corpus. If Navarrete was concerned with saving the honor of his nation and the historical reputation of its monarchy through the fuller revelation of its history, U.S. writers were interested in the creation of their own new national heroes. That Columbus was to be for the United States the consummate heroic figure was neither challenged nor debated; it seemed to be a given well beyond the time of Irving's death.[136] In Irving's view, to be truly exemplary this American hero had to be historical, not fictional. His personal writings reveal his concern about achieving that objective: he was aware that critical readers would expect him to indulge his imagination and be careless about particulars; he expressed repeatedly the imperative to transcend his works of "mere imagination" in *Columbus;* and he reiterated his hope that the work would reach a broad public.[137] If the book were to have broad didactic value, its reading as history was essential.

Although today we might describe Irving's goal as the creation of a "legendary hero" who should not be "forced to descend out of the realm of myth," in Irving's own time his version of the heroic was viewed as human and historical.[138] The "deathless renown" that William Cullen Bryant envisioned for Irving was realized, thanks not only to his folkloric accounts of Granada and the environs of Tarrytown but also to his biography of Columbus. Although his work was not known (except by its detractors) as a product of original research using previously unknown sources, it was recognized for decades as a work of historiographic authority. When it began to lose its standing as the most authoritative historical treatment of Columbus in the 1880s, a new period of its influence began (or continued) with its use in the schools, either as direct reading or as a conceptualization that filtered into generations of college, secondary, and primary school texts. (Severn Wallis had understood well the role that *Columbus* would play in U.S. general education.)

Thus in the 1890s Irving's *Columbus* entered another phase of its long life. "The Students' Series of English Classics," published in Boston under the motto "The best preparation to the study of an author is to read what he has written," provides a pertinent example. Isaac Thomas, the editor of the series' 1894 *Selections from Washington Irving* (and principal of Hillhouse High School in New Haven, Connecticut), observed in reference to the series' motto that "happily the fashion of Manuals of Literature is passing away, and we are learning to become acquainted *with* authors rather than to know *about* them." In his preparation of the anthology of Irving's writings he noted that Irving was now considered in some quarters antiquated but was, at the same time, always described as "genial . . . as if it were a small thing to be able to give pure pleasure and enjoyment." Thomas lauded Irving's works for their "belief in the possibility of chivalrous actions" and other worthy endeavors "marred by neither pedantry nor pretension."[139]

Even in the form of anthologized selections, the coherent narrative entities that Irving had created in his original works lent themselves to successful reproduction. Thomas's choice for the "English Classics" series, which was intended for grammar school use, was the complete chapter of "Columbus's Discovery of Land, 1492" (book 3, chapter 4), not from the 1829 abridgment but from the author's revised 1849 edition.[140] In the predawn of October 12, 1492, Columbus waited aboard ship, contemplating his accomplishment and the challenges that lay ahead:

> The great mystery of the ocean was revealed; his theory, which had been the scoff of sages, was triumphantly established; he had secured to himself a glory durable as the world itself. It is difficult to conceive the feelings of such a man, at such a moment; or the conjectures which must have thronged upon his mind, as to the land before him, covered with darkness. . . . A thousand speculations . . . must have swarmed upon him, . . . wondering whether the morning light would reveal a savage wilderness, or dawn upon spicy groves, and glittering fanes, and gilded cities, and all the splendor of Oriental civilization.[141]

The expectant, heroic dimension of this piece is paramount, and it captures the promise of new revelations and future gains so seductive to a U.S. readership peering over its own new frontiers. This anticipatory outlook was a dominant Irving motif, and it was still current three decades later in a college textbook series.

The Yale University "Chronicles of America" series of the 1920s provided further new life for the work. The 1890s did not herald the diminution of *Columbus*'s pedagogical influence. Paradoxically, the evidence of its persistence is found in the very volume that announced its waning scholarly authority. Irving's legacy is prominently in evidence. The book's paperback cover, emblazoned with the Yale University seal, exhorts the reader, "Let Us Now Praise Famous Men." The opening pages describing Columbus's character effectively paraphrase Irving's portrayal of Columbus, though mitigating the positive value of certain qualities that Irving attributed to Columbus and leavening the negative value of others.[142] The summary at the end of this textbook account of Columbus's career brings down by a few notches the exalted character of his heroic profile, but heroic the admiral remains nonetheless:

> The discoverer of America strikingly illustrates the aphorism that the world's great men, so far from having commonly been men of learning, have often been but glorified enthusiasts. . . . To say of Columbus that he was not conspicuous for learning is but to repeat that his chief powers were moral not intellectual. Patience, endurance, tenacity, energy, and will—these, despite his ignorance, made him great. Cupidity and vanity, entailing boastfulness and craft, we have noted as his chief weaknesses; but as to cupidity the record is perhaps less vulnerable than it is at times represented.[143]

This 1920s interpretation echoes Irving's characterization of Columbus, making explicit the distinction of thinkers versus doers so fundamental to Irving's interpretation. The romantic historians' emphasis on active experience and the popular figure of the self-made man prevail a full century after their emblematic portrayal in Irving's biography.

The romance and adventure wrapped up in such versions of Christopher Columbus persisted, with variations, until the 1970s when critical views of Columbus and his actions toppled him decisively from his pedestal. What began in the post–civil rights, post–Vietnam era as a simple undoing turned into a complete inversion of the Columbus phenomenon. The unheroic became the antiheroic, which in turn produced a new kind of larger-than-life phenomenon. Columbus, as described in a popular high school textbook of the early 1990s, for example, has become a monstrous antihero, the aforementioned "Renaissance Darth Vader who ushered in five centuries of imperialism by enslaving, raping and butchering the native Caribs who greeted his 1492 voyage."[144]

Washington Irving would be doubly appalled, not only at the content and meaning of this new Columbus but at the thought that he, Irving, had made its emergence possible by launching onto the scene of early North American letters in the 1820s a vivid, memorable, and larger-than-life Columbus. Despite the numerous versions of the life of Columbus in print in collections and anthologies before 1828, it was Irving who gave the admiral a recognizable face, a head filled with great and grave thoughts, and a will to travel from shore to shore—of the English-speaking world. More important, Irving initiated the whole course of modern Columbian historiography—with all its controversies, contradictions, and antiheroics—by introducing the concept of the discovery of America as a grand accident.

Washington Irving gave Columbus an American personality, and, by the force of his half-century's work and his unprecedented editorial success, Irving gave to the United States the impress of his own personality as well. Universally described as affable, elegant, and kind, with "faith in his fellow-men, a kindly sympathy with the lowest, without any subservience to the highest,"[145] Irving's public persona—seemingly straight from the world of romance itself—exercised an influence over the story of Columbus that was far greater than the whole body of earlier narratives. William Thackeray once remarked that the respect and affection enjoyed by Irving in the United States was a national sentiment.[146] In the final analysis the greatest evidence of Irving's Americanism was his Hispanism; through the latter he gave to Anglo-America two of its most notable founding figures—the Genoese mariner of the Renaissance and the gentleman from Tarrytown of the new republic.

On his U.S. tour in 1842 Charles Dickens went to the White House to meet President John Tyler and encountered an otherwise motley group of visitors "of very many grades and classes" and "grotesque attire." Dickens found them nevertheless laudable in one important regard. While waiting for their respective interviews with White House officials, they abandoned the "noisy orators and officers of state" to flock around the newly appointed minister to the Court of Spain, Washington Irving. Expressing their gratitude for "the store of graceful fancies he had poured out among them," their comportment revealed a "refinement of taste and appreciation of intellectual gifts, and gratitude to those men who, by the peaceful exercise of great abilities, shed new charms and associations upon the homes of their countrymen, and elevate their character in other lands." Dickens thus praised his friend Irving, "the man of quiet pursuits," with the exhortation "long may he dispense such treasures with unsparing hand; and long may they remember him as worthily!"[147]

Irving's *Columbus* helped to fulfill the hope that Dickens so warmly expressed. Among those "new charms and associations" that Irving shed upon the homes of his countrymen, *Columbus* stands out. In the end the most serious charges leveled against the work pointed to the attributes that originally guaranteed and now explain its longevity. Its "high color," its dramatic and episodic narrative, and its adherence to the tried-and-true sequence of events already familiar to readers of earlier accounts are essential to that formula. Its reticence to comment overtly on historical causality nevertheless embedded a deeper causality in the actions of Columbus's narrative persona. Its good-versus-evil dynamic in the contest between Columbus and Ferdinand—a legacy of the oldest biography of the admiral—conspired to make Columbus a foundational figure of Anglo–North American history.

The legacy of Washington Irving's romantic Hispanism was far reaching.

One wonders if through his literary efforts his real search had been not for the prizes awarded him as the United States' first professional writer but rather for a narrative lingua franca (romance? biography?) capable of engaging not only his North American compatriots "of very many grades and classes" but also his European audiences. To be a national writer with an international audience is, after all, always an American aspiration. It is in this regard that Washington Irving may be called one of the founders of Anglo–North American Hispanism and his *Columbus* one of its most abiding monuments.

Notes

An earlier version of this chapter appeared as "Early Anglo-American Hispanism in the 'Columbian Encounter' of Washington Irving and Martín Fernández de Navarrete," in *Preactas de la I Conferencia Internacional "Hacia un nuevo humanismo,"* ed. José Manuel de Bernardo Ares, 2 vols. (Córdoba: Universidad de Córdoba, 1997), 1:5–40.

1. Stanley T. Williams, *The Spanish Background of American Literature,* 2 vols. (1955; rpt., Hamden, Conn.: Archon Books, 1968), 2:4, 43; Washington Irving, *Cuentos de la Alhambra,* trans. José Ventura Traveset (Barcelona: Edicomunicación, 1997).

2. Washington Irving belonged to the first generation of U.S. writers whose other notable figures were James Fenimore Cooper and William Cullen Bryant; the second, stronger generation of U.S. writers included Ralph Waldo Emerson, Herman Melville, Edgar Allen Poe, and William Hickling Prescott.

3. Three authors discuss the common twentieth-century literary assessments of Irving's works: Stanley T. Williams, *The Life of Washington Irving,* 2 vols. (New York: Oxford University Press, 1935); William L. Hedges, *Washington Irving: An American Study, 1802–1832* (Baltimore: Johns Hopkins University Press, 1965); and Edward Wagenknecht, *Washington Irving: Moderation Displayed* (New York: Oxford University Press, 1962).

4. Washington Irving, *The Alhambra: A Series of Tales and Sketches of the Moors and Spaniards,* 2 vols. (Philadelphia: Carey and Lea, 1832), 1:33.

5. Ibid., 1:89–97.

6. Irving's "Spanish" works include the *Voyages and Discoveries of the Companions of Columbus* (1831) and the posthumously published *Spanish Papers* (1866) in addition to the previously mentioned accounts of Columbus's voyages to America, the war of the conquest of Granada, and the lore of the Alhambra. Although widely read and reprinted, *Astoria; or, Anecdotes of an Enterprise beyond the Rocky Mountains* (1836) was a major critical disappointment.

7. In a commemorative conference marking the centenary of Irving's death, Spanish scholars noted that Irving himself has become part of the legend of the Alhambra. See Francisco Ynduráin Hernández, "Washington Irving, primer hispanista americano," in *Washington Irving (1859–1959),* Anejos del Boletín de la Universidad de Granada: Conferencias 9 (Granada: Universidad de Granada, 1960), 51. Outside the rooms

Irving inhabited near the Court of Lindaraja is the inscription "Washington Irving escribió en estas habitaciones sus cuentos de la Alhambra en el año de 1829" (In these rooms Washington Irving wrote his stories of the Alhambra in the year 1829) (Williams, *Life of Washington Irving*, 1:358).

8. James Monroe's two-term presidency provided the immediate backdrop to Irving's history of Columbus: the acquisition of the Floridas from Spain in 1819–21, the recognition of the new Latin American states of Central and South America in 1822, and the announcement of the Monroe Doctrine on December 2, 1823. Declaring that the Old World and the New World had different systems and that they should remain distinct spheres, the United States asserted unilateral protection over the entire Western Hemisphere. The United States could not have backed up this policy militarily in 1823, and in 1833 it did not oppose the British occupation of the Falkland Islands or its other encroachments into Latin America. In 1845 and 1848 President James Polk reiterated the Monroe principles, warning Britain and Spain to stay out of Oregon, California, and Mexico's Yucatan Peninsula. The "manifest destiny" of the United States was thus firmly ensconced decades before John O'Sullivan coined the phrase in 1845 to prophesy "the fulfillment of our manifest destiny to overspread the continent allotted by Providence." See *New Encyclopedia Britannica*, 32 vols., 15th ed. (Chicago: University of Chicago Press, 1992), 8:269; Frederick Merk, *Manifest Destiny and Mission in American History* (1963; rpt., Cambridge, Mass.: Harvard University Press, 1995), chaps. 1–4.

9. Gilbert Sewall, director of the American Textbook Council, observed that "Columbus has undergone what is perhaps the most dramatic reworking of any major historical figure in memory" and noted that the assault began in the 1970s. See Sam Dillon, "Schools Growing Harsher in Scrutiny of Columbus," *New York Times*, October 12, 1992, pp. 1A, 7B.

10. Elected a member of the Board of Visitors of the College of William and Mary in 1779, Jefferson wrote a bill amending the constitution of the college that failed to win enactment by the Virginia Assembly (Roy J. Honeywell, *The Educational Work of Thomas Jefferson* [Cambridge, Mass.: Harvard University Press, 1931], 205–10). He was nevertheless able to implement its curricular changes while resident in Williamsburg as governor of Virginia. This included substituting the modern languages for instruction in Latin and Greek (College of William and Mary, *The History of the College of William and Mary from Its Foundation, 1693 to 1870* [Baltimore: John Murphy, 1870], 66; Lyon G. Tyler, "Early Courses and Professors at William and Mary College," *William and Mary Quarterly* 14:2 [October 1905]: 76–77). Jefferson recalled these changes decades later: "When I was a Visitor, in 1779, I got the two professorships of Divinity and grammar school put down, and others of law and police, of medicine, anatomy and chemistry, and of modern languages substituted" (Thomas Jefferson to Joseph C. Cabell, in Nathanial Francis Cabell, ed., *Early History of the University of Virginia as contained in the letters of Thomas Jefferson and Joseph C. Cabell* [Richmond, Va.: J. W. Randolph, 1856], 207; see Honeywell, *Educational Work*, 54–56).

11. In the "Report of the Commissioners Appointed to Fix the Site of the University of Virginia," August 4, 1818, Jefferson and his colleagues incorporated Spanish into the

modern language curricula alongside French, Italian, German, and Anglo-Saxon (the latter for its philological value to modern English). They observed: "The Spanish is highly interesting to us, as the language spoken by so great a portion of the inhabitants of our continents, with whom we shall probably have great intercourse ere long, and is that also in which is written the greater part of the earlier history of America" (Cabell, *Early History*, 440).

12. "Spain: Her History, Character, and Literature: Vulgar Errors—Their Extent and Sources," *Southern Literary Messenger* 7 (1841): 441. The writer is Severn T. Wallis, who in the early 1840s was Irving's harshest critic.

13. This survey of Anglo–North American interest in Hispanic culture summarizes Williams, *Spanish Background*, 1:28–32, 44–47; 2:273–75.

14. Daniel Walker Howe observes that New England Whigs such as Alexander H. Everett and William Hickling Prescott were attracted to the study of Spain because it provided a negative example as a country that had failed to progress (Howe, *The Political Culture of American Whigs* [Chicago: University of Chicago Press, 1979], 74). Richard Kagan develops this line of argument in his essay (chapter 1) in this volume.

15. Michel-Rolph Trouillot, "Good Day Columbus: Silences, Power and Public History (1492–1892)," *Public Culture* 3, no. 1 (1990): 7, 8n.12.

16. John G. Cawelti, *Apostles of the Self-Made Man* (Chicago: University of Chicago Press, 1965), 43–46.

17. Martín Fernández de Navarrete, *Colección de los viajes y descubrimientos que hicieron por mar los españoles desde fines del siglo XV*, in *Obras de D. Martín Fernández de Navarrete, tomos I–III*, ed. Carlos Seco Serrano, 3 vols., Biblioteca de Autores Españoles 75–77 (Madrid: Atlas, 1954–64).

18. Williams, *Spanish Background*, 2:12, 296n.25. About the Spanish language Irving extolled: "There is an energy, a beauty, a melody and richness in it surpassing in their combined proportions all other languages that I am acquainted with" (*Washington Irving and the Storrows: Letters from England and the Continent, 1821–1828*, ed. Stanley T. Williams [Cambridge, Mass.: Harvard University Press, 1933], 114).

19. Besides writing his books on Columbus and the fall of Granada during his stay in Spain, Irving began and advanced work on the *Voyages and Discoveries of the Companions of Columbus* (1831), *The Alhambra* (1832), *Mahomet and His Successors* (1848), and the posthumously collected *Spanish Papers* (1866).

20. Irving identified the gentleman who "gave us permission to occupy his vacant apartments in the Moorish palace" as "the governor of Alhambra," who subsequently abandoned its lofty hill to reside in the center of Granada "for the more convenient despatch [*sic*] of his duties." It is unclear from the context whether Irving's reference to the "present commander, Don Francisco de Salis [Solís?] Serna," is that same governor (Irving, *The Alhambra*, 1:39, 44). Williams identifies Irving's Alhambra host as "General O'Lawler, Governor of Granada" (*Life of Washington Irving*, 1:362). Irving was appointed first secretary of the U.S. legation in London by his friend Louis McLane II, minister to the Court of St. James (*Letters of Washington Irving to Henry Brevoort*, ed. George S. Hellman [New York: G. P. Putnam's Sons, 1918], xlv).

21. Williams, *Spanish Background*, 2:44. Irving served in his "honorary" diplomatic post during the absolutist reign of Fernando VII (1823–33) and as minister to the Court of Spain during the personal reign of Isabella II (1843–68).

22. Irving, *The Alhambra*, 1:81–82.

23. Obadiah Rich, *Bibliotheca Americana Nova; or, A Catalogue of Books in Various Languages, Relating to America, Printed since the Year 1700* (London: O. Rich, 1835), 2:209.

24. Williams, *Life of Washington Irving*, 1:324. John Murray published the original four-volume edition of Washington Irving's *A History of the Life and Voyages of Christopher Columbus* (London, 1828; hereafter cited as *Columbus*) and G. & C. Carvill brought it out soon afterward in three volumes (New York, 1828). In 1829 Irving prepared and published an abridged version in one volume (New York: G. & C. Carvill, 1829). The *Voyages and Discoveries of the Companions of Columbus* was first published separately in London in 1831. A few years after Navarrete's death Irving brought out a full and augmented third edition under the title *The Life and Voyages of Christopher Columbus to Which Are Added Those of His Companions*, rev. ed., 3 vols. (New York: G. P. Putman, 1849). An identical version followed in London shortly thereafter under the title *The Life and Voyages of Christopher Columbus Together with the Voyages of His Companions*, 3 vols. (London: John Murray, 1849; hereafter cited as *Life and Voyages*). The simultaneous U.S. and British publications were executed by Irving in order to preserve copyright at a time when international copyright protection did not exist (Stanley T. Williams and Mary Ellen Edge, *A Bibliography of the Writings of Washington Irving: A Check List* [New York: Oxford University Press, 1936], xi, 69, 72).

25. William Robertson's 1777 *History of America* had been the first (and last) English-language history of Columbus before the beginning of the new era of Columbian scholarship launched by Navarrete. Robertson's work stood for a long time as the common source for the English view of the admiral. Robertson had used as his principal sources the published chronicles of Hernando Colón, Pietro Martire d'Anghiera, Gonzalo Fernández de Oviedo, Francisco López de Gómara, Antonio de Herrera y Tordesillas, and, indirectly through Herrera, the *Historia de las Indias* of Bartolomé de Las Casas.

26. John Harmon McElroy, introduction to Washington Irving, *The Life and Voyages of Christopher Columbus*, ed. John Harmon McElroy, in volume 11 of *The Complete Works of Washington Irving* (Boston: Twayne, 1981), xvii–xviii. See Williams and Edge, *Bibliography of the Writings*, 69–83.

27. Justin Winsor, *Christopher Columbus and How He Received and Imparted the Spirit of Discovery* (Boston: Houghton Mifflin, 1891), 55–59; Carlos Seco Serrano, "Introducción: Vida y obra de Martín Fernández de Navarrete," to Navarrete, *Colección*, in Seco Serrano, *Obras de D. Martín Fernández de Navarrete*, 1:xlviii.

28. Henry Harrisse held Irving's *Columbus* in high esteem: "L'oeuvre de Washington Irving est plus que littéraire. C'est une histoire écrite avec jugement et impartialité, que laisse bien loin derrière elle toutes les descriptions de la décourverte du Nouveau-Monde publiées avant ou depuis" (The work of Washington Irving is more than literature. It is a history written with judgment and impartiality that leaves far behind it all descriptions of the New World published before or since) (Harrisse, *Christophe*

Columb, 2 vols. [Paris: Ernest Leroux, 1884], 1:136). Harrisse's book, however, marked the beginning of a trend toward a more critical view of Columbus, later exemplified by the works of Henry Vignaud (*Toscanelli and Columbus* [1902], *Études critiques sur la vie de Colomb* [1905], and *Histoire critique de la grande entreprise de Christophe Colomb* [1911]). See Irving Berdine Richman, *The Spanish Conquerors: A Chronicle of the Dawn of Empire Overseas,* Chronicles of America 2 (New Haven, Conn.: Yale University Press, 1921), 218.

29. Williams and Edge, *Bibliography of the Writings,* 69–83.

30. Marcelino Menéndez y Pelayo, "De los historiadores de Colón," in *Estudios y discursos de crítica histórica y literaria 7,* in *Obras completas de Menéndez Pelayo 12,* dir. Miguel Artigas (Madrid: Consejo Superior de Investigaciones Científicas, 1942), 104–5, my translation.

31. This is Williams's typology (*Spanish Background,* 2:278–85).

32. While Prescott and Irving today are generally considered in contrast to one another as authors of different types of literature (history and historical romance, respectively), as early Anglo-American Hispanists the features of U.S. romantic writing that they shared are more significant than their differences. See Rolena Adorno, "Creadores de historia y progreso: Comentario," *Op. Cit. Revista del Centro de Investigaciones Históricos de la Universidad de Puerto Rico* 9 (1997): 109–27.

33. This survey of tendencies in romantic American historiography summarizes David Levin, *History as Romantic Art: Bancroft, Prescott, Motley, and Parkman,* Stanford Studies in Language and Literature 20 (Stanford, Calif.: Stanford University Press, 1959), ix, 7–23.

34. Levin cites Parkman's statement to illustrate how the U.S. romantic historians attributed the fulfillment of historical progress to puritanism (Levin, *History as Romantic Art,* 35).

35. Ibid., 38–39.

36. Ibid., 11.

37. Irving, *Columbus,* 1:iv. When writing *Columbus* he expressed his anxiety about its potential success and its importance as an American topic: "If it fails to interest the public I shall be grievously disappointed. The subject appear[e]d to me of great importance, especially to our country" (Irving to Thomas W. Storrow, January 3, 1827, Madrid, in *Washington Irving and the Storrows,* 106). I define Irving's Americanism as his pursuit of service to his country through his literature and his search for the best ways to exercise his literary gifts, which were aspirations he often expressed, as here, in his private journals and personal letters. William Hedges similarly characterizes Irving's Americanism not by literary theme but by the cultural tensions that he experienced, namely, between bourgeois and aristocratic attitudes, romantic and classical impulses, and a general uncertainty about the function of the writer in a commercial society (Hedges, "The Theme of Americanism in Irving's Writings," in *Washington Irving: A Tribute,* ed. Andrew B. Myers [Tarrytown, N.Y.: Sleepy Hollow Restorations, 1972], 34). To these factors I would add Irving's concerns about the function of a U.S. writer in an *international* society. The years he spent abroad placed him in the unusu-

al situation of explaining the United States to Europeans and Europe to Americans—all in the era of romanticism. I would argue that his work may best be understood as the search for a narrative lingua franca of international intelligibility.

38. Irving to Storrow, August 16 and October 26, 1826, Madrid, *Washington Irving and the Storrows*, 94, 100.

39. Quoted in Williams, *Life of Washington Irving*, 1:312–13.

40. *Washington Irving and the Storrows*, 133n.1.

41. Böhl supported his family by working as a manager for the William Duff Gordon wine company, producers of fine sherry, in Puerto de Santa María.

42. On the Irving-Caballero relationship see Stanley T. Williams, "Washington Irving and Fernán Caballero," *Journal of English and Germanic Philology* 29 (1930): 352–66; Stanley T. Williams and E. H. Hespelt, "Two Unpublished Anecdotes by Fernán Caballero Preserved by Washington Irving," *Modern Language Notes* 49 (1934): 25–31.

43. Böhl had strongly criticized Spanish subservience to French culture in a number of areas. Irving, meanwhile, confined his criticism to more tame remarks about how contemporary Spanish theater "bent its neck to the yoke of French dramatic rule" (Williams, *Life of Washington Irving*, 1:350–51).

44. Ibid., 1:348, 373.

45. *Washington Irving and the Storrows*, 79.

46. *The Journals of Washington Irving (Hitherto Unpublished)*, ed. William P. Trent and George S. Hellman, 3 vols. (Boston: Bibliophile Society, 1919), 3:10, 51–55.

47. Irving, *Columbus*, 1:v–vi.

48. This would have been Pedro de Larreátegui y Ramírez de Baquedano (1801–66), the ninth duke of Veragua, descended from the admiral's son Diego Colón. See Harrisse, *Christophe Colomb*, 2:292, 294.

49. Irving, *Columbus*, 1:vi–vii.

50. Ibid., 1:v (emphasis added). Rich's library was Irving's main source of materials. Shortly after he started work on *Columbus*, Irving remarked: "His [Rich's] house is crammed with books of the most interesting kind, such as could only be found scattered in national libraries. All these are as absolutely at my command as though they were my own, and he is eager to procure me anything else that I may have occasion for" (Irving to Storrow, April 14, 1826, Madrid, in *Washington Irving and the Storrows*, 79). A year later he wrote: "Since my arrival in Spain I have been completely immersed in old Spanish literature. My residence under the roof of Mr. Rich the American Consul has been particularly favourable to my pursuits; he is a diligent collector of rare works and has the most valuable works in print and manuscript of the Spanish writers" (Irving to Henry Brevoort, April 4, 1827, Madrid, *Letters of Washington Irving*, 411–12).

51. Williams, *Life of Washington Irving*, 1:473n.48.

52. See Williams, *Life of Washington Irving*, 2:303; Williams, *Spanish Background*, 2:14.

53. Irving to Storrow, April 14, 1826, Madrid, *Washington Irving and the Storrows*, 79–80.

54. "Although there were many books, in various languages, relative to Columbus, they all contained limited and incomplete accounts of his life and voyages; while nu-

merous valuable tracts on the subject existed only in manuscript or in the form of letters, journals, and public muniments. It appeared to me that a history, *faithfully digested from these various materials,* was a desideratum in literature" (Irving, *Columbus,* 1:iv [emphasis added]).

55. See, for example, Irving's *Columbus* (bk. 1, chaps. 4, 6). In studying three of Irving's post-*Columbus* works on the American West (*A Tour on the Prairies* [1835], *Astoria, or Anecdotes of an Enterprise Beyond the Rocky Mountains* [1836], and *The Adventures of Captain Bonneville* [1837]) as examples of "adventurous enterprise," Peter Antelyes links the notions of personal adventure and territorial expansion. He sets forth the explicit association of "adventure" with economic enterprise, noting that the first English-language usage of the term in the fifteenth century referred to financial risks taken in the oceanic transport of goods. See Peter Antelyes, *Tales of Adventurous Enterprise: Washington Irving and the Poetics of Westward Expansion* (New York: Columbia University Press, 1990), 3. As my reading of *Columbus* makes clear, Irving engaged the theories of "adventurous enterprise" in his works on the Spanish exploration of the Caribbean well before his return to the United States in 1832.

56. Alexander H. Everett faulted Irving for underrating the merit of Columbus's religious vision, and he attributed this perceived lacuna to Irving's "merely superficial view" of the state of the world at the time (Everett, "Irving's Life of Columbus," *North American Review* 28 [1829]: 131).

57. We have had to wait until the appearance of Alejo Carpentier's 1979 novel, *El arpa y la sombra,* for a brilliant satire of these gaps and inconsistencies in Columbus's writings.

58. Citing directly from Las Casas's handwritten account of the first voyage transcribed in Navarrete's first volume, Irving pointed out that while the sovereigns "smiled at this sally of the imagination" (y vuestras Altezas se rieron), the quest for Jerusalem was nevertheless "a deep and cherished design of Columbus." Irving emphasized the scant attention paid by the monarchs to this objective, which Columbus "meditated throughout the remainder of his life, and solemnly provided for in his will." Irving continues: "In fact, he considered it as one of the great works for which he was chosen by heaven as an agent, and he afterward looked upon his great discovery as but a preparatory dispensation of Providence to promote its accomplishment" (Irving, *Columbus,* 1:168–69 [bk. 2, chap. 8]).

59. Levin, *History as Romantic Art,* 40–41.

60. Irving credentials Columbus as a nonmaterialist by characterizing him as disinterested in financial reward. In dramatizing one of Columbus's final interviews with Ferdinand after the fourth voyage, Irving insists: "It was, in fact, on the subject of his dignities alone that Columbus was tenacious; all other matters he considered as of minor importance. In a conversation with the king, he declared that he had no desire to enter in any process or pleading. He was willing to put all his privileges into the hands of the king, and to receive out of the dues arising from them, whatever his majesty thought proper. He prayed only that the matter might be speedily decided; that he might retire to some quiet corner, and seek the repose that his great fatigues and infirmities required.

All that he claimed without qualification or reserve, were his official dignities, assured to him under the royal seal with all the solemnity of a treaty" (Irving, *Columbus*, 4:32–34 [bk. 18, chap. 3]). If Columbus was tenacious regarding his rank and privileges, it was "not from a mere vulgar love of titles, but because he prized them as testimonials and trophies of his achievements" (Irving, *Columbus*, 4:51 [bk. 18, chap. 5]).

61. Ibid., 4:42.

62. Ibid., 4:56–58 (bk. 18, chap. 5).

63. Ibid., 4:57–58.

64. Ibid., 4:53–54.

65. Ibid., 4:58–60.

66. Ibid., 4:25, 30 (bk. 18, chap. 3).

67. See, for example, Irving, *Columbus*, 1:434 (bk. 5, chap. 7).

68. Ibid., 4:47 (bk. 18, chap. 4).

69. As Williams summed up the reviews that appeared in English in 1828–30, "the all-embracing sentimental tradition of the age approved Washington Irving's only attempt at serious history" (Williams, *Life of Washington Irving*, 2:302–4). See also Haskell Springer, *Washington Irving: A Reference Guide,* Reference Guides in Literature 6 (Boston: G. K. Hall, 1976), 22–27.

70. Washington Irving, *Diary, Spain, 1828–29,* ed. Clara Louisa Penney (New York: Hispanic Society of America, 1926), 90.

71. Williams, *Life of Washington Irving*, 1:356, 383n.88, 492n.179; McElroy, introduction to Irving's *Columbus*, xviii, lxxxv; *Visions of Washington Irving: Selected Works from the Collections of Historic Hudson Valley* (Tarrytown, N.Y.: Historic Hudson Valley, 1991), 30–31.

72. The range of Irving's friendships with artists and the immense popularity of his writings as themes for U.S. painters and graphic artists resulted in illustrations for his work by an unprecedented number of famous and nearly famous artists (David M. Sokol, "Washington Irving: Friend and Muse to American Artists," in *Visions of Washington Irving*, 15, 25). See also Jules David Prown, "Washington Irving's Interest in Art and His Influence upon American Painting," master's thesis, University of Delaware, 1956; James T. Callow, *Kindred Spirits: Knickerbocker Writers and American Artists, 1807–1855* (Chapel Hill: University of North Carolina Press, 1967).

73. Washington Allston to Gulian C. Verplanck, March 29, 1830, quoted in Jared B. Flagg, *The Life and Letters of Washington Allston* (New York: Charles Scribner's Sons, 1892), 237. Allston's proposal was never realized. After six years of deliberations Allston decided that he could not accept the commission. The remaining four panels, to join the four by John Trumbull that were already in place, ultimately were painted by Robert W. Weir, William H. Powell (Irving supported him for the commission), John Vanderlyn (another friend of Irving), and John G. Chapman. All four artists are regarded as second rate by modern critics, and none of the compositions has a Columbian theme (Callow, *Kindred Spirits*, 46–49; Sokol, "Washington Irving," 17, 22–23). Emanuel Leutze's *Ferdinand Removing the Chains from Columbus* (1843) and Abraham Woodside's *Columbus at the Court of Ferdinand and Isabella* (1846) nevertheless drew

inspiration from Irving's *Columbus*. Irving must have been disappointed in Allston's failure to accept the Capitol commission as well as his inability to finish his masterwork, *Belshazzar's Feast*. Irving considered Allston's increasingly recognized artistic merits "to possess more than any contemporary the spirit of the old masters" (Washington Irving, *Spanish Papers and Other Miscellanies, Hitherto Unpublished or Uncollected*, ed. Pierre M. Irving, 2 vols. [New York: G. P. Putman, Hurd and Houghton, 1866], 2:150).

74. *Irvingiana: A Memorial of Washington Irving* (New York: Charles B. Richardson, 1860), xxvii.

75. Everett, "Irving's Life of Columbus," 108–10.

76. Ibid., 110.

77. Ibid., 126–27. Although decades later Harrisse praised Irving's work in his published history of Columbus, Harrisse nevertheless observed in his private memoirs that Irving's *Columbus* lacked the foundation, that is, "the underlaying," or "the why and wherefore of events," that Harrisse deemed "essential to every important historical composition" (quoted in Williams, *Life of Washington Irving*, 2:303).

78. Irving, *Columbus*, 1:vii–viii (emphasis added).

79. Everett, "Irving's Life of Columbus," 127–28.

80. Ibid., 128–30.

81. Navarrete, introduction to *Colección*, in *Obras I*, 46b; Navarrete, prologue to *Colección*, in *Obras II*, 13b, my translation.

82. Navarrete may have had in mind works such as Robertson's outline sketch of Columbus in his 1777 *History of America* or Juan Bautista Muñoz's notable *Vida del almirante* in his unfinished *Historia del Nuevo Mundo* (1793). Muñoz's biography of Columbus was incomplete insofar as he had not had the opportunity to introduce the necessary supporting documentation (Seco Serrano, introduction to Navarrete's *Obras I*, xlviii).

83. Navarrete, prologue to *Colección*, in *Obras II*, 13b.

84. Navarrete, introduction to *Obras I*, 51a–57b.

85. Irving, *Columbus*, 4:116 (appendix 3).

86. Hernando Colón, *The Life of the Admiral Christopher Columbus by His Son Ferdinand*, trans. Benjamin Keen (1959; rpt. New Brunswick, N.J.: Rutgers University Press, 1992), 3–4, 15–28 (chaps. 1, 6–9); Irving, *Columbus*, 1:60, see 53–65 (bk. 1, chap. 5]). See also Francisco Morales Padrón, "El descubrimiento de América según Washington Irving," in *Washington Irving (1859–1959)*, 81–86.

87. Navarrete, introduction to *Colección*, in *Obras I*, 62, 254a (cartas de don Cristóbal Colón).

88. Navarrete wrote the remarks that seem to affirm his royalist political loyalties shortly after Fernando VII's 1823 reinstitution of the absolutist regime that would prevail until that monarch's death in 1833. Navarrete had received royal appointment to the directorship of the Depósito Hidrográfico in 1823; in 1825 he expressed his gratitude and loyalty to the monarch who allowed him independence in carrying out his historiographic work aimed at revindicating Spain's maritime imperial history. Also in 1825 Navarrete was

elected director of the Real Academia de la Historia by its members; he was reelected six times and died in that post in 1844. The longevity of his intellectual leadership, from the final period of Fernando VII's absolutist reign through the civil wars over the royal succession, suggests that Navarrete was regarded as a source of equanimity and stability and became a reference point for moderates once the path to greater liberty was opened after Fernando VII's death (Carlos Seco Serrano, "Fernández de Navarrete y la historia de los descubrimientos," in Instituto de Historia y Cultura Naval, *XI Jornadas de historia marítima: Martín Fernández de Navarrete, el marino historiador (1765–1844)*, Cuadernos monográficos del Instituto de Historia y Cultura Naval 24 [Madrid, 1995], 30–34). Navarrete has been characterized today as a late Spanish exemplar of Enlightenment values and a "survivor of that generation that desired change without war and transformation by means of voluntary acquiescence and compromise" (Gonzalo Anes y Álvarez de Castrillón, "Fernández de Navarrete, académico de la historia," in Instituto de Historia y Cultura Naval, *XI Jornadas de historia marítima*, 73).

89. Irving wrote, "There is a certain meddlesome spirit, which, in the garb of learned research, goes prying about the traces of history, casting down its monuments, and marring and mutilating its fairest trophies. Care should be taken to vindicate great names from such pernicious erudition. It defeats one of the most salutary purposes of history, that of furnishing examples of what human genius and laudable enterprise may accomplish" (Irving, *Columbus*, 1:64–65 [bk. 1, chap. 5]).

90. Here Irving's experience of nineteenth-century Spain is also pertinent. His first sojourn in Spain (1826–29) occurred during the "ominous decade" of Fernando VII's absolutism and its attempts to crush all vestiges of the liberal opposition. His second stay (1842–46), as minister to the Court of Spain, occurred during the regency of General Baldomero Espartero and the personal reign of Isabella II. These years were marked by dictatorial military influence and armed insurrection; they have been identified with the emergence of polarizing political sentiments that would characterize the national ideologies of twentieth-century Spain. See Jesús P. Martínez, *Historia de España, vol. II: Edades moderna y contemporánea* (Madrid: Ediciones y Publicaciones Españolas, 1963), 71–73.

91. "New Documents Concerning Columbus," *North American Review* 24 (April 1827): 290.

92. Ibid., 286–87.

93. Ibid., 292.

94. Navarrete reminded his readers that he had earlier criticized Hernando Colón for his "devious astuteness" regarding the origins of his family, their homeland, and other related matters. Now he pointed out that Hernando's writing displayed "more the affection of a son than the impartiality of a historian." He emphasized the point by citing a memorable quotation from Padre Juan de Mariana to the effect that love, like hate, blinds that faculty of the soul that governs understanding and leads to the distortion of truth. Navarrete added that this danger affected the writers of fiction in general as well as those who wrote about the lives and deeds of their fathers and forefathers (Navarrete, prologue to *Colección*, in *Obras II*, 11).

95. Ibid., 11b–12a. As a common topic for the contemporary historical novel, Navarrete cited the conquest of Granada, which may be a veiled reference to Irving's *Conquest of Granada*. Whether the book had already appeared or not (the official publication date was May 9, 1829), Navarrete knew that Irving was at work on a popular account of those events. Irving identified his work as a "romantic chronicle" and planned to publish it under the pseudonym of Fray Antonio Agapida. He was chagrined when his London publisher, John Murray, affixed his real name to the title page of the first edition (Williams, *Life of Washington Irving*, 1:346). Irving had no doubt wished to distance himself as the author of the historical *Columbus* from the *Granada*, to which he had endeavored to give "something of the effect of a work of imagination" (*Washington Irving and the Storrows*, 134). In Navarrete's view Irving's novelistic impulse vitiated not only the *Conquest of Granada* but also the disinterested narration of Spanish ultramarine history in his *Columbus*.

96. Navarrete, prologue to *Colección*, in *Obras II*, 11b–12a.

97. Ibid., 12a.

98. Williams, *Spanish Background*, 1:44–45; 2:5.

99. Irving's English translation of Navarrete's remarks accompanies his transcription of the original Spanish text (Irving, *Life and Voyages*, 1:x–xi).

100. "Spain: Her History, Character, and Literature," 231–39. See McElroy, introduction to Irving's *Life and Voyages of Christopher Columbus*, xxiv–lxxx; Williams, *Spanish Background*, 1:67–69, 339.

101. "The *Knickerbocker*, Mr. Irving, and Sr. Navarrete," *Southern Literary Messenger* 9 (1843): 16.

102. *El Pensamiento* was edited by the poet José de Espronceda, Miguel de los Santos, and Ros de Olano, with whom Gil y Carrasco collaborated in 1841. Gil y Carrasco's poetry was published in the 1830s in *El Español*, a journal directed by Irving's translator, the novelist José García de Villalta. See Jorge Campos, "Introducción: Vida y obra de Enrique Gil y Carrasco," in Enrique Gil y Carrasco, *Obras completas*, ed. Jorge Campos, Biblioteca de Autores Españoles 74 (Madrid: Atlas, 1954), xiii–xiv.

103. Irving, *Columbus*, 1:v; "Navarrete on Spain," *Southern Literary Messenger* 7 (1841): 233–34.

104. "Navarrete on Spain," 233–35.

105. Ibid., 236.

106. Ibid., 235–38.

107. Irving, *Columbus*, 1:vi.

108. "Spain: Her History, Character, and Literature," 441–49.

109. Ibid., 442–47.

110. Ibid., 443, 449.

111. Gil y Carrasco, *Obras completas*, 546, 548.

112. Ibid., 544–47.

113. Ibid., 547.

114. "Spain, Popular Errors—Their Causes—Travellers," *Southern Literary Messenger* 8 (1842): 305–6 (emphasis added).

115. Quoted in Williams, *Life of Washington Irving,* 2:128–29.

116. "Editor's Table," *Knickerbocker Magazine* 20, no. 1 (1842): 97; "Editor's Table," *Knickerbocker Magazine* 20, no. 2 (1842): 194–97.

117. "Mr. Washington Irving, Mr. Navarrete, and the *Knickerbocker,*" *Southern Literary Messenger* 8 (1842): 727, 729–33.

118. "Editor's Table," *Knickerbocker Magazine* 20, no. 6 (1842): 586–87; "*Knickerbocker,* Mr. Irving, and Sr. Navarrete," 15–16 (emphasis added).

119. Wagenknecht, *Washington Irving,* 81.

120. Irving, *Life and Voyages,* 1:viii, x; see also Irving, *Columbus,* 1:v.

121. Irving, *Columbus,* 1:64–65 (bk. 1, chap. 5).

122. "I feel vexed at this shabby attempt to purloin this work from me, it having really cost me more toil and trouble than all my other productions and being one that I trusted would keep me current with my countrymen; but we are making rapid advances in literature in America, and have already attained many of the literary vices and diseases of the old countries of Europe" (Irving to Brevoort, December 20, 1828, *Letters of Washington Irving,* 420–21; see also Williams, *Life of Washington Irving,* 1:355).

123. Irving to Philip J. Forbes, October 25, 1852, Collection of the New-York Historical Society, New York.

124. Williams first cited the letter to Forbes and thus was the first to reference Irving's knowledge of *The World Displayed* (Williams, *Life of Washington Irving,* 1:21, and *Spanish Background,* 2:9). The English-language collection of travels was for Williams an example of the readings out of which Irving's early love of England grew. Wagenknecht later quoted Irving's letter to Forbes and noted that the "*Life and Voyages of Columbus* may be said to have begun when that same boy [Irving] pored over the geographical narratives in *The World Displayed*" (Wagenknecht, *Washington Irving,* 182). My reading of Williams led me to connect Irving's reading of *The World Displayed* with his *Columbus,* which Williams himself had not done. Wagenknecht's insightful remark, which I discovered late, was borne out by the analysis I had already done on the common sources of *The World Displayed* and Irving's biography.

125. William L. Hedges, "Irving's *Columbus:* The Problem of Romantic Biography," *Americas* 13 (1957): 132n.21.

126. Irving, *Columbus,* 4:48–73 (bk. 18, chap. 5); *World Displayed,* 1:141 (chap. 5).

127. *World Displayed,* 1:81 (chap. 2).

128. Williams, *Life of Washington Irving,* 1:355.

129. See Springer, *Washington Irving,* 21–24.

130. "Notice of *Life and Voyages of Christopher Columbus* (abridged)," *Brooklyn Daily Eagle,* March 12, 1847, cited in Springer, *Washington Irving,* 44; ibid., 67.

131. William Hickling Prescott, *History of the Reign of Ferdinand and Isabella, the Catholic,* 5th ed., 3 vols. (1838; Boston: Charles C. Little and James Brown, 1839), 1:xi–xii; 2:133–34 (pt. 1, chap. 16, endnote). Prescott's views echo Irving's understanding of his own efforts. While Irving described his work as containing "many curious particulars not hitherto known concerning Columbus" and as having "thrown light upon some parts of his character which have not been brought out by his former biogra-

phers," he also prided himself on having "labored hard to make the work complete and accurate as to all the information extant relative to the subject." His targeted audience was broad and popular: "I have sought to execute in such a manner as would render it agreeable to the general reader" (quoted in Wagenknecht, *Washington Irving,* 183).

132. William Cullen Bryant, *Life, Genius, and Character of Washington Irving* (New York: G. P. Putnam, 1860), 28.

133. According to Bryant, Irving's rewriting, which he later apparently regretted, had been prompted by Slidell Mackenzie's comment that the original version of the narrative suffered from an "unequal" style (Bryant, *Life, Genius, and Character,* 29).

134. Ibid., 45–46.

135. Ibid., 46.

136. See Richman, *Spanish Conquerors,* 218–20.

137. Irving to Storrow, April 14, 1826, December 1, 1827, and February 23, 1828, *Washington Irving and the Storrows,* 78–81, 122–23, 127.

138. Hedges, "Irving's *Columbus,*" 134; Hedges, *Washington Irving,* 245. See also Wagenknecht, *Washington Irving,* 184.

139. Isaac Thomas, preface to *Selections from Washington Irving,* ed. Isaac Thomas, Students' Series of English Classics 17 (Boston: Leach, Shewell, and Sanborn, 1894), iii, v.

140. *Selections from Washington Irving,* 269–80; Irving, *Life and Voyages,* 1:143–53.

141. *Selections from Washington Irving,,* 279–80.

142. On Columbus's imagination Richman wrote: "He was masterful and imaginative, but his masterfulness tended to ungenerousness and his imagination to vagary and mischievous exaggeration" (Richman, *Spanish Conquerors,* 14). On the sinister character of the admiral's vanity and cupidity, the textbook stated: "It is probable, however, that the sinister in him has by recent writers been somewhat over-magnified" (ibid.).

143. Ibid., 59–60.

144. Dillon, "Schools Growing Harsher," p. 1A.

145. Thomas, preface to *Selections from Washington Irving,* iv–v.

146. Quoted in Ynduráin Hernández, "Washington Irving," 51. Irving met Thackeray in 1852–53 when the latter was on a lecture tour in the United States. Thackeray visited Irving at Sunnyside and marveled at the "universal veneration" in which the U.S. writer was held (Williams, *Life of Washington Irving,* 2:203, 209, 213).

147. Charles Dickens, *American Notes* (1842; rpt., Gloucester, Mass.: Peter Smith, 1968), 150.

3

George Ticknor's *History of Spanish Literature*
Thomas R. Hart Jr.

No one did more to establish the national and popular character of Spanish literature than George Ticknor. Born in Boston in 1791, Ticknor graduated from Dartmouth College in 1807 (figure 3.1). He read law in Boston and was admitted to the bar in 1813 but practiced for only one year. In 1815 he began a period of study at the University of Göttingen in Germany. A letter from President Kirkland of Harvard offering him a professorship caused him to prolong his stay in Europe in order to visit Spain. He began teaching at Harvard in 1819 and remained there until his resignation in 1835. His *History of Spanish Literature* appeared in 1849; in 1864 he published a biography of his close friend William Hickling Prescott, who had died two years before. Ticknor died in Boston in 1871.[1]

Ticknor's three-volume *History* became the standard work on the subject upon its publication and retained that position for at least half a century. There are several later editions as well as translations into French, German, and Spanish. Ticknor explains his aims in a letter to Sir Charles Lyell that accompanied a presentation copy of his *History:* "I have been persuaded that literary history . . . should be made, like civil history, to give a knowledge of the *character of the people* to which it relates. I have endeavored, therefore, so to write my account of Spanish literature as to make the literature itself the exponent of the peculiar culture and civilization of the Spanish people.[2]

Lionel Gossman reminds us that "as late as the eighteenth century, . . . history was still a literary genre. Voltaire and Gibbon had no doubt that they were 'writers' in a genre with a pedigree as noble and almost as long as epic or tragedy. In the last century, Michelet and Burckhardt also thought of themselves

Figure 3.1. Thomas Sully's *George Ticknor (1791–1871), Class of 1807*, 1831, oil on canvas, 91.5 × 71.1 cm (Hood Museum of Art, Dartmouth College, Hanover, N.H.; gift of Constance V. R. White, Nathaniel T. Dexter, Philip Dexter, and Mary Ann Streeter)

as writers."[3] So did the American romantic historians, none more so than Ticknor's friend William Hickling Prescott. In a modest way, so too did Ticknor himself. In a letter to his nephew George Ticknor Curtis, he takes care to point out that his work is not addressed to specialists but to the general reader: "As you read, please to bear in mind that my book is an attempt to make literary history useful, as general reading, to a people like the American, by connecting it with the history of civilization and manners in the country to which it relates. Whether I have succeeded is another question; but you will not judge me as I wish to be judged, unless you take this for what the Germans call your 'stand-punct' [*sic*]."[4]

Ticknor's New England contemporaries often expressed a similar desire to be "useful." In his notebooks, Prescott constantly reminds himself of the need to interest his readers. In a note of July 3, 1828, confirming "for the hundredth time" his decision to write the book that would be published in 1837 as *History of the Reign of Ferdinand and Isabella*, Prescott vows that his work "shall aim . . . at a popular rather than erudite compilation" and is confident that it "may be made novel, elegant, useful & very entertaining."[5] Reviews of Ticknor's *History* by his friends make the same point. George S. Hillard, who was chosen by Ticknor's family to prepare *Life, Letters, and Journals* for publication, observes that Ticknor "aimed to produce a book . . . which shall be found in the drawing-room as well as in the study" and has, therefore, tried "to present the literature of Spain as the true exponent of its civilization and the manners of its people, and to infuse into it that animating life-blood which flows from the great national heart of the country."[6]

In the preface to his *History* Ticknor presents it as an entirely new work:

> In the interval between my two residences in Europe [1817–19 and 1836–38] I delivered lectures [on Spanish literature] to successive classes in Harvard College; and on my return home from the second, I endeavored to arrange these lectures for publication. But when I had already employed much time and labor on them, I found—or thought I found—that the tone of discussion which I had adopted for my academical audiences was not suited to the purposes of a regular history. Destroying, therefore, what I had written, I began afresh my never unwelcome task, and so have prepared the present work, as little connected with all I had previously done as it, perhaps, can be, and yet cover so much of the same ground.[7]

In reality, however, Ticknor never subjected his text to a sweeping revision. The main lines of his *History* are already firmly established in the *Syllabus of a Course of Lectures on the History and Criticism of Spanish Literature* that he published in 1823, while a comparison of the *Syllabus* with the manuscript lectures now in the Harvard University Archives reveals that the lectures follow the *Syllabus* very closely and that they are similar in many ways to the *History* of 1849.[8]

It is, of course, true that Ticknor discusses many more books and writers in the *History* than in the lectures. He began to collect Spanish books during his first visit to Madrid in 1818 and, although he never returned to Spain, continued to add to his collection throughout his life and even afterward, since he provided funds for posthumous purchases after his collection became the nucleus of the Ticknor Collection in the Boston Public Library. He could build such a large library because he had private means. Before accepting appointment as the first Smith Professor of the French and Spanish Languages and Literatures at Harvard, he wrote his father, Elisha, asking for assurance that he would not have to live on a professor's salary, and his financial position became even more secure after his marriage to Anna Eliot on September 18, 1821. David Tyack observes that "Anna's inheritance of $84,349.50 from her father, coupled with George's modest legacy from Elisha, who died in 1821, enabled the Ticknors 'to live at ease with unpretending elegance'" and notes that several other scholars of modest means, including Henry Wadsworth Longfellow, who succeeded Ticknor as Smith Professor, also married wealthy women.[9]

Despite the enormous accumulation of new materials, the basic plan of Ticknor's *History* remains the same as in his Harvard lectures. Hundreds of passages repeat sentences, paragraphs, and even whole pages with only slight changes in wording. Here is one such passage; the Harvard lecture is on the left, the *History* on the right:

The cavalier and heroick drama of the Spanish theatre is, therefore, unlike all that is found on any other stage. It takes no cognizance of ancient examples, for they could not be applied to materials and feelings so entirely modern and romantic—it borrowed nothing from the drama of Italy or France for it was in advance of both, when its final form and character were settled—and as for England though Shakespeare and Lope were contemporaries and there are many points of resemblance between them, they and their schools had undoubtedly not the least influence on each other. It is, therefore, entirely national and popular.[10]	The Spanish theatre, in many of its attributes and characteristics, stands, therefore, by itself. It takes no cognizance of ancient example; for the spirit of antiquity could have little in common with materials so modern, Christian, and romantic. It borrowed nothing from the drama of France or of Italy; for it was in advance of both when its final character was not only developed, but settled. And, as for England, though Shakespeare and Lope were contemporaries, and there are points of resemblance between them which it is pleasant to trace and difficult to explain, still they and their schools, undoubtedly, had not the least influence on each other. The Spanish drama is, therefore, entirely national.[11]

Another passage illustrates the emotional response to ruins that David Levin notes among the American romantic historians.[12] Once again the Harvard version is on the left:

The gradual decay and final disappearance of any language brings with it melancholy thoughts which are, in some sort, peculiar to it. It seems, as if a portion of the world's intelligence were extinguished—as if we were cut off from a part of the intellectual inheritance, to which we had an equal right with those who destroyed it, and which it was a personal injury to us that they did not pass down unimpaired, as they themselves received it. This feeling pursues us, even when, as in the Greek and Latin, the people that spoke it had risen to the full heights of their	For the slow decay and final disappearance of any language bring with them melancholy thoughts, which are, in some sort, peculiar to the occasion. We feel as if a portion of the world's intelligence were extinguished; as if we were ourselves cut off from a part of the intellectual inheritance, to which we had in many respects an equal right with those who destroyed it, and which they were bound to pass down to us unimpaired as they themselves had received it. The same feeling pursues us even when, as in the case of the Greek and Latin, the people that

refinement, and left behind them monuments by which all posterity can measure and share their glory— but our regret is much deeper, when the language of a people is cut off in its youth, before its character has been fully developed, and when its literature is hardly beginning to appear—at the very moment, when all is promise and hope, and before any thing is ripened and settled into its final forms and most graceful and beautiful proportions. And this was singularly the misfortune and the fate of the Provençal and the dialects it called forth.[13]

spoke it had risen to the full height of their refinement, and left behind them monuments by which all future times can measure and share their glory. But our regret is deeper when the language of a people is cut off in its youth, before its character is fully developed; when its poetical attributes are just beginning to appear, and when all is bright with promise and hope. This was singularly the misfortune and the fate of the Provençal and of the two principal dialects into which it was modified and molded.[14]

It is hard to see why Ticknor insisted that his *History* represents a complete revision of his lectures, which had already firmly established his reputation as an authority on Spanish literature. Prescott, in the *North American Review* in July 1837, speaks of "Mr. Ticknor's beautiful lectures before the classes of Harvard University, still in manuscript, [which] embrace a far more extensive range of criticism than is to be found in any Spanish work, and display, at the same time, a degree of thoroughness and research which the comparative paucity of materials will compel us to look for in vain in Bouterwek or Sismondi."[15] Ticknor read the lectures to Prescott in the fall of 1824 and thus perhaps helped persuade him to abandon his projected history of Italian literature and choose a Spanish subject instead. More than twenty years later, in his review of Ticknor's *History* in the same journal, Prescott remarks that "Mr. Ticknor has profited largely by the former discussion of this subject in his academic lectures. Not that the present book bears much resemblance to those lectures,—certainly not more than must necessarily occur in the discussion of the same subject by the same mind, after a long interval of time. But this interval has enabled him to review, and no doubt in some cases to reverse, his earlier judgments, and his present decisions come before us as the ripe result of a long and patient meditation."[16] It is difficult to say whether Prescott was making a point Ticknor himself wanted stressed or whether he really was mistaken about the extent of the changes in the lectures Ticknor had read to him a quarter of a century earlier.

Why did Ticknor want readers of his *History* to think he had made extensive changes in his Harvard lectures? Prescott gives a hint in a letter of April 10, 1844, to Count Adolphe de Circourt in which he says, "Since his return from his last visit to Europe [in 1838], [Ticknor] has occupied, or rather amused himself—he courts the Muses now with something more of a Platonic love than in his earlier days—with writing anew on a different plan and in more extended and much more thorough manner a history of Spanish literature. . . . When I speak of his finishing his great work, I beg you not to understand that the time is drawing near. Heaven knows if we shall ever see it, for to say the truth he seems to grow more and more fastidious and more indifferent to publication."[17] Prescott may exaggerate Ticknor's indifference to publication. For a man of Ticknor's social position and scholarly achievements there was a moral obligation to write and a social obligation to publish. Ticknor may have felt that his apparent idleness after his resignation from Harvard in 1835 demanded some kind of explanation, especially since Prescott, despite recurrent problems with his eyesight, had published during the same period his *History of the Reign of Ferdinand and Isabella* (1837), *The Conquest of Mexico* (1843), and *The Conquest of Peru* (1847).[18]

What the people of Boston thought was of immense importance to Ticknor, just as what he thought was important to them, or at least to the aristocratic circle in which he moved. His nephew Charles Eliot Norton observes in a letter to Thomas Carlyle that "Mr. Ticknor deserved all his success; he was a 'scholar and a gentleman' and had an attractive, if not very deep, nature. His very defects—the worst of which were lack of imagination and lack of humor—served him in conventional society."[19] Ticknor's *History* demonstrates the continued vitality of the peculiarly Bostonian conception of "usefulness," so important in his youth when, as William Charvat points out, "wealth and social position carried with them an obligation of social leadership or cultural distinction."[20] Ticknor's *History* is in part an attempt to meet that obligation, and his interpretation of Spanish literature and the Spanish character constantly reflects the Federalist and Unitarian standards of the Boston society in which he played a leading role for half a century.

Richard L. Kagan observes that Prescott understood Spain as the antithesis of the United States: "Just as Prescott cherished the notion of 'American exceptionalism,' the idea that his own country possessed a unique history that destined it for greatness, Spain was equally exceptional but seen from the inverted perspective of a nation separated from the European, that is, Protestant, mainstream and consequently bereft of the progress and prosperity that flowed in its wake."[21] Ticknor shared these views. His determination to make his *History* "useful, to a people like the American" meant drawing up a balance sheet of the virtues and defects of Spanish civilization in terms that suggest an implicit, and occasionally explicit, contrast with developments in the United States. To this Ticknor adds a contrast between Spain and France. His lectures on French literature, written at about the same time as his lectures on Spanish literature and addressed to the same audience of Harvard undergraduates, show that he conceived the essential qualities of the two literatures in opposition to one another.

Anti-French feeling was widespread in the Boston circles in which Ticknor grew up. Charvat remarks that "Prescott's group were exposed, in their youth, to the world-wide reaction against the French Revolution. The great movement of French liberalism in political, social, and religious thought . . . received a serious setback when it became apparent that such thought was a potential threat to government, property, and organized religion."[22] "When Napoleon was rejected from France," Ticknor wrote to his father in May 1815, "every man in Christendom, of honest principles and feelings, felt as if a weight of danger had been lifted from his prospects."[23] In his sixties, he recalled that as a boy he had read an early edition of Jacques Mallet du Pan's *Considerations on the Nature of the French Revolution* (1793) "and received a direction to my opinions on that subject which I think has not been materially altered since."[24] The entries Ticknor made in his journal during his first visit to France show that his prejudices were, if anything, strengthened by firsthand knowledge of French society. "This morning I left Paris," he wrote on September 2, 1817, "and I have not left any city with so little regret."[25]

Ticknor saw no difference between the French society of his own day and that of the court of Louis XIV. He noted in his journal on May 14, 1817, after an evening at Benjamin Constant's, that "this is precisely the sort of society that used to assemble in the coteries of the times of Louis XIV and XV, and it required no great effort of the imagination to persuade me that I was at a *soirée* of those periods. Everything this evening was purely French; the wit, the criticism, the vivacity, even the good-nature and kindness, had a cast of nationality about them which in France is called amiability, but which everywhere else would be called flattery."[26] In a letter of August 12, 1817, to Dr. Walter Channing he praises Molière but then adds, "Do not misunderstand me. I do not regret that we have none of this comedy in English, for I deprecate the character and principles out of which it grows, and should lose no inconsiderable proportion of my hope for England and America, if they had reached or were approaching that ominous state of civilization and refinement in which it is produced."[27] Twenty years later Ticknor had not changed his mind. During his second visit to Europe in 1838 he noted in his journal that

the tone [of the French theater] is decidedly lower, more immoral, worse than it was twenty years ago; and when it is recollected how much influence the drama exercises in France on public opinion, it becomes an important fact in regard to the moral state of the capital and country. The old French drama, and especially the comedy, from Molière's time downwards, contained often gross and indelicate phrases and allusions, but the tone of the pieces, as a whole, was generally respectable. The recent theatre reverses all this. It contains hardly any indecorous phrases or allusions, but its whole tone is highly immoral.[28]

In the French lectures Ticknor is troubled less by the immorality of French literature than by its exclusiveness: "The French, in its essential features, is a literature of elegant society—a literature of graceful, courtly refinement—a literature, in short, of the higher classes . . . rather than a literature which has gone forth from the rich and abundant soil of the great mass of the People. . . . This is certainly an extraordinary state of things—and, when compared with what is found in other literatures, it may be considered in some degree an unnatural state of things." The other literatures of modern Europe "are national in their character—and they were all bro't forth in a soil free for the purposes of Poetry where manners sprung up wild and unconstrained, and where the whole body of the People furnished in its due proportions the different materials that went to form the deep feeling of the literature . . . where the class was marked by its prejudices and its circumstances—and where the whole nation had one costume of national manners, which passed into its literature and became a part of its national feeling and character."[29]

Like other New England critics in this period, Ticknor stresses the writer's obligation to make his work accessible to all classes and thus to serve as a force for social stability. His ideal is not a classless society but a society in which all classes share the same moral and political principles. It was a society of this kind that he believes shaped Spanish literature in its best period and that he thinks particularly evident in the theater of Lope de Vega (1562–1635), to whom he gives nearly twice as much space as to Cervantes: "The Spanish drama in its highest and most heroic forms was still a popular entertainment. . . . Its purpose was, not only to please all classes, but to please all equally."[30]

The good writer is representative of his nation; therefore, good writing must be national. Edward T. Channing, one of Ticknor's closest friends, asserts that "so long . . . as a country is proud of itself, it will repel every encroachment upon its native literature. . . . Intimacy with other nations, especially if they are polished, and the leaders of fashion, will tempt men to imitate them in every thing. But a nation should keep itself at home, and value the things of its own household. It will have but feeble claims to excellence and distinction, when it stoops to put on foreign ornament and manner, and to adopt from other nations, images, allusions, and a metaphorical language, which are perfectly unmeaning and sickly, out of their own birth-place."[31]

Ticknor's treatment of one such case of Spanish "intimacy" with another, more polished nation—the attempt of Juan Boscán (1487?–1542) and Garcilaso de la Vega (1501?–1536) to introduce Italian forms into Spanish poetry—shows how closely his point of view resembles Channing's. He censures Boscán for taking "for his models foreign masters, who, though more advanced than any he could find at home, were yet entitled to supremacy in no literature but their own. . . . The original and essential spirit of Italian poetry could no more be transplanted to Castile or Catalonia than to Germany or England."[32] Boscán might "have done more for the literature of his country than he did"; as for Garcilaso, Ticknor insists that "it would have been better for himself and for the literature of his country, if he had drawn more from the elements of the earlier national character and imitated less the great Italian masters he justly admired. . . . It would have given a freer and more generous movement to his poetical genius, and opened to him a range of subjects and forms of composition, from which, by rejecting the example of the national poets that had gone before him, he excluded himself."[33]

While Ticknor accepts the principle that good literature must be national, he does not believe that a work must be judged by the moral and aesthetic standards of the time and place in which it is written. The clowns (*graciosos*) in Lope de Vega's plays are "demanded by the taste of the age," but "nothing in any age can suffice for their justification."[34] Ticknor treats the playwright Pedro Calderón de la Barca (1600–1681) similarly: "we are not to measure Calderón as his contemporaries did. We stand at a distance too remote and impartial for such indulgence; and must neither pass over his failures nor exaggerate his merits."[35]

Ticknor's critical principles rest mainly on the neoclassical theories of such eighteenth-century British writers as Lord Kames and Hugh Blair. The latter's *Lectures on Rhetoric and Belles Lettres,* first published in 1783, was widely used as a textbook in New England schools and colleges during Ticknor's youth and for many years afterward.[36] Ticknor tells us that when Prescott determined to make his name as a writer he "studied as if he had been a school-boy, Blair's *Rhetoric.*"[37] Blair's *Lectures* is, to some extent, an abridgment and simplification of Kames's *Elements of Criticism.*[38] Kames's *Elements,* like Blair's *Lectures,* was often reprinted in America and, like the latter, appeared in a variety of annotated or abridged editions for school use.

Ticknor's remarks on Lope's *graciosos,* "whose ill-advised wit is inopportunely thrust, with their foolscaps and bawbles, into the gravest and most tragic scenes," show how close his critical position is to that of Kames and Blair.[39] Blair attacks Shakespeare for his "grotesque mixtures of serious and comic in one piece."[40] Kames asserts that "wit and ridicule make not an agreeable mixture with grandeur. . . . In a rapid succession, which approaches to co-existence, [dissimilar emotions] will not be relished."[41]

Ticknor's harsh criticism of Luis de Góngora (1561–1627) offers another example of his reliance on neoclassical precepts. The "most obvious feature" of Góngora's poetry is that it "consists almost entirely of metaphors, so heaped one upon another, that it is sometimes as difficult to find out the meaning hidden under their grotesque mass as if it were absolutely a series of confused riddles."[42] As an "extreme case" of Góngora's abuse of metaphor, Ticknor cites a passage from the *Soledad primera* in which the poet, "speaking of a lady whom he admired," calls her "a maiden so beautiful that she might parch up Norway with her two suns and bleach Ethiopia with her two hands."[43] Ticknor would certainly have agreed with Blair that "resemblance, which is the foundation of the metaphor, [should] be clear and perspicuous, not far-fetched, nor difficult to discover," and that difficult metaphors are "always displeasing, because they puzzle the reader and instead of illustrating the thought, render it perplexed and intricate."[44]

The British tradition, in which almost all New England critics were brought up, insists that literature is communication and that its function is to teach. For Blair, "the ultimate end of all poetry and indeed of every composition, should be to make some useful impression on the mind."[45] The writer is a moral teacher, and the critic's task is to judge him on moral grounds.

In one of his many literary memoranda Prescott reminds himself that "the *human character* is the most interesting subject of contemplation to *every* reader. . . . A leading object of my history should be the exhibition of character whether of the times or of individuals." Ticknor surely would have agreed with Prescott that "interest is created out of character."[46] He gives biographical details for major writers before discussing their works and often ends his treatment with a paragraph on the writer's "character." He concludes his three chapters on Cervantes by insisting that

if we would do him the justice that would have been dearest to his own spirit, and even if we would ourselves fully comprehend and enjoy the whole of his *Don Quixote,* we should, as we read it, bear in mind, that this delightful romance was not the result of a youthful exuberance of feeling and a happy external condition, nor composed in his best years, when the spirits of its author were light and his hopes high; but that—with all its unquenchable and irresistible humor, with its bright views of the world, and its cheerful trust in goodness and virtue—it was written in his old age, at the conclusion of a life nearly every step of which had been marked with disappointed expectations, disheartening struggles, and sore calamities; that he began it in a prison, and that it was finished when he felt the hand of death pressing heavy and cold upon his heart.[47]

When Ticknor speaks of *Don Quixote*'s "bright views of the world and its cheerful trust in goodness and virtue," he attributes qualities to the novel that he believes belong to its author. Ticknor is determined to present *Don Quixote* as a happy book because, like other New England critics who share his Federalist and Unitarian sympathies, he believes that writers have an obligation to be cheerful, since pessimism marks them as dissatisfied with the established social order and irreligious to boot. Christians are cheerful because they know that God is good; pessimism is a sign of lack of faith. Charvat suggests that the stress upon optimism in the literary criticism of this period is an indication of a widespread reaction against Calvinism.[48] Hillard notes that Ticknor was "brought up in the doctrines of Calvinistic Orthodoxy, but later serious reflection led him to reject those doctrines; and soon after his return from Europe [that is, when he was in his late twenties] he joined Dr. Channing's church, of which he continued through life a faithful member."[49] Elsewhere Hillard observes that Ticknor's "natural cheerfulness . . . [was] cultivated as a part of the requirements of manliness and kindness, and of religion; therefore, though he was often disposed to be anxious and to exercise great caution in the affairs of daily life, he was never depressed or discontented."[50]

Ticknor's stress on the character of the writers he studied goes hand in hand with his readiness to assess the moral value of their work. He was above all a judicial critic, and his judgments were based as much on moral as on aesthetic criteria. David Tyack reports that "while Ticknor was lecturing on Shakespeare in Boston, his minister, William Ellery Channing, urged him to 'speak in the character which I always wish you to sustain, of a true friend of the moral as well as the intellectual progress of your fellow creatures.' He warned him against making Iago too interesting or creating sympathy for Romeo and Juliet, 'who are greatly criminal when abandoning themselves to one passion.'"[51]

Channing can find no fault with Ticknor's treatment of the humanistic comedy *Celestina* by Fernando de Rojas (1473?–1541): "Large portions of it are foul with a shameless libertinism of thought and language. Why the authority of church and state did not at once interfere to prevent its circulation seems now hardly intelligible. Probably it was, in part, because the *Celestina* claimed to be written for the purpose of warning the young against the seductions and crimes it so loosely unveils; or, in other words, because it claimed to be a book whose tendency was good."[52]

Nevertheless, Ticknor was less ready than one might expect to insist that a moral book must present only morally irreproachable actions. He does not subject Juan Ruiz's fourteenth-century *Libro de buen amor* to the same condemnation as *Celestina,* even though Don Melón's attempt to win the favors of Doña Endrina with the help of the go-between Trotaconventos is similar to Calisto's pursuit of Melibea and probably reflects dependence on a common source. Ticknor calls the anonymous sixteenth-century novella *Lazarillo de Tormes* "a work of genius," although he says that its protagonist has "so small a stock of honesty and truth, that neither of them stands in the way of his success," and that "at last, from the most disgraceful of motives, he settles down as a married man."[53] He was perhaps inclined to treat *Lazarillo* kindly because it offers "a pungent satire on all classes of society" and because he admired its presumed author, the historian and poet Diego Hurtado de Mendoza (1503–75), an attribution now regarded as uncertain.[54]

We should be wary of saying that Ticknor's political and religious views determined his attitude toward individual writers and works, since later scholars often found the same qualities he identified. Ticknor gives an extended account of Cervantes's captivity in Algiers, praising his courage and optimism and his "universal good-nature."[55] Modern biographers make the same point. Melveena McKendrick speaks of Cervantes's "natural optimism" during his captivity and asserts that his "repeated escape attempts, the resistance to intimidation and threats of torture, reveal a character of unusual initiative, stamina and energy, . . . realistic as well as optimistic, above all a character capable of standing up to adversity in a way few men can."[56] Richard Predmore mentions "the unique example he set of courage, steadfastness and generosity" while a slave in Algiers.[57] Similarly, when Levin tells us that Prescott conceived *The Conquest of Mexico* as "an epic in prose, a romance of chivalry" and quotes him as saying that Cortés's "'life was romance put into action,'" we should bear in mind that Cortés's contemporary Bernal Díaz sees the conquistador in the same way in his *Historia verdadera de la conquista de la Nueva España* (1632).[58]

Ticknor's Cervantes is very different from Marcel Bataillon's nostalgic survivor of the age of Charles V.[59] Although I believe that Bataillon's interpretation is preferable, there is nothing absurd about Ticknor's. So fine a critic as Erich Auerbach asserts that "the 'something' which orders the whole [of *Don Quixote*] and makes it appear in a definite, 'Cervantean' light . . . [is] an attitude toward the world . . . in which bravery and equanimity play a major part."[60] If Ticknor's cheerful Cervantes owes as much to his political and religious views as to Ticknor's reading of *Don Quixote,* then Pierre Vilar's very different Cervantes, who offers a penetrating insight into the "decadence" of his country, owes as much to Vilar's Marxist interpretation of seventeenth-century Spanish history as to anything in the text of the novel.[61] The fundamental aim—to portray Cervantes's character by drawing inferences from his novel—was the same for Bataillon, Auerbach, and Vilar as it was for Ticknor.

Ticknor's *History* was immediately recognized as a vast improvement on the work of his predecessors Bouterwek and Sismondi in large part because he had read many more Spanish books than either of them. Many of Ticknor's judgments are repeated in Ernest Mérimée's *Précis d'histoire de la littérature espagnole* (1908), the third edition (1922) of which was translated into English as *History of Spanish Literature* (1930) by S. Griswold Morley after Mérimée's death in 1924.[62]

Like Ticknor, Mérimée believes that "Spanish literature, considered in its long historical development, presents a markedly national character."[63] His assertion that "the older poetry, and by that I mean particularly the popular forms, had roots deep driven into the soil, and drew thence its racy sap" might be, though it is not, a quotation from Ticknor's *History*. *Don Quixote* "is very Spanish, because it incarnates the essential types of the race and the . . . chief traits of the national soul."[64]

Mérimée's critical judgments sometimes seem as wrongheaded as Ticknor's and are often similar in tone. Mérimée allots a single paragraph to Saint John of the Cross (in a chapter on nonfictional prose in the Golden Age!), although he asserts that "there is no greater poet in this period."[65] He is even less willing than Ticknor to concede the greatness of Garcilaso: "The languishing pastoral is too artificial for us. . . . Imitation of a dozen sources no longer passes for a merit, but is regarded rather as a sign of weak inventiveness. Yet there is no denying the fact: this poet who died so young had an enormous influence on the language and on letters. . . . His language is always cited as one of the purest forms of Castilian, and his delicate and harmonious art makes one forget that the theme, as always in the pastoral, is commonplace."[66]

Ticknor's *History*, of course, was never intended to be a textbook. Its nearest equivalent in the twentieth century is Gerald Brenan's *The Literature of the Spanish People*, published almost exactly a hundred years later. In his preface, Brenan presents his work in terms very much like those Ticknor uses:

> Perhaps it is desirable that I should say something of the various objects I have had in mind in writing this book. The first has been to persuade English readers to sample the delights of Spanish literature. . . . Both history and geography have combined to give it a character unlike that of other European countries. . . . Literary history is, in one respect, merely a branch of a total history that includes in its various departments political history, social history and the history of art. With this in mind I have taken any opportunities that seemed to be offered for showing in what way Spanish literary works are to be regarded as an expression of the national spirit in successive ages and, incidentally, to use this for throwing light on the character of the Spanish people.[67]

Brenan, of course, is not consciously following Ticknor's example. His decision to stress "the character of the Spanish people" is perhaps the best way to present a foreign literature to readers who cannot read its masterpieces for themselves. This is Prescott's view. He praises Ticknor because "instead of presenting a barren record of books,—which, like the catalogue of a gallery of paintings, is of comparatively little use to those who have not previously studied them,—he illustrates the works by the personal history of their authors, and this, again, by the history of the times in which they lived."[68] We should not be too quick to assume that Ticknor's decision was solely the result of his association with the romantic historians who played such a significant role in the intellectual life of nineteenth-century New England.

Notes

1. Further biographical details are given in Robert L. Gale's entry "George Ticknor" in *American National Biography,* ed. John Garraty and Mark C. Carnes, 24 vols. (New York: Oxford University Press, 1999), 21:643–45. For more detailed treatments see Orie William Long, *Literary Pioneers: Early American Explorers of European Culture* (Cambridge, Mass.: Harvard University Press, 1935), 3–62; David Tyack, *George Ticknor and the Boston Brahmins* (Cambridge, Mass.: Harvard University Press, 1967); and Stanley T. Williams, *The Spanish Background of American Literature,* 2 vols. (New Haven, Conn.: Yale University Press, 1955), 2:44–77.

2. George S. Hillard, *Life, Letters, and Journals of George Ticknor,* 2 vols. (Boston: James R. Osgood, 1876), 2:253–54.

3. Lionel Gossman, *Between History and Literature* (Cambridge, Mass.: Harvard University Press, 1990), 3.

4. Hillard, *Life, Letters, and Journals,* 2:254.

5. *The Literary Memoranda of William Hickling Prescott,* ed. C. Harvey Gardiner, 2 vols. (Norman: University of Oklahoma Press, 1961), 1:90.

6. George S. Hillard, writing in *The Christian Examiner,* January 1850, p. 122.

7. George Ticknor, *History of Spanish Literature,* 3 vols. (New York: Harper, 1849), 1:ix–x.

8. George Ticknor, *Syllabus of a Course of Lectures on the History and Criticism of Spanish Literature* (Cambridge, Mass.: Printed at the University Press by Hilliard and Metcalf, 1823). Ticknor's unpublished lectures—cited hereafter as "Lectures"—may be consulted in the Harvard University Archives, George Ticknor Papers (shelf list available in the repository). For further information, see my doctoral dissertation, "A History of Spanish Literary History, 1800–1850" (Yale University, 1952), and my article "George Ticknor's *History of Spanish Literature:* The New England Background," *Publications of the Modern Language Association* 49 (March 1954): 78–79.

9. Tyack, *George Ticknor,* 90. The phrase "to live at ease with unpretending elegance" is quoted from Hillard, *Life, Letters, and Journals,* 1:335.

10. Ticknor, "Lectures," n.p.

11. Ticknor, *History,* 2:452–53.

12. David Levin, *History as Romantic Art: Bancroft, Prescott, Motley, and Parkman* (Stanford, Calif.: Stanford University Press, 1959), 7.

13. Ticknor, "Lectures," n.p.

14. Ticknor, *History*, 1:343–44.

15. William H. Prescott, "Cervantes" (*North American Review*, July 1837), reproduced in his *Biographical and Critical Miscellanies* (Philadelphia: J. B. Lippincott, 1883), 117. [Editor's note: Prescott is referring to two European writers, Friedrich Bouterwek (1766–1828) and J. C. L. Sismonde di Sismondi (1773–1842)].

16. Prescott, "Ticknor's *History of Spanish Literature*," in *Biographical and Critical Miscellanies*, 680, quoting from his *North American Review* article.

17. *The Correspondence of William Hickling Prescott, 1833–1847*, ed. Roger Wolcott (Boston: Houghton Mifflin, 1925), 458.

18. See Tyack, *George Ticknor*, 187–92. Tyack notes that Ticknor's motto was *Labor ipse voluptas* (work itself is pleasure).

19. Quoted in Tyack, *George Ticknor*, 155–56.

20. William Charvat, introduction to *William Hickling Prescott: Representative Selections*, ed. William Charvat and Michael Kraus (New York: American Book, 1943), xxi.

21. Richard L. Kagan, "Prescott's Paradigm: American Historical Scholarship and the Decline of Spain," *American Historical Review* 101 (April 1996): 424.

22. Charvat, *Prescott*, xii.

23. Hillard, *Life, Letters, and Journals*, 1:49.

24. Ibid., 2:274.

25. Ibid., 1:134.

26. Ibid.

27. Ibid., 1:150.

28. Ibid., 2:140.

29. George Ticknor, "General Plan of a Course of Lectures on the French Language and Literature," n.p., Harvard University Archives, George Ticknor Papers.

30. Ticknor, *History*, 2:451.

31. Edward T. Channing "On Models in Literature," *North American Review* 3 (July 1816): 208.

32. Ticknor, *History*, 1:485–86.

33. Ibid., 1:495.

34. Ibid., 2:245.

35. Ibid., 2:397.

36. William Charvat, *The Origins of American Critical Thought, 1810–1835* (Philadelphia: University of Pennsylvania Press, 1936), 44. [Editor's note: Hugh Blair (1718–1800) was a Scottish Presbyterian minister who taught rhetoric and belles lettres at the University of Edinburgh.]

37. George Ticknor, *The Life of William Hickling Prescott* (Boston: Ticknor and Fields, 1864), 59.

38. Helen Whitcomb Randall, *The Critical Theory of Lord Kames*, Smith College Studies in Modern Languages No. 22 (Northampton, Mass.: Smith College, 1944), 82. [Ed-

itor's note: Henry Home, later Lord Kames (1696–1782), was a prominent Scottish lawyer and philosopher.]

39. Ticknor, *History,* 2:245.

40. Hugh Blair, *Lectures on Rhetoric and Belles Lettres,* 2 vols. (London: W. Strahan et al., 1783), 2:523 (lecture 46). Harold F. Harding edited a two-volume facsimile edition, published by Southern Illinois University Press in 1965.

41. Henry Homes [Lord Kames], *Elements of Criticism,* 3 vols. (London: Printed for A. Millar; Edinburg: A. Kincaid and J. Bell, 1762), 1:377.

42. Ticknor, *History,* 2:523–24.

43. Ibid., 2:525.

44. *Lectures,* 1:303 (lecture 15).

45. *Lectures,* 2:361 (lecture 40).

46. *Literary Memoranda,* 1:117, 2:70.

47. Ticknor, *History,* 2:118–19.

48. Charvat, *Origins,* 19.

49. Hillard, *Life, Letters, and Journals,* 1:327.

50. Ibid., 2:496.

51. Tyack, *George Ticknor,* 149.

52. Ticknor, *History,* 1:267.

53. Ibid., 1:511.

54. Ibid., 1:550.

55. Ibid., 2:60n.16.

56. Melveena McKendrick, *Cervantes* (Boston: Little, Brown, 1980), 78, 88.

57. Richard Predmore, *Cervantes* (New York: Dodd, Mead, 1973), 90.

58. Levin, *History as Romantic Art,* 164–65; J. H. Elliott, "The Mental World of Hernán Cortés," in *Spain and Its World, 1500–1700: Selected Essays* (New Haven, Conn.: Yale University Press, 1989), 30.

59. Marcel Bataillon, *Erasmo y España: Estudios sobre la historia espiritual del siglo XVI,* trans. Antonio Alatorre, 2 vols. (Mexico City: Fondo de Cultura Económica, 1950), 2:401.

60. Erich Auerbach, *Mimesis: The Representation of Reality in Western Literature,* trans. Willard R. Trask. (Princeton, N.J.: Princeton University Press, 1953), 355.

61. Pilar Vilar, "Le temps du Quichotte," *Europe* 34 (1956): 3–16; available in English as "The Age of Don Quixote," in *Essays in European Economic History, 1500–1800,* ed. Peter Earle (Oxford: Clarendon, 1974), 100–13.

62. Ernest Mérimée, *History of Spanish Literature,* trans. S. Griswold Morley (New York: Henry Holt, 1930).

63. Ibid., 594.

64. Ibid., 168, 309.

65. Ibid., 266.

66. Ibid., 162–64.

67. Gerald Brenan, *The Literature of the Spanish People* (Cambridge: Cambridge University Press, 1951), xi–xiii.

68. Prescott, *Biographical and Critical Miscellanies,* 679–80.

∼ 4

"Longfellow's Law": The Place of Latin America and Spain in U.S. Hispanism, circa 1915

James D. Fernández

> There are too many occasions on which one has to listen to doubts, to defend [our field's] worthiness, to apologize. And every one of those incidents springs from the general public ignorance of things Spanish and from lack of prestige.
> —J. Warshaw, 1919

> Spanish teachers in our country have no traditions and no idols to adore. We are just now writing our textbooks and training our teachers. The future will judge us.
> —Aurelio M. Espinosa, 1921

Original Displacements

In December 1826 a young Bostonian on the grand tour of Europe received a letter from his father, offering the following advice: "Such are the relations now existing between this country and Spanish America that a knowledge of the Spanish is quite as important as French. If you neglect either of these languages, you may be sure of not obtaining the station which you have in view." The son received the letter in Paris, heeded his father's advice, and headed straight for Madrid. About four months later he would write back from the capital of Spain: "I have not seen a city in Europe which has pleased my fancy so much, as a place of residence."[1]

This well-behaved son was none other than the great U.S. poet and Hispanist Henry Wadsworth Longfellow (figure 4.1). Longfellow's filial obedience paid off; after perfecting his Spanish in Madrid, he returned to the States, first to occupy the newly established chair of modern languages at Bowdoin College

Figure 4.1. Self-portrait by Henry Wadsworth Longfellow en route from Málaga to Granada, 1827. (MS AN 1340 [172]; by permission of the Houghton Library, Harvard University)

and later to be appointed the Smith Professor of French and Spanish at Harvard. The first endowed chair in modern languages and literatures in the United States, the Smith chair had been established at Harvard in 1815 by the Boston merchant Abiel Smith and had been first held by the great Hispanist George Ticknor. "From the establishment of this professorship dates the rise of a teacher of modern languages to the position of a college officer; from this time on, he could expect to be regarded as a member of the faculty."[2] Interestingly, the first four holders of the Smith chair were accomplished Hispanists (Ticknor, Longfellow, Lowell, and Ford).

It turns out that the 1810s and '20s in the northeastern United States were years of burgeoning interest in the Spanish-speaking world. The "relations now existing between this country and Spanish America" to which Longfellow's father referred are obviously the political and commercial opportunities offered by the emancipation of Spain's New World colonies. As Edith Helman puts it, Americans "saw the advantages of South American independence, the obvious economic advantages of having a market for . . . surplus agricultural and manufactured products, and new sources of raw materials."[3]

These pragmatic concerns were translated into a greatly fortified interest in the Spanish language and the Spanish-speaking world. The University of Pennsylvania and William and Mary, at the behest of Benjamin Franklin and Thomas Jefferson, respectively, had introduced the study of Spanish into their curricula in the eighteenth century. But the subject had its first real academic boom in the United States in the second and third decades of the nineteenth century, the decades of the independence of the Latin American republics, the decades surrounding the 1823 establishment of the Monroe Doctrine.[4]

As is evident in the letter from Longfellow's father, at the origins of U.S. interest in Spanish is the view that Spanish is an American language, with a history and, most important, a future as such. As Longfellow's response to his father's advice shows, however, this interest in the American language called Spanish, for complex reasons worthy of careful consideration, was translated in practice into an interest in the language, literature, and culture not of Latin America but of Spain. A double displacement would seem to be at work here: from Latin America to Spain and from language/politics/commerce to literature/history/culture. In a sense, although the eyes of pragmatism looked south, the gaze of students and scholars became fixed toward the east.[5]

I invoke this early U.S. vogue for things Spanish and the double displacement that underwrites it—"Spanish, for commercial and political reasons, is an important American language; we shall send our children to Europe to study Spanish culture and civilization"—because I believe that it contains a set of issues and tensions that have characterized the history of Hispanic studies in the United States, right up to the present day. To acknowledge my indebtedness to Richard Kagan's important essay, "Prescott's paradigm," I will call the most central of these issues "Longfellow's law," according to which *U.S. interest in Spain is and always has been largely mediated by U.S. interest in Latin America.*[6] The purpose of this essay is to explore in some detail one moment in the history of this "law": the years on either side of World War I, which coincided with what arguably was the biggest and most dramatic surge in the history of Spanish studies in the United States.

In the case of the 1820s boom in Spanish studies, the displacement from Latin America to Spain was hardly perceived as such. For these early promotors of Spanish studies, "there was no division between the Spanish and the Spanish-American language and culture. In order to learn Spanish, you read the works of the great Spanish writers. And in reading Spanish literature, you learned about the Hispanic mind and character in America as well as in the Peninsula."[7] In the case of the boom in interest in Spanish that coincided with World War I, however—less than two decades after a war between the United States and Spain—the documents show that the displacement was being contested. In the debates that raged during these years the centrality of Spain to Hispanic studies in the United States is not so much something that may be assumed but rather something to be argued, at times with revealing emphasis.[8]

The American Association of Teachers of Spanish (AATS) was founded in the midst of this circa-1915 surge in U.S. interest in Spanish. The initial volumes (1917–21) of the association's journal, *Hispania,* provide an extraordinary perspective on these debates, whose effects, to a large degree, can still be felt today in Hispanic studies in this country. At issue in these debates are the historical, intellectual, and institutional articulations between the United States, Spain, and Latin America, between commerce and culture, and between politics and academic inquiry. In what follows I attempt to offer an overview of these debates as they were manifested in the first five years of *Hispania,* with the hope of bringing to light a crucial but little-known moment in the history of Hispanism, and of helping us take stock of where we are today.

By Popular Demand: A National Need of Spanish

In the July 1915 issue of the *Yale Review* Frederick Bliss Luquiens begins his article, "The National Need of Spanish," by pointing out a coincidence of events that had gone relatively unnoticed one year before: on August 5, 1914, the same day that the United Kingdom declared war on Germany, the U.S. steamer *Cristóbal* became the first cargo-carrying ship to make the ocean-to-ocean voyage through the Panama Canal. "Now . . . we may realize that the two events constitute one of the most striking coincidences in history. . . . The declaration of war meant the immediate diminution of South America's trade with Europe in general and Germany in particular. The opening of the canal at last put Ecuador, Peru and Chile commercially within our reach. It seemed as if the hand of fate at one and the same moment were opening the door of South America to us, and closing it upon Europe."[9] In words that resonate with the advice offered by Longfellow's father, the article then presents a forceful and thoroughly pragmatic argument in favor of the teaching of Spanish in U.S. schools: "To the study of [Spanish], our present relations with South America have given a new and paramount value, which entitles it to as much respect, even from practical men, as the study of engineering or stocks and bonds."[10]

Luquiens goes on to decry the scarcity of opportunities for U.S. high school and college students to study Spanish in 1915:

[Spanish] is not studied because it is not taught. In the face of the ever-growing demand, our educators are unmoved. According to information from the Bureau of Education, there are in the whole United States only 765 secondary schools which teach it! And the majority of these are either technical or commercial schools, or schools in border States. In our colleges, the election of Spanish is restricted by arbitrary and artificial rules, such as requirement of the previous study of French or German, or even of both. . . . Many of our colleges, moreover, refuse to accept Spanish as a credit for entrance, which renders more difficult still its introduction into

secondary schools. Upon our educators, from college presidents to school princi-
pals, rests the responsibility of meeting what may be called the national need of
Spanish.[11]

Apparently, the educators soon listened, if not to Luquiens, at least to the
clamorous "ever-growing demand" for Spanish instruction. Just two years later
the inaugural issue of *Hispania*, published by the newly founded AATS, would
refer to Spanish as "an educational field which is growing so rapidly that its
unorganization threatens to become disorganization and confusion."[12] A
Spaniard who witnessed the wartime expansion of Spanish would write back
to his colleagues in Spain: "Since 1916 the study of Spanish has grown with such
speed and in such proportions that it cannot be measured by the criteria we
are accustomed to in Europe. The universities witnessed the arrival of thousands of students to their Spanish classes; the high schools, hundreds of thousands."[13] The "Notes and News" sections of *Hispania*'s first years record the
progress of what—with true missionary zeal—is occasionally referred to as
"the work"; "from Butte, Montana comes the news that enrollment in Spanish is nearly seven times as great as in 1915 when the work was started"; "Spanish
has been recently introduced in the intermediate schools of New York, Chicago, St. Louis, New Orleans, San Francisco, Los Angeles, and other large cities
of our country"; "at the University of Kansas a department of Hispanic Languages and Literatures has been created, with a staff of 6"; "Spanish has been
put on an equal basis with French and German in Lehigh University and Simmons College"; "the Spanish section of the Department of Romance Languages
at the University of Minnesota has grown since September, 1914, from 95 to
459 in 1917–18. There are in the department three Spanish American teachers:
Mr. Balbino Dávalos, Mr. Pedro Henríquez Ureña, and Mr. Enrique Jiménez."[14]

One of the many crucial larger issues embedded in these discussions about
Spanish as an object of study is that of the responsiveness—or lack thereof—
of U.S. educational institutions to "popular will": the relationship between
societal demand and academic supply. Luquiens refers to the ever-growing
"bottom-up" demand for instruction in Spanish; the people demand high
school Spanish; the expansion of high school Spanish necessitates more Spanish in college.[15] Indeed, the founders of the AATS openly and emphatically
portray themselves as the stewards of a popular will: "The citizens of this country steadily and insistently demand instruction in Spanish for their children.
The high school, which is the 'college of the people,' must and does meet that
demand and will continue to meet it. . . . [The accusation that Spanish is assuming a disproportionate importance in our schools] is one that we must face
serenely and say 'Let the people decide.'"[16]

But claiming to be the curator or interpreter of popular will would prove to be a double-edged sword, particularly within the more prejudiced and elitist halls of U.S. academia. "Numbers," and the bottom-up demand for Spanish, probably always have been the field's greatest strength and its greatest vulnerability. At this crucial moment in the history of Hispanism a tremendous amount of energy—and ink—were spent attempting to maximize the benefits and minimize the liabilities that went with being the "people's choice." Two strategies in particular, aimed at harnessing, disciplining, and legitimating the popular demand for Spanish stand out in these early issues of *Hispania*: the linking of the study of Spanish with questions of patriotism and national security, especially powerful and sensitive issues in times of war; and the attempt to create intellectual and cultural prestige for the study of Spanish and the Hispanic world. As I will show, these two core strategies generated a tension— perhaps a constitutive tension—at the heart of Hispanic studies: the national interest argument leads to an emphasis on the Americanness of Spanish; the cultural prestige dilemma leads many Hispanists to bracket or downplay the language's utilitarian value (and, consequently, its Latin American vector) and to highlight the "Old World" culture of Spain.

Patriotism and Pedagogy

During the first postwar meeting of the AATS, President Lawrence Wilkins would look back on the association's first three years of existence: "War times were indeed inauspicious times in which to undertake the organization of our society. The world cried out for sterner things in America than a society of Spanish teachers. The sterner things were given in abundant measure by our country. And be it said at this time that many members of our society, some in khaki here and in France . . . have taken an active part in the all-important and serious work of war, now so magnificently won by the forces of right and justice."[17] The war is in some way inscribed on virtually every page of the early issues of *Hispania,* from "Notes and News" items—"the many southern California friends of [Los Angeles Spanish teacher] Miss María G. de López are proud to know that she has gone to France as an *ambulancière*"—to the reproduction of a War Time Conference Resolution: "As teachers of the foreign modern languages we pledge ourselves to refrain from the use of any book . . . which . . . tends to weaken in the minds of our youth the American ideals of Liberty, Democracy and Humanity."[18]

The "all-important and serious work of war" was, of course, carried out in the trenches of Europe, but battles were waged on the homefront as well.[19] During his tenure as president of the association, Wilkins would frequently sound the note of the patriotic mission and contributions of teachers of Spanish: "For the teachers of Spanish comprehend clearly that theirs is in essence a patriotic duty at all times. Besides offering themselves for participation in war service, they felt, I am sure, that in teaching Spanish well and effectively they are contributing much to the welfare of the country."[20] Again and again Wilkins would emphasize the notion that the study of Spanish was being promoted solely in the interests of the United States: "*Los Estados Unidos ante todo, y el bien de sus ciudadanos!* [The United States above all else, and the well-being of her citizens!] We do not wish our young people to become so saturated with Spanish culture that they will prefer it to that of their own country. . . . If we cannot teach Spanish without unduly lauding a foreign nation to the belittlement of our own, then let us close up shop for once, and I, for one, will go back to the farm— even though wheat bring [*sic*] only a dollar a bushel or less."[21]

These emphatic claims for the patriotic import of Spanish instruction ought to be read in the context of concurrent accusations that much instruction in German, then the most-taught foreign language in U.S. schools, was in fact subversive. Wilkins was himself the inspector of modern languages for New York City's board of education, and during World War I, he had recommended the elimination of German-language instruction from the city's high school curriculum. Spanish would pick up most of the students who would have opted for German. Wilkins again invokes the vox populi as the motor of his decision to banish German:

> The American people of today and of many generations to come will be in no mood to listen to pleas that German be taught so that young Americans may read at first hand Goethe, Schiller, or Lessing. . . . The German language, the German literature, German art, German universities, German science, German culture and the entire German civilization have been vastly over-rated here and in other lands. We have had far too much teaching of German in our schools. It was fast becoming the second language of our nation. And I personally believe that it was taught chiefly for the purposes of furthering propaganda originating in Berlin.[22]

If the newfound affection for Spanish was a spontaneous and popular phenomenon—and therefore practically irresistible—so too was the sudden and potent aversion to German. Another contributor to an early issue of *Hispania* would be even more graphic in his linking of popular will and the elimination of German from U.S. classrooms: "German *went* from our schools because the bulk of the American people were convinced that some of its advocates had sinned against this country and would have no more of it."[23]

According to Wilkins, one of the principal missions of this new association would be to take advantage of the largely utilitarian popular demand for Spanish instruction in order to transform it into the foundation of national—and even hemispheric—security: "our joy we can truthfully say is not a selfish one, is not merely because the favoring winds have veered in our direction, but it is based in the fact that our citizens are, *consciously or unconsciously*, laying, by their desire to study Spanish, the most inspiring and secure basis for real Pan-Americanism."[24] Elsewhere, Wilkins writes: "We have in this country overrated the value of German and underrated the value of Spanish, as media of discipline and culture. The highest interests of our own people and of all the peoples of all the Americas demand that the youth of our land become acquainted at the earliest possible moment with Hispanic civilization. Hispanic peoples, Hispanic literature and language, all taught so as to contribute to the betterment of our own national life. They will then be trained and cultured in the way the times demand and they will help to spread in this hemisphere in a most effective manner not Pan-Germanism, but Pan-Americanism."[25] The popular demand of Spanish is linked with the popular repudiation of German. Teaching Spanish, harnessing the popular will, disciplining the conscious or unconscious desire of U.S. citizens—these are not just jobs; they are patriotic duties.

Discipline, Culture, and Prestige

In the opening essay of the "Organization Issue" of *Hispania*, titled "On the Threshold," Wilkins enumerates those factors that, in his estimation, have led to the sudden boom in popular interest in Spanish and things Hispanic. To wit: "The very erroneous belief that Spanish is easy"; "the prejudice that exists against German, a natural phenomenon accompanying a war against Germany"; the slow realization that "we Anglo-Saxons may . . . have overestimated our 'superiority' . . . to our fellow Americans in the republics to the south of us"; and "in the first place . . . stimulus from the business world."[26]

With these as the principal factors bringing about the surge in interest in Spanish, it is not hard to imagine the formidable resistance that these early promotors of the language must have faced, particularly in the more rarefied and elitist circles of colleges and universities. By the accounts of the founding participants of twentieth-century U.S. Hispanism, instruction in Spanish came into popular demand in large measure because the language was seen as an easy-to-learn wartime substitute for a discredited language and as a skill helpful in making a buck. As for the other factor mentioned by Wilkins—the supposed popular interest in revising received notions about the "Hispanic character"— this optimistic assessment is repeatedly contradicted on other pages of these early issues of *Hispania*: "The truth is that we have a tremendous mass of inertia and a popular feeling of indifference to work against. We are handling the language of a nation whose unfortunate colonial experiences and luckless military conflicts with our own tend to create feelings of repugnance, if not of scorn; of races, whose psychology, social evolution, and contributions toward progress we do not understand and appear to be in no hurry to understand; of peoples whom custom persuades us to look upon as backward."[27] Spanish is perceived as easy; Spanish is a convenient, wartime "substitute" for German;[28] Spanish is of commercial interest; Spanish is the language of an underestimated race—clearly, these "assets" are at the same time liabilities, and the better part of the pages of the first issues of *Hispania* are dedicated to exploring, refuting, or nuancing them.

In the early twentieth century "discipline" and "culture" are what justified the inclusion of the study of modern foreign languages in the high school and university curricula. Inasmuch as the notion that Spanish is an easy language calls into question the "disciplinary" value of learning the language, it represents a powerful attack on the suitability of Spanish as an object of study in nontechnical, noncommercial secondary and postsecondary education. The scholars who published in the early issues of *Hispania* could therefore not let this notion go uncontested. They challenge the misperception by explaining two of its possible origins: Because Spanish has most often been acquired by Americans as a second or third foreign language, it only *seems* easier; and the spelling of Spanish—unlike that of French and English—had successfully been rationalized and made relatively uniform, giving the language a superficial appearance of simplicity. Hispanists were quick to point out the profound irony here: one of the most remarkable achievements of Spanish civilization— the effective normalization of the Spanish language—was being used as evidence of the inferiority of the language and its speakers. Defenders of Spanish will play up the language's complexities and the subtleties to argue that its acquisition provides adequate exercise for the brain: "The advocates of German told us (and still tell us, some of them) that the study of the German language produces more brain loops than does the study of any other modern language; that the intricacies of noun and adjective declensions and of word order develop in some way mental powers that can not be developed in French, or Spanish, or Italian. . . . Because of its pronunciation, grammar, idioms, vocabulary and sentence structure, Spanish affords an excellent medium for imparting that particular kind of mental discipline which is given by linguistic study. . . . The study of this language will develop as many brain loops as will the study of Sanscrit or Russian."[29]

But the attacks on the "cultural value" of teaching and learning the Spanish language were what would most preoccupy the promoters of Spanish studies during World War I. Following an unfortunate and fallacious line of logic that can still be detected today in some academic circles, the worldliness of the demand for Spanish—its popularity, its traceable links to hemispheric politics, to business, to the supposedly culturally deprived "New World"—was precisely what called into question the cultural worthiness of Spanish as a field of study. In 1915 many believed that Spanish had no place outside the "commercial schools." Even "friends" and "natural allies" of the AATS, like Ernest Hatch Wilkins, the Petrarch scholar and occasional teacher of Spanish at the University of Chicago, expressed serious reservations about the proliferation of Spanish courses on these grounds:

> That Spanish should be widely studied I agree; but that it should be studied in such overwhelming numbers is but added evidence to the old indictment that we Americans see only that which is at hand. That Spanish should be studied for its literary value I agree, but I believe that no sane critic who knows the several European literatures and languages would rank Spanish literature with Italian or with French in universal value. That Spanish should be studied for its commercial returns I agree, provided that it be studied in commercial courses. . . . Is it well . . . that 3,000 [university] students should be studying Italian and that 200,000 should be studying Spanish? . . . I believe the time has come in the college world when Italian should be deliberately developed and Spanish should be deliberately checked.[30]

With friends like these, who needs enemies? The enemies were there, though, stating a less nuanced version of the same argument: "He is a bold man who will claim that Spain ranks with England, France, America, or Germany in any element of greatness. Its literature is far inferior to that of Italy. The average educated Englishman, American, German or Frenchman credits Spain with only one great author—Cervantes—and only one great work—Don Quixote."[31]

This predicament led the *Hispania* Hispanists to agree on the need to articulate a "Spanish program" in order to establish "prestige" for their subject. The uncomfortable model for this program would turn out to be none other than German, a language that in a relatively short time had become the most studied modern foreign language in the United States and an indispensable feature of a distinguished education.[32] In an article titled "The Spanish Program," J. Warshaw asks: "What brought about this surprising condition? 'German efficiency,' probably, first of all, and next, the application of common-sense principles of organization, cooperation and coordination. Our great lesson, I believe, lies there, and however regrettable it may be that we should turn to anything German for guidance, we must be willing to profit by experience wherever found, hoping, of course, to assimilate only the good and reject the bad."[33] In a remarkably straightforward and self-conscious way, the author goes on to outline a program for manufacturing prestige for Spanish, in essence an advertising campaign: "The extraordinary vogue of German was largely the result of efficient advertising for prestige. The popularity of French, too, has been due to prestige; but it has needed very little active propaganda in our days. German prestige was made. Spanish prestige must be made. There is no other way out."[34]

Warshaw's prescriptions for prestige include devising a "closely coordinated species of informational machinery" in order to disseminate answers to the "prestige questions which the ubiquitous inquirer" asks about the cultural worthiness of Spanish: "Has the Spanish world ever produced a surpassing genius in any field? Can you point to a world-famous Spanish engineer, chemist, mathematician, physicist, artist, poet, zoologist, lawyer, financier, statesman? . . . Have Spanish countries contributed vitally to the advancement of civilzation? What do we owe Spanish? Why should we study Spanish?"[35] Curiously, tellingly, the author seems to pose questions to which he does not have the answer: "We do not know much about the prestige-value of Spanish, and it is precisely this prestige value which is uppermost in any comparisons of the foreign languages as school subjects. . . . We . . . should know the answers; and we should try to make such information as commonplace as breakfast-foods. How to do this, we may learn from the Germans. Of course it would be a great pity if the questions were unanswerable!"[36]

The U.S. Hispanists would receive help in formulating answers to these prestige questions from a number of Spaniards. Américo Castro, who would go on in the 1940s to become a leader of U.S. Hispanism, contributed an article to *Hispania* that seems, from its title, like a response to the "Who's Who" in Spain that the U.S. educators had called for: "El movimiento científico en la España actual" (Scientific Enterprises in Today's Spain).[37] The preeminent Spanish philologist Ramón Menéndez Pidal sent a long letter to the officers of the AATS, wishing them well and offering them authoritative, scientific evidence of the cultural importance of the Spanish language and of the necessary and natural centrality of Spain in U.S. Hispanism. The letter was printed in the first issue of *Hispania*.

Indeed, the "prestige problem" that afflicted Spanish as an object of study in the United States—its utilitarian ties to popular demand and to Latin America—would provide Spain and Spaniards with a unique opportunity to play an essential role in the configuration and promotion of the field.

Ever since the loss of Spain's last American colonies—Cuba and Puerto Rico—in 1898, many Spanish intellectuals and institutions had strenuously tried to reaffirm Spain's spiritual and cultural ties with—some would say, "tutelage over"—its offspring in the New World. In Latin America as well, many intellectuals, in the face of post-1898 U.S. hegemony in the hemisphere, had taken to reaffirming the continent's links to Spain, to a Hispanic *raza. Hispanidad,* as this affirmation of essential Hispanic values shared by Spain and Latin America is known, has often been seen as being in direct conflict with pan-Americanism, or the affirmation of a North-South hemispheric unity of purpose and destinies shared by the nations in the Americas. *Hispanidad* is generally thought of as a reaction against U.S. cultural, economic, and political imperialism; pan-Americanism is normally seen as part of an effort to eliminate any claims that Europe might have on the future of the American hemisphere.[38]

These categories and projects nevertheless would play themselves out in peculiar ways in U.S. educational circles in the teens, when interest in Latin America was coded as being primarily—or even exclusively—driven by economics, whereas interest in Spain was marked as being driven purely by culture. The strength and clarity of these associations were remarkable. In *El hispanismo en Norteamérica* (1917) Miguel Romera-Navarro, a Spaniard teaching at the University of Pennsylvania, would state matter-of-factly: "Hispanism in North America is made up of two clear and parallel streams; one is purely literary, and flows particularly toward Spain; the other is economic in character, and is aimed at Latin America."[39] Given this set of factors, if the civic, patriotic imperative of the Hispanists publishing in *Hispania* inclined them toward the discourse of pan-Americanism, the "prestige dilemma" that they faced would seem to push them toward the premises of *Hispanidad.*[40]

In this regard one of the most significant and symptomatic texts published in the early issues of *Hispania* is in the form of a long letter written by the young Spanish philologist Federico de Onís and addressed to his colleagues on the faculty at the University of Salamanca. An agent of Spain's attempt to collaborate and capitalize on U.S. interest in Spanish, de Onís took a leave of absence from his home institution to assume a post at Columbia University in the midst of the Spanish frenzy. De Onís soon became a privileged witness to what he calls the *fiebre colectiva,* or collective fever, the frenzy to learn Spanish.[41] In the letter, which occasionally reads like the wartime dispatch of an advance scout, de Onís offers a diagnosis of the cause of this fever that is worth quoting at length:

> There has always been a small but select group of individuals in the United States that has made of our Spain an object of their love and devotion. The names of Washington Irving, Longfellow, Prescott, Ticknor, Lowell, and Howells come immediately to mind. When, in 1914, those great nations involved in the European war were forced to abandon their foreign trade, the United States saw, with keen instinct, the unique possibility of taking over those markets and developing in them their own commerce and export industry. It was then that a collective frenzy began to manifest itself, the ardent desire to learn Spanish. The Spanish language was the tool that would permit North Americans to understand, and carry out commerce with,

Hispanic America. But to carry out commerce properly is a difficult task. Knowing the language is not enough; one must also know the nations that speak it, their tastes, their character, their traditions, their psychology, their ideals; in order to achieve this, one must know their history, their geography, their literature, their art. The Latin American nations are the offspring of Spain; one must, then, go to the source and become knowledgeable about Spain.[42]

De Onís goes on to point out the remarkably circuitous logic that underlies this interest in Spain—somewhat like a trip from New York to Buenos Aires via Madrid—and praises the American spirit for its ability to produce such logic:

> The North American mentality is capable of such circuitous loops [*tales rodeos*] when it wishes seriously to undertake an action, and this is the reason for its success and efficiency. This is how this popular fad, which looked to the Spanish language as a tool for commerce and wealth, came to join with that other more traditional movement, one consisting of a select and disinterested group of scholars, writers and artists, a group of intellectuals or lovers of the Spanish soul. Both movements, though entirely different in their origins and in their natures, have been successful in coming together and have complemented each other. Thanks to the existence of a school of philologists and critics specializing in the Spanish language, it has been possible to contain and direct the popular movement which initially rose up so forcefully and unexpectedly.[43]

The philologist clearly senses the potential returns for Spain in this vision of the field, according to which the representatives of culture/disinterestedness/Spain would "channel" and "direct" the commercial/utilitarian/Latin America–oriented flow of the boom in Spanish studies.[44]

De Onís ends his letter by listing and describing the "enemies" of U.S. Hispanism or, perhaps it would be more accurate to say, the enemies of Spain's role in U.S. Hispanism. On a clear scale of bad to worst, some feel that Spanish simply should not be taught in the schools—these are so few and viewed as so extremist that they pose no real danger; then there are those "*de peor especie*" (of a worse species) who, while recognizing the language's commercial importance, deny any cultural value to the study of Spanish, and thus "cancel any favorable effects that [America's interest in Spanish] might have for Spain"; finally, there are the most dangerous of enemies, the "internal enemies" who argue that, because the true U.S. interest lies in Latin America, "*¿Qué nos importa España?*" (What do we care about Spain?). De Onís accuses these "*hispano-americanistas a ultranza*" (hard-core hispano-americanists) of trying to separate "today's popular current, which looks for a way of approaching the Latin American nations with practical ends in mind, from the traditional, disinterested stream that led United States citizens to the source, to Spain."[45]

Final Displacements

Federico de Onís imagines a pure, crystalline stream of U.S. Hispanism, originating in men like Prescott and Longfellow and flowing, untroubled, right through the nineteenth century and to his time. The representatives of the original, pristine stream supposedly practiced an aristocratic and disinterested brand of scholarship, focused on the soul of Spain, and undisturbed by worldly interests, popular demands, or any other contingencies of the moment.

Nonetheless, both Prescott's paradigm and Longfellow's law suggest that such a vision of the field is largely illusory. Kagan has taught us how Prescott, when writing "about the Spain of Ferdinand and Isabel, . . . was also writing about the young United States."[46] And I have shown how Longfellow certainly had the "relations now existing between this country and Spanish America" on his mind as he prepared himself to occupy the station to which he aspired. Indeed, a close look at any of the definitive moments in the history of U.S. interest in Spanish reveals that politics—turmoil and opportunity in the New World, or the rearticulation of the ties between Europe and the Americas—have always conditioned, in subtle and not-so-subtle ways, the shape and intensity of U.S. interest in things Spanish.

There are those who would like to be able to narrate the now two-centuries-old "rise of Spanish" in terms of the immanent value of great cultural figures: Cervantes, Darío, Unamuno, and Borges. But the archive that documents the rise of Spanish practically imposes other, much more worldly headings. The Latin American wars of independence and the Monroe Doctrine; the Mexican War; the Spanish-American War of 1898;[47] World War I and pan-Americanism; World War II and the Good Neighbor policy; the Cuban Revolution and the cold war; the influx of millions of Spanish speakers into the United States in the last few decades—these are some of the major forces that have driven enrollments and shaped the institutional will to include Spanish in the U.S. curriculum. Despite these hemispheric realities, Spain, for complex reasons—only some of which I have addressed in this chapter—has occupied a remarkably privileged position vis-à-vis Latin America in that curriculum.

In postulating the heuristic device that I have somewhat frivolously labeled Longfellow's law—U.S. interest in Spain is and always has been largely mediated by U.S. interest in Latin America—I do not mean to endorse some coarse version of materialist determinism, according to which economics or geopolitics immediately determine the shape of cultural artifacts or courses of study. On the contrary, I hope to have demonstrated that a number of complicated and dynamic factors thoroughly mediates the way in which these complex forces come to be expressed in curricula. Shifting cultural and academic values and structures; changing and insidious forms of prejudice and racism; intersecting and conflicting national and international projects—nationalisms, *europeísmo, Hispanidad,* pan-Americanism, or globalism, for example; the efforts and talents of exceptional individuals; the demands of an ever-changing population in the United States—all these things have shaped the way "Spanish" has been brought forth as an object of study in the United States in general and, in particular, have helped determine the places occupied by "Spain" and "Latin America" within that field of study. I hope to have shown that the places assigned to "Latin America" and "Spain" in Hispanic studies are linked in complex ways and are subject to constant shifting. These places are neither natural nor necessary; they cannot be designated as coordinates of latitude and longitude, nor as branches and sub-branches of a genealogical tree.

Notes

1. Edith F. Helman, "Early Interest in Spanish in New England (1815–1835)," *Hispania* 29, no. 3 (April 1946): 340.

2. J. R. Spell, "Spanish Teaching in the United States," *Hispania* 10, no. 1 (May 1927): 150.

3. Helman, "Early Interest in Spanish," 344.

4. See Spell, "Spanish Teaching in the United States," for information about the introduction of Spanish as a course of study at U.S. colleges and universities: Pennsylvania, 1750; William and Mary, 1788; Dickinson, 1814; Harvard, 1816; Virginia, 1825; Bowdoin, 1825; Yale, 1826; Amherst, 1827; Williams, 1827; Columbia, 1830; College of New Jersey (Princeton), 1830; University of the City of New York (NYU), 1832.

5. Spell writes—approvingly, it would seem: "The influence of the attitude of the Harvard professors toward Spanish determined to a large extent the type of study followed in most of the schools in the United States; even the institutions which urged the study of the language from the most utilitarian motives used texts whose purpose was to introduce students to the treasures of Spanish literature. Never throughout the century did Harvard cater to the practical calls for Spanish; no text dealing with Mexico or South America was ever issued; and no member of the faculty who taught Spanish ever traveled in Spanish America" (Spell, "Spanish Teaching in the United States," 151–52).

6. Kagan writes, "What I call 'Prescott's paradigm' is an understanding of Spain as America's antithesis . . . Spain's principal attraction [as a topic for a U.S. historian] was that its history, especially in the Habsburg era—the period that Prescott regarded as its nadir—represented everything that his America was not. America was the future—republican, enterprising, rational; while Spain—monarchical, indolent, fanatic—represented the past" (Richard L. Kagan, "Prescott's Paradigm: American Historical Scholarship and the Decline of Spain," *American Historical Review* 101 [April 1996]: 430).

Kagan argues that this paradigm has conditioned a good deal of U.S. historiographical writing about Spain, from Prescott to the twentieth century.

7. Helman, "Early Interest in Spanish," 346.

8. For example, Federico de Onís writes, "'Spain belongs to the past; we are more concerned with the present and the future, which lie in Hispanic America. We shouldn't even go to Spain to study its language.' All of this, and more like this, has been said and written repeatedly, and has been defended with such vehemence that we can only explain it as issuing from a blind hatred towards Spain. How else can we understand the persistence of such fierce battles waged in defense of something which does not exist: a Hispanoamerican language?" (de Onís, "El español en los Estados Unidos," *Hispania* 3, no. 5 [November 1920]: 281 [my translation]).

9. Frederick Bliss Luquiens, "The National Need of Spanish," *Yale Review*, June 1915, p. 699.

10. Ibid., 706–7. The opening of the Panama Canal and the commercial opportunities it offered to U.S. entrepreneurs are among the many war-related phenomena frequently cited in the period as driving U.S. interest in Spanish: "The demand in South America since August, 1914, for our capital and the much greater need here than before of South American raw material—hides, sugar, coffee, etc.,—the Pan-American Financial Congress, the establishment of the International High Commission, its trip through South America and its labors toward sytematization of bank discounts, credits, consular invoices, etc., the establishment in Hispanic America of nine branches of the National City Bank of New York authorized by the Federal Reserve law of the United States, the growth in shipping facilities between our ports and those of South America, as, for instance, the recent establishment of a direct line of five steamers between New York and Valparaíso,—all of these things are either causes or effects of the, for us, rather well-concerted effort to 'capture the South American trade'" (Lawrence Wilkins "On the Threshold," *Hispania*, organization issue [November 1917]: 5).

11. Luquiens, "National Need of Spanish," 709.

12. Lawrence Wilkins, "The President's Address," *Hispania* 2, no. 1 (February 1919): 38.

13. De Onís, "El español en los Estados Unidos," 276 (my translation).

14. *Hispania* 1, no. 2 (March 1918): 109, 110; *Hispania* 1, no. 4 (December 1918): 257 (two quotes), 258.

15. "There should be available to these [high school] teachers [of Spanish] in every college and university advanced courses in the language and literature of Spain and Spanish America. Our Association can surely take steps to urge and encourage the establishing of such courses in the higher institutions" (Wilkins "On the Threshold," 8).

16. Lawrence Wilkins, "The President's Address," *Hispania* 4, no. 1 (February 1921): 31.

17. Wilkins, "President's Address" (1919), 36.

18. *Hispania* 1, no. 2 (March 1918): 108; *Hispanis* 2, no. 1 (February 1919): 46.

19. In the remarks he made before the AATS in December 1919, Francisco Yanes, assistant director of the Pan-American Union, rhetorically linked the "foreign" and "domestic" battles fought by Hispanists: "If the labor of teachers is a thankless task to begin with, it has become even more so recently. The energy that has been invested in

the study of Spanish, and the great success with which it has spread all over the United States, have given rise to rivalries and planted the seed of discord, which, falling on fields fertilized with ignorance or bad faith, has produced nothing more than weeds that obstruct the path that had once been clear. You know better than I the reasons for these events, and you also know who is responsible for them. Those of you who fought as good citizens on the battlefields of Europe and defeated the enemy may now defeat this other enemy that threatens you here in your own country" (Francisco J. Yanes, "Remarks of Mr. Francisco J. Yanes," *Hispania* 3, no. 1 [February 1920]: 29).

20. Wilkins, "President's Address" (1919), 37.

21. Wilkins, "President's Address" (1921), 29.

22. Lawrence Wilkins, "Spanish as a Substitute for German for Training and Culture," *Hispania* 1, no. 4 (December 1918): 207.

23. Henry Grattan Doyle, "'Tumefaction' in the Study of Spanish," *Hispania* 3, no. 3 (May 1920): 106. Elsewhere in the same article Doyle bristles at the suggestion that enrollments in Spanish be artificially checked and again plays the patriotism card: "The proposed artificial restriction of Spanish is . . . not only impracticable and futile, as all such attempts at artificial restriction must necessarily be in a progressive, Anglo-Saxon country, but it is undemocratic and in essence un-American—an attempt by the few to determine what is good for the many" (136).

24. Wilkins, "On the Threshold," 6; emphasis added.

25. Wilkins, "Spanish as a Substitute for German," 221. Elsewhere Wilkins writes: "It behooves us, as teachers of Spanish particularly, to ever bear in mind that it is first of all for the good of our own land that we teach Spanish. And while we appreciate and teach Spanish traditions, literature and language, we do so to help our own citizens to a still higher place as leaders in the world; not as leaders in selfish commercial conquest, nor primarily as leaders in financial operations, nor as leaders in military aggrandizement, but as leaders in the great fraternity of democracy which exists in a more untrammeled state in the New World than in the old. Here is our opportunity. Here is our work" (Wilkins, "President's Address" [1919], 38).

26. Wilkins, "On the Threshold," 3.

27. J. Warshaw, "The Spanish Program," *Hispania* 2, no. 5 (November 1919): 225.

28. Wilkins chafes at the use of the word *substitute:* "When I accepted the invitation of Professor Fife to speak on the topic, 'Spanish as a Substitute for German for Training and Culture,' it seemed to me unfortunate that two of the words in the topic bore a certain flavor of ill-repute. I refer to 'substitute' and 'culture.' Then I reflected that if such be the case, it is not the fault of us American teachers. Substitute, in the form of 'Ersatz,' and 'culture' in the guise of 'Kultur,' had not their origin in our land or language. Substitutes and substitutes for substitutes are offered today in Germany. These substitutes, be they chopped straw for wheat flour, mendacity for truth, paper for cloth, militarism for national freedom, composition for leather, piracy and murder for international law, the 'good old German god' for the true God, are all substitutes of an inferior for a vastly superior article, quality and principle. It is in no such sense, I assure you, that I offer Spanish as a substitute in our educational scheme. I offer

a superior for an inferior article to provide training and culture for American youth" (Wilkins, "Spanish as a Substitute for German," 205–6).

29. Ibid., 206, 213.

30. Quoted in Doyle, "'Tumefaction' in the Study of Spanish," 133.

31. Ibid., 139.

32. "Somebody, certainly, was responsible for the German invasion. It began at a date within the memory of men now living and was victorious within fifty years after it had started. It was no more anonymous than a ballad, which is anonymous only because we do not happen to possess the name of the composer or of his emendator. What part the German government played in arousing enthusiasm by underground means will probably never be accurately known; but it is not at all difficult to conjecture the influence wielded by teachers of German" (Warshaw, "Spanish Program," 227).

33. Ibid., 225.

34. Ibid., 227. The issue of advertising and propaganda is clearly a sensitive one for these Hispanists both because of the German question (accusations that German teachers were agents of propaganda) and because of the "intellectually suspicious" popular demand for Spanish. "We ought never to descend to the position of mere propagandists and act as though we considered our own language specialty to be the only subject that should occupy the student's attention" (John D. Fitz-Gerald, "The Opportunity and the Responsibility of the Teacher of Spanish," *Hispania*, organization issue [November 1917]: 12). "I am convinced that we can best win the confidence of other schoolmen by showing a tendency to higher standards, as a body, and a certain distaste for mere numbers for which, in the opinion of many of our colleagues, we show only too great an anxiety" (J. Warshaw, "Concerted Action in Spanish," *Hispania* 4, no. 2 [March 1921]: 119). "This Association has made no propaganda for increasing the study of Spanish and need not do so. Public men, the newspapers, the public in general, have made and will continue to make all the propaganda necessary to induce people to study the language. . . . But we must make dignified propaganda among our fellow educators, specialists in other subjects, and among administrators in schools and colleges, in an endeavor to make crystal-clear what are the benefits to be derived from Hispanic Studies" (Wilkins, "President's Address" [1921], 31).

35. Warshaw, "Spanish Program," 226.

36. Ibid., 227.

37. Actually, Castro's "response" probably disappointed Warshaw, who wanted support for the premise that he forwarded with some trepidation: "That the Spanish world should not have produced its fair quota of uncommon men, illustrious deeds, and both practical and theoretical contributions to civilization, would be an anomaly almost impossible to account for, given the traditional Spanish character" (Warshaw, "Spanish Program," 1919, 235). Castro begins his essay by citing Giner de los Ríos: "We are indebted to the world; we would need to give back to other nations at least one one-hundredth part of what we received from them," and goes on to affirm: "It is certainly too soon to speak overseas of what is done in Spain [in terms of science]. But I have decided to write, with the thought that though the absolute value of our scientific

James D. Fernández

productivity is very small, the knowledge of what we are currently doing in the field of science might always be of interest to Hispanists" (Américo Castro, "El movimiento científico en la España actual," *Hispania* 3, no. 4 [October 1920]: 185 [my translation]).

38. On *hispanismo* and pan-Americanism see Frederick B. Pike, *El Hispanismo, 1898–1936: Spanish Conservatives and Liberals and Their Relations to Spanish America* (South Bend, Ind.: University of Notre Dame Press, 1971). Pike's description of the changing attitudes of some liberal Spaniards vis-à-vis the United States during World War I is pertinent here: some Spanish liberals "abandoned the hope . . . that Spain could serve as the mediator between Spanish America and Europe and thereby encourage the flow of European capital and cultural influences into the New World so as to block United States hegemony. Instead, they envisioned a role for Spain as the intermediary between the United States and Spanish America. . . . A few Spanish liberals believed that transformations in United States cultural values had reduced, and in the future might eliminate that country's threat to the Hispanic spirit. Thus Federico de Onís . . . took the hispanista movement in the United States as a happy indication that the country was beginning to appreciate and seek for itself a more spiritually oriented culture" (158–59).

39. M. Romera-Navarro, *El hispanismo en Norteamérica* (Madrid: Renacimiento, 1917), 5 (my translation).

40. This superimposition of projects and premises—Hispanism and Pan-Americanism, the Hispanic world is essentially different, the Hispanic world is essentially similar—leads to some interesting characterizations of the links between the United States and Latin America. One way to reconcile difference and sameness is through the notion of complementarity: "In order to understand the Spanish peoples of Spain and the new world we must, therefore, study their literature in all its manifestations. When we understand well the culture and civilization of these people . . . we shall have taken the first step in the direction of lasting progress and lasting peace and good will between the two great civilizations of the western hemisphere, the Anglo-Saxon civilization of the north with its great material prosperity, its scientific efficiency, its practical aspect, its democracy of opportunity, its love of peace and work, its wonderful educational system and its practical sense of justice, and the Spanish civilization of the south, with its love of the traditional virtues, its lofty idealism, its humanism, its love for family ties and veneration of motherhood, its artistic temperament, its deep religious instinct, and its new scientific and educational activities" (Aurelio M. Espinosa, "On the Teaching of Spanish," *Hispania* 4, no. 6 [December 1921]: 279–80).

41. De Onís, "El español en los Estados Unidos," 275.

42. Ibid., 272 (my translation).

43. Ibid., 276 (my translation). De Onís's characterization of the situation, according to which "culture/Spain" is not so much opposed to "business/Latin America" but rather enlisted—in a circuitous way—in the service of business, closely parallels the remarks of another early contributor to *Hispania*: "It is hoped that young America, in turning to the study of Spanish, will not limit her interest to the merely commercial

140

aspect of our international relations. The Hispanic American likes to be treated as a man, not merely as a business. He likes to be understood morally, intellectually, socially, as well as commercially, and he likes to have people know that he has antecedents and forebears, and is not like Topsy who 'never did have no father and mother but jus' grew.' In other words, he likes to have others acquainted with the history of his own country, with its literature, art, institutions, and general culture, and with that of the mother land" (Fitz-Gerald, "Opportunity and the Responsibility," 12).

44. De Onís points out some secondary benefits that the U.S. interest in Spanish may produce for Spain in fascinating and passionate terms worth citing: "A great deal of interest and curiosity has arisen, regarding the current realities of the Spanish-speaking nations, especially concerning their present and their future, while in previous years the only thing of interest about these countries was their past, their history. . . . At the bottom of every historical fact lies an economic factor; this is not to say that everything in this world is about economics. We have witnessed the United States approaching us with an acute awareness that we are the repository and creators of a civilization. And at our first encounter, without any effort on our part, this civilization has invaded their house. Making the United States aware of us, having them judge us and interpret us will be the first step. From now on, any *hispano* who participates in a creative or organizational activity will feel the gaze of the world upon him, and any localism or ruralism, any of the irresponsible superficiality that generally characterizes our politicians, our writers and our artists, will disappear. We shall repair our own relationships collectively in order to withstand with dignity the foreigner's gaze; we will rise from the moth-eaten pillows of our eternal siesta, leaving aside our petty family disputes" (de Onís, "El español en los Estados Unidos," 283–84 [my translation]).

45. Ibid., 279, 281 (my translations).

46. Kagan, "Prescott's Paradigm," 428.

47. Spell writes, "The Spanish American War and the consequent acquisition of new territory seemed to act as an eye-opener on the magnates of the commercial circles in the United States. For the first time, apparently, they caught a glimpse of the time when they must turn to the great undeveloped areas of South America as a field of investment for their money and a market for their goods. The first step to that end which suggested itself was simple: more people in the United States must learn the Spanish language. As a result of this conviction came the general introduction of Spanish into the secondary schools of the country. Each wave of contacts brought the same result, but each time on a larger scale: in the twenties [1820s] Spanish was introduced in some of the high schools and academies; at the close of the Mexican War, into the high schools of Baltimore and Boston; after 1898, its introduction was general in all parts of the country" (Spell, "Spanish Teaching," 155).

5

Archer Milton Huntington, Champion of Spain in the United States

Mitchell Codding

During the first half of the twentieth century, Archer Milton Huntington (1870–1955) did more than any other individual to influence and advance the field of Hispanic studies in the United States (figure 5.1). Perhaps his best-known and most lasting contribution is The Hispanic Society of America, the "Spanish Museum" that he founded in 1904, which over the course of fifty years he came to fill with his collections of Hispanic paintings, decorative arts, books, manuscripts, maps, prints, and photographs. By the time of his death in 1955 the Hispanic Society had published under his direct supervision more than two hundred monographs by the society's curators, along with other internationally noted scholars, on virtually all facets of Hispanic culture. Through his financial sponsorship countless Hispanists were able to conduct their research and publish the fruits of their scholarly labors—in many instances in journals that he also supported, such as the *Revue hispanique,* the *Romanic Review,* and the *Art Bulletin,* as well as the series Bryn Mawr Notes and Monographs under the editorship of Georgiana Goddard King. In recognition of Huntington's scholarship and of his invaluable contributions to the advancement of Hispanic studies, Huntington received honorary degrees from Yale, Harvard, Columbia, and the University of Madrid; membership in all the major Spanish royal academies, as well as most of the national academies of Latin America; appointment to the governing boards of numerous museums, including Spain's Casa del Greco and the Casa de Cervantes, both of which he helped found, the Museo Romántico, the Instituto de Valencia de Don Juan, the Museo Sorolla, and the Museo Nacional de Arte Moderno; and the award of every

Figure 5.1. Archer M. Huntington (1870–1955), ca. 1900. (The Hispanic Society of America, New York)

conceivable Spanish and Latin American medal of honor or distinction, the most notable of which were Spain's Orders of Charles the Third, Alfonso the Twelfth, Isabel the Catholic, Plus Ultra, and Alfonso the Tenth.[1]

Despite his public prominence, and in large part as a result of it, Archer Huntington was in fact a very private man, who in all his numerous endeavors repeatedly declined personal recognition for his contributions. As the only son of one of the richest men in the United States, Collis Potter Huntington (1821–1900), builder of the Central Pacific Railroad and the Newport News Shipbuilding and Drydock Company, Archer Huntington learned at a relatively early age to zealously conceal from the public eye all details of his private life and finances. Consequently, the personal accounts of his early fascination with the Hispanic world and his subsequent studies, the beginnings and formation of his collections, and the evolution of his concept of a Spanish museum remain largely anecdotal or have been gleaned from *A Note-Book in Northern Spain*[2] and his later publications.

We do know that from the age of twelve Huntington assiduously kept diaries of his thoughts and daily activities, but unfortunately later in life he chose to discard most of the diaries from his youth. The voluminous correspondence that he maintained with his closest friend and confidant, his mother, Arabella Duval Huntington (1850–1924), which he began in earnest on his first trip to Spain in 1892 and continued until her death in 1924, has survived in part and provides a wealth of insights into his changing vision of his role and that of the Hispanic Society in the advancement of Hispanic studies. Much of the details of his life before 1900 might have been lost were it not for his mother, who in 1920, on her seventieth birthday, wrote to her son requesting that he compile a detailed memoir of their life together based upon his notes and letters. The devoted son complied, and the resulting autobiographical narrative, taken in part from original diaries no longer extant, which he augmented with subsequent details and commentaries, now serves as the primary source on the most significant period in Huntington's formation as a Hispanist and museum builder. His memoirs, or the Huntington "diaries" as they have come to be called, were used by Beatrice Gilman Proske for her brief biography of Archer Huntington published by the Hispanic Society in 1963; however, with the exception of a few quotations, the diaries remain unpublished almost in their entirety. These documents provide an invaluable resource for examining Huntington's evolution as a Hispanist, his methods and philosophy behind the formation of his collections, and his concept of the purpose of the Spanish museum as it progressed from a youthful dream to the functioning realities of the Hispanic Society. Only through his diaries can we come to know and understand this very private man, for they reveal not only his contemporary appraisal of events but the unique perspective of the fifty-year-old Hispanist reexamining his life and accomplishments for his mother. In order to take fullest advantage of his diaries, I will quote his own words whenever possible.[3]

Born in New York City on March 10, 1870, Archer Huntington spent his earliest years, in the absence of his father, surrounded by his mother, grandmother, other adult relatives, and household servants. As a child of privilege, he attended the best private schools, received the benefit of personal tutors, and enjoyed the experiences and education afforded by foreign travel. In school he learned the customary Greek and Latin, English history and literature, but at home he took up readings in French history with his mother, who had become well versed in French art and letters. By his own admission he was not above the temptations of common mischief but on the whole was a rather solitary and bookish child. Huntington recalled his first exposure to the Spanish language in the late 1870s while on a visit to his mother's relatives in San Marcos, Texas. In the autobiographical narrative prepared for his mother in 1920, he wrote: "And here it was that I first heard Spanish talked by our [Mexican ranch hands]. To my surprise they actually seemed to understand each other. I even learned a few words myself which no Castilian would ever hail with friendly understanding" (1870s). His first trip to Europe in the summer of 1882 resulted in a constant series of cultural and intellectual awakenings that were to shape the course of his life. In this summer of discoveries he took up the habit of keeping diaries, and in London he recorded his beginnings as a collector:

On June 20, a very important event took place. I solemnly state in my diary that I took a ride on a tram in the morning, to which statement I annexed the words "and got some rare coins." Little did I know that a collector had been born in me, and that with 2 shillings, resulting in 7 small pieces of copper, I had entered the pathway which those demented souls who collect follow so assiduously.

On June 22, I find that I bought more coins, and started to make a list of them. When I think of the years of cataloging and listing that have followed, this too seems to indicate a fated choice of occupation. (1882)

It was also in London, only two weeks later, that a chance purchase in a bookstore initiated his lifelong interest in Spain. He wrote, quoting from his original diary:

On July 2 we went to "Sefton Park and saw some birds in cages. Then to a book store and bought a book by G[eorge]. Borrow.[4] It is called the *Zincali* and is about the gypsies of Spain. The most interesting book I have found here. Spain must be much more interesting than Liverpool. Our courier Quinlan is going to get me more books by this Borrow."

"This Borrow!" Dear Lady do you remember my later contacts with the books of this Borrow? Now manuscripts of his are in the vault at the Hispanic Society and all is well.

Soon I became quite enthusiastic about Borrow. Here was something new. Adventure, and all alive, and when years later I went to Spain it was as though I were not entirely in a new world. I read him over and over. Perhaps this was a first step, and I owe to this strange person credit as an influence in the days ahead. The Bible in Spain followed, and I was launched on a sea of wonder and questions. Johnny Appleseed had passed my way. (1882)

In the days that followed, first in London and then in Paris, Huntington discovered his passion for art and museums. From his London diary entry for July 12, 1882, he quotes:

Went to the National Gallery with Wallace.[5] Never saw anything like it. Could spend a month here. After lunch I came back again until it closed. I never knew there were such pictures. My feet gave out and I went home.

Read the catalogue until I could not see any more and went to bed. I think a museum is the grandest thing in the world. I should like to live in one.

I cut out all the pictures I can get to make a newspaper museum. I think you can do it with small wooden boxes with no tops. You could look down into them and the pictures are on the inside. And many would be from Spain. (1882)

In Paris on August 12 he experienced the world of art and museums to the fullest extent possible for a child of twelve, as he recalls:

"I went to the Louvre this morning." It seems a statement simple enough, but even today, as I look back at this experience, I know that it was a very vital one. Those miles of pictures! I left Quinlan, the courier, and walked and wondered. After a while I could not see more pictures. I felt stupid and ill, and I sat down and rested. And then of a sudden "my illness passed away and I wasn't tired any more, and I wanted to sing." There was something about all of these mysterious objects that stirred and excited me. It was like a rapid visit to many countries, and the meeting of strange persons, and walking in new landscapes. I knew nothing about pictures, but I knew instinctively that I was in a new world. (1882)

Two years later in New York his first "museum" took shape, with the art clipped from newspapers and magazines and displayed in seven wooden boxes made into seven galleries.

Inspired by Borrow's *Zincali* and other books by this author, Huntington began his formal instruction in Spanish at home at fourteen, at first two days a week, then six, with a female tutor from Valladolid whom he enticed into telling him of her native city and Spain. His now obsessive interest in Spain carried over into his first efforts at creative writing and his first encounters with Spanish literature. From his diary for 1884 he wrote:

> This year was the birth of a great work—my novel. The earth trembled. I chose Roderick the Goth as hero, and filled many many pages with battles and the deeds of mighty men. Roderick himself would have been surprised.
>
> Many years later, on a cleaning up expedition among overgrown files, I came upon it, and sadly dropped page by page on the open fire. What the world has lost!
>
> Adventure now filled me with yearning for high deeds, the rescue of bereaved maidens, and I read Amadis of Gaul. The trees became giants, the great house a castle of dreams. (1884)

In the summer of 1887 Huntington made his second trip to Europe, again to London and Paris, although this time accompanied by both his mother and father, whose social and business obligations left the teenager free to explore further the great museums and to continue his firsthand education in art history. On this trip he clearly had discovered the usefulness of photographs for furthering his studies::

> My photograph collection now fills 4 trunks and is rather a problem. I am leaving it here in storage and will get it on the way home. Most of the books have gone already.
>
> The photographs form a sort of diary and I have a book of notes on them. One grows to realize how much may be learned from them, and they bear the details which our memories cannot keep for us. Anything which is easily available and which stores up such a vast mass relieves the memory for something else. (1887)

In Paris, aside from further artistic revelations at the Louvre in the presence of the *Venus de Milo,* Huntington was struck with the idea of purchasing an entire collection of coins from a dealer, about six hundred in all, which he proceeded to carry out. Having discovered the economic efficiency of this method for rapidly expanding his collection, it became his preference in all future transactions as a collector.

On his return to New York at seventeen he tentatively entered the world of business on October 13, 1887, copying letters at a new desk in his father's private office. For the next two years he continued his apprenticeship, learning the intricacies of his father's financial empire, though his spare time was devoted to poetry, the study of Spanish art, and dreams of his own museum. Summarizing his diary for 1889, Huntington wrote:

> Now I wrote poetry continuously, mostly bad—(and cremated), and studied shorthand—a pure amusing waste of time, but a recreation. Later I invented a system of my own, also hours wasted.
>
> No little time went to the History of Spanish Art and Architecture these days. But art that one cannot see cannot be understood, and we learn only names and words. (1889)

He continued by quoting from the original diary: "'If I ever build a museum it will be a comfort to know that I could not help it, and what a comfort when we are sure of being on the wrong road and know it is always the right one because we *had* to take it'" (1889).

By January 1889 Huntington had already concluded that he had little affection for the world of business, which at this point provided him with only the relatively uncreative task of managing the transportation empire that his father had built. In March 1889 he traveled with his parents on a business trip to Mexico, where for the first time he directly experienced Hispanic culture, dined with Porfirio Díaz in Chapultepec Castle, and finally reached a decision that would profoundly alter the course of his life.[6] Describing the significance of this journey, he wrote:

> The trip to Mexico, short as it was, was a sort of strange awakening. You kept asking why I was so quiet. If you could have guessed what sort of sea your boy was tossing upon, you need not have asked. Mexico was a revelation. From books I had gathered impressions of it and California had already given me broken bits of meaning, but when the reality suddenly came! This, of course, was my first encounter with something which was to fill my whole life, and all at once I felt a curious, feverish eagerness. In all the years to come I would be forever looking back at these days of discovery, short as they were, and quite aware that here I took my first step toward unguessed goals quite hidden from me but toward which I was instinctively drawn. From now on the road was clear, and I no longer cared about the stupid criticisms

to which I had been subjected. The plan to be a business man in which I had acquiesced showed itself to be a taking of the wrong road. And my museum dreaming became clear and took on new forms. (1889)

In December 1889 Huntington's father offered to turn over to him as soon as possible the management of the Newport News Shipyards, thus forcing him to make a final decision about his career plans. The following month Archer Huntington took the first step toward turning his dream into reality:

> The 26th [of January] was a momentous day, for I went down to discuss with Captain Lachlan my giving up of the office. To say that he was shocked, and I hope disappointed, was to put it mildly. I explained that after all, a young fool like myself, who is chiefly interested in Spanish and museums, is not quite the person to launch a thousand ships. He had great difficulty in restraining the expression of what he really thought about literature and art, but we got through it after a while and, I think, remained friends. I went over it again on the following day, and during the night he had evidently reorganized his forces to attack my silly notions. However, I had been building some breastworks myself, and said good-bye and left the office.
>   On the 27th and 28th at home & took off piece by piece my spiritual maritime clothing, put on an imaginary Spanish sombrero and began working in earnest. Of course I knew what a disappointment all this would be to you and father, but I am afraid it has to be, as I am about as useful for the upbuilding of a great shipyard as an elephant darning lace. One must love a thing to do it. (1890)

Now officially committed to Hispanic studies and his museum, Huntington set about cataloging his Spanish library, which in February 1890 already numbered almost two thousand books. By the end of that year he had begun planning his museum. On November 8, 1890, he wrote: "I am working on more plans for a museum which will amuse you. I would like to know how much wall space is wasted in U.S.A. museums by windows. The windows of an art museum should be pictures" (1890). Once his intentions were known, Huntington suffered the ridicule of friends and family for having chosen such a seemingly worthless vocation. The reaction of his older cousin Henry E. Huntington, on a visit in December 1890, was typical:[7] "Saw H. E. Huntington today, and he asked me many questions about books, of which he knows very little. In fact he is rather frankly contemptuous of book collecting and especially my own. He repeated several times, "But why Spain?" And rather laughed at me. I told him he had better begin himself, but he laughed again, and said he thought he could do better with his time. (Yet he had a change of heart did he not?)" (1890). A more poignant encounter took place on January 1, 1891, during a visit to the American Museum of Natural History. Huntington recalled:

> Friends had already as you know begun to try to divert me to other fields. You

may recall the efforts of our good friend Morris K. Jesup who looked upon Spain and particularly Spanish letters and art as a worn out and undesirable field and did what he could to bring me to an understanding of the importance of science, and scientific research.[8]

It was on January 1 of this year that I visited him at his Museum with father and he made clear that my place was there and not in what he indicated was a "dead and gone" civilization, the study of which would bring me small reward or satisfaction. I told him I was not seeking a reward, that rather had hopes of presenting a picture by book or otherwise of what was, had been, and might be. I did not venture to use the word Museum which had filled me with a dream for so long.

My father watched me as we talked and when we turned back home he said— "Archer I can see that you know what you want, and I believe you can do it. Go on as you like and do the thing well." I shall not forget those words. (1891)

The idea of a museum focusing on the artistic and intellectual achievements of a single people was relatively new, and the very novelty of Huntington's career plans may have been the source of the dismissive responses of his relatives and peers. Large national museums such as the British Museum (founded 1753), Musée du Louvre (1793), Museo Nacional del Prado (1819), and Smithsonian Institution (1846) had sprung up throughout Europe and the Americas, but their focus tended to be more universal than national in scope. To be sure, during the course of the nineteenth century museums with specific national, and frequently historical, themes also had come into existence. These included the Museo Nacional de Historia (Mexico City, 1825), National Portrait Gallery (London, 1856), Musée de l'Histoire de France (Paris, 1867), and Tate Gallery (London, 1897). Yet Huntington's idea of a museum emphasizing a comprehensive view of a single culture or race was somewhat unique, and comparable institutions such as the Musée National des Arts Asiatiques–Guimet (Paris, 1889) and Oriental Institute Museum (Chicago, 1894) were only then in the process of being established. If Huntington had a clear model, it was the British Museum, an institution that, though not limited to British culture, at least endeavored to gather multiple aspects of human artistic and intellectual endeavor under a single roof. Furthermore, Huntington's Spanish museum, like the British Museum, was to incorporate a library, together with a large number of works of art. In this respect Huntington's planned museum of Spanish culture was truly innovative and certainly without precedent in the United States.

With these aims in mind, as well as in anticipation of his first trip to Spain, Huntington spent most of 1891 immersed in the intensive study of Arabic with a tutor. Though seemingly unrelated to the necessities of travel in Spain, Arabic too formed part of Huntington's larger scheme of Hispanic studies:

I did not study Arabic with any desire to use it as a major help in the future but, for a better understanding of Spanish and the Spaniard, one has to have it. And how many doors it opened and how much time it saved me.

I had already chosen a period and soon I was to be at work on a translation of the poem of the Cid and as the other flowers grew in my garden, it became in each case easier to get that general view which was to make possible the working out of my one object—a Museum which more or less should present the culture of a race and its chronological backgrounds.

And now soon I shall be in Spain and this is the last year of preparation. As I look back I can see that all the years have been somewhat unconsciously mere preparation. (1891)

While certain of his own path, Huntington had yet to convince his peers of the value of his scholarly pursuits and the goal of a Spanish museum. He recorded in the diary for 1891:

> But it is always the Museum. Charles [Pratt Huntington, his architect cousin] says he can't see it unless I want to get my name on something. This enraged me.
>
> To place one's name on a donation be it a building or subscription is an artificial and flimsy door to fame. The human race is full of creators, but it is their acts and not the name of some rotting corpse in a cemetery which are interesting. There are quite enough names of the living to remember in everyday existence without converting human minds into a book of lists. The greatest creators are unknown, even those who invented the wheel, the plow or the axe. (1891)

Not all of 1891 was dedicated to Arabic and planning for his long-awaited trip to Spain. In February he made a brief visit to Cuba, from which he gained "many new Spanish impressions," along with a trunk full of literature. That same year he also reported on a highly significant acquisition for his Spanish library: "Another shoal of gleaming 1st Editions has swum into my ken: I have sat on the bank and baited my hook with little golden certificates for some time & cast near where I saw them last and, behold, bites! Now twelve of the dear little yellow vellum backs are peering at me from shelf 3! Congratulations, please. I will not bore you with their XV and XVI century names. But bend your head while I whisper: Three are *unique!*" (1891).

In 1892 at last the time had come for his trip to Spain. Huntington busied himself with surgical studies for the eventuality of serious physical harm in some remote region of Spain. He also began work on his edition of the *Poem of the Cid*,[9] and he furiously compiled notes for the journey. In February he wrote: "I am in a maze of work day and night. A note book which I call *Questions* lies on my table and grows fatter day by day. These are the things I want to find out about Spain, books, pictures, architecture, etc. But chiefly I must know the people and see them as they are, and as they were. The two lock and define each other" (1892). By March he was all but dying of anticipation, writing:

> The thing now is to get to Spain. I am so stuffed with questions that if I do not get there soon I shall forget—or burst.
> The first trip must be cities, the country and the people. Then book collecting and Library work and last History and Archaeology. They will overlap of course but it is best to go with a plan to cover several trips. (1892)

Finally in June he set off for Spain in the company of his paid scholarly companion, the Hispanist W. I. Knapp, a professor at Yale University.[10] On July 4, 1892, the last day of their journey before arriving in Spain, Huntington exclaimed:

> "At last! We are on the train leaving Paris. Every click of the rails plays an accompaniment to a dream come true. All these years! Well I must prepare to repaint my picture. Surely the thing I am about to find will be quite unlike what I have built up. I can see Spain ahead dotted with palaces and fortresses, with cathedrals and walled cities, with bearded warriors and great ladies. Of course it is all wrong. Isabella the Catholic will not be in Madrid and I am sure to miss Visigoths and Almanzor.
> "But there will be footprints."
> As I had little to bring and much to gather I rather feared my introductions and put off using them. It was just as well in the end for I met everyone I wanted to see and laid foundations for friendships which have lasted through years.
> With what kindness and willingness these friends have helped me. How many pitfalls I have avoided and how often they have saved me weeks and days. There is a curious spontaneous generosity which the Spaniard possesses and which I have deeply felt. Men of all ranks aided me and those I now met as friends have remained friends indeed. My love of things Spanish already had its roots in the soil but my love of the Spaniard was now to flower into something of great beauty and my gratitude has grown with the years. (1892)

The adventures, experiences, and impressions of this first trip to Spain were recorded by Huntington in minute detail in a copious succession of letters to his mother. Five years later these very letters were to become, with some expurgations, *A Note-Book in Northern Spain*.

The contacts made on his first trip to Spain proved extremely advantageous to his collections, because they resulted in a flood of offers and new acquisitions. On the formation of his library and collection of art, Huntington wrote in 1894:

> As to myself, I doubt the certainty which others possess. I have been rather reckless in buying and while many have led me to a work of art I bought only on my

own feeling. The collection of the Society to be, which was gradually taking form in some detail, must express my faults and mistakes in no small degree. I had to rely on the long preparation. In the years immediately following 1894, I believe I could have told at once where almost any famous painting of Spanish origin could be found in Europe or the peninsula. I had seen most of them. This was helpful at a later time when I began to buy seriously. My notes and lists were full and there were photographs and books. Painting of course, is the simplest and the most difficult of the arts. In the crafts any fool with money may be a collector and may learn facts and figures. . . .

As to money, it is the fashion to treat it with a certain contempt by those whose existence often depends upon it. Money has given us chiefly our colleges, museums, and hospitals.

Books flowed in now from Europe and my collection grew steadily. The problem of the catalogue became a serious one. But the greatest waste of time is in endless luncheons and dinners. They not only distract while you are enjoying them but the effect lingers and wastes other hours. (1894)

In the coming years these unwelcome distractions only multiplied. On August 6, 1895, he married his divorced cousin Helen Gates Criss in London, and on their return they entered immediately into New York's social life of endless luncheons, dinners, and musical and theatrical performances. Not all these distractions were unwelcome, for he fondly remembered the evenings spent in the home of the editor of *Century* magazine:

The Friday evenings at the Gilders were charming.[11] Mrs. Gilder was the soul of those gatherings and everyone worth while in Arts and Letters was there. Everyone loved Mrs. Gilder, and the crowded rooms were always full of compliments and her charm. The talk was far better than at the Players. Gilder was a sort of royalty and his power as editor of a great magazine was wide. I went regularly when I was in New York, and not a few friendships grew out of meetings there. These were the days when I came to know Mark Twain and to admire him. The slow deliberate old man had a power of his own, and one admired his simplicity and quick replies. Everyone talked of Mark Twain, and he had a host of friends. (1895)

That same year, in collaboration with the De Vinne Press, he began to publish what has come to be known as the "Huntington Reprints," a series of facsimiles of rare books and manuscripts taken primarily from his own library, in the hope that these valuable texts might be preserved and made available to scholars.[12] While on his honeymoon in Geneva in 1895 he noted:

The idea of the facsimiles I am happy to say was not a mistake and they have been very well received.

This method of reprinting and saving rare editions is going to be more important as time goes on. (1895)

The following spring saw his return to Spain, and his library grew by leaps and bounds, as he observed on March 8, 1896, in Madrid: "Books and more books. The days when I had to search are over. They tumble in. Dealers, friends, and strangers bring them. And now come first editions and other flowers of type" (1896).

In February 1897 his father made the couple a gift of a small estate named Pleasance in Baychester, on the shore of Long Island Sound in the Bronx, on the heels of which followed the gift of three Spanish paintings from his father's collection, including Antonis Mor's portrait of the duke of Alba. Finally, Huntington had space for a proper library, and its planning and construction filled the remainder of the year. This endeavor provided valuable practical experience for the eventual design and construction of his Spanish museum. On November 13, 1897, he reported on the progress of this labor of love:

> Work goes on steadily at Pleasance in the library. The wire gratings, gas, electric fixtures, and what not, make work impossible during the day, but I am getting a good practical library building, fireproof, damp proof and top lighted. The building is 80 ft. long and 40 ft. high, with galleries and a central portion 40 ft. by 40 ft. There is no plaster on the walls and there will not be any. The floors are brick, there is a fine, big fireplace, and all is well.
>
> As I had found it a much better plan than [the noted architect] Richard Hunt's and as my ideas of a library and his did not meet it is certainly well that he did not build or plan it. He would never have approved of my somewhat radical ideas. (1897)

His library completed and installed at Pleasance, and the first volume published of his edition of *Poem of the Cid,* Huntington set off for southern Spain in 1898 to focus on archaeology and books. The diary for this trip, compiled primarily from letters to his mother, by itself could have produced several major publications, but Huntington chose not to do so. Describing the goals of this trip, he stated:

> *This* is a *book trip.* My claws are sharpened, and I carry a large bag. In Sevilla there is material to be had. There are some splendid collections nesting by the Guadalquivir. Frankly I am tired of angling in the shallow streams of the north. Perhaps I may this time catch something larger even than a *merluza* [hake].
>
> We collectors! This fish line is baited with a museum, and at least some crabs are even now trying to crawl into my net. Vague of outline it indeed may be, and no doubt too much may slip in, but on this trip it is books, books, and yet again books! Easier than omnivorous feeding.
>
> It is pleasanter indeed to do one's hunting alone on one's own accord, rather than to sit in stuffy auction rooms waiting for jewels to gleam. Yet even those sordid places of battle I ever recall with unholy joy.
>
> Of pictures on this trip I shall have nothing to say, nor even time to look at them.

Ahora no se hace caso de esas. They are for another day. Moreover, as you know, I buy no pictures in Spain, having that foolish sentimental feeling against disturbing such birds of paradise upon their perches. Let us leave these beloved inspiration builders where they were born or dwelt, for to Spain I do not go as a plunderer. I will get my pictures, *outside*. There are plenty to be had.

You ask my plans. I answer *books*. I know very clearly indeed what I am after. My lists are made. The idea of the museum of which I told you grows so great that I cannot see around it. Already I see the librarian at his desk, the objects in cases, pictures and tapestries on walls, each a flower from fields wherein I have loved to walk; the whole something of a cross section in miniature of the culture of a race. It is no longer a dream. It has become somnambulistic, and I begin to feel that it can be done. (1898)

Further defining his conception of the Spanish museum, Huntington added:

My collecting has always had for it a background—*you* know—a museum. The museum which must touch widely on arts, crafts, letters. It must condense the soul of Spain into meanings, through works of the hand and spirit. It must not be a heaping of objects from here or there or anywhere until the whole looks like an art congress—half dead remnants of nations on an orgy. One outline of a race. And one gathering of faithful expositions and kindly, educated Trustees! And true research.

I am collecting with a purpose and you know that purpose quite well. That small compact Museum of Spanish culture will take all the time left me in this world. Others can then come and write beautiful books hot off the shelves—and still others may write books hot off these. I wish to know Spain as Spain and so express her—in a museum. It is about all I can do. If I can make a poem of a museum it will be easy to read.

As I have often said I venture to flatter myself that I am not a "collector," rather an assembler for a given expression. To be sure this is not altogether unlike the book maker, but I find these good scholars wonderfully equipped with spongy facts, but insight and discrimination can only be had at first hand. One must almost *be* a Spaniard to understand him—*almost*! And if you do not understand him how can you feel the story of his culture, how know what to use and what to discard. You see my job is marked out and I have no choice but to continue.

There is one thing of which I am certain, that the study of a book—Spain or any book-country is too often saving fat and letting the meat go. If I ever have a museum, the staff shall know works and *refranes* and shall have met native creatures near to men—from mule to bed-bug. They shall pursue a word and its feathery meanings as an Englishman seeks the brush of a fox; they must block the burrows of escape and ride off with the trophy. Then they may write about their Spain. I think women should do it. (1898)

The books that Huntington so eagerly sought on his 1898 trip he found in

Seville in the library of the famous bibliophile Manuel Pérez de Guzmán y Boza, marqués de Jerez de los Caballeros, and he described it in raptured detail:

> The Marquis of Jerez and his brother Tserclaes each have books. Books indeed! The library of Jerez is the more interesting to me, naturally, for it has so much that I am looking for in Spanish letters, and would save me years of hunting were it mine. But of course I suppose that is out of the question. He long ago refused Quaritch, when the latter had made him a good offer for that time, and yet here is one wing, with the feathers all on, waving at me!
>
> As I sat in the high library, with the friends of Jerez, and we discussed these books it seemed to me that the hero of every romance I had ever read floated out of some early edition and joined the group! Many in Sevilla who knew, collected or loved were there. It was a wonderful *tertulia* [party].
>
> In this amazing library not alone the essence of books filled the air. Pictures were discussed and photographs passed around the big table. The duke of Alba had sent a batch from Madrid with new ideas and attributions. But it was the books that added a skylight with sun to the room!
>
> Jerez would slyly slip a little volume before me and point out its condition. Many of his books have been bound in Paris but they gained nothing in that for me. Bindings are bindings alone. And fantastic flourishes on modern leather are not better than simple vellum.
>
> At a late hour Jerez, Marín, and I were still fumbling books and manuscripts in Jerez's library. I should like to be able to tell you my feelings. Of course, the experience for me is like nothing else on earth. I feel like an old time gold miner who has run upon a pocket of nuggets in a sluggish stream and, my soul, but they do shine! Now don't make any guesses. Just hold your breath and wait. If—if—if—. And here I close this Lady and the Tiger letter, to let your curiosity send forth cries of pain. (1898)

Huntington had indeed found the mother lode, but he would have to wait another four years before he could stake his claim.

The other goal of his 1898 trip was the pursuit of ancient Spain, as he wrote: "Do you remember what I said of Itálica, and my hope of being able to do some work there? I want to get a little closer to Roman Sevilla, to Hispalis. This will be done in much the same spirit which urged me to work in surgery,—*not* to be a surgeon, and as in all the other not-to-bes. In this case, not to be an archaeologist" (1898). Upon reaching Itálica, he was immediately seduced by its atmosphere of antiquity, which he lyrically described:

> Went out for a first visit to Itálica, through a storm of flowering trees. There rose up about me the strange perfumed sense of the past, and the present became the interminable hallway by which I was passing to something always just out of reach.

I was but leaving new footprints in that long corridor. Footprints that others need not ponder.

Itálica enveloped me. It was a place of whispers. The dead had retreated here and taken up an abode in the winds of forgotten street corners, in the calling of far-off church bells, in the curious longing of mysterious faces, among the fallen battlements of a dead past.

On what were streets one might almost hear cries that Arabs uttered a thousand years ago, mingled with Latin footsteps of earlier Roman soldiers and the clink of armor. On other days the gray sky closes down like a shifting pall, the shining walls of ghost buildings seem to lean toward one as if eager to hear new echoes of the lost world outside.

The student, the archaeologist, the traveler died within me.

I became filled with the breath of ancient things that are never really ancient but seize upon the heart with a realism which remakes the present, as though it had those strange new messages to whisper, which Romans and Moors had thought young in the First and Tenth Centuries. Itálica is itself alone a mere vestige of itself. I was a part of it for a moment, and all that I had read about it came back to me. Kings, nobles, ladies, retainers, Romans, Arabs, Greeks, and Goths, tread the unreal streets and ruins. (1898)

The treasures unearthed in his excavations at Itálica, a venture cut short by the outbreak of the Spanish-American War, along with the artifacts acquired from Jorge Eduardo Bonsor's excavations at Carmona, soon formed the core of the archaeological collections of Huntington's Spanish museum.[13]

As he had hoped, his travels through Spain in 1892, 1896, and 1898 had given him new insight into the Spain that had escaped him in books. By 1898 he had come to the realization that his years of study of Hispanic culture had produced only a sterile, academic, and incomplete portrait of Spain. Through personal interaction with individuals from all levels of Spanish society, and in particular those of the countryside, Huntington felt that finally he had discovered the soul of Spain in its people:

> You know how, in the past years, I have been saturated with the history of Spain. And how dear it was to me! I worked in a vast world of things, dates, men and actions. I could turn a quotation in its shell as a spoon finds the yolk of an egg. And all this information was hard boiled and shining. I felt as though I knew as many happenings of the past as a priest knows of the by-ways of heaven. Happenings that never happened! Motives that never entered the minds of the dead were as easy to my tongue as the newspaper's false news of yesterday. . . .
>
> I came to Spain, and talked to Spaniards and saw that I had lacked the *clue,* the clue of insight. So, at one time traveling in the *coche de San Fernando,* at another on the back of a mule, I wandered over the Peninsula, and let the clues unfold into cer-

tainties and at last watched large bits of history dissolve before my eyes as ice warm water. I came to know the living Spaniard and what he could *not* have done. For the Spaniard of today and his ancestor of yesterday, Iberian, Roman, Goth or Arab, are like all humans, true brothers under the skin, and the spirit whispers of the departed still linger in eyes and form, in gesture and pattern of thought, in faith and superstition, in dress and dreams. And just as today you may encounter a troglodytic person on Broadway or Piccadilly so, in Galicia you may meet a Suabian or lunch in Sevilla with a reclad spirit of one of the Abencerrages.

The ignorance of people regarding Spain! There are good reasons for this.

They visit it much less and find it less comfortable than other countries and, when they do go there, follow a too well worn track, and do not speak the language. Spain has for them a fixed pattern of sentimentalism and contemptability.

It is in the back country that Spain can be known, in the bare lands that once were covered with great forests and are now inhabited by a scattered and tradition filled population, one which has preserved the true type better than elsewhere.

These amazing peasants, whose struggle for existence is a hard one indeed, are men and women of another age, but fine men and women for all that, erect, preserving an independence and character of truth and honesty which fills one's heart with a sense of freshness and integrity—if you draw near with integrity.

I talk with everyone, one ear drinking in figures of speech the other cocked for the location of some rabbit warren of books. From these talks I learn so much more than I can get from many a more instructed friend. Here are the sources of the national values. The blood that runs in these veins is the national blood undiluted by recent contacts with the world outside. (1898)

Huntington spent the next six years in a flurry of activities, including the publication of about forty facsimiles of rare books, although his primary focus remained the creation of the Spanish museum. His goal came even closer to reality in January 1902 with the purchase of the much-coveted library of the Marqués de Jerez de los Caballeros. While aware that the acquisition of this invaluable library would inevitably be the subject of controversy in Spain, Huntington remained confident in his belief that this would ultimately lead to the advancement of Hispanic studies. In the diary for 1902 he wrote:

As you may imagine the Jerez Library sale was not long in becoming news in Sevilla. [V. F.] Johnston[, British vice consul at Seville,] wrote on January 17th that it was already about town, and letters came from friends all over Spain. Many regretted it as a loss to the country, and said so frankly, but one or two grasped its influence to spread in America knowledge of Spanish letters. Of course on the whole Spain loses nothing.

It has been a great and glorious blessing to me to be able in this way to hasten my collecting, saving me many a month of search for books otherwise unobtainable.

Certainly the making of this library has become one of the most laborious and delightful undertakings imaginable, and here I have obtained material which could never be duplicated. (1902)

On the eve of the foundation of his Spanish museum, Huntington again traveled to Europe in search of more objects to fill out the already impressive collections. In January 1904 he wrote:

> The stay in Paris was active. I was collecting furiously but carefully in view of the necessary completion of those lines chiefly in book collecting and minor arts. I collected always with the view to definite limitations of the material to be had, always bearing in mind the necessity of presenting a broad outline without duplication. These limitations greatly aided me by reduction of the number of pieces adequate to present a comprehensive whole, and I often astonished my dealer friends by refusing an object which most collectors would have seized upon with enthusiasm. Moreover, I was most eager to complete those lines of which I had serious knowledge, for I had already learned by experience that the dealer is not so much the collector's friend as his own. (1904)

Finally, with land purchased in upper Manhattan (on 155th Street at Broadway) and an initial endowment set aside, on May 18, 1904, Huntington executed the foundation deed for a public Spanish library and museum, to be called The Hispanic Society of America. The object of this institution was the "advancement of the study of the Spanish and Portuguese languages, literature, and history." The immediate public response in the United States to this grand endeavor was one of skepticism, as Huntington wrote, "When the H.S.A. had come to notice in the press in 1904, without a *torbellino de aplausos* [resounding applause], many people were amused at the new form of fad by a rich man" (1904). In contrast, Spaniards responded to the announcement enthusiastically, with offers of all types of assistance:

> The flood of offers of books, pictures, and what not has risen to something of a tempestuous sea. They come from everywhere and in every tongue, but on the whole not much of first class order appears. Spain I find, to my surprise, is peopled with individuals thoroughly competent to fill positions in the new society, who either recommend themselves or have their friends do so. One gentleman from Logroño explains to me carefully that his knowledge of leather and its uses in bookbinding is more profound than usual. Another said that he is best informed about the roads of Spain; and the third places at my disposition his bibliographical knowledge of the cock fight. While I do not have to answer the whole brood, much of it has to be attended to for the sake of politeness.
>
> All this however has its value, for now and again I pick up something, a book, a tile, a bit of pottery and what not. (1904)

In little more than a year the building was in place, but he spent two more years directly supervising the careful arrangement of the collections. With the formal inauguration of the Hispanic Society on January 20, 1908, Huntington at last had in place the vehicle through which he could pursue his fixed purpose of being the champion of Spain in the United States (figure 5.2). The doors of the society had been open to the public for only a few months when Huntington again set off for Europe, where he was to happen upon the paintings of Joaquín Sorolla, on exhibition in London.[14] In his diary entry of May 13 he noted: "To the Grafton Galleries to see the Sorollas. As I was working out an idea about these I listened with interest to 'GM' [George Moore] opinions.[15] He was silent for a while. The pictures had made an impression clearly. Suddenly he burst out: A well equipped man this, well equipped indeed—but harsh, very harsh. He inveighed against the harshness but kept admitting the startling qualities of the Spanish painter" (1908). Given the tremendous influence that this encounter ultimately would have upon the lives of Sorolla and Huntington, as well as the Hispanic Society, it is unfortunate that he failed to record his own impressions. He unquestionably was captivated by Sorolla's work, for he immediately initiated plans through agents in London for an exhibition at the society the following year.

Figure 5.2. The Hispanic Society of America, 1908. (The Hispanic Society of America, New York)

Their first meeting took place at the Savoy Hotel upon Sorolla's arrival in New York on January 24, 1909, as Huntington recalled in his diary:

> Arrived N.Y. 2 p.m. Lorraine. Sunday Jan. 24.09. I did not go to meet them as I was going to lunch with Helen [Huntington]. . . . Went to see them at the Savoy at 5. Found his wife daughter & son with him. He was all excitement over his arrival. Had a young american painter with him who has a studio in Wash[ington] Sq[uare] & who went to meet him on his arrival. He gave me very pleasant messages from the king and insisted on hurrying off to the H.S.A. to see the pictures. Expressed his satisfaction at the hanging which I had done & made many suggestions. Pointed out to me the "very best" work he had sent *in five instances*! (1909)

As they worked around the clock through the following days in preparation for the opening of the exhibition on February 4, a close friendship quickly developed between Huntington and Sorolla. On January 31 Huntington recorded in his diary:

> S[orolla] has had a frensy of picture hanging. The men are worn out. At first, I made some suggestions but these I saw he did not like. Fortunately he has forgotten what I said and now nearly all have been accepted as his own. I am still in doubt about the placing in the upper floor. But that must be his affair not mine. Every one has had to work night and day. Dr. [Winfred] Martin & I have been in the building until 3 in the morning over the catalogue, but it has taken shape at last.[16] S[orolla] is perfectly willing that we should kill ourselves if we like. He has only one earthly idea and that is his art. It is delightful. He works as I love to work so all is well between us. I think though that I have been able to tire even him a bit, which is also delightful! (1909)

Their labors were rewarded beyond their greatest expectations. The exhibition was an immediate sensation, attracting nearly 160,000 visitors from February 4 through March 8. Huntington's first special exhibition had been an unparalleled success, conferring international recognition and acclaim upon both Sorolla and the Hispanic Society. Under the auspices of the society the Sorolla Exhibition then traveled to the Buffalo Fine Arts Academy and the Copley Society of Boston. The success of this exhibition encouraged Huntington and Sorolla to arrange for another exhibition of his work two years later at the Art Institute of Chicago and at the City Art Museum of Saint Louis. During the next twenty years Huntington and the Hispanic Society sponsored a number of significant temporary loan exhibitions, yet none approximated the popular appeal or the influence of the Sorolla Exhibition. In a letter to his mother after the closing of the exhibition in New York, copied in his diary, Huntington expresses unabashed pride in his accomplishments:

I will not bore you any more about the Sorolla Exhibition. It came upon New York rather stealthily as I had planned. How much it had cost me in time, labor, patience! It was called a triumph. The artists looked upon it as an invasion. The collectors welcomed it as an opportunity to burnish brazen names more highly by association. The dealers secretly snarled & wrote me enthusiastic messages. One said: "Spain sank low in our defeat of her, she has replied with the lightnings of art."

Everywhere the air was full of the miracle. People quoted figures of attendance. There was eternal talk of "sunlight". Nothing like it had ever happened in New York. Ohs and Ahs stained the tiled floors. Automobiles blocked the street.

Orders for portraits poured in. Photographs were sold in unheard of numbers. And through it all the little creator sat surprised, overwhelmed yet simple and without vanity, while I translated to him the rising tide of press enthusiasm. And Clotilde his small Valencian wife, with the pained drawn face of those who dwell with the great, folded her little hands meekly & drank of the tide of glory tremulously, nervously smiling, bewildered and happy, as more than a hundred people crowded into the small building to pay tribute to her husband. And then it was all over; the doors were closed and the packing began, for the pictures must soon start upon their pilgrimages to other galleries.

So you have the Hispanic Society's first serious presentation of itself to New York and the artist gained the wherewithal for the fulfillment of his dream of a home in Madrid to be built as a museum for later days. (1909)

Energized by the recent triumph, Huntington renewed his search for books and art objects for the Hispanic Society, adhering to his grand scheme of building library and museum collections that would touch upon all facets of Hispanic culture. Even though Sorolla and others encouraged him to buy in Spain, Huntington maintained his long-established policy of acquiring significant early works of art only outside the peninsula. Huntington personally purchased the bulk of the society's museum collections from major art dealers and on occasion at auction in Paris, London, and New York. In fact, the same policy applied in general to library acquisitions, as he acquired few rare books and manuscripts in Spain after he bought the Jerez library. He preferred instead to purchase whole collections at a time that had been expressly prepared as printed catalogs for Huntington and the Hispanic Society by the antiquarian book dealer Karl W. Hiersemann of Leipzig. For a period of ten years, from the founding of the Hispanic Society until the outbreak of World War I, Huntington dealt almost exclusively with Hiersemann, which allowed him to add rare books and manuscripts by the thousands to the library.

As part of the all-encompassing vision for his institution, Huntington approached Sorolla in 1910 with a proposal for a commission for the Hispanic Society of a series of large historical paintings that would provide a comprehensive panorama of Spain and Portugal. As Huntington related to his mother in his diary for 1910, the historical theme of the society's "big decoration" was soon abandoned in favor of one focusing on the provinces of Spain, one more in tune with Sorolla's innate talents:

> I have been in the midst of a continual rush for buying, and Spanish things are plentiful. They are not always of the best, but good enough in many cases. Sorolla always talks of the things to be had in Spain, and in October was urgent that I go there. However, I have explained to him that I do not care to buy much of importance in Spain, owing to the fixed rule that I have been following in buying outside of the Peninsula only. The things come to Paris eventually and one is saved the long bargaining which is enough to drive one mad. It is an inheritance from an Oriental background. But I do not go to Spain to buy (with the exception of books).
>
> On the 30th of October I visited you at the Bristol. . . . Later I talked with Sorolla about the big decoration for the Hispanic Society, and we changed the plan to one of provinces, peasants, and cities of the Peninsula.
>
> Sorolla is ill. He seems to have caught a bad cold painting Princess Troubetzkoy. I should have anticipated a fever. Sorolla today asked me whether I would consider being made a Grandee of Spain. I looked at him in some amazement, not being quite sure whether he was serious or not. He assured me that he was serious. And I had to explain that for an American this was out of the question. I rather think Sorolla did not know exactly what he was suggesting. . . .
>
> We returned to the question of the decoration, and finally decided upon a series of landscapes of the provinces, emphasizing costume, and he was very delighted, because the idea of historical work had given him a bit of a chill as it meant research and material with which he was unfamiliar. But this new plan left him free to select his own subjects and details. I tied no strings to the proposal and emphasized nothing beyond the vague treatment of provinces, and he is to have a free hand. Tears came in his eyes, and I felt that our problem was solved. We said good-by as we are separating probably for a long time. (1910)

On April 30, 1911, Sorolla wrote to Huntington accepting the commission for twenty-nine panels representing the regions of Spain. Following further revisions to the overall design, they signed a contract in Paris on November 26 that required Sorolla to provide the Hispanic Society within a period of approximately five years a decoration painted in oil measuring from three to three-and-one-half meters in height by seventy meters in length, depicting contemporary life in Spain and Portugal.[17] As Sorolla began work on the large canvases, along with the portraits destined for the Hispanic Society, Huntington and Charles Pratt Huntington formalized plans for the western addition to the main building that would house Sorolla's monumental work.

Huntington continued to add to the society's now-extensive museum collections, buying works by both early and contemporary artists. While in

Madrid in 1912, he visited King Alfonso XIII and Queen Victoria Eugenia de Battenburg, who inquired into his acquisitions of Spanish art. His response, by now customary, assured the monarchs that he had no intention of depriving Spain of its artistic heritage: "We lunched at the Palace today, and the King brought up the question of my purchase of Spanish art. I explained to him, although I am sure he already knew it, that I only purchased books in Spain, as I felt that Spanish paintings should remain where they were. So many had drifted abroad that it was perfectly easy for me to obtain all the necessary types without robbing Spain. The Queen seemed pleased with the idea" (June 17, 1912). Huntington fully appreciated the concerns of the Spanish monarchs, for he was more than familiar with the insatiable appetite for European art and culture of his fellow Americans. Musing on this subject while in Paris the following year, he wrote:

> I am not very enthusiastic about the American idea of living "abroad." Go there & get their culture if possible, Yes. But as no American can *think* like these Europeans it is not wise to moor too closely to their dock. I am glad to have escaped the temptation.
>
> For the artist one must make exception. The idea of Art is a powerful stimulant in Europe. Art there has had all the experiments and is still trying. The artistic life must of course find its expression in the physical background of nations. And the physical background of Europe is distressful. Art will pay for this, in confusion.
>
> So now I gather what I can for the Museum. So much is going to America. However the *greatest* art is still in Europe—to remain I think until another Napoleon becomes a collector!
>
> . . . [The architect Ogden] Codman & I went over to Schultz's Spanish "patio" which is for sale. A piece of plunder of some interest. Not for me however. Hearst would be quite fool enough to buy it I think. The old age of Hearst should be given up to the elimination of an unclean spirit. But Saint Cyriacus is no longer with us![18] (October 24, 1913)

The outbreak of World War I in Europe effectively brought to an end Huntington's active pursuit of acquisitions for the Hispanic Society. By war's end Huntington had for the most part lost interest in substantially expanding the art, rare book, and manuscript collections of the society, perhaps in part because he realized that years of work still lay ahead in researching and cataloging the material already amassed. He also had begun to sense the passing of an era, one in which many of the greatest art collections in the United States had been built. On his return to Paris in 1918 he observed:

> The question which I find very interesting at this moment is that of the future of American collecting of Art. The very greatest types have it must be confessed not gone to us. Although some very fine examples are in the U.S.A. . . . the growing

antagonism to the rich will be felt. The great what may be called transcontinental period is over. And for all we may say, Art collecting has been chiefly home decoration and vanity badges. The museum is taking the place of the collector—*is* the collector in a sense—and the volcanic dealer's fires die down. (May 17, 1918)

For Huntington and the Hispanic Society one major acquisition, however, did await completion: Sorolla's commission on the provinces of Spain. From the beginning Sorolla had faithfully reported to Huntington his progress and successive revisions to the content and design of the "paneaux." When Huntington returned to Madrid in 1918 after an absence of four years, he was delighted with Sorolla's decoration for the Hispanic Society as it neared completion, but he was somewhat dismayed to find that Sorolla no longer was the robust artist he had encountered on his last visit. Because of Sorolla's declining health and the rapidly changing world of contemporary art, Huntington sensed that the conclusion of Sorolla's great work for the society also signaled the conclusion of the great artist's career, writing:

To see Sorolla this morning with D.H. [Douglas Huntington, a cousin]. Found him with Clotilde and Elena and the boy (who now speaks English well).[19] We saw the work for the H.S.A. which has advanced wonderfully. This is going to be exactly what I had hoped and wanted—a presentation of Spain by provinces. It has educational as well as art value and will fill the place made for it admirably. I am again glad that S[orolla] would not handle the historical scheme of which we first talked. I should have known that he could not, with this he has full liberty to be himself. . . . S[orolla] has taken his theory of painting to its limit & for that alone it will stand.

S[orolla] is not too well. He is thinner & softer and I am alarmed about him. He kept saying that the H.S.A. had given him his great chance, but there is a general let down and he is very tired.

I had hoped that the return to out-of-doors would have kept him fit but there is I fear something organic.

Clotilde smiling, nervous & retiring is older and still dresses in bright yellow, which with her coloring is not bad. Poor dear C[lotilde]. She has had all the trials of family and genius and her little thin body has put up quite as fine a struggle as that of her distinguished husband. Without her he might have got no where.

In these days when the art pattern is changing for the worse S[orolla] feels the change but he is not discouraged or convinced of a better way. He is S[orolla] & that is enough. Well, I agree.

The daughter is very quiet & simple but is I think a bit restless under too much restraint. There is a faint touch of something akin to sullenness.

We went over each picture slowly and explored the house in detail. He is very proud of the house & calls it his His[panic] Soc[iety]. He has a dream of its future as a S[orolla] museum & I think something of the kind may be brought about one of these days, but I hope in the distant future.

I am afraid S[orolla] has done his work. There is too clear a change in his physical condition & the sense of fatigue points a bit too clearly. But the work is done & may God bless him & his. (January 1, 1918)

With the completion of Sorolla's work for the Hispanic Society at hand, Huntington also saw a chapter of his own life coming to a close. In a letter to his mother from 1919 he wrote: "I am about through at last as a collector. Only now & then a book perhaps. But let the others go to it. I have never felt enthusiasm for 'general' collecting—and the H.S.A. shows that. One subject is enough, don't you think? No you do not for I could tempt you any day with a Van Dyke or, better, a Rembrandt" (August 19, 1919). This same year Huntington began plans for a visit by Sorolla and exhibitions of his work in the United States in the autumn of the following year; however, Sorolla's sudden crippling illness in the summer of 1920 abruptly halted all plans and unfortunately ended any hope that the great artist would ever see his monumental *Provinces of Spain* installed in the room that came to bear his name (figure 5.3).

A letter written by Huntington to his mother on December 6, 1920, provides an enlightening epilogue to these diaries, which trace the evolution of the great Hispanist from the inception of his museum and library through its general completion. Though satisfied with his creation, he had come to recognize with time not only his own limitations but those of his institution. In contrast to

Figure 5.3. Inauguration of the Sorolla Room, 1926. (The Hispanic Society of America, New York)

the unbridled enthusiasm of the early diaries, youthful ideals and dreams had yielded to the realities of administration, as he wrote:

> I am at Pleasance today, writing a report to the Hispanic Society Trustees for the Minutes, which I have just finished, and which is the usual dull reading. On the whole, I think the Hispanic Society is doing very well. You will be interested to know that the staff is gradually taking shape, and some day I hope that we may issue through them a fine set of monographs. I hope to get each one interested in a single subject, so that they may become expert in each case along a definite line. I am more than ever convinced that this is a women's work, and at first can be only research,—later we may develop monographs of importance, and already we appear to be on the road. When I first made the collections, you will remember that the whole field of Hispanics lay before me, and my dream was its classification and presentation by myself, but dreams are dreams, and the administration has taken its toll of my time, and money, of which I had far too much, and to which you have added your share, has been the greatest thief of all. Really, my dear old lady, one cannot carry the burden of wealth and climb mountains. In the days when I worked on *The Cid,* I was free, and comparatively poor, and the ten years that I spent on that laborious job, with Arabic and other languages as a side issue, were filled with a glorious sense of accomplishment. The building of museums, with all their infinite detail, does not stir the same emotion, and in this I can only feel that I am but preparing the way for others. I suppose this is wrong and that I ought to be just as enthusiastic in one field as the other, but I did want to do creative work, and 8 to 10 hours a day must be had to do it. However, I do not think you will be ashamed of your infant's ventures into museum building, for, after all, creative work is a gamble, and I may have set the value of my ability on a pedestal. Now and again I am able to write a poem or an introduction, and the history no longer tempts me. Well, we will see. (1920)

Huntington's plans for the staff of the Hispanic Society shortly would come to fruition just as he had envisioned. He had recently hired a group of young women in their twenties to work in the Library Department, all recent graduates with degrees in library science from colleges like Simmons in Boston or Gallaudet in Washington, D.C. After they had been employed for only a few months as librarians, Huntington assembled them one day and told them of his plans to form a museum department composed of specialist curators for each major area within the collections. He proceeded to offer them the opportunity to select a new field of specialization, which they eagerly accepted: Elizabeth du Gué Trapier (paintings and drawings), Beatrice Gilman Proske (sculpture), Alice Wilson Frothingham (ceramics), Florence Lewis May (textiles), and Eleanor Sherman Font (prints). Along with Clara Louisa Penney, bibliographer in manuscripts and rare books, they began to research and catalog the society's collections, an almost endless task that would take them decades to complete. As Huntington had hoped, in time they became experts in their fields, first issuing catalogs of the collections, followed by scholarly monographs, many of which remain fundamental references, such as Proske's *Castilian Sculpture* (1951), May's *Silk Textiles of Spain, Eighth to Fifteenth Century* (1957), and Frothingham's *Spanish Glass* (1963).

Even though Huntington never was able to fulfill his dream of returning to scholarly research, he did continue his "ventures into museum building." In 1920 a new wing was added on the east side to serve as the reading room and to house the collection of prints. Following his second marriage, in 1923 to the noted sculptor Anna Vaughn Hyatt, Huntington began to plan for the addition of appropriate permanent sculpture on the terrace in front of the society. The addition of yet another building for galleries and storage on the north side of the terrace provided the proper setting for Anna Huntington's sculpture, and in 1927 her monumental equestrian bronze of El Cid was placed in the lower terrace, immediately becoming the unofficial symbol of the Hispanic Society.

In the years that followed, the collections of the society continued to grow through purchases and gifts, many from its founder, although Huntington himself no longer aggressively acquired works. As would be expected, in his final years he became less involved in the daily operations of the society, yet he retained total administrative authority as president until his death in 1955. In addition to financial bequests, Huntington's final gift was a treasure trove of drawings, manuscripts, and rare books that he had reserved for himself over the years in a personal vault within the library. His greatest legacy to Hispanic studies remains the Hispanic Society, with its invaluable museum and library collections. Today his "Spanish Museum" not only remains an essential resource for the study of Hispanic culture in all its varied manifestations but through its vast collections offers infinite research opportunities for future generations of scholars. In this sense, as Huntington had speculated in the 1920 letter to his mother, his greatest contribution to Hispanism indeed was "preparing the way for others."

Notes

1. For details see Beatrice Gilman Proske, *Archer Milton Huntington* (New York: Hispanic Society of America, 1963).

2. Archer Milton Huntington, *A Note-Book in Northern Spain* (New York: G. P. Putnam's Sons, 1898).

3. All the quotations that follow are taken from the Huntington diaries and correspondence files located in the Huntington Archives at The Hispanic Society of Amer-

ica in New York. Because both the diary pages and correspondence are filed chronologically, it is only possible to cite them by date.

4. George Henry Borrow (1803–81), the English linguist and author, traveled through Portugal, Spain, and Morocco from 1835 to 1839 as an agent for the Bible Society of London and as a correspondent for London's *Morning Herald* (1837–39). The first book resulting from his travels and adventures in Spain was *The Zincali; or, An Account of the Gypsies in Spain* (London: J. Murray, 1841). Two years later he published what would become his most famous work, *The Bible in Spain; or, The Journeys, Adventures, and Imprisonments of an Englishman, in an Attempt to Circulate the Scriptures in the Peninsula* (London: J. Murray, 1843), a highly original and insightful account of contemporary Spain.

5. Wallace served as a hired chaperone for the young Archer during his stay in London.

6. Porfirio Díaz (1830–1915), president of Mexico (1876–80; 1884–1911), was well acquainted with Archer's father, Collis P. Huntington, who recently had built the Mexican International Railroad, a branch line in northern Mexico of the Southern Pacific Railroad. Archer recounts in his diary entry for March 15, 1889, that at a formal dinner with the president in Chapultepec Castle he had suffered the embarrassment of fainting, presumably brought on by heat and altitude. Díaz later served as a member of the advisory board of the Hispanic Society from 1905 to 1914.

7. Henry Edwards Huntington (1850–1927), nephew of Collis P. Huntington, shared the management of the Central Pacific Railroad in the 1890s from his office in San Francisco. After Collis died in 1900, Henry received one-third of his uncle's estate and moved his offices to Los Angeles, where he developed an extensive interurban railway system that greatly contributed to the rapid growth of the city. Henry retired at the age of sixty to devote himself to his book and art collections and his estate in San Marino. In 1913 he married Arabella Huntington, Collis's widow, and together they developed the collections that now comprise the Huntington Library, Art Collections, and Botanical Gardens in San Marino.

8. Morris Ketchum Jesup (1830–1908), a New York banker and philanthropist, was one of the founders of the American Museum of Natural History and served as its president for more that a quarter century from 1881 until his death.

9. Archer Milton Huntington, ed. and trans., *Poem of the Cid*, 3 vols. (New York: G. P. Putnam's Sons, 1897–1903).

10. William Ireland Knapp (1835–1908) left a professorship in modern languages at Vassar Female College in 1867 to spend the next eleven years in Spain researching sixteenth-century Spanish literature. During this time he published editions of the works of Juan Boscán (1875), and of the poems of Diego Hurtado de Mendoza (1876–77), for which Spain awarded him the Royal Order of Isabel la Católica in 1877. Knapp returned to the United States and joined the faculty of Yale University, where he held a permanent chair, Street Professor of Modern Languages, from 1880 until 1892. Knapp is best known for his famous biography *Life, Writings and Correspondence of George Borrow*, 2 vols. (New York: G. P. Putnam's Sons, 1899).

11. Richard Watson Gilder (1844–1909), a preeminent figure in New York literary circles, was managing editor of *Scribner's Monthly* (1870–80) and, under its later name, editor-in-chief of *Century* (1881–1908). Gilder and his wife, Helena, were justly famous for their weekly salon attended by the most notable artists and writers of the day.

12. The fifty-four "Huntington Reprints" were reproduced through a photogelatin process under the supervision of Edward Bierstadt and printed at the De Vinne Press. After the founding of the Hispanic Society in 1904, successive facsimiles appeared with the society's imprint. The series included such noted works as Alonso de Ercilla y Zúñiga's *La Araucana* (Madrid, 1569); *Cronica del famoso cauallero Cid Ruy diez campeador* (Burgos, 1512); García de Resende's *Cancioneiro, ge[ne]ral* (Lisbon, 1516); Johanot Martorell and Martí Johan de Galba's *Tirant lo Blanc* (Valencia, 1490); Miguel de Cervantes's *El ingenioso hidalgo Don Quixote de la Mancha* (Madrid, 1605); and *Celestina* (Burgos?, 1499?).

13. Jorge Eduardo Bonsor (1855–1930), a British national born in Lille, France, conducted excavations at Bell Beaker, West Phoenician, and Roman sites around Carmona, near Seville, from 1880 until 1907. One of the most distinguished archaeologists active in Spain at the turn of the century, Bonsor formed part of the European generation that definitively established archaeology as a scientific discipline. Archer Huntington acquired a major portion of the Hispanic Society's archaeological collection from Bonsor, the proceeds from which permitted Bonsor to fund his ongoing excavations. A number of Bonsor's most significant studies eventually were published in English by the Hispanic Society, such as *Tartesse* (1922); *Early Engraved Ivories . . . from Excavations by George Edward Bonsor* (1928); *The Archaeological Expedition along the Guadalquivir 1889–1901* (1931); and *An Archaeological Sketch-Book of the Roman Necropolis at Carmona* (1931).

14. Joaquín Sorolla y Bastida (1863–1923), born in Valencia, was Spain's most internationally prominent painter in the first decades of the twentieth century. Known as the "painter of light" for his masterful technique of capturing the bright sunlight of Valencian seascapes and beach scenes in his bravura style of plein air painting, Sorolla was an equally skilled portraitist who was commissioned to paint many of the most notable figures of his day in Spain and the United States, including King Alfonso XIII, Pío Baroja, Miguel de Unamuno, Louis Comfort Tiffany, and President William Howard Taft. Sorolla achieved his greatest fame and financial success, both in Europe and the United States, following the 1909 exhibition at the Hispanic Society.

15. George Augustus Moore (1852–1933), an Irish novelist and essayist, in his early years studied painting in Paris, befriending many of the French impressionists. The product of this experience was the collection of essays *Modern Painting* (1893). Moore's lifelong interest in art is also reflected in his fiction. In his novels, such as *A Mummer's Wife* (1883), *Esther Waters* (1894), *The Untitled Field* (1903), and *The Brook Kerith* (1916), Moore is best known for the psychological portraiture of his characters and his purity of style.

16. Winfred R. Martin (1853–1915) served as librarian of the Hispanic Society from 1907 until his death in 1915.

17. Sorolla's commission for what is now known as *The Provinces of Spain* (1911–19) ultimately consisted of fourteen huge canvases depicting contemporary regional costumes and customs of the major provinces of Spain. Huntington originally had conceived of this commission as a series of canvases presenting the history of Spain. As Sorolla was uncomfortable with this historical approach, which would have required considerable research, they finally agreed upon a series of paintings emphasizing the most typical regional costumes and traditions of Spain. Sorolla spent eight years traveling throughout Spain, making innumerable sketches for later reference in his studio, in search of the ideal settings, models, and inspiration for what he called his "Vision of Spain." Unfortunately, Sorolla died before seeing his greatest work installed at the Hispanic Society in 1926.

18. Ogden Codman (1863–1951), architect and interior decorator, was one of the major proponents of the classical and colonial revival styles of the gilded age in the United States. Together with Edith Wharton, Codman wrote the important book on classical interior decoration, *The Decoration of Houses* (1897). Codman worked primarily in Boston, Newport, and New York, and his clients included Frederick Vanderbilt and John D. Rockefeller, as well as Archer Huntington, for whom he constructed a townhouse at 3 East 89th Street and renovated the adjoining townhouse at 1083 Fifth Avenue (1913–17), now the National Academy of Design.

The Spanish "patio" mentioned by Huntington was the Patio de la Infanta from the Renaissance palace built in 1546 for the *converso* merchant banker Gabriel Zaporta in Zaragoza. The sculptural elements of this plateresque masterpiece have been attributed to Martín Tudela. The Zaporta palace was demolished at the beginning of the twentieth century, and the Patio de la Infanta was acquired by the Paris art dealer M. Fernand Schultz. It was repatriated in 1958 by the Caja de Ahorros y Monte de Piedad de Zaragoza, Aragón y Rioja, and after a quarter century in storage was reconstructed in its headquarters in Zaragoza.

William Randolph Hearst (1863–1951), the newspaper and magazine publisher, was already famous in 1913 for his voracious acquisition of historic European interiors, art, and artifacts destined for the decoration of his castle, whose construction began in 1922 at San Simeon, California.

Saint Cyriacus, a Roman martyr during the reign of Emperor Diocletian (284–305), gained fame as a healer and exorcist while imprisoned in Rome. Credited with having freed the emperor's daughter, as well as the daughter of the king of Persia, from demonic possession, Saint Cyriacus consequently has been invoked in the Catholic faith against diabolical possessions.

19. Huntington here refers to Sorolla's wife, Clotilde, his daughter, Elena, and his son, Joaquín.

~~ 6

Georgiana Goddard King and A. Kingsley Porter Discover the Art of Medieval Spain

Janice Mann

Just at the moment when art history in the United States began to emerge as a systematized discipline distinct from archaeology, art criticism, and aesthetics, a number of scholars employed at prestigious East Coast universities left the better traveled roads of classical Greece, Renaissance Italy, and Gothic France to strike off into the virtually uncharted territory of medieval Spain. In the first decades of the twentieth century Georgiana Goddard King (1871–1939) of Bryn Mawr College (figure 6.1) and Arthur Kingsley Porter (1883–1933), who taught first at Yale and then at Harvard University (figure 6.2), were among those who regularly left their comfortable offices to seek out obscure sites in remote areas of rural Spain.

King and Porter were part of the vanguard of professionalized art history in the United States. They had been preceded since the mid-nineteenth century by such U.S. scholars as Charles Eliot Norton (1827–1908), who had examined the fine arts as the means to moral edification and cultural refinement, but not until after the turn of the century did the systematized study of the history of art begin in earnest.[1] No less an art historian than Erwin Panofsky typifies this moment of U.S. art history as animated by "the spirit of discovery and experimentation" and "a spirit of youthful adventurousness."[2] James Ackerman characterizes the art historical scholarship of this moment as "distinguished by an extraordinary perseverance and enthusiasm in the search for unknown monuments and documents, especially when they were to be found in inaccessible places."[3] Panofsky believed that the ebullience of U.S. art history in the 1920s was encouraged by a shift of power from one side of the

Figure 6.1. Georgiana Goddard King (1871–1939). (University Archives, Canaday Library, Bryn Mawr College)

Figure 6.2. Arthur Kingsley Porter (1883–1933), taken ca. 1930 at Glenveagh Castle. (Harvard University Archives)

Atlantic to the other. As the United States emerged as a full-fledged world power in the later years of World War I, able to play a decisive role even in European affairs, the United States came into contact with Europe in an active rather than a passive way for the first time. The military, political, and economic clout of the United States engendered an increased sense of entitlement to intellectual territory understood before the war as the domain of Europeans.[4] Free from the centuries-old national allegiances and prejudices of Europeans, U.S. scholars, at least according to Panofsky, approached the Old World's cultural heritage with greater impartiality, often moving into areas that their transatlantic counterparts had not bothered to explore.

The art of medieval Spain, needless to say, beckoned enticingly to U.S. art historians of the early twentieth century. The field was barely known to serious scholars and much maligned as unoriginal by amateurs.[5] In the early twentieth century the rest of Europe perceived Spain as unprogressive and hopelessly rustic and therefore not worthy of intellectual consideration. This very lack of modernity, I would claim, enhanced Spain's appeal for U.S. art historians like King and Porter. Although their scholarship claimed a positivistic objectivity founded on a sound empirical basis, it was to a great extent generated by the romantic and escapist sentiments that colored the views of many educated Anglo-Saxon East Coast Americans recoiling from what they perceived as the increasing coarseness of their country during the first decades of the twentieth century.[6] Spain and its Middle Ages appealed to U.S. art historians as seemingly more authentic and profound than their own time and country.

King spearheaded U.S. interest in the architecture and sculpture of medieval Christian Spain.[7] For her day, she was a well-educated woman, graduated from Bryn Mawr College with a bachelor's degree in English in 1896. She stayed on to pursue graduate work in political science, philosophy, and English until 1898, when she left for a semester of study at the Collège de France in Paris. In 1906 King returned to Bryn Mawr after seven years of teaching at a private school for girls in New York. Shortly thereafter she founded the college's art history department in 1914. In a 1937 interview given on the occasion of her retirement, King disclosed the romantic attitude that motivated her preoccupation with the sculpture and architecture of medieval Spain. She declared herself a "real Hispanophile" and spoke of how the country's "black magic" was still for her "the most exciting thing in the world."[8] With open sentimentality she informed the interviewer, "I came there last and it still trails clouds of glory for me, as the last love always does. It has not yet become a part of the general scheme of things as Siena, for instance, has."[9] In other words, the lure of the unbeaten path, along with her understanding of the place as a mysterious land of enchantment, drew King to Spain.

King's most ambitious work, *The Way of Saint James,* is also the most revealing in terms of her attitudes toward Spain, art history, and the Middle Ages.[10]
Begun in 1911, *The Way* examines the medieval monuments lining the road that
pilgrims followed from Toulouse to Saint James's shrine at Santiago de Compostela.[11] The work is divided into four books printed in three volumes. *Book
I: The Pilgrimage,* gives a thorough account of medieval sources discussing the
pilgrimage to Santiago. *Book II: The Way,* which forms the bulk of the text, gives
an account of King's trip with her companion, whom she calls Jehane, along
the road from Toulouse, across the Col de Somport, and through northern
Spain to Santiago. The results of King's rigorous art historical investigations
are woven together with the more personal account of her trip. "Jehane" perhaps euphemistically refers to King's real travel companion, photographer, and
collaborator, E. H. (Edith) Lowber, who took some of the photographs used
in *The Way.*[12] Their journey provides more than just a framing device for the
history and analysis of the architecture and sculpture encountered along the
route. King's observations of her own times link the present with the past,
revitalizing all that lay inanimate there.[13] Santiago de Compostela, including
the medieval church, the modern town, history, and folklore, is described in
Book III: The Bourne. A brief tying up of loose ends is provided by *Book IV:
Homeward,* which discusses the Pórtico de la Gloria, a handful of sites in Galicia, and finally the passage back to France through the historic pass at Ron-
cevaux. Throughout *The Way* King weaves together the present with the past,
the legendary with the historical, and her personal experiences with her more
objective scholarly account.

King was the first art historian to examine the idea that the pilgrimage to
Santiago stimulated artistic creation and cultural exchange, although she is
seldom given credit for it. Later, after more esteemed male art historians such
as A. Kingsley Porter and Emile Mâle adopted and deployed this conceptual
framework in a heated quarrel about the national origins of Romanesque
sculpture, it became a standard art historical paradigm.[14] The ultimate source
of inspiration for this approach to medieval creativity was the French philologist Joseph Bédier, who claimed that the free movement of jongleurs and pilgrims along the pilgrimage routes generated and disseminated the chansons
de geste.[15] Unlike Bédier, who could formulate his ideas from written texts,
King had to travel along the route followed by the pilgrims in order to gather
the material for *The Way.* This made for a different kind of understanding of
the Middle Ages and their relationship to the present. For King the road carried one back through time as well as across geography.[16] It is both the means
to, and the repository of, history.

Written in an age before art history was subject to a set of regulatory regimes that prescribed a problem-solving teleology, *The Way of Saint James* is more descriptive than analytical. Occasionally, King offers deductions about dates and sources of style or motifs, but her main task is to reveal unknown and obscure buildings and make them familiar to the reader through her words. Her text never focuses on an art historical monument in isolation. The process of getting to the site; the setting, not simply the geography of the site but the surrounding people, aromas, and sounds; and the present social and historical contexts of the building are all parts of the discussion. For instance, in her treatment of the Romanesque church of Santa María in Santa Cruz de la Serós, King describes "the purple starlight" of the early morning, the flowers by the riverside, loggers at their work, and the sound of water rushing through an irrigation system and into the fields.[17] Against this backdrop of the present, King describes the medieval convent church in prolonged detail, concluding that its tympanum, copied from that of Jaca, is "Benedictine, twelfth century, regional."[18] Next she gives an account of the founding of the convent and its subsequent history; and finally, she returns to the present, describing the village, its few art treasures, and her departure. By situating her comments about the medieval church and its history in the anecdotal immediacy of the present, King erases the distance between the Middle Ages and her own day. Santa María and the other medieval churches that she treats live in the here and now rather than in the cool detachment of the past.

For King nowhere are the Middle Ages more alive in the present than at Santiago de Compostela. It is "the bourne, the end of heart's desire . . . like places you have come to in a dream and remember that you have known them long ago."[19] She overlays the modern with the medieval by focusing on its legacy in the present, the bells ringing, candlelit churches, religious rituals, relics, legends, and the vestments of the clergy. She tends to ignore the middle class and focuses instead on the upper and lower reaches of society, the archbishop surrounded by cardinals, royalty accompanied by soldiers and canons in the order of Santiago, or peasants and beggars "tricked out in calico capes sewn over with scallop shells, and staffs on which the gourd is reduced to a symbolic knob."[20] Cars, trains, cameras, and other clear signifiers of modernity, while mentioned elsewhere in her account, all but disappear from her discussion of Santiago. King intersperses her text with the observations made by pilgrims from other eras that harmonize with her own, creating an intertextuality that reinforces the notion of the timelessness of Santiago and the universality of the pilgrimage experience.[21]

King understood the pilgrimage to Santiago as transcendental. She wrote that it predated Christianity and was in fact as old as the human race.[22] This paralleled her understanding of Spain itself as timeless.[23] The road's magnetic draw was rooted in the very forces of nature that summoned the pilgrim. "Along that way the winds impel, the waters guide, earth draws the feet. The very sky allures and insists."[24] The pilgrimage cannot really be rationally comprehended but only accounted for by mystics who "can tell how journeys to such shrines are made: *The way is opened before you, and closed behind you.* Simple, that: believe it or not, it happens. So with Compostella it draws you."[25] The poetry of King's words seems calculated to mobilize the imagination rather than the intellect of the reader and thereby to communicate a kind of knowledge not wholly dependent on fact.

King found poetry in the prosaic as well as the profound. She frequently stops the flow of her scholarly account to relate a personal encounter with the "picturesque." For example, she diverges from a description of the cathedral of Santiago de Compostela to say how she saw a peasant in pilgrim's dress: "with an ecstatic face, who looked a little like S. Francis. His head was the same shape, and his brown frock helped the illusion. For a long time I watched him praying, and when he got up and went out I ran after and asked leave to photograph, readily yielded: then he asked an alms. Why not? Give and take is fair."[26]

Although her evocative prose imbues these vignettes of Spanish daily life with a sense of dignity, they are nevertheless generated by King's understanding of Spain as "still unspoiled and romantic."[27] Yet they are more than just a romanticized anthropology; they serve to foreground the medieval architecture that King discusses in the present, making it and its history relevant to the early twentieth century and creating a putative continuity between past and present.

King valued the emotional response to art, nature, the sacred, and personal encounters. Writing at a time before intellectual discourses such as deconstruction or political shifts such as the collapse of the British Empire forced authors to question the objectivity of Eurocentric values, King believed in the universality and transcendental nature of qualities such as the "aesthetic" or the "spiritual." But at the same time much of her commentary is grounded in the subjective. In *The Way of Saint James* King's personality and gender frequently break through the surface of her scholarly text. Given that she lived in a female scholarly community, and that her closest emotional ties were with her two sisters and her travel companion, Edith Lowber, it should come as no surprise that King's account of the pilgrimage is clearly gendered. Her text expresses as much interest in Spanish women in both the present and the past as it does in men. The accomplishments of medieval Spanish queens, such as Doña Mayor of Navarre, find as revered a place in King's account as do those of their husbands.

King's eye is equally engaged by contemporary Spanish women, and she often notes them, their concerns, and habits, for instance:

Every little town has these little churches, that stay open after dark for a few veiled, whispering women. They have a special feeling, like the scent of dried leaves, like the taste of night air, like the hushed Friday evening of the return from Calvary in Ribalta's painting. To Spanish women they are very comfortable. The subdued glow of light, the warm smell, the rustling human figures, offer something of the attraction of the hearth, without the *ennui* of home. The great point is that in church one is never bored; that prayers lull, like the nursery rocking-chair. . . . It will be hard to break the women of the habit, at winter nightfall, while men are in the cafés, of going to church.[28]

Drawing from travel literature, and working in the early years of art history before its methods became dogmatic, and before more scientifically minded Europeans came to dominate the field in the United States, King describes her experience as a woman researcher in the field without reserve. To this extent she exposes much of the process by which she constructs her narrative. She makes clear how gender can complicate research when she relates a story of how a young male guide maligned her moral character for coming alone with him on a trip on horseback to remote sites around Villafranca.[29] In an account of her stay in Pamplona she points out to the reader how socially prescribed gender roles make life unpleasant for the female researcher, especially on long winter evenings: "For a woman alone, they are hard. She has been out seeing things while the daylight lasted and is honestly tired. . . . She cannot walk up and down the pavement, in the light of shop windows, as men are doing. She goes back to her room at the hotel. There she cannot go to bed to keep warm, for dinner is still three hours away; she makes her tea, then fills a rubber hot-water-bottle, and wrapping it and herself in a rug lies down under a faint electric bulb to read and shiver and not dare to doze."[30]

King's amalgam of the personal with the scholarly and the past with the present confused at least one reader of *The Way of Saint James.* An anonymous reviewer in the *London Times Literary Supplement* opined that King had been unable to "make up her mind whether to write a series of rather romantic travel sketches or a serious work of research, and she confused the two."[31] Rather than stemming from indecision or conflict, King's dialogistic method simply exposes the private experiences in which she formulated her scholarly observations. For an author writing before postmodern critical theory, King shows a remarkable awareness of the fictional contingencies of scholarship and the importance of personal positioning. In the foreword she unreservedly acknowledges that she has made "one straight story out of three years' wanderings, and places visited and revisited."[32]

In chapter 1, entitled "Intentions," King writes that she followed the Pilgrim Way at first in order "to discover and record" the impact of foreign sources,

especially French, on Spanish medieval architecture.[33] But her purpose shifted in the process of investigation and grew "long since from a mere pedantic
exercise in architecture, to a very pilgrimage."[34] In other words, a rational academic task evolved into a journey that was spiritual and colored what she saw.
She may have sought facts, but what she experienced was in part transcendental. Sadly, the personal grounding of King's work caused it to lose credibility
with the next generation of art historians, whose art historical methods were
more regimented.

King explored the dual frontiers of art history in the United States and the
field of Spanish medieval art. Her love of opening up new territory persisted
to the end of her career. Her only doctoral student, Delphine Fitz Darby, described her when she was in her sixties and impaired by a stroke, "yet hoping
for one last trip—this time to Portugal, then a nation less attractive to travelers than was neighboring Spain. But G.G. loved to pioneer."[35] King's place at
the forefront of her discipline and her self-image as a trailblazer led her to
unexplored intellectual territory. Geography, discovery, and art history sometimes elided in King's mind, as is evident in what she wrote to Gertrude Stein:
"I saw they have excavated [some] of the palace of the Western Caliphs at
Cordova—it was immensely picturesque & vined & the scraps of stone &
pottery had beauty absolute besides the exciting implications: it was more
wonderful as landscape than Tiryns or Knossos or Mycenae or I suppose I felt
it more."[36] Her romantic nature drew her to the obscure and the transcendental. She found both in the land and the Romanesque art of Spain.

Where Georgiana Goddard King has been all but forgotten in the field of
Spanish Romanesque, the life and work of Arthur Kingsley Porter have become
the stuff of legend.[37] As Linda Seidel has aptly pointed out, Porter's mysterious disappearance during a storm from his isolated cottage on the island of
Inish Bofin off the coast of Donegal in 1933, when he was at the height of his
career, contributed to the mythification of his life and work.[38] Unlike King, who
was a Hispanophile interested in every aspect of Spanish cultural production
throughout her career, Porter devoted only a portion of his scholarly career
to Spanish Romanesque art, beginning around 1920 and trailing off after his
first trip to Ireland in 1928. Nevertheless, it was he who made Spanish Romanesque art and architecture seem significant and worthy of widespread
study, in art historical circles in the United States and in Europe.

Born in Stamford in 1883 to an old Connecticut family, Porter lived in a world
of economic privilege.[39] His father, Timothy, had intended to become a minister, but during the Civil War he abandoned the church for the more lucra-
tive career of banking.[40] Kingsley, having prepared at the Browning School in

New York, followed the family tradition of attending Yale like his father; brothers, Blatchly and Louis; and his uncles and cousins.

After his graduation from Yale in 1904, Porter was destined to become a junior partner in the law firm of his brother Louis until his life was derailed by a transcendental experience inspired by an aesthetic encounter with medieval architecture. Unlike Georgiana Goddard King, who confessed her intense personal responses, Porter never publicly disclosed the epiphany that changed his life. It was only revealed after his death in a memorial tribute by his devoted wife, Lucy, who wrote: "One day in front of the Cathedral of Coutances there suddenly 'shined a light round him' and it was if he were in trance. When he awoke he knew he could never be a lawyer."[41]

In the fall of 1904 Porter entered the Columbia School of Architecture instead of his brother's law firm. During his two years there he began researching his first book, *Medieval Architecture: Its Origins and Development,* published in 1909.[42] Except for what he might have learned during his architectural training, Porter had no formal preparation for the book. He was essentially a self-taught amateur. Subsequently, Porter taught art history at Yale intermittently from 1915 to 1919 in the History Department. At the same time he pursued a bachelor of fine arts degree at Yale, which he received in 1917. Finally, Porter settled in Harvard's Department of Fine Arts, where he taught from 1921 to 1933.

In the summer of 1920 Porter visited northern Spain for the first time.[43] He was in the midst of researching his ten-volume *Romanesque Sculpture of the Pilgrimage Roads,* subsequently published in 1923. He invited both Bernard Berenson and Georgiana Goddard King to join him and Lucy on this excursion. His letter of invitation to Berenson clearly reveals that Porter perceives Spain as an art historical wilderness, just waiting to be claimed:

> It would be amusing to follow the route of the Lombard masters, as nearly as convenient, and see what we can see along the road [to Santiago de Compostela]. . . . There are a quantity of glorious things all through the region which I am on fire to see. Possibly you might even be tempted to recross the frontier into Spain. You have recently skimmed the cream, but that country is so little known it might not be an entire waste of time to browse around. I am hopeful that Puig y Cadafach [*sic*] of Barcelona may know of some interesting and unknown things.[44]

Porter's paradoxical wish to know the unknown suggests that knowledge of Spanish monuments on the part of Spanish scholars, such as Puig i Cadafalch, did not really count. Apparently, King's publications had done little to map this virgin territory in Porter's mind, either. For her part King seems to have seen Porter as something of a neophyte. As Berenson had, she declined his offer to travel in Spain. She explained why to Archer Huntington: "Kingsley Porter has invited me to motor with him and his wife for awhile in Spain—but I guess I won't. I want to work, not to instruct. He is very nice but I am too busy."[45]

After his first trip was over, Porter wrote to Berenson with enthusiasm: "The whole thing was an exciting experience, and I feel it has singularly widened for me the Romanesque horizon. I am now at the stage where I begin to realize all the things we didn't see, and all the books we didn't read, so that a return in the near future, with I trust less hurry seems inevitable."[46] Porter did indeed return to Spain, and his visits resulted in seven articles devoted to Spanish medieval art, including his polemical "Spain or Toulouse? And Other Questions" (1924); several chapters of *Romanesque Sculpture of the Pilgrimage Roads* (1923); and *Spanish Romanesque Sculpture* (1928), which he wrote at Berenson's urging.[47] Porter perceived Spain as a place left behind by the modern developments that he believed were destroying the United States. He was drawn to Spain for professional reasons but also by his romantic image of Spain, similar to King's, as timeless and quaint, albeit on the verge of corruption by modernity. This is made abundantly clear in Porter's 1924 description of his visit to the area around Jaca in Aragon: "Jaca turned out to be one of the paradises on earth, as unspoiled as a beneficent God and inspired Middle Ages left it. . . . I fear we saw Jaca about its end. A railway is in construction across the port of Aspe and they are building a great summer hotel and an automobile road to San Juan de la Prua [*sic*] is under construction and other things equally fatal. San Juan itself is in the throes of a restoration which will reduce it to the condition of the alleged medieval monuments of France and Italy."[48]

Within this edenic land Porter fashioned a romanticized role for himself that was as much knight in shining armor, pilgrim, and pioneer as it was scholar. For instance, in his foreword to Mildred Stapely Byne's *The Sculptured Capital in Spain* (1926), he confesses that what has spurred the writing of his text "is the desire to point a moral."[49] His quest is to rescue the "mistreated" art of Spain from the abject position assigned to it by ignorant and prejudicial scholarship. With a romantic self-righteousness and an almost religious zeal, he seeks to right the wrong through impassioned rhetoric like the following: "It turned out that this so-called backward and uncreative race [Spaniards], the artistic dregs of Europe, always incapable of originating and content to lick the platters of more gifted neighbours, had in reality preceded and excelled the rest of the Occident during half of the Middle Ages; that it had been producing architecture of high technical perfection at a time when Italy and France and England and Germany were sunk in barbarism."[50]

The same crusading enthusiasm and self-righteous tone appear in all of Porter's works on Spanish medieval art written throughout the 1920s. For instance, in "Pilgrimage Sculpture" he defends Spanish art from nationalistically biased French scholars, claiming that "if the author was French, he has found at Toulouse originality, power, inventiveness; in Spain thoughtless copying of French motives."[51] In "Spain or Toulouse? And Other Questions," a lengthy review of Emile Mâle's *L'art religieux du XIIe siècle en France,* Porter attacks the French art historian's nationalistic attitude while presenting himself as the noble defender of the innate creativity of Spanish medieval art. He challenges Mâle's conviction that Toulouse was the generating center of Romanesque sculpture, contending that, "where he has written Toulouse we should often rather read Spain or Burgundy."[52] In "The Tomb of Doña Sancha and the Romanesque Art of Aragon" and "Iguácel and More Romanesque Art of Aragon," Porter calls attention to the significance of this previously "unrecognized school of Romanesque art," which in his opinion flourished before that in Toulouse.[53] In this article he is both discoverer and defender.[54] In "Leonesque Romanesque and Southern France," a review of Manuel Gómez-Moreno's *Catálogo monumental de España: Provincia de León,* Porter asserts with confidence, "On the whole, art seems to have flowed from Spain into Roussillon as steadily and overwhelmingly as it did from Spain into Toulouse."[55]

Porter's longer works, *Romanesque Sculpture of the Pilgrimage Roads,* only portions of which were devoted to Spanish art, and *Spanish Romanesque Sculpture,* also promote early dates for Spanish Romanesque sculpture. In these books as in his articles Porter used a conceptual strategy that depended on written documents, detailed comparative visual analyses made on site, and the evidence of abundant photographs to promote his belief in the precocity of Spanish Romanesque and likewise to refute the claims of French archaeologists who held that all Romanesque art originated in southern France.[56] Unlike King, he is little concerned with affect, meaning, or historical context but mainly occupied with dating, classifying, and ordering Spanish Romanesque art in order to establish a chronology that gives Spanish art a place equal to that of France.

Neither book swayed French archaeologists, such as Emile Mâle, Marcel Aubert, or Paul Deschamps, who remained wedded to the belief that Toulouse provided the origin for the alleged revival of monumental sculpture that occurred in the eleventh century. According to Stephen Nichols, French medievalists considered it their patriotic duty to demonstrate the origin of their national identity in both language and art.[57] They were compelled by the desire to fashion a glorious medieval past without rival.[58] In the atmosphere of exaggerated patriotism after World War I, their predisposition to see the origins of Romanesque sculpture in France went unchallenged at home. The extent to which their investment in French primacy was a personal one is revealed in the comment of the eminent French archaeologist Camille Enlart on hearing that Mildred Byne, a friend of Porter's and an amateur historian of Spanish art, had accepted the early dates being assigned to the Asturian churches in Oviedo. Byne relayed Enlart's doleful comment to Porter: "An answer in the affirmative brought from him the following: Eh bien! Si vous avez raison toute ma vie d'archéologue ne compte pour rien" (well then, if you are right, my career as an archaeologist is worthless).[59]

Unlike the French, Porter had no national medieval past to reclaim in honor of his country. His theories about the rise of Romanesque sculpture in southwestern France and northern Spain professed an international spirit that denied the existence of boundaries. In 1923 he suggested that "the art on either side of the frontier [between France and Spain] is precisely the same. One style stretched from Santiago along the pilgrimage road to Toulouse and Moissac and Conques. This art is neither French nor Spanish. It is the art of pilgrimage."[60]

In Porter's conception the pilgrimage to Compostela functioned as a crucible in which a new artistic style was created through the amalgamation of different styles from various origins, as opposed to Mâle's notion of a conduit that delivered fully formed French art into a Spanish cultural wasteland. King held an opinion somewhere between the two. Although she accused some French scholars of exaggerating the amount of French influence in Spain, claiming they could not get "the sound of [their] own town belfry out of [their] ears," she readily acknowledged that French masons and sculptors contributed to the appearance of Spanish Romanesque churches.[61] She believed that "art cannot be imported, only the moulds of it," and that foreign characteristics were soon acculturated and turned into something Spanish.[62]

Although his scholarship was not motivated by overt nationalism as was Mâle's, Porter's national identity played a role in forming his views on Romanesque art. Porter, as I noted earlier, likened the pilgrimage to Santiago to a kind of crucible in which artists from all over Europe met and shared ideas.[63] His notion of the pilgrimage roads as a "melting-pot," in which intercultural exchange produced a new amalgamated art, resembles the way the United States imagined itself during Porter's lifetime, which roughly coincided with the huge influx of immigrants beginning in the 1880s and lasting through the mid-1920s. The term *melting pot,* used to describe the reconfiguring of the U.S. populace during the great wave of immigration, was originated by a play of the same name that was written by Israel Zangwill and performed in both New York City and Washington, D.C., in 1908. It is unclear whether Porter saw the play, but its extensive publicity assured his knowledge of it. Mary, the wife of Porter's friend Bernard Berenson, saw the play in Washington, D.C., seated beside President Roosevelt and Zangwill. Both the Zangwills and the Porters were friends of the Berensons so they may have been acquainted with each other.[64]

In *The Melting-Pot* Zangwill's protagonist, an idealistic Jewish émigré composer, repeatedly describes the United States as "God's Crucible, the great Melting-Pot where all the races of Europe are melting and re-forming!" and "where the roaring fires of God are fusing our race with all others."[65] In the afterword to the 1914 edition Zangwill explained that "the process of American amalgamation is not assimilation or simple surrender to the dominant type as is popularly supposed, but an all-round give-and-take by which the final type may be enriched or impoverished."[66] Porter projected this peculiarly American sense of nationhood onto the formation of Romanesque sculpture. European nationalism may be absent from his texts, but he does not replace it with a neutral internationalism, as is so often suggested. Instead he substitutes a vision of the United States in an act of unconscious cultural imperialism.[67]

At times Georgiana Goddard King also understands Spain in terms of the United States. For instance, she describes the railroad tracks running through the frontier between France and Spain from Bedous to Jaca as having been laid down like the trails of Native Americans, or she compares the Pyrenean pine woods to those in the Adirondacks and the whitewashed halls of an Aragonese spa to nineteenth-century examples in Virginia.[68] She even imagines Santiago de Compostela in terms of a U.S. amusement park, saying: "In the great years, and at the height of the season, this church must have been—God forgive me!—rather like Coney Island . . . immense crowds kept arriving, and tramping through, like a dozen Cook's parties in a day, and everything had to be shown to them, and everything explained."[69] These, however, are specific one-to-one comparisons that inform the foreign by illustrating it in terms of the familiar, and they do not serve as the basis for any of the paradigms that shape the larger issues of King's work.

Like King, Porter often combines the notions of scholarly investigation and pilgrimage. In *Romanesque Sculpture of the Pilgrimage Roads* he states: "The modern pilgrim to Santiago journeys those long, but delicious kilometers, not entirely, nor even chiefly, to admire the miracles of scholarship already performed, nor even in the hope (inevitably present, however fatuous) of himself assisting at others. One feels, as nowhere else, wrapped about by the beauty of the Middle Ages. One is, as perhaps never before, emotionally and intellectually stimulated."[70]

These statements imply that, for Porter, scholarly production was not the only goal. Experiencing the transcendental and transformative power of the art of the Middle Ages was equal in significance. His desire for this spiritualizing exercise should come as little surprise, considering that an epiphanic experience initiated his career as an architectural historian.

The powerful appeal of the medieval and Spain was to some extent grounded in the national identity of King and Porter. From earlier generations of Americans they inherited an understanding of Spain as picturesque and as a place where the sublime and the exotic could be experienced in the everyday. The first wave of U.S. intellectual interest in Spanish culture, history, politics, and literature reached its apex in the 1820s and 1830s.[71] Americans of this era came to know Spanish culture through travel books such as Henry Wadsworth Longfellow's *Outre-Mer* (1833–34); Washington Irving's *Legends of the Alhambra* (1832), and Caleb Cushing's *Reminiscences of Spain, the County, Its People, History, and Monuments* (1833).[72] These established for Americans, albeit mainly those in New England, a paradigm of a romanticized Spain that was charmingly backward and still slightly tinged by the vestiges of an orientalized past. For instance, in *Outre-Mer* Longfellow explores the Spanish character, informing his readers that Spaniards are generous, dignified, and religious but also ignorant, melancholy, slovenly, and superstitious.[73] In *The Legends of the Alhambra* Washington Irving intertwines the last poignant moments of Spain's Islamic past with colorful folk tales and his observations of contemporary Spain, which he represents as quaint and unmarred by modern notions of progress. These writers establish an epistemological claim for Spain as exotic and charmingly backward but therefore a place of uncommon authenticity—a place where "real life" could still be observed.[74]

Irving, with *The Life and Voyages of Christopher Columbus* (1828) and *The Conquest of Granada* (1829), and William H. Prescott, with *The History of Ferdinand and Isabella* (1837), introduced Americans to Spanish history. George Ticknor did the same for Spanish letters with his *History of Spanish Literature* (1849). Prescott, according to Richard Kagan, established a dominant paradigm that understood Spain as backward as juxtaposed to a progressive United States.[75] Columbus, for these nineteenth-century scholars, was the connection that intimately linked the destinies of Spain and America. This ostensible connection and his more progressive national image were the factors that gave Prescott the confidence to be the first U.S. scholar to write a new history of a country other than his own and Ticknor to be the first American to write a critical survey of a European literature.[76] Both scholars understood Spain as a once fertile but now fallow field, abandoned and readily available for plowing. While their attempts at chronicling Spanish literature and history were scholarly, they were not free from romantic attitudes, especially concerning the Middle Ages, as Kagan has ably demonstrated.

Unlike their compatriots of earlier generations, it was northern more than southern Spain, and the earlier rather than the late Middle Ages that interested Porter and King, but their attitudes retained much in common with the U.S. scholars of the previous century. Coincidentally, like Ticknor and Prescott, these fledgling art historians formulated a new discipline with the raw material provided by the past of Spain, the only European nation with a distinguished artistic past so lacking in modernity that it could still be construed as a frontier.

Although rigorous in their art historical investigations, neither King nor Porter questioned their presuppositions about the country they visited. The yearning for romance that attracted them to the Iberian Peninsula is also what drew them to study the art of the Middle Ages. According to T. J. Jackson Lears, late nineteenth- and early twentieth-century American enthusiasm for the Middle Ages arose from antimodernist sentiments that encouraged an idealized view of the medieval spirit as childlike in its innocence, vitality, and lack of ethical confusion. For the affluent white educated class of old-stock eastern elites to which Porter and King belonged, the perceived authenticity and unambivalent faith of the Middle Ages provided a cultivated safe haven from the aggressive, less refined, contingent, and industrial society emerging around the turn of the century.

Porter and King were constantly eager to look over the next hill and around the next mountain, both literally and figuratively, in terms of the art historical field. Both were moved to discover unpublished monuments and to break new ground. Metaphors of the pioneer and the frontier surface frequently in contemporary assessments of the careers of King and Porter. John Beckwith, for instance, wrote a review of Porter's books entitled "Kingsley Porter: Blazing the Trail in Europe," and one of King's obituaries twice refers to her as a pioneer. While these references are essentially poetic, they point the way toward another motivation behind Porter's and King's interest in the art of medieval Spain.

King, born in 1871, and Porter in 1883 experienced one of the most significant shifts in Americans' understanding of their national identity, the closing of the American frontier. The 1890 census reported that the United States no longer possessed a frontier—a western boundary where civilization met the wilderness. At the World's Columbian Exposition of 1893, Frederick Jackson Turner, one of the nation's foremost historians, whose late career overlapped with the beginning of Porter's at Harvard, addressed the significance of the frontier and its closing in the formation of U.S. culture. He asserted that the most significant factor in the forming of an American national identity was the constant westward movement of the frontier.[77] According to Turner, the challenges of life on the untamed frontier forged Europeans into independent, self-reliant Americans whose intellects were characterized by the strength, practicality, restless nervous energy, dominant individualism, buoyancy, and the exuberance that comes with freedom.[78]

With the frontier at home closed, U.S. art historians of Porter's and King's generation could have been seeking for one elsewhere. The rugged landscape of the Pyrenees, frequented by U.S. art historians studying medieval Spain during the teens and twenties, was as sparsely populated and physically daunting as any spot in the newly tamed American West. There lay a scholarly field virtually untilled, full of unknown monuments just waiting to be explored.

Porter was drawn repeatedly to inaccessible places and the marginal areas of his discipline. For instance, before turning to medieval Spain, he was preoccupied with the early Romanesque buildings of northern Italy; afterward he was lured by the even remoter beauties of the Donegal wilds, where he disappeared without a trace in 1933. He consciously aspired to be a trailblazer. In 1923 he admits to Berenson, "The delight of discovery is for me one of the keenest. I fear I find a certain satisfaction in feeling that no one has been before me."[79] The sad dilemma into which such sentiments eventually led him are evident in the draft of a letter written to two of his colleagues in which he expresses his desire to resign his Harvard post, declaring: "With the great development of archaeology in the last few years the complexion of things has changed. It is no longer a field for a pioneer, but for co-operative production. The peculiar advantages I once possessed no longer count."[80] In his nostalgia for the days when he could move alone and freely into an unpopulated intellectual territory, constantly discovering monuments unknown to art historians, Porter echoed a loss felt by many Americans at the closing of the western frontier. Like Turner describing the end of the availability of free land in the Wild West, Porter seems to express a conviction that the experience that produced him was no longer available to others. When he could no longer be the first to till the soil, he withdrew from the field.

The Spanish Civil War (1936–39) and subsequently Franco's repressive fascist regime all but halted U.S. art historical interest in medieval Spain until the 1970s. By the time the civil war broke out, Porter had been missing for three years and King, already in poor health, had turned to Portugal. Ironically, Walter W. S. Cook (1888–1962), who followed King and Porter to the Iberian Peninsula in the 1920s in search of unknown medieval frescoes, panel paintings, and altar frontals, contributed further to the decline in interest in medieval Spain. As the administrator of New York University's Institute of Fine Arts, established in 1932, Cook hired German émigrés, such as Erwin Panofsky, Walter Friedlaender, Karl Lehmann, and Richard Krautheimer, after the Nuremberg Decrees in 1933 forced Jewish academics from their posts in Germany.[81] Long past its formative stage, the art history that the Germans brought with them was uniform in the canon of works that merited study and in its belief in the existence of objective, scientific methods. Their Old World sophistication, multilingualism, erudition, and confidence in the precision of their methods held an overwhelming appeal for the U.S. art historical community. In no time their regimented discipline supplanted the amateurish art history of King and Porter. For the transplanted Germans, whose methods and preferences dominated the field until the late 1970s, medieval Spain held no interest.

They ignored King's scholarship. Her facile ability to shift from the present to the past, and from the personal to the objective, led at least one later art historian to dismiss her work as "stream of consciousness" scholarship.[82] Her personal accounts were not seen as a means to the significant but as unmethodical, unobjective, and therefore invalid. Porter's reputation fared somewhat better. His scholarship, enmeshed with that of eminent European art historians such as Paul Deschamps and Emile Mâle, was part of the mainstream discourse on the formation of Romanesque sculpture. While most scholars have rejected his early dates for Spanish monuments, his books continue to be valued for the encyclopedic scope of their excellent photographs, and some of the paradigms he established continue to shape the field. Examining the pilgrimage roads as a site of extraordinary artistic creation, whether the inception of this paradigm is credited to King or Porter, remains a vital way of shaping the study of Romanesque architecture and sculpture of Spain, France, and Italy.

Notes

1. For the first decades of art history in the United States, see Craig Hugh Smyth and Peter M. Lukehart, eds., *The Early Years of Art History in the United States* (Princeton, N.J.: Princeton University Press, 1993); Erwin Panofsky, "Three Decades of Art History in the United States," in *Meaning in the Visual Arts* (1955; rpt., Chicago: University of Chicago Press, 1982), 321–46; Colin Eisler, "*Kunstgeschichte* American Style: A Study in Migration," in *The Intellectual Migration*, ed. Donald Fleming and Bernard Bailyn (Cambridge, Mass.: Harvard University Press, 1969), 544–629; and James S. Ackerman and Rhys Carpenter, *Art and Archaeology* (Englewood Cliffs, N.J.: Prentice Hall, 1963).

2. Panofsky, "Three Decades of Art History," 327, 329.

3. Ackerman referred to the scholars of this era as the "second generation" of art historians in the United States (James Ackerman, "Art History in America," in Ackerman and Carpenter, *Art and Archaeology,* 191).

4. Panofsky, "Three Decades of Art History," 327–28.

5. Sweeping negative comments like the following were common before the turn of the century: "There is nothing in Spanish painting until the time of Velásquez and the school terminates with Murillo. Sculpture does not flourish at all and architecture is borrowed" (Daniel Cady Eaton, "Lectures on Italian Painting and Art," cited in Priscilla Hiss and Roberta Fansler, *Research in the Fine Arts in the Colleges and Universities of the United States* [New York: Carnegie, 1934], 48).

6. See T. J. Jackson Lears, *No Place of Grace: Antimodernism and the Transformation of American Culture, 1880–1920* (1981; rpt., Chicago: University of Chicago Press, 1994).

7. For a complete biography of King see Susanna Terrell Saunders, "Georgiana Goddard King (1871–1939): Educator and Pioneer in Medieval Spanish Art," in *Women as Interpreters of the Visual Arts, 1820–1979*, ed. Claire Richter Sherman with Adele M. Holcomb (Westport, Conn.: Greenwood, 1981), 209–38.

8. H.F.F., "Miss King to Return to Live in Bryn Mawr," *College News*, February 24, 1937, 3.

9. Ibid.

10. Harold Wethey commented that "*The Way of Saint James* is the most complete expression of the author's mind and personality; it is a cloth woven of her numerous and varied interests, interests which she transformed into something peculiarly her own through the creative powers of her imagination" (Wethey, "An American Pioneer in Hispanic Studies: Georgiana Goddard King," *Parnassus* 11 [November 1939]: 33).

11. Five years earlier she had already begun to explore how the pilgrimage routes led French and Lombard masons and sculptors into Spain in search of employment. See Georgiana Goddard King, "French Figure Sculpture on Some Early Spanish Churches," *American Journal of Archaeology* 19 (1915): 250–67.

12. In 1919 and 1920 King and Lowber traveled in Spain at the expense of the Hispanic Society. King was paid $3,500 for her research and writing, and Lowber was paid $1,000 for her photographs (Georgiana Goddard King to Archer Milton Huntington, April 16, 1919, unpublished letter in King file, Hispanic Society of America [hereafter cited as HSA]).

13. Rhys Carpenter described King's process of scholarship by saying that King "believed the scholar's function to be one of creative reinterpretation, a personal revitalization of all that had lapsed into the inanimateness of the past" (Carpenter, "Faculty Tribute to Miss King," *Bryn Mawr Alumnae Bulletin*, June 1939, p. 8).

14. See Janice Mann, "Romantic Identity, Nationalism, and the Understanding of the Advent of Romanesque Art in Christian Spain," *Gesta* 36 (1997): 156–65.

15. Joseph Bediér first presented his ideas in lectures in 1904 and 1905 and subsequently in the four volumes of *Les légendes épiques*, published between 1908 and 1914. King quotes a long passage from the third volume of this work, which discusses how the *Chanson de Roland* reflects a knowledge of the pilgrimage to Santiago de Compostela (Georgiana Goddard King, *The Way of Saint James*, 3 vols. [New York: Hispanic Society of America, 1920], 1:30–31).

16. In an article published during the years that King was working on *The Way*, she wrote, "Where the Romans marched, ran the roads of the Middle Age, and there, today, the railways lay down their lines of steel. That, for instance, which runs from Salamanca to Astorga, keeps yet, for the traveler, a curious frontier feeling. To the right lies all of known Spain; to the left, mountains and then something vaguely imagined as Portuguese. Just so the road, which it scarcely supersedes, will have felt to Ferdinand the Great, and his ill-fated son, King Sancho, and his ill-used daughters Doña Urraca

and Doña Elvira" (Georgiana Goddard King, "Early Churches in Spain," *Journal of the American Institute of Architects* 6 [1918]: 559).

17. King, *The Way,* 1:165.

18. Ibid., 1:169.

19. Ibid., 1:3, 17–18.

20. See especially her description in volume 1 of a mass in the cathedral (27–33).

21. For example, see vol. 1, pp. 143–44.

22. She states, "Paleolithic man had moved along it, and the stations of a living devotion today he had frequented" (King, *The Way,* 1:22).

23. She described Spain in *Heart of Spain* as a place where "time has no power upon her beauty, which was ordained before time was. The twilight of the ages is luminous upon her; she broods, aloof and fair, a place of enchantments" (Georgiana Goddard King, *Heart of Spain* [Cambridge, Mass.: Harvard University Press, 1941], 67).

24. King, *The Way,* 1:22.

25. Ibid., 1:24–25.

26. Ibid., 3:23.

27. Ibid., 1:407.

28. Ibid., 2:66–67.

29. "Three days out, he mentioned that his friends all said a woman who would go off that way was not worth . . . I never quite made out the phrase, though I have heard it, first and last, three times or four, but spoken always rapidly, and under the breath. The idea is, that she could not be worth much. In fine, he was fatally compromised by coming. Then I turned in the saddle and laughed 'Boy,' said I, 'I am forty-two, old enough to be your mother. I can't compromise you, nor you me'" (King, *The Way,* 2:380).

30. Ibid., 1:261.

31. "Pilgrims of Saint James," *London Times Literary Supplement,* December 30, 1920, p. 890.

32. King, *The Way,* 1:iii.

33. Ibid., 1:iv, 3.

34. Ibid., 1:22.

35. Delphine Fitz Darby to Suzanne Lindsay, May 27, 1989, University Archives, Canaday Library, Bryn Mawr College.

36. King to Gertrude Stein, November 25, 1927, Gertrude Stein and Alice B. Toklas Collection, Yale Collection of American Literature, Beinecke Rare Book and Manuscript Library, Yale University.

37. For comments on the development of Porter's legend, see Linda Seidel, "Arthur Kingsley Porter: Life, Legend, and Legacy," in Smyth and Lukehart, *Early Years of Art History,* 97–110.

38. Ibid., 97.

39. Porter was descended from Daniel Porter, who came to the United States from England around 1640. "Arthur Kingsley Porter," *The National Cyclopedia of American Biography,* 62 vols. (New York: James T. White, 1898–1984), 40:572–73.

40. "Louis Hopkins Porter," *National Cyclopedia of American Biography*, 35:169.

41. Lucy Kingsley Porter, "A. Kingsley Porter," *Medieval Studies in Memory of A. Kingsley Porter*, ed. Wilhelm R. W. Koehler (Cambridge, Mass.: Harvard University Press, 1939), xi. Coincidentally, Henry Adams was also extremely moved by Coutances. He wrote, "No other cathedral in France or Europe has an interior more refined—one is tempted to use the hard-worn adjective, more tender—or more carefully studied" (Henry Adams, *Mont Saint-Michel and Chartres* [1904; rpt., New York: Houghton Mifflin, 1933], 50). It is unlikely that Porter had seen *Mont Saint-Michel and Chartres* because it originally was published in a very limited edition.

42. A. Kingsley Porter, *Medieval Architecture: Its Origins and Development*, 2 vols. (New York: Baker and Taylor, 1909). Porter says he actually wrote the book as a full-time occupation between 1906 and 1909 (*Sexennial Record of the Class of 1904, Yale College*, ed. G. Elton Parks [New Haven, Conn.: Yale University Press, 1911], 204).

43. Porter informed Bernard Berenson that he had decided to accept the job offered him by Harvard but with some mixed feelings, saying, "As I see things, an official position, like a social background (or what passes for such) or a real reputation, is of value in that it does save time and energy which would otherwise be wasted in the effort to assert one's self. But this official label of an university position is bought only at the price of time and energy. How does the balance stand?" (Arthur Kingsley Porter to Bernard Berenson, January 9, 1920, Harvard University Archives [hereafter cited as HUA]; all quotations from Porter's correspondence appear courtesy of the Harvard University Archives).

44. Porter to Berenson, January 14, 1920, HUA.

45. King to Archer Huntington, April 1, 1920, HSA.

46. Porter to Berenson, July 26, 1920, HUA.

47. Porter wrote to Berenson, "You have done lots of nice things to me, but never anything for which I am more grateful than pushing me into the Spanish Romanesque field once more. I have seldom worked at anything with such breathless interest as this new book" (Porter to Berenson, November 11, 1925, HUA).

48. Porter to Berenson, May 24, 1924, HUA.

49. A. Kingsley Porter, foreword to Mildred Stapely Byne, *The Sculptured Capital in Spain* (New York: W. Helburn: 1926), 5.

50. Ibid., 8.

51. A. Kingsley Porter, "Pilgrimage Sculpture," *American Journal of Archaeology*, 2d ser., 26 (1922): 7–8.

52. A. Kingsley Porter, "Spain or Toulouse? And Other Questions," *Art Bulletin* 7 (1924): 4.

53. A. Kingsley Porter, "The Tomb of Doña Sancha and the Romanesque Art of Aragon," *Burlington Magazine* 45 (1924): 165–79, and "Iguácel and More Romanesque Art of Aragon," *Burlington Magazine* 52 (1928): 115–27.

54. Porter casts himself in the role of the discoverer of both the Doña Sancha sarcophagus (although he acknowledges it is known in Spain) and Nuestra Señora de Iguácel.

55. A. Kingsley Porter, "Leonesque Romanesque and Southern France," *Art Bulletin* 8 (1926): 250.

56. Berenson may have introduced Porter to detailed Morellian analysis as the basis for deducing observations about style and authorship. [Editor's note: The Italian art historian Giovanni Morelli formulated this particular mode of analysis in his *Della pittura italiani: Studi storico critici—Le gallerie Borgehese e Doria Pamphelli en Roma* (1897).] Although they had corresponded since 1917, Porter and Berenson did not meet until 1919. Around this time Porter grew less interested in architecture and more interested in pictorial art.

57. Stephen Nichols, "Modernism and the Politics of Medieval Studies," in *Medievalism and the Modernist Temper,* ed. Howard Bloch and Stephen Nichols (Baltimore: Johns Hopkins University Press, 1996), 32.

58. See my comments on Emile Mâle in "Romantic Identity," 61.

59. Mildred Stapely Byne to Arthur Kingsley Porter, September 27, 1922, HUA.

60. A. Kingsley Porter, *Romanesque Sculpture of the Pilgrimage Roads,* 3 vols. (1923; rpt., New York: Hacker Art Books, 1969), 1:193, and "Pilgrimage Sculpture," 1n.1.

61. King, *The Way,* 1:10.

62. Georgiana Goddard King, *Pre-Romanesque Churches of Spain* (Bryn Mawr, Pa.: Bryn Mawr College, 1924), 205.

63. A. Kingsley Porter, "Rise of Romanesque Sculpture," *American Journal of Archaeology,* 2d. ser., 22 (1918): 422.

64. Ernest Samuels, *Bernard Berenson: The Making of Legend* (Cambridge, Mass.: Harvard University Press, 1987), 67.

65. Israel Zangwill, *The Melting-Pot* (New York: Macmillan, 1924), 33, 95.

66. Ibid., 203.

67. In the mid-1920s Porter moved away from the "melting-pot" concept and toward the "generating center" as a way of explaining the advent of some Romanesque art. He claimed the school of Aragon, although showing some outside influence, was "essentially local and autochthonic." His comments about León as a center of artistic creation that radiated influence almost echo those of Mâle about Toulouse. He writes, for instance: "One suspects indeed that León was the artistic focus of Spain. . . . And one even suspects that it was the artistic focus of considerably more than Spain," and "throughout the entire eleventh and part of the twelfth century the great current of art in Europe is moving from the south to the north" (Porter, "Tomb of Doña Sancha," 175, and "Leonesque Romanesque," 236, 250).

68. King, *The Way,* 1:144–45, 175, 205.

69. Ibid., 3:173.

70. Porter, *Romanesque Sculpture of the Pilgrimage Roads,* 1:171.

71. Norman P. Tucker, *Americans in Spain: Patriots, Expatriates, and the Early American Hispanists, 1780–1850.* (Boston: Boston Athenaeum, 1980), 1.

72. For a more comprehensive view see Stanley T. Williams, *The Spanish Background of American Literature,* 2 vols. (New Haven, Conn.: Yale University Press, 1955).

73. Henry Wadsworth Longfellow, *Outre-Mer and Drift-Wood*, vol. 7 of *The Works of Henry Wadsworth Longfellow* (Boston: Houghton Mifflin, 1910), 140–41.

74. Longfellow stated, "There is so little change in Spanish character, that you find everything as it is said to have been two hundred years ago" (*The Letters of Henry Wadsworth Longfellow*, ed. Andrew Hilen, 6 vols., [Cambridge, Mass.: Belknap Press of Harbard University Press, 1967], cited in Richard L. Kagan, "Prescott's Paradigm: American Historical Scholarship and the Decline of Spain," *American Historical Review* 101 [April 1996]: 426).

75. Kagan, "Prescott's Paradigm," 430.

76. Ibid., 423, 432.

77. Richard White has noted how Turner defined U.S. culture as progressive like the westward-moving frontier but that progress was achieved paradoxically by repeatedly moving from civilization into the primitive wilderness (White, "Frederick Jackson Turner and Buffalo Bill," in *The Frontier in American Culture*, ed. James R. Grossman [Berkeley: University of California Press, 1994], 25).

78. Frederick Jackson Turner, *The Frontier in American History* (1920; rpt., Tucson: University of Arizona Press, 1986), 37.

79. Porter to Berenson, autumn 1923, HUA.

80. Porter to Edward Forbes and Paul Sachs, August 29, 1929, HUA.

81. See Harry Bober, "The Gothic Tower and the Stork Club," *Arts and Sciences* 1 (1962): 2.

82. John Williams, cited by Saunders in "Georgiana Goddard King," 231.

7

Before the Latin Tinge: Spanish Music and the "Spanish Idiom" in the United States, 1778–1940

Louise K. Stein

In a letter to an Italian correspondent in 1778, Thomas Jefferson complained that though music was "the favorite passion of my soul . . . fortune has cast my lot in a country where it is in a state of deplorable barbarism."[1] Jefferson was not alone; two other seriously musical founders, John Adams and Benjamin Franklin, along with a number of other leading citizens through to the mid-nineteenth century, also noted that the pursuit of a musically sophisticated American high culture had fallen to the side of the road that led to political independence and much-valued "progress."[2] "Civilized behavior and liberty coexist with great difficulty," commented an early nineteenth-century French visitor to Philadelphia, after an evening at the theater. This perception of a conflict between Old World elegance and American democratic rusticity, between bracing American rationalist progress in government and industry and "barbarism" in the arts,[3] seems to have persisted as a troubling dichotomy in the long period in which the Republic's musical life lacked anything like the systems of patronage and supportive social and economic structures that remunerated musical performance and composition in Europe. Fundamental aspects of the reception history of musical repertories in the United States are bound up with the somewhat conflicted history of "art" or "classical" music (musical composition, performance, patronage, administration, and reception) as an American phenomenon.[4]

Though Jefferson and his colleagues most likely did not know it, the first music of European extraction to be heard in North America was undoubtedly Spanish—military music and Latin-texted sacred music, both plainchant and polyphony, as performed and taught by mid-sixteenth-century Spanish missionaries to Native Americans in the southwestern regions of what became the United States. At the same time the reports of Spanish clerics contain the first European descriptions of the musical instruments and musical performance in the culture of Native Americans.[5] The earliest Spanish missions to include musical training of the natives were established in what is today New Mexico. The missionaries established a network of about twenty-five missions by the end of the seventeenth century, the sites for the earliest European musical pedagogy in North America. The missionaries taught Roman Catholic sacred music (with Latin and Spanish texts) that included the vernacular *villancicos* and perhaps even secular songs and instrumental music in areas of the southern and southwestern United States (Florida, Texas, New Mexico, and, after 1769, southern California) through the eighteenth and early nineteenth centuries.

In contrast, during the colonial and revolutionary eras the musical life of the cities along the eastern seacoast, and later of the Midwest, emulated English and French musical centers, while musical education was tied closely to Protestant religious practice and fomented by the many "singing societies" that were founded to strengthen piety and devotion through community-based musical experience. From about 1730 there are records of public concerts and musical theater in the colonies, though preachers viewed secular musical performance warily, and it was largely in the hands of "immigrant professionals and gentleman amateurs."[6] Nevertheless, eighteenth-century Americans danced to the same French minuets and gavottes that were enjoyed in London or at Madrid, Versailles, and other European courts. But the scope of professional music making in North America was anything but lavish. Musicians in North America worked as performers and teachers in a public marketplace where their survival depended on attracting paying customers. The musical life of the courts and cathedrals in the Spanish colonies in Latin America (where the Church, the municipal governments, and the viceregal courts and aristocratic households employed musicians) was undoubtedly more elaborate, if less democratic, than that of colonial and revolutionary America. For example, while large-scale court operas in Spanish and Italian had already been performed in Lima and in Mexico City before 1715, only ballad opera, a particularly British and nonspectacular kind of partly sung middle-class musical theater on a smaller scale, flourished in the North American colonies as an "unpretentious entertainment with simple songs, enjoyable to all."[7]

Writing from his newly declared democracy, Benjamin Franklin was aware of the difficulties inherent in the emulation of a "superior" musical culture, when he noted in a letter of 1775 to a Spanish prince, the Infante don Gabriel Antonio de Borbón:

... as yet the Muses have scarcely visited these remote Regions. Perhaps, however, the Proceedings of our American Congress, just published, may be a subject of some curiosity at your Court. I therefore take the Liberty of sending your Highness a Copy, with some other Papers, which contain Accounts of the successes wherewith Providence has lately favoured us. Therein your wise Politicians may contemplate the first efforts of a rising State, which seems likely soon to act a part of some Importance on the stage of human affairs. . . .[8]

In Franklin's day evidence for a positive reading of Spain's contribution to the history of music had been provided in the brief section on Spain offered in *A General History of Music* (1789) by the English writer Charles Burney (acknowledged as the first modern musicologist), in his evaluation of sixteenth-century sacred music in Europe. Burney had similarly considered sixteenth-century English, German, French, Italian, and Dutch sacred music. His contemporary John Hawkins (*A General History of the Science and Practice of Music,* London 1771) was perhaps more representative of the uninformed majority, stating that Spaniards had made "a slow progress" as musicians— an opinion that Burney countered with a full seven pages about late fifteenth- and sixteenth-century Spanish composers and musical theorists.[9] His principal factual source was the *De musica libri septem* (1577) of Francisco Salinas, the learned humanist professor of music at the University of Salamanca. Burney rightly credited Salinas with original contributions to musical humanism (the rediscovery and understanding of ancient Greek music) and reproduced examples from Salinas's important section on classical and Spanish poetic meters in music. While Burney enjoyed only limited access to Spanish musical sources, beyond the published treatises and printed musical anthologies he could find in London or studied during his extensive travels, he cited the numerous Spanish singers who had swelled the ranks of the papal chapels in Rome as evidence that Spain's contributions to sixteenth-century musical life in Europe had not been "scanty" at all.[10] He knew enough of Spanish sacred music to cite works by the most prominent Spanish composers of that period (such as Cristóbal Morales, Francisco Guerrero, and Tomás Luis de Victoria), though the only Spanish musical examples published in this part of *A General History of Music* were taken from Salinas's treatise. Though Burney wrote a "general history of music for British readers," and not a "universal history for an international audience," educated music lovers in the United States from the 1780s on into the early nineteenth century surely would have known Burney's work.[11] But Burney's case for Spain's musical history was built on his appreciation for the learnedness of its musical Renaissance (music historians refer to the fifteenth and sixteenth centuries with the term *Renaissance*) and accomplishments in Roman Catholic sacred music. Thus his appreciation might have been lost on many readers in North America, where musical life was shaped by Anglo-Germanic Protestantism.

The extent to which Spanish music was heard by eighteenth- and nineteenth-century U.S. audiences outside the Southwest has not been thoroughly researched. It is possible, and to my mind likely, that Spanish dances and ballads traveled north and east with the ubiquitous Spanish guitar (*guitarra española*), as they had traveled back and forth between the Hispanic New World and the old, as well as around Europe, in the late sixteenth, seventeenth, and early eighteenth centuries.[12] However, most historians of the instrument take mentions of the guitar in early to mid-eighteenth-century North American documents to be references to the English guitar ("gittar"), or cittern, a wire-strung instrument with a different tuning and technique.[13] For example, among the works collected or composed by William Selby from London (organist of the King's Chapel in Boston from 1782) and published in *The New Minstrel*, a musical publication for which he sought subscriptions in 1782, and his now lost *Apollo and the Muse's Musical Compositions*, were sonatas for flute and concerted pieces for violin, both with "guitar" accompaniment.[14] Slightly later in Philadelphia, the French composer and cellist Henri Capron gave concerts on the guitar and taught "ladies and gentlemen in the art of singing and playing on the Spanish and English guitars, recording the most approved method of the finest masters in Europe." The guitar was easy to tune and to carry around, and it was "now considered not only as a desirable but as a fashionable instrument."[15]

This vogue for the guitar in the United States coincided with what was happening in Europe, where Spanish popular songs and dances had become quite the rage in easy arrangements as salon pieces. In Boston between 1798 and 1802 a Mr. Francis Mallet offered music lessons on the "English and Spanish" guitars, as did Dr. George K. Jackson in 1812, M. Antoine Mathieu in 1818 (he also sold Spanish cigars), and Luke Eastman in 1819.[16] In early nineteenth-century Boston, where the guitar was heard frequently in concerts as an accompanying instrument, the "Spanish guitar" was a featured novelty in concerts by a visiting Italian musician, Signor Pucci, in 1814.[17] The emblematic "genuineness" of Spanish guitar music brought the instrument "into the circle of fashion" in Europe, especially in France, and this fashion spread to the United States.[18] Farther west, in cowboy lands and lore "from Texas to California, guitars of the open range frequently had Spanish antecedents."[19] The first guitar manual published in North America appeared in 1820 in Charleston, South Carolina, and included instructions on the Spanish and English guitars.[20]

By 1846, more than a decade after the priests had been sent back to Spain and the missions of the Southwest closed down, the "musical activity in the

[Spanish] settlements had ceased." Nevertheless, "Spanish-language singing traditions flourished as separate and distinct from the English-language ones" in the American Southwest in the late nineteenth and early twentieth centuries.[21] In California in the last decades of the nineteenth century "before the Gringo Came," according to the journalist and music-lover Charles Lummis:

> . . . there was no paying $5 to be seen chattering in satin while some Diva sang her highest. There was no Grand Opera—and no fool songs. There were Songs of the Soil, and songs of poets and of troubadours, in this far, lone, beautiful, happy land; and songs that came over from Mother Spain and up from Step-mother Mexico. . . . The Folksong of the Spanish blood—whether in the old Peninsula, or in the New World that Spain gave to the Old—has a particular fascination, a naïveté, and yet a vividness and life, a richness of melody, with a certain resilience and willfulness—that give it a pre-eminent appeal. It has more Music in it—more Rhythm, more Grace.[22]

Working between about 1885 and 1904 in New Mexico and California, Lummis recorded about three hundred songs in Spanish with guitar accompaniment, and these were transcribed in 1904–5 by the composer and music critic Arthur Farwell (another visitor from the East Coast).[23] Lummis and Farwell published only fourteen of the songs, with piano accompaniment and English translations for the lyrics, in their anthology of *Spanish Songs of Old California* (1923). These songs have been recently characterized as having spicy triplet rhythms and an ethos devoted to the contemplation of pleasure and sensual enjoyment. For Richard Crawford their aesthetic, and the dramatic "closeness of love and death" that they reveal, was the antithesis to the idealized Victorian slant of most of the English lyrics of songs of the late nineteenth-century United States.[24]

In the first two decades of the twentieth century, a few folklorists in addition to Lummis were collecting and publishing Spanish-texted songs in the United States. Publishing in 1917, Eleanor Hague recalled that J. F. McCoy had issued ten Spanish songs as sheet music in Santa Barbara; Sturgis and Blake had published *Songs of the Pyrenees* in Boston and New York; and sheet music was to be found "in any music store" for two songs of Spanish America, "La paloma" and "La golondrina." Hague listed a few other songs available in the United States and noted in her collection *Spanish-American Folk-Songs*, "I have been able to trace only five of these melodies back to Spain; but I do not like to say positively that more of them might not be found in the mother country, although I have searched diligently through many volumes of Spanish folk-music."[25] The "many volumes" that Hague consulted in her search for the Iberian musical roots of the songs, however, were published in Madrid or Paris, where collections of Spanish songs were still enjoying a certain vogue. In New

York in 1918 Carl Van Vechten, a music critic fascinated with Spanish music, suggested another source of Spanish folk songs: the "Spanish catalogue of the Victor Phonograph Company offers a splendid opportunity for the study of Spanish and gipsy folk-music . . . even gipsy songs, conceived in esoteric scales, sung by gipsies, accompanied by the guitar."[26] Spanish songs sounded "a world of romantic adventure" for Lummis, for Eleanor Hague, and for others who compiled such anthologies.[27] It was probably also true for those who bought them and learned something about Spanish music from them in the 1920s and beyond. Invoking the stereotypes of the audible landscape through the "land of Coronado, de Vargas, Alvarado, De Vaca, Oñate, Fray Marcos and the heroic Father Serra," a later anthologizer asked, "Who can resist the plaintive harmonies of the guitar, the haunting love story poured out in song?"[28]

An exoticized "Spanish idiom" with popular or folkloric gestures and guitar-inspired sounds was most likely already familiar to Americans in the mid-nineteenth century (even outside the Southwest). It became an identifiable part of U.S. art music in the works of the composer and piano virtuoso Louis Moreau Gottschalk (1829–69), whose "Spanish idiom" was designed to be novel and evocative. Gottschalk grew up in New Orleans but made the obligatory voyage to the European home of "cultivated music" as a young man, when he studied and performed in Paris from 1842 to 1853. As early as 1845 he had begun to borrow from American Negro music in his piano pieces "to achieve local color."[29] Gottschalk performed for Queen Isabel II of Spain before he was ever heard in Chicago, but this should be no surprise. European success was essential for the legitimation of U.S. musicians. Back home there just was not much of a concert scene for Gottschalk to participate in. The United States was still viewed as a place rife with invention in industry and agriculture but not the arts.[30] About the same time that Gottschalk began to think about leaving Europe, in 1853, a New York critic reviewing an orchestral concert noted, "With encouragement, America can produce musical wonders as well as reaping machines."[31] In 1851 the influential French composer Hector Berlioz admired the "nonchalant grace of tropical melody" in Gottschalk's piano fantasies, acknowledging that exotic American elements fed what Berlioz termed the European "passion for novelty."[32] Gottschalk also composed music based on tunes he encountered on his concert tours, especially Cuban sounds and melodies from the West Indies and after his tour of Spain in 1851–52 composed some "Spanish" pieces with evocative sounds and titles: *El sitio de Zaragoza*, *La jota aragonesa*, *Marcha real española*, *Manchega*, *Canto del gitano*, and *Minuit à Seville*.[33]

U.S. concert audiences heard "Spanish" music as interpreted through the filter of performances by non-Spaniards, among them an Italian known as

Pucci, the Frenchman Capron, and the American-born Gottschalk; and the first ballads in Spanish published in the United States reached performers in the deliberately but dubiously "authentic" versions arranged for voice and piano by the U.S. composer Arthur Farwell. Pucci's concerts and other such performances of Hispanic music in the young republic may have been mere novelty shows, but this raises an important point: it was precisely the novelty, exoticism, and sensual color of Hispanic music and of the virtuoso Spanish guitar repertory that brought "the Spanish sound" to the attention of impresarios, performers, conductors, and audiences in North America. Even for musicians who admired and cultivated the Hispanic idiom, such as Lummis and Farwell, the lure of the Spanish sound was its association with "romantic adventure." The very novelty that Europeans found attractive in Gottschalk's deliberately American pieces was contributed by their perceived authenticity: here was a real live visitor from the New World performing art music based on what were authentically "American" musical materials. But the novelty that most Americans heard in the Spanish guitar pieces performed by Signor Pucci, or the "Spanish" piano pieces by Gottschalk, was pure novelty. Whereas European audiences heard Spanish guitar music as genuinely and authentically Spanish in performances by the likes of the Spanish guitar virtuoso Fernando Sor and others, U.S. concert audiences consistently basked in the novelty of "Spanish" music heard through the filter of arrangements. This kind of adaptation is a persistent trait in the performance history of European music in the United States before the twentieth century, to be sure. But the reception of Spanish music in the United States cannot be understood without acknowledging that various kinds of adaptation may have contributed to a lively but pernicious trivialization of Spanish art music.

⁓

If U.S. listeners were introduced to Spanish music largely through arrangements and recomposition, U.S. musicologists of the early twentieth century also received a somewhat tinted view of Spain's musical past. The judgments of nineteenth-century European musicologists, both foreign and Spanish, were often confused about Spain's early contribution to the history of music. A number of musical sources from the Middle Ages and the early Renaissance were unknown until the last years of the nineteenth century, and the notation of many of the known musical sources was difficult to decipher. The priest and musical scholar Hilarión Eslava, whose *Lira sacro-hispana* was published in 1856, even admitted, "It is true . . . that not even we can present works or treatises from the fifteenth century to demonstrate our well-founded opinions."[34] Noted connoisseurs of Spain's artistic culture, such as Antonio Ponz and Louis

Viardot, for example, did not bring music into their narratives. Viardot, a specialist in Spanish art and director of the Italian opera in Paris, who married the singer Pauline García (Viardot), daughter of the famous singer Manuel García, felt a special attraction to the musical history of Spain, though he acknowledged that "nothing, absolutely nothing, has been written about Spanish music."[35] Few professional writers on music in the late eighteenth and nineteenth centuries experienced Spanish musical culture at first hand, and even fewer ventured into Spanish libraries and archives.

Among those mid-nineteenth-century music historians whose writings shaped the narratives of musical history that were brought to and taught in the United States, the German Robert Eitner and the Austrian August Wilhelm Ambros largely based their meager consideration of Spanish music on the composers and musicians included in the Belgian François-Joseph Fétis's *Biographie universelle des musiciens* (1835–44).[36] Fétis lengthened the lists of names that had been compiled by eighteenth-century writers such as Burney, and in its second edition (1860–65) his *Biographie universelle* included information from the recently published work of Spanish scholars, many of whom he corresponded with.[37] Fétis's *Biographie universelle* was most likely among the reference works that could be found on the shelves of important libraries in the United States, and his *Musique mise à la portée de tout le monde* was translated into English for the Boston Academy of Music as *Music Explained to the World; or, How to Understand Music and Enjoy Its Performance.*[38] Another Belgian, François-Auguste Gevaert, a composer and highly respected scholar of early music who later was honored with induction into the Order of Isabella la Católica, traveled in France, Italy, Germany, and Spain in 1849–52 and produced a report on Spanish music for the Belgian Royal Academy (*Rapport sur l'état de la musique en Espagne*, 1851) that was to spark an important polemic.[39] Gevaert declared that in all its history, Spain had produced only church music and popular music and that polyphony (which he and others then and since have considered an elevated category of musical creation and a hallmark of the Renaissance "style" in music) had been cultivated in Spain only from the time of the arrival there of Flemish musicians in the early sixteenth century. In short, Gevaert found Spain's musical culture, past and present, to be less than ideally civilized from a European point of view.[40]

At about the time that Gevaert visited Spain in 1850, the principal venues of art music in the musical life of Spanish cities were dominated by non-Spanish music and musical genres (especially Italian but also French and Austro-German). A number of leading Spanish musicians were troubled by this state of affairs and reacted strongly indeed to Gevaert's negative assessment of their musical inheritance.[41] Very much a man of his times, the composer Mariano

Soriano Fuertes y Piqueras (1817–80), a modestly successful composer in the Spanish genre of the *zarzuela,* wrote the first complete history of Spanish music to be published.[42] He pursued scholarship in order to argue forcefully in favor of a nationalist Spanish musical agenda, though he was not a professional musicologist (he had taught solfège at the Madrid conservatory and held a series of administrative positions, including the directorship of the Gran Teatro del Liceo in Barcelona). His *Historia de la música española desde la venida de los fenicios hasta el año 1850* (1855–59), was a response to the poor opinions of his country's music expressed by outsiders. For Soriano Fuertes, as for many of his contemporaries, national characteristics came forth in musical styles: "la música tiene patrias," such that Spain's music had its own indigenous musical language.

Full of errors, Soriano Fuertes's history was considered an embarrassment by a slightly younger group of Spanish musicians and scholars, who, though they took up the cause of constructing the national musicology and a national history of music, called for musical scholarship to be based more rigorously on primary sources (*"documentos originales"*). Evidence for the industry with which Spanish scholars pursued a positivist course can be found in the many volumes and boxes of notes, musical transcriptions, and documents collected by the leading figure of his age in Spanish music, Francisco Asenjo Barbieri (1823–94), the first musician to be awarded a seat in the Real Academia Española.[43] Barbieri was highly successful as a composer of theatrical music, and his efforts on behalf of Spanish music took many forms. More libertine than pious and more political than religious, Barbieri worked especially to promote and study native Spanish genres that were nonreligious: the *zarzuela,* the first Spanish operas, the music of the *comedia nueva,* the *romances,* and so on. Barbieri's monumental transcription and edition of the so-called *Cancionero musical de palacio,* published in 1890, opened the way for a broader consideration of early Spanish music.[44] Through this songbook Barbieri demonstrated to musical scholars beyond the Pyrennees that an entire repertory of secular polyphony, in musical settings of high-class poetry, was cultivated in Spain before the sixteenth century. Here was proof that Spanish royalty had supported both exquisitely profane and pious musical creations (he had assumed that the *Cancionero* reflected the patronage of Ferdinand and Isabella); here was proof that, just as Spanish poets were original in their use of native elements and forms, Spanish composers worked with their own musical forms and turns of melody. What is more, his voluminous *Cancionero musical de los siglos XV y XVI* offered proof that Spanish music had enjoyed a copious and individual effervescence that predated the so-called Golden Age of Spanish sacred music of the sixteenth century. Until his discovery the latter had been virtually the only celebrated moment in Spain's musical past (though Gevaert's report had implied that even the credit for this should go to the Netherlanders!).[45]

Though Barbieri never completed his own history of Spanish music, his legacy to scholars of Spanish music in his own time and in ours has been considerable. Among those who benefited directly from Barbieri's work was the composer and musicologist Felipe Pedrell (1841–1922), who, though not as erudite as Barbieri and less brilliant as a musician and scholar, was highly successful as a teacher and promoter of the cause of Spanish music. Pedrell was largely self-taught in music, and during his time abroad in Rome and Paris (1876–78) he began to become interested in early music and in musicology. In the 1880s in Barcelona, Pedrell founded three musical periodicals (*Salterio sacro-hispano, Notas musicales y literarias,* and *La ilustración musical hispano-americana*), and it was through these that he began to publish music by earlier Spanish composers. His most important contributions to the history of Spanish music are, in fact, his illustrated annotated catalog of the music collection of the Biblioteca de Catalunya (*Catàlech de la Biblioteca musical de la Diputació de Barcelona* (1909), his edition of the works of Tomás Luis de Victoria (1902–13), and most especially his collections of musical transcriptions such as *Hispaniae schola musica sacra* (1894–98), the *Teatro lírico español anterior al siglo XIX* (1897–98), the *Antología de organistas clásicos españoles* (1908), and the *Cancionero musical popular español* (1918–22). Pedrell's deeply romantic enthusiasm for the cause of Spanish music often led him into factual or conceptual errors, as demonstrated in his two most important prose publications, *Los músicos españoles en sus libros* (1888) and *Por nuestra música* (1891). The latter, despite its scholarly deficiencies, was especially influential. His theories to the effect that a nationalist music should be based on the nation's national songs influenced (indeed, practically nurtured) Spanish composers such as Isaac Albéniz, Enrique Granados, and Manuel de Falla.[46] Falla's "homage" to Pedrell explains with delicacy how Pedrell's romantic vision served both to bring Spain's musical history to the attention of scholars around the world and to allow Spanish composers who embraced modernism to find a new path toward an authentically national musical idiom. Falla wrote that Pedrell was the one "through whose works Spain has again joined the circle of Europe's musical nations."[47]

In summary, the controversies about Spain's musical past and its authenticity took root in the eighteenth century and are spattered with accusations to the effect that Spain had been constantly receptive to the musical contributions of other nations but had not made an original contribution.[48] When the renowned and highly influential German music critic Edward Hanslick wrote disparagingly of Spain's musical history in 1891—"Hardly any other civilized nation in music history has erected so few milestones [and] left behind so few traces, as has the Spanish [nation]"—he mirrored the point of view held by a century of European musical criticism and by the standard German and French musical reference works and encyclopedias.[49] Sir George Grove, editor of the first *Dictionary of Music and Musicians* (1878–90), later excused the brevity of the entry for Spain under "Schools of Composition" with the comment that "nobody knows anything about Spanish music."[50] The only moment of Spain's musical history to merit a mention in the Grove article is the sixteenth century, where "The Spanish School" is dismissed in about 260 words as a mere transplantation: "The Roman origin of The Spanish School is so clearly manifest, that is it is unnecessary to say more on the subject than has been already said. . . . Spanish Singers of good Voices were always sure of a warm welcome in Rome," where they learned the art of counterpoint from the "Flemings there domiciled, and afterwards from the Romans themselves." Fortunately, Spanish singers "not infrequently carried [contrapuntal polyphony] back with them to Spain" and "so completely are the Spaniards identified with the Romans, that the former are necessarily described as disciples." With characteristic patriotism the next paragraph informs readers that contrapuntal polyphony was practiced in the typically superior culture of England "at an earlier period than even in the Netherlands."[51]

The defensive attitude that such assertions engendered in Spanish scholars seems to have boiled to the surface in the 1920s, in the work of two musicologists who had been among those Spanish musicians who studied with Pedrell and who were fully convinced of the need for a national music and a national musicology. To understand how Spanish music fit into the nascent field of musicology in the United States, the influence of these two, Rafael Mitjana and especially Higini Anglés, needs to be considered. They brought Spanish musicology into the international arena just as the International Musicological Society was being founded and at the same time that U.S. musicologists began to accelerate their own process of self-definition.

Mitjana (1869–1921) belonged to the *generación del '98,* and was among those intellectuals calling for a national renewal in arts and letters while pushing toward a reassertion of Spain's national character. Mitjana was, like Charles Seeger and others in the United States in the same period, a well-traveled, highly musical gentleman scholar in search of his country's musical identity and acutely aware of the dichotomies that ran through its musical life. He studied with Pedrell in Barcelona and later with Saint-Saëns in Paris (though Mitjana also studied law and took up diplomatic service as his career) and contributed the large and important article on Spain to the prestigious *Encyclopédie de la musique* (1920).[52] During his travels in Europe and elsewhere, Mitjana searched for examples of Spanish music in foreign libraries. Among his contributions to the reconstruction of Spain's musical history were his discovery of the so-called *Cancionero de Upsala* (a musical anthology whose repertory was composed largely for the court of the duke of Calabria in Valencia, though the collection was printed in Venice in 1556) and the presentation of documents for the biographies of Spanish composers of the fifteenth, sixteenth, and even seventeenth centuries (such as Juan del Encina, Tomás Luis de Victoria, Antonio de Cabezón, and Bartolomé de Selma y Salaverde). In his enormous essay "La Musique en Espagne" (completed 1914 but published 1920), Mitjana attempted to bring the history of Spanish music up to the European standard. Carrying on the Pedrellian project, Mitjana worked zealously to "wrench the national music out of the quicksand in which it found itself and liberate it from foreign tyranny."[53] By "national music" Mitjana did not refer to "the spontaneous musical art of the people" (el arte espontáneo del pueblo) but only to "the products of a cultivated art that is reflexive and refined" (los productos del arte culto, reflexivo y refinado), which in the case of Spain was nevertheless shaped to some extent by melodies of the traditional "national" popular song ("la canción popular ha ejercido siempre una influencia extraordinaria, fecunda y provechosa, sobre la música española" [the popular song has always an extraordinary fecund and fruitful influence upon Spanish music]).[54] However carefully he documented his work, it was soaked through with an unabashed nationalism: from the very first pages, phrases such as "autoctonous art" and "essential racial traces" shape Mitjana's militant discourse. Nevertheless, his history shows considerable erudition and includes copious musical examples, many of them transcriptions taken from the earlier editions and anthologies of Eslava and Pedrell. Because Mitjana's essay was published in French (an accepted language in U.S. scholarly and academic circles) rather than Spanish, and the *Encyclopédie de la musique* was surely among the tomes that U.S. libraries purchased as they stocked their musical reference shelves, Mitjana's version of Spain's musical history was undoubtedly read by U.S. scholars.[55] It was the best survey of Spanish music available in the 1920s. Indeed, some of the best-known and most frequently performed pieces from the Spanish early music repertory were brought together for Pedrell's earlier anthologies and then used as illustrations for Mitjana's essay—Miguel de Fuenllana's setting of the romance "Paseábase el rey moro"; variation pieces from Diego de Ortiz's *Tratado de glosas;* Juan Vázquez's setting of "¿Con qué la lavaré?"; Juan Hidalgo's charming ensemble song "Quedito, pasito."

The profile of the Catalan priest Higini Anglés (1888–1969), Pedrell's most important apprentice, could not be more different from Mitjana's, though Anglés's work was also directed to recovering Spain's musical heritage as a "national" project. He was also the first professional musicologist that Spain produced, though he was a Roman Catholic priest, and his scholarship was exclusively rigorous and focused. His research into early Spanish music began around 1918, and within a few years he had studied musicology at the universities of Freiburg and Göttingen (1923–24). He was to return to Germany for the years of the Spanish Civil War and lived in Munich from 1936 to 1939. After the war Anglés served the national musical agenda from his several administrative positions, organizing musicology as a narrowly controlled discipline in Spain, and his work had an immediate and galvanizing effect on the history of Spanish music in the international arena.[56] His prestige on the international level was considerable: he was honored with memberships in numerous scientific and musical societies in the 1940s and 1950s and served as vice president of the International Musicological Society (an organization largely guided by Anglo-German musicology) from 1933 to 1958. In this position he came into contact with musicologists teaching in the United States.[57]

Anglés showed that Spain had a rich and original tradition of early music. His paper for the International Musicological Society congress in Vienna in 1927 (about the now-familiar "Codex Las Huelgas" from the thirteenth-century monastery of that name) proved that Spain had had an independent tradition of polyphonic music in the late Middle Ages.[58] This startling information revealed a possible musical complexity (a much-valued commodity in the standard musicology of the day, steeped as it was in the vapors of a romantic and postromantic aesthetic) in the early music of Spain, causing a large crack to form in the edifice of ignorance that surrounded the history of Spanish music.

Thanks to the documentary work of Barbieri, Mitjana, and Anglés, the collections and transcriptions of music brought together and published by Eslava and Pedrell, and the publications of institutions such as the Consejo Superior de Investigaciones Científicas and the Biblioteca de Catalunya, it was at least theoretically possible for scholars at home and abroad to begin to study early Spanish music. But along with this entirely positive result, the nationalist project left its indelible marks on their work. Although Spanish scholars had invested in the nationalist musical project in order to open a reconsideration of Spain's place in the realm of art music, the brand of musicology that was officially promoted by government-sponsored organizations in Spain in the decades after the Spanish Civil War was primarily interested in Spain's musical past as an expression of religious orthodoxy.[59] This point of view was not one that the fathers of U.S. musicology were sympathetic to.

The birth of musicology as a discipline in the United States before World War I can be traced to the pioneering work of several U.S. gentleman scholars and college professors who fully identified "musicological endeavor with the

European landscape."[60] Among those who shaped early musicology in the United States, the Boston-bred and Harvard-educated Charles Seeger was later to show an interest in both U.S. and Hispanic music. Though his early career was directed mostly toward composing and conducting, Seeger offered the first U.S. courses in musicology in 1916 at the University of California at Berkeley. From around 1913 Seeger defined musicology as comprising "the whole linguistic treatment of music—the manual instruction, the historical study, the music-research of the psycho-physical laboratory, the piece of music criticism." In Seeger's early appraisal the musical and music-historical disciplines in Europe (especially in France, Germany, and Austria) were showing "vigorous growth," while in the United States "practically nothing has been done, owing partly to a prejudice against the musicological point of view itself."[61] For Seeger the positivist historical study of music that was under way in European universities (and in Spain) was problematic because an emphasis on "history" had led away from "systematic" musical work (analysis and criticism), and "contact between the living art and its study has been poor."[62] Early in the history of U.S. musicology, he called for attention to "the music and music activity actually existing in the United States," regardless of "cultural idiom or social standing," and he encouraged both scholars and composers to work with what could be called authentically American musical materials.[63]

In the 1920s and early 1930s U.S. and Spanish musical scholarship were kindred spirits to some extent. As they retrieved the gleaming vessels of their musical past, and sought to anchor their work in an indigenous authenticity, Spanish composer-scholars were already doing what Seeger urged Americans to do in his early efforts to legitimize, analyze, popularize, and historicize "music that expresses or characterizes the American people." Seeger's suggestion that U.S. composers make use of indigenous musical materials, such as folk tunes, in composing a national art music was, of course, something that many Spanish musicians were already invested in.[64] And when Seeger and others, most notably Oscar G. Sonneck, began to shape an American musicology from an American musical perspective, Spanish scholars had already been fighting much the same ideological battle but with the odds stacked more heavily against their success. Spanish scholars and papers on Spanish music were not strongly represented at international gatherings in the early twentieth century, though 1930 seems to have been a banner year. When the International Society for Musical Research held its first congress in Liége in 1930, four of the forty-two volunteer papers were on Spanish music. One was presented by Higini Anglés (the official representative from Spain and a member of the International Musicological Society council), two others were given by his Spanish colleagues, and one was by the British journalist John B. Trend, who had already published an important book on Spanish music.[65]

In the United States the most influential musicologists were trained in Germany, and they brought European predilections with them when they took on professorships in this country. When the American Musicological Society was founded in 1934, only three of the fourteen founding members had not studied or been born in Europe (one was Charles Seeger). In 1930 the first professorship in musicology was designed at Cornell University especially for Otto Kinkeldey (1878–1966), a U.S. scholar who, though primarily educated in New York, had completed his doctorate in Berlin in 1909. Kinkeldey studied and worked in Germany at the highest professional levels before World War I made it impossible for him to remain there. The first U.S. doctoral degree in musicology was awarded in 1932 at Cornell to his student, J. Murray Barbour (1897–1970), an American who was trained mainly in the United States but also in Cologne and Berlin and who for most of his academic career taught at what is now Michigan State University.[66] Coincidentally, Barbour's dissertation, "Equal Temperament: Its History from Ramis (1482) to Rameau (1737)," did touch on the subject of Spanish Renaissance musical thought, because Spanish musical theorists had made such an undeniable contribution to his subject.[67]

The legacy of nineteenth-century Europe was to shape the history of music in the United States as nothing more or less than the history of the great musical achievements of major Austrian, French, German, and Flemish composers of the past. In the first decades of the twentieth century, though Seeger and others began to question the European monopoly on the nation's cultivated taste, serious "modern" musicologists were still trained in this science of music at German universities. Oscar Sonneck, the prolific scholar who organized the music division at the Library of Congress in Washington, D.C., was born in the United States but raised and educated in Germany. Active as well on the international scene, Sonneck stands out as a true pioneer; though he researched many European subjects, he is mostly remembered as a U.S. musicologist who meticulously anthologized historical documents about his country's musical life.[68] As the nearest thing to an official representative of the unpopulated field of U.S. musicology, Sonneck worked to establish a forum for documentary musical scholarship in the United States. In this practical objective he was a dedicated positivist, but he was not picky about the nationality or geography of anyone else's musical focus.[69] Because so little was circulating in the way of musical scholarship on any topic, an eclectic inclusiveness characterized musicology in the United States before World War II, and during this period the music of Spain and the music of the United States were mixed along with all sorts of other subjects into the grab bag of topics that scholars worked on. The early reports of the American Musicological Society (AMS) also include scattered references to papers on Spanish music given at regional meetings: in 1936 George Boylston Brown of Rochester, New York, read two papers about Spanish folk music and dance at meetings of the western New York chapter. In 1938 and 1939 Charles Warren Fox presented his findings, entitled "Accidentals in *Vihuela* Tablatures" and "The Masses of Cristóbal Morales," at meetings of the western New York chapter. In December 1938 at the annual national meeting of the AMS in Washington, D.C., a study of Spanish music was first presented at a national meeting, when the exiled Spanish composer and critic Adolfo Salazar, then living in Washington, read "The Music in the Primitive Spanish Theatre to Lope de Vega and Calderón."[70] Two papers on Spanish music were given at the annual national meeting of the AMS in Cleveland in 1940: Otto Gombosi gave his paper, "The Cultural and Folkloristic Background of the *Folia*," and Isabel Pope gave hers, "The Musical Development and Form of the Spanish *Villancico*." In 1941 Eleanor Hague, who had been collecting Spanish and Hispanic-American folk songs, presented "Regional Music of Spain and Latin America" to the southern California chapter of the AMS. Another important contributor to U.S. musical Hispanism, Gilbert Chase, a seasoned critic but not a professional scholar, presented "Guitar and Vihuela: A Clarification" to the southeastern chapter in 1940 and a paper about the Renaissance composer Juan Navarro to the same chapter in 1943.

Though a few scholars were interested in particular aspects of Spanish musical history (the history and derivation of Spanish folk dances, sixteenth-century *vihuela* music, and sixteenth-century Spanish sacred music), Spain did not have a compelling role in the history of music as constructed by the dominant traditions of French and German musical scholarship, and as taught to the first U.S. students of musical history. For Europeans, as for U.S. audiences imbued with European values, Spanish music and U.S. music were both peripheral to the history of "art music"; they were most interesting as folk traditions and as concert fare only when served up as exotic novelties.

Spanish and Latin American music of the "art" or "classical" tradition have been curiously unattractive to the mainstream of U.S. musical study, in part because of the ways in which the discipline of musicology was shaped in the United States in its second formative period. In the Hitler years "the influx of refugees from Europe transformed music along with so many other aspects of American artistic and intellectual life."[71] When formerly persecuted scholars came to the United States in search of a new start, their historical and intellectual forays were nurtured by the music they knew and revered. For the newcomers historical positivism (as opposed to what today would be called "criticism") offered not only a safe retreat from the myriad dangers of political subjectivity but a secure anchor for the intellectual freedom that they had paid dearly to cultivate. The musical past of General Franco's fascist Spain was not high on the list of priorities for the émigré scholars who had fled fascism, as they joined U.S. professors and formed departments, established publication projects, and organized scholarly meetings. And unless they could read Spanish, they probably knew little about what Spain's musical history had to offer.

As musicology became institutionalized at major universities, "most of the powerful professors of the postwar period . . . were members of the European diaspora."[72] Their baggage included well-entrenched traditional musical tastes and values in favor of European art music. They were engaged with music primarily as scholars, not as composers or as writers of the snazzy popular criticism that was the daily work of most U.S. writers on music earlier in the century. Heirs to the aesthetic and didactic traditions of European universities, the evidence of any country's musical past was to be found in the *output* of its composers. The history of art music was the history of musical *composition,* valued above musical *performance* and *improvisation,* so that particular musical features (such as technical complexity, organicism of conception, strong formal outlines) were considered desirable. These predilections, together with a general ignorance of the historical record where Spain was concerned, meant that Spanish music was not a topic much discussed in classrooms in the United States.

The first history of Spanish music to be published in the United States was written by an impassioned music critic from Cedar Rapids, Iowa, who was not a musicologist. It reflects both the paucity of information available in English and the understanding of Spain's musical history as reducible to an early moment of musical glory characterized by a rigid Catholicism and orthodoxy in the far-away sixteenth century.[73] Although the author of this history, Carl Van Vechten (1880–1964), was not a musicologist, he had been graduated from the University of Chicago in 1903 with a bachelor's degree in English. During his seven years in Chicago he had devoted himself to writing and to music—studying scores, playing the piano, singing, attending concerts and rehearsals, meeting musicians, and going to clubs, though he did not enroll in any music courses at the university. He studied Latin, French, German, and English literature but not Spanish. After graduation he worked as a reporter for the Hearst paper, the *Chicago American,* and in 1906 moved to New York to take a job as assistant music critic at the *New York Times* (under Richard Aldrich).[74] Van Vechten was prolific and popular in New York, among those busy critics who wrote freelance criticism about music and dance for the genteel U.S. public before musicology existed as such in the United States.[75] He even published an article, "Shall We Realize Wagner's Ideals?" in the second issue of the *Musical Quarterly,* a new U.S. journal of musicology edited by Oscar Sonneck.[76] That Sonneck, a pioneer in U.S. musicology, a solid documentary scholar, composer, and erudite music lover, included Van Vechten's musical criticism in several issues of his journal speaks volumes about the timeliness and appeal of Van Vechten's early essays. As he is famous for demonstrating in his later career, Van Vechten did not at all represent the conservative establishment. He was "the loudest, most insistent voice calling for recognition of the musical revolution. At a time when the names of Stravinsky, Satie, Ornstein, and Schoenberg were unknown to many and anathema to the remaining few, Van Vechten was a defender of their experiments and a champion of their art."[77] His was the first article on Igor Stravinsky to be published in the United States, and he was the first to write about the Russian Ballet in New York (he has even been called America's first dance critic).[78] He was an intellectual with a nose for fashion and a penchant for taking on promising underdog causes. An early crusader in the cause of interracial harmony and a devotee of African-American culture, he was to become an influential patron and supporter of such writers in the Harlem Renaissance as Langston Hughes, though one of his many novels, *Nigger Heaven* (1926), was divisively controversial.[79] In later life Van Vechten became a photographer and captured just about everybody who was anybody in his portraits.[80] His favorite subjects were the African-American celebrities and artists of the 1930s, 1940s, and 1950s, but among his portraits are some of Spanish, Latin American, and American Hispanic artists as well, including the painter Joan Miró (1935), the Spanish pianist José Iturbi (1933), and a number of dancers—the Spanish flamenco dancer Vicente Escudero (1933), the Mexican choreographer and dancer José Fernández (1939), the flamenco star La Argentinita (1940), the Dominican-born U.S. dancer Francisco Monción (1944), the Chilean Hernán Baldrich (1962), and the American Rosa Rolando (Covarrubias) among them.[81]

A man of many "firsts," when he took on Spanish music for one of his early books, Van Vechten was characteristically striking out as an independent avant-garde intellectual, with a topic that he and his publisher and friend, Alfred E. Knopf, believed would sell his book as a popular success (the book is dedicated to Knopf's wife, Blanche). In fact, the project was designed to make money. Unable to pay the alimony of $738 demanded by his first wife, Van Vechten had spent some time in the Ludlow Street Jail in 1915. Financial problems still plagued him while he was writing *The Music of Spain* and even after it was published. In a letter of February 7, 1919, to his brother, Ralph Van Vechten, a prominent Chicago banker, Carl Van Vechten explained defensively that although he had published five books in three years (the first had appeared in

December 1915) and his work was receiving accolades from noted writers of the day, he and his second wife (the actress Fania Marinoff) were "absolutely without money." In the same letter he noted that he had received an offer to publish *The Music of Spain* in French translation and that a trip to Spain to write a book was among the projects that he would likely be unable to start "owing to petty financial annoyances."[82]

Van Vechten had not been to Spain when he put together *The Music of Spain,* and he was somewhat confused about what the early history of Spanish music had to offer, but he had done his homework.[83] He read what he could find on the subject of Spain's musical past and present and concluded (following the article in Grove's *Dictionary*) that "the early religious composers of Spain deserve a niche all to themselves, be it ever so tiny. . . . There is, to be sure, some doubt as to whether their inspiration was entirely peninsular, or whether some of it was wafted from Flanders, and the rest gleaned in Rome."[84] The messy authenticity question here bubbles innocently forth in Van Vechten's consideration of early Spanish music at roughly the same time that it was bothering Charles Seeger and a few others interested in constructing the musical past of

Figure 7.1. Encarnación López Julvez, "La Argentinita" (1895–1945), as photographed by Carl Van Vechten in 1940. This influential Spanish dancer who collaborated with Manuel de Falla and Federico García Lorca made her U.S. debut in 1930. Her understated performances of authentic Spanish dance in an age of exotic stereotypes helped establish Spanish ballet as a legitimate concert form. (Photograph by Carl Van Vechten; reproduced with the kind permission of the Van Vechten Trust)

the United States. Though Van Vechten did not list his bibliography, notes scattered throughout his text show that he drew information from several kinds of sources. He relied heavily on Albert Soubies's three tiny volumes on the history of Spanish music, "La Musique d'Espagne," from *Histoire de la musique dans les different pays d'Europe* (1886–1906), published in Paris. Soubies (1846–1918) too was a music critic rather than a scholar, but his twelve volumes on musical history, arranged by geographical regions, were stuffed with facts, names, dates, and classifications. In 1900 "La Musique d'Espagne" provided a highly readable, positively enthusiastic evaluation of Spain's musical history, despite its errors and the absence of any musical examples. Others of Van Vechten's sources were also in French, including essays published in France by J. Jean Aubry; the published letters from Spain of the nineteenth-century French composer Emmanuel Chabrier (1841–94), which had appeared in French as journal articles from 1909 to 1911; and collections of Spanish folk songs issued in Paris, Madrid, and Seville in the 1870s and 1880s (in French). Van Vechten had also consulted the few scholarly articles on Spanish musicians published in *Grove's Dictionary of Music and Musicians* and the travel essays about Spain by nineteenth-century writers such as Richard Ford (1845 and 1846) and John Hay (*Castilian Days*, 1871). Van Vechten's admiration for several different books and essays by Havelock Ellis (including *The Soul of Spain*, 1908 and 1915) also comes through clearly. Among Spanish writers, he mentions excerpts translated from Soriano Fuertes's *Historia de la música española,* and several items by Felipe Pedrell. Van Vechten specifically mentions Pedrell's *Teatro lírico español* anthology, as well as Pedrell's *Por nuestra música* (1891) in the French translation by Bertal. According to Van Vechten, Pedrell's *Músicos contemporáneos y de otros tiempos* was available at the library of The Hispanic Society in New York, and the piano score of Granados's *Goyescas* "now reposes in the Museum of the Hispanic Society."[85]

Writing his short book on Spanish music in New York between 1915 and 1918 (the year in which his book was published was also the year of publication of the first issue of the *Hispanic American Historical Review*), Van Vechten responded to current fashion. The book was a critical success; it was deemed "indispensable to libraries," and Van Vechten was praised as having "a perfect knowledge of the material." Unfortunately, it did not sell widely and the "meager royalties" that came in were not enough to alleviate Van Vechten's financial woes.[86] This is surprising, given the rage for things Hispanic that Van Vechten himself reports as characterizing the cultural scene in New York. His chapter called "Spain and Music" (dated New York, March 20, 1916) tells us that Spanish song and dance had lately been all the rage, just as "highly coloured paintings by Sorolla and Zuloaga" were on exhibit in "private and public galleries," and interest in paintings by Goya and El Greco was on the rise. As proof of the great success garnered by Spanish artists and their creations, he mentions performances by the singers Emilio de Gogorza, Andrés de Segurola, Lucrezia Bori, and María Barrientos, and piano pieces by Isaac Albéniz, Joaquín Turina, and Enrique Granados (though the performers of these were not Spanish). The recital of Spanish dance performed at the New York Winter Garden by Isabel Rodríguez "quite transcended the surroundings and made that stage as atmospheric, as a *maison de danse* in Seville," though "the amazing *Spanish* dances of Anna Pavlowa" also fanned the flames of the new taste for things Spanish.[87] Van Vechten noted a few extracts from Spanish musical theater that had been applauded in Europe as well—the *polo* "Yo soy contrabandista" from Manuel García's monologue opera *El poeta calculista* (1805), and the "Carceleras" from Ruperto Chapí's *zarzuela, Las hijas de Zebedeo* (1889).[88]

Included in *The Music of Spain* is a short essay from 1917, in which Van Vechten reviewed with frenetic enthusiasm and self-confessed "verbal explosion" a musical revue called *The Land of Joy,* with music by the Spanish composer Joaquín Valverde y San Juan (1875–1918), that had been performed at the Park Theater in late October and early November 1917. The revue must have been a success, for the score was published soon after as "a musical operetta" in a bilingual piano-vocal edition in New York in 1918 by G. Schirmer (the music publishing house whose director of publications in 1918 was none other than Oscar G. Sonneck). Though the revue was a sort of "sublimated form of *zarzuela*" calculated to hold its audience captive and appeal to all classes of listeners, for Van Vechten "the whole entertainment, music, colours, costumes, songs, dances, and all, is as nicely arranged in its crescendos and decrescendos, its prestos and adagios as a Mozart finale."[89] Van Vechten noted that the presence of native "Spaniards in the first-night audience gave the cue, unlocked the lips and loosened the hands of us cold Americans." Impressed by the energy of the performers, especially the dancers known as "La Argentinita" and "Doloretes," Van Vechten wrote of their "gipsy fascination" and "abandoned, perverse bewitchery." The experience led him to wonder about the much-beloved Spanish sound as composed and performed by non-Spaniards, and he mused, "What we have been thinking of all these years in accepting the imitation and ignoring the actuality, I don't know."[90]

Van Vechten's devotion to the unsung glories of Spanish music and dance was sparked especially by the Spanish idiom, which allowed him to think of Spanish music as exotic and non-European: "The resemblance between negro and Spanish music is very noticeable. . . . Spanish melodies, indeed, are often scraps of tunes, like the African negro melodies. . . . Whoever was responsible, Arab, negro, or Moor . . . the Spanish dances betray their oriental origin in their complexity of rhythm (a complexity not at all obvious on the printed page, as so much of it depends on dancer, guitarist, singer, and even public!), and the *fioriture* which decorate their melody when melody occurs."[91]

On the other hand, he assured his readers that "the repertoire of the concert room and the opera house is streaked through and through with Spanish atmosphere and, on the whole, I should say, the best Spanish music has not been written by Spaniards, although most of it, like the best music written in Spain, is based primarily on the rhythm of folk-tunes, dances and songs." For Van Vechten musical authenticity called for the incorporation of natively national musical materials (folk tunes and rhythms), though his list of "the true Spanish tunes" is actually a catalog of non-Spanish pieces, beginning with Chabrier's *España* and *Habanera*, and Debussy's *Ibéria*. Ravel's *Rapsodie espagnole* was "as Spanish as music could be," and Van Vechten noted, "It is French composers generally who have achieved better effects with Spanish atmosphere than men of other nations."[92]

The "Spanish idiom" was popular and remained familiar to U.S. listeners through non-Spanish pieces in the standard concert repertory. When looking for ways to broaden the audience for contemporary art music in New York in the 1930s, the composer Aaron Copland even resorted to borrowing from a Hispanic idiom—tunes and rhythms he remembered from his visit to a dance hall in Mexico in 1932, and tunes from a Mexican *cancionero* (or songbook) and a collection of Mexican folklore—for his piece *El salón México*. Copland wrote some years later: "It seemed natural to use popular Mexican melodies for thematic material; after all, Chabrier and Debussy didn't hesitate to help themselves to the melodic riches of Spain. There was no reason I should not use the tunes of the hispanic land on our southern doorstep. My purpose was not to quote literally, but to heighten without in any way falsifying the natural simplicity of Mexican tunes."[93] This passage from the scholar John H. Mueller, writing at Indiana University as a social aesthetician as late as 1951, is more representative of attitudes about French composers and Spanish music that were already well entrenched in the United States (the emphasis is mine):

> Ethnologists well know that these national forms, although often the objects of intense loyalty, differ from one another not because of any inherent racial predisposition, but because they developed in *cultural isolation* in response to innumerable local conditions and circumstances. . . . Occasionally these *aboriginal* motifs have had an appeal even to other nations as *quaint and exotic* themes. Indeed, it has been said that the best "Spanish" music has been written by Frenchmen: Debussy, Ravel, Lalo, Bizet, Chabrier, who did much to popularize the Spanish idiom. Spain furnished the rhythms, France the technical and professional equipment to incorporate them into more pretentious forms.[94]

Aside from Van Vechten's book and the work of folklorists in the Southwest, the "Spanish idiom" was attractive to concert goers but did not inspire much U.S. scholarship on Spanish music. Professional scholarship among Spaniards focused on late medieval and Renaissance Catholic sacred music, which did not intersect in the U.S. concert repertory with music composed "in the Spanish idiom." It is safe to speculate that U.S. scholarship on early Spanish music did not develop beyond a sort of descriptive musical criticism because its sources were published in Spanish and concerned a repertory that did not fulfill the concert-going public's expectation of what "Spanish" music sounded like.

Perhaps in order to bridge this gap, The Hispanic Society of America published the British journalist John B. Trend's *The Music of Spanish History to 1600* as part of its Hispanic Notes and Monographs series.[95] Trend's small book was designed as "a history and a guide-book to Spanish music, something after the manner of Ford's inimitable *Handbook for Travellers in Spain and Readers at Home.*"[96] Though he had studied music with Edward Dent, Trend was not a musicologist or a professor when he wrote this book (though in 1933 he became professor of Spanish at Cambridge University). He intended to popularize early Spanish music. To do so he emphasized the exotic "Moorish" elements of medieval Spanish music, purportedly the audible counterparts to the images and architectural elements that were being rediscovered by Trend's contemporaries in art and literature. For Trend early Spanish music was unique because it was receptive to both oriental and Western European "influences." Building on the work of Barbieri, Trend described and illustrated the music of the *romancero,* such that his book went beyond Van Vechten's in presenting early Spanish musical culture as heterogeneous and not exclusively religious. Most important, Trend's tiny guidebook had a scholarly dimension and erudition that set it apart from Van Vechten's. Trend consulted primary sources, offered musical transcriptions, and did not limit his bibliography to English- or French-language sources. Though more rigorously scholarly than Van Vechten, Trend revealed a tendency toward antiquarianism that was not at all typical of U.S. writings on music around 1920. Also pertaining to this vein of romantic positivist scholarship, despite its sometimes fantastic historical errors, is the abridged version of Julián Ribera's *Music in Ancient Arabia and Spain,* translated from the Spanish by Eleanor Hague and Marion Leffingwell, which offered "a vivid but entertaining picture of a period which, at least in English, has always been a complete blank."[97]

The very novelty with which so much Spanish music was presented in the United States caused it to be left out of most of the historical narratives and period textbooks that came to present the "standard," or canonical, history of Western art music—which unabashedly celebrates the history of technical innovation in musical composition. The principal textbooks published in the United States for studying music history in college and conservatory classrooms are devoted to individual "style" periods or chronological segments about the history of European musical composition. Reading these texts, the categories of music (genres, forms, composers, and geographical regions) considered for each period and thus the geography of the history of music as taught in the United States in the latter half of the twentieth century become clear. Not surprisingly, because of its marginal status in the standard historical narratives spun by U.S. music historians, Spanish music is more likely to be included in music texts published before the 1960s or in the 1990s than in those published during the intervening decades, the boom years of U.S. textbook publishing in music.

The texts devoted to medieval music typically offer a couple of pages about Spain (the most extensive treatments are those in Gustave Reese, *Music in the Middle Ages* [1940], and Richard H. Hoppin, *Medieval Music* [1978]). They invariably mention Mozarabic chant and its geographical isolation and consider briefly another anomalous creation, the Galician-Portuguese *Cantigas de Santa María*.[98] Both repertories can be distinguished clearly from music of a more obviously pan-European derivation (though musicologists would now concede that attempts to describe Europe as a musically unified place in the Middle Ages were and are of dubious value). They are thus "exotic" even to the ears of medievalists.

In texts about Renaissance music, Spanish music receives somewhat more attention, though the tendency has been to evaluate all Renaissance music and musical cultures against the style-defining technical characteristics of Franco-Flemish music, with musical institutions and aesthetics measured according to paradigms set by Italy as the nurturing geographical cradle of a supposedly European musical mainstream. Two influential books from the 1950s—Gustave Reese's *Music in the Renaissance* (1954), the principal reading for several generations of music students, and Alec Harman's *Medieval and Early Renaissance Music* (1958)—characterize Spain as receptive and describe the spread and development of Franco-Flemish, French, and Italian genres in the Iberian Peninsula but pay less attention to the music of Spanish composers or to Spanish performance traditions (though admittedly Reese's coverage of Spanish music was broader and more detailed than most).[99] The contributions of Spanish composers to the Latin-texted sacred repertory in the "golden" centuries of Spain's cultural history are recognized in more recent texts, along with the existence of Spanish secular genres such as the *romance,* the *villancico,* and the *ensalada.*[100] But because these handy histories have focused on the production end of music—the work of composers in internationally circulating repertories—to the detriment of other approaches that might emphasize traditions of performance (such as improvisation), patronage, and administration of music in the fifteenth and sixteenth centuries, areas in which Spain demonstrated innovation and even leadership, the full extent of Spain's contribution to early modern musical history is as yet unacknowledged in the standard accounts.

For the period 1600 to 1800 the best-known textbooks on Western music leave the impression that Spain had no musical life at all in precisely the period in which the cultivation of art music was high on the list of cultural achievements everywhere else. Among textbooks on baroque music (music of the seventeenth and early eighteenth centuries), only one, Manfred Bukofzer's notoriously detailed *Music in the Baroque Era* (1947), mentions Spanish music at all, and its coverage is limited to a highly general and problematic three-page description of music on the Iberian Peninsula and in New Spain.[101] For the period generally referred to as the classic era (dominated by Haydn, Mozart, and the young Beethoven), the texts of Theodore E. Hager (1969), Leonard G. Ratner (1980), and Julian Rushton (1986) do not mention Spanish music or take into account musical life in Spain. Philip Downs's text (1992) provides a two-page description of the keyboard music of Antonio Soler, and Reinhard G. Pauly's widely used book in the Prentice Hall History of Music series (1988) contributes three sentences to a description of the keyboard music of this same composer.[102] Among textbooks devoted to music in the romantic era (the nineteenth century, from which most of the standard concert repertory is drawn), those of Rey M. Longyear (1969) and Carl Dahlhaus (1989) do not include any reference to Spanish music or composers. Leon Plantinga's 1984 book includes a very brief description of late nineteenth-century Spanish musical nationalism.[103] In his widely used text published in 1947, Alfred Einstein made manifest the taste and suppositions of his own day by devoting his few pages on Iberian music to its significance as a "national" style.[104]

Spanish composers made an undeniably rich and well-known contribution to the early twentieth-century international concert repertory. Although Spanish art music enjoyed a vibrant period early in the century (what a recent textbook has referred to as "a new Renaissance in Spanish music"), Spanish music is not mentioned in a number of surveys of twentieth-century music.[105] In Marion Bauer's 1933 text (with subsequent editions in 1934 and 1947), Spanish music receives two pages in a chapter concerned with nationalism based on folk music, and a later paragraph is devoted to the impressionist style in Spain; following this example, perhaps, Eric Salzman (1967) devoted one page to the music of Spanish nationalism and two pages to the music of Latin

American composers (Carlos Chávez, Silvestre Revueltas, and Heitor Villa-Lobos).[106] In William Austin's 1966 textbook the names of some Spanish composers are listed without a discussion of their music.[107] In those texts on twentieth-century music that do include coverage of Spanish music (usually under the heading of "Other Countries"), Spanish musical nationalism and Manuel de Falla are the focus.[108] Glenn Watkins's *Soundings: Music in the Twentieth Century* (1995) includes two pages on the music of de Falla in a chapter covering "emerging national aspirations" of the early twentieth century.[109]

My compressed survey of the standard U.S. textbooks is meant to make clear that certain aspects of Spain's musical history have retained at least a small place in only a few of the standard histories of Western music used in U.S. classrooms during the years in which the musicological canon was taught to eager prospective musicologists.[110] Early in the history of U.S. musicology, in the 1920s and 1930s, an interest in Spanish folk music, in musical nationalism, and in the somewhat exotic or highly original contributions of medieval Spain shaped the coverage that Spanish music was likely to receive, and things have not changed much since those days. In music as in other fields, Spain is permitted to be a land of exotic color and difference, and its musical history has been shaped by this expectation. In the United States, as in Spain in the early twentieth century, concert audiences were more familiar with an exotic or novel "Spanish idiom" than with modern Spanish music. Further, the notion that "some of the best Spanish music was written by French composers" has persisted from the days in which the "Spanish idiom" was cultivated by Spanish nationalist composers under French tutelage.[111] Most kinds of Spanish music, whether they were narrowly national or not, were neither studied nor marketed as music that would appeal to a general audience.

Whatever was happening in the world of musicological scholarship, the "Spanish idiom" was probably the most powerful of the forces that shaped international views on Spanish musical culture, because musical performances reached and affected more people in the United States and in Europe than did the published writings of musicologists and polemicists. A survey of the repertories of the major U.S. orchestras in the late nineteenth and early twentieth centuries (to about 1940) shows that they took up the "Spanish idiom" most frequently in works composed by non-Spaniards.[112] Spanish music was rarely performed by major orchestras in the United States, with the exception of a few pieces by Isaac Albéniz, Enrique Granados, and Manuel de Falla. These were the biggest Spanish names on the concert stage internationally, and, because the repertories of U.S. orchestras were modeled on European ones anyway, it is no surprise to find a few of their pieces on concert programs. "The first orchestras in North America were founded by European immigrants who wanted to continue to hear and play the great orchestral music of their cultural traditions," and "the origin of many orchestras—as well as other arts organizations—was also in a movement to separate high art from popular culture."[113] These orchestras emerged from an "aesthetic ideology that distinguished sharply between the nobility of art and the vulgarity of mere entertainment."[114] In the United States from the mid-nineteenth century forward, orchestras and chamber music societies performed mainly music by the great names from the Austro-Germanic tradition.[115] "The number of American orchestras grew slowly in the two decades before World War I; they were manned by German musicians essentially, and often rehearsals were conducted in the German language."[116] Among the favorite orchestral pieces, the most frequently performed were the symphonies of Beethoven, Brahms, and Mendelssohn, overture arrangements from Wagner operas, the tone poems of Liszt (especially *Les Preludes*), and several decades later the tone poems of Richard Strauss. The repertory of the Philharmonic Society of New York was especially rich, as this was both "the oldest established orchestra in the country" and the "first organization capable of performing a classic symphony whose members banded together for that specific purpose."[117]

The programs of both the New York Philharmonic and the Boston Symphony Orchestra show that in the late 1920s and early 1930s the choices of artistic directors and audiences called for an increase in coloristic program music. This trend permitted a handful of highly colored "nationalist" pieces by Spanish composers to be pulled into the standard repertory in the United States, as elsewhere. The first composition by a Spanish composer to be performed in New York, in the concert series of the Symphony Society of New York (which was later absorbed into the New York Philharmonic), seems to have been Pablo de Sarasate's *Ziguernerweisen,* op. 20 (which was premiered in Leipzig in 1878), a delicately elegant virtuoso piece for violin and orchestra, performed on December 10 and 12, 1905, with Jan Kubelik as soloist.[118] Only two seasons before this the Spanish violinist Enrique Fernández Arbós performed his own *Tango,* op. 6, with the Boston Symphony Orchestra (October 23, 1903). *Tango* clearly made it onto the Boston program because Arbós was concertmaster of the orchestra during the 1903–4 season. The Sarasate piece, a favorite still among virtuoso violinists, probably was chosen for New York two years later because the guest soloist requested it.

The visits of talented Spanish performers and composers to the United States most likely helped the cause of Spanish music.[119] Certainly, the New York sojourn of the composer-pianist Enrique Granados influenced the programming of the major concert venues in that city. Granados's *Goyescas* was the first opera in Spanish ever to be produced at the Metropolitan Opera House (January

1916). "The Nightingale" (a song for voice and piano arranged from *Goyescas*) was performed on a New York Philharmonic concert in 1916, and "Intermezzo" and "Epilogue" from *Goyescas* were given their U.S. premiere on March 10–11, 1916, in Philadelphia by the Philadelphia Orchestra. In New York to supervise the rehearsals of *Goyescas*, Granados played a concert of his own music with the cellist Pablo Casals, another Spaniard, on January 24, sponsored by the Society of the Friends of Music. According to the review by Richard Aldrich, Granados "played with brilliancy and power." Of course, the critic also noted that "there were also the languor, the smoldering fire, the tenderness and passion which belong in this music, by which it is marked with Spanish character even more than the rhythms and certain of the melodic traits that run through it."[120]

Among Spanish musicians who were influential in the United States, the violinist, conductor, and composer Enrique Fernández Arbós (1863–1939) was a tireless advocate of his country's music.[121] Before coming to the United States, Arbós had made a name for himself in Europe as a virtuoso violinist. He was a professor of violin at the Royal College of Music in London and in 1904 became principal conductor of the recently founded Orquesta Sinfónica de Madrid. He later conducted major orchestras in Barcelona, Budapest, London, Paris, Prague, and Rome and was noted especially as an interpreter of new music. He conducted the first performance of Stravinsky's *The Rite of Spring* in Spain, albeit in 1932, nearly two decades after it was composed (1913), and conducted the Madrid premiere of Manuel de Falla's *Noches en los jardines de España* (1916), a piece that reached the United States in 1924 as *Nights in the Gardens of Spain*.

Before finally settling in Madrid in 1916, Arbós visited the United States several times and had warm collegial relations here with a number of orchestras (he conducted in Buffalo, Chicago, Detroit, Cleveland, New York, St. Louis, San Francisco, Los Angeles, and Hollywood).[122] "Most Americans had never heard Spanish music until Arbós introduced it in city after city."[123] As I have mentioned, he was concertmaster of the Boston Symphony Orchestra in the 1903–4 season. He conducted the Symphony Society of New York in a series of concerts from March 22 to April 1, 1928, and conducted the U.S. premiere of his orchestration of the Albéniz "Triana" from the *Iberia* suite in two concerts, thus introducing this now-beloved piece to U.S. music lovers through his access to a major venue ("Triana" was the most popular of the nine pieces from *Iberia* that Arbós orchestrated). Though Albéniz had visited the United States as an adolescent in 1872–73 (on a runaway tour of the Americas that he had begun as a stowaway on a ship bound for South America), it appears that his music was first popularized in the United States through the wildly acclaimed Italian pianist Alfredo Casella's arrangement of and performance as soloist in the *Rapsodía española,* op. 70 (1887), with the New York Philharmonic in 1922–23 and with the Boston Symphony in 1923. Arbós also brought with him Ernesto Halffter's *Sinfonietta* (1925) for its U.S. premiere by the Symphony Society of New York on March 22 and 25, 1928, though this piece (which is less folkloric) did not capture the imagination of the U.S. public and performers in the same way that the Albéniz pieces did. In the winter of 1929 Arbós was guest conductor of the Boston Symphony (under Serge Koussevitzky) and took advantage of this position to program a number of unusual Spanish works in his three appearances with the orchestra in 1929 and again in 1931 (see especially the entries for January 1929 in table 7.1).

Table 7.1. Performances of Spanish Music and Music in the Spanish Idiom by Principal U.S. Orchestras to 1950

Year	New York	Boston	Chicago
1887		Lalo, *Symphonie espagnole,* op. 21 (vln. and orch.)	
1888	[NYSS: Bizet, "Seguidilla" from *Carmen*]		
1890		Lalo, *Symphonie espagnole*	
1894		Liszt, *Rapsodie espagnole* (arr. Busoni)	
1896		Bizet, Suite from *Carmen*	
1897		Bizet, Suite from *Carmen* Lalo, *Symphonie espagnole* Chabrier, *España*	
1898			
1899			
1900		Lalo, *Symphonie espagnole*	
1901			
1902			
1903		E. Fernández Arbós, ***Tango,*** for vln., op. 6 (Arbós soloist)	
1904		Lalo, *Symphonie espagnole*	
1905	[NYSS: Sarasate, ***Ziguernerweisen*** for vln. and orch. (soloist J. Kubelik)]		
1906			
1907	[NYSS: Chabrier, *España*]	Lalo, *Symphonie espagnole* (Kreisler soloist) Chabrier, *España* (twice)	
1908	[NYSS: Moszkowski, *Malagueña*]	Rimsky-Korsakoff, *Capriccio español,* op. 34	

Table 7.1. Con't.

Year	New York	Boston	Chicago
1909	[NYSS: Ravel, *Rapsodie espagnole*]	Rimsky-Korsakoff, *Capriccio español*	
1910	1910–11 Chabrier, *España* (cond. G. Mahler) [NYSS: Lalo, *Symphonie espagnole*, Dec. 4, 1910, vln., Jaroslav Kocian]		Lalo, *Symphonie espagnole* (Oct. 28–29, 1910; vln. Jaroslav Kocian)
1911			
1912	[NYSS: Dec. 8, Lalo, *Symphonie espagnole*]	Chabrier, *España*	
1913	Josef Stransky, cond., 1913–14: Bizet, "Aria for Micaela" from *Carmen* Rimsky-Korsakoff, *Capriccio español* Liszt-Seidl, *Spanish Rhapsody* Sarasate, ***Ziguernerweisen,*** for vln. and piano		
1914	1914–15, Chabrier, *España* [Jan. 6, 1914: Lalo, *Symphonie espagnole* (arr. vln. and piano; Aeolian Hall recital, J. Thibaud, vln.)] [NYSS: Debussy, *Ibéria*]	Ravel, *Rapsodie espagnole* Rimsky-Korsakoff, *Capriccio español*	
1915	1914–15: [NYSS: Bizet, "Dances" from *Carmen;* Chabrier, *España*] Moszkowski, *Malagueña* Rimsky-Korsakoff, *Capriccio español* 1915–16: Bizet, "Aria for Micaela" from *Carmen* Rimsky-Korsakoff, *Capriccio español* Lalo, *Symphonie espagnole*	Chabrier, *España* Lalo, *Symphonie espagnole* Rimsky-Korsakoff, *Capriccio español*	
1916	1916–17: Chabrier, *España* Bizet, "Aria for Micaela" from *Carmen* Rimsky-Korsakoff, *Capriccio español* Moszkowski, *Malagueña* Granados, "The Nightingale" from ***Goyescas*** (song with piano)	Chabrier, *España* Albéniz, ***Catalonia,*** suite 1 Ravel, *Rapsodie espagnole*	

Table 7.1. Con't.

Year	New York	Boston	Chicago
1917	1917–18: Chabrier, *España* Rimsky-Korsakoff, *Capriccio español* Esplá, **Veille d'armes de Don Quichotte**		
1918	1918–19: Chabrier, *España* Rimsky-Korsakoff, *Capriccio español* [NYSS: Lalo, *Symphonie espagnole* (Seidel)]	Rimsky-Korsakoff, *Capriccio español*	
1919	1919–20: Chabrier, *España* (3 times) Rimsky-Korsakoff, *Capriccio español* [NYSS: Lalo, *Symphonie espagnole* Turina, **La procesión del Rocío**]	Chabrier, *España* Apr. 18: world premiere, R. Laparra, *Un Dimanche Basque,* piano and orch. (Laparra soloist) Ravel, *Rapsodie espagnole*	
1920	1920–21: Lalo, *Symphonie espagnole* (vln. and orch.; Joan Manén soloist) Rimsky-Korsakoff, *Capriccio español* (twice)	Lalo, *Symphonie espagnole*	
1921	12–30: Falla, "Three Dances" from **El sombrero de tres picos**		
1922	[NYSS: "Seguidilla" from *Carmen* Debussy, *Ibéria*] 1922–23: Lalo, *Symphonie espagnole* (J. Thibaud, soloist) Albéniz (arr. Casella), **Rapsodia española** for piano and orch.		Debussy, *Ibéria* Chabrier, *España*
1923	1923–24: Chabrier, *España* [NYSS: Falla, "Three Dances" from **El sombrero de tres picos**]	Albéniz (arr. Casella), **Rapsodia española** for piano and orch. (Casella soloist) Ravel, *Rapsodie espagnole* Salzedo, **Enchanted Isles** (harp and orch.; Salzedo soloist) Turina, **Danzas fantásticas**	Albéniz (arr. Casella), **Rapsodia española** for piano and orch. (twice; Casella soloist and guest cond.)
1924	[NYSS: Rimsky-Korsakoff, *Capriccio español*] 1924–25: Chabrier, *España* (twice)	Lalo, *Symphonie espagnole* (Thibaud soloist) Falla, **Noches en los jardines de España** (Mar.)	

Table 7.1. Con't.

Year	New York	Boston	Chicago
	Rimsky-Korsakoff, *Capriccio español*	Falla, **El amor brujo** (Oct.) Rimsky-Korsakoff, *Capriccio español*	
1925	[NYSS: Ravel, *Alborada del gracioso*] 1925–26: Ravel, *Rapsodie espagnole* (3 times)		
1926	[NYSS: Jan. 17 Falla, **Noches en los jardines de España** (piano and orch.; soloist Gieseking)] Dec. 23–24: Falla, **Noches en los jardines de España** (piano and orch.; soloist Schmitz)	Falla, "Three Dances" from **El sombrero de tres picos** Dec. 31: Falla, **Concerto** for harpsichord, flute, oboe, clarinet, vln., cello (U.S. premiere)	
1927	[NYSS: Ravel, *Alborada del gracioso* Albéniz, **Catalonia**] Oct. 22–23: Falla, **Noches en los jardines de España** (piano and orch.; soloist Schmitz) Nov.: Debussy, *Ibéria*	Falla, **El amor brujo**	
1928	[NYSS: Albéniz, excerpts from **Iberia** Ravel, *Alborada del gracioso* Ravel, *Rapsodie espagnole* Debussy, *Ibéria* Falla, **El amor brujo** Granados, "Intermezzo" from **Goyescas** E. Halffter, **Sinfonietta**] Mar.: Falla, **El amor brujo** (Braslau, contralto) 1928–29: Cassadó, *Catalonian Rhapsody* Ravel, *Rapsodie espagnole* Nov. 23, 25, 26: Debussy, *Ibéria*	Ravel, *Rapsodie espagnole*	
1929	Dec. 19, 20: Falla, "Three Dances" from **El sombrero de tres picos**	1–18: Turina, **La procesión del Rocío** 1–18: Ravel, *Alborada del gracioso* 1–18: E. Halffter, **Sinfonietta** 1–18: Albéniz, **Iberia** suite (arr. Arbós)	

Table 7.1. Con't.

Year	New York	Boston	Chicago
		Falla, "Three Dances" from ***El sombrero de tres picos*** 12–6: Ravel, *Bolero* Ravel, *Rapsodie espagnole*	
1930		Falla, ***Noches en los jardines de España*** Falla, "Three Dances" from ***El sombrero de tres picos*** Ravel, *Rapsodie espagnole* Rimsky-Korsakoff, *Capriccio español*	
1931	Dec. 23, 24, 26, 27: Falla, "Three Dances" from *El sombrero de tres picos*	Albéniz, "Al Albaicín," and "Navarra" from ***Iberia*** (arr. Arbós) Falla, ***El amor brujo***	
1932	1932–33: Debussy, *Ibéria*	Rimsky-Korsakoff, *Capriccio español* Ravel, *Rapsodie espagnole*	
1933	1933–34: Debussy, *Ibéria*	Falla, "Three Dances" from ***El sombrero de tres picos***	
1934	April: Falla, ***El amor brujo*** (Braslau, contralto) Dec.: Ravel, *Rapsodie espagnole* (3 times)	Rimsky-Korsakoff, *Capriccio español* Falla, ***El amor brujo***	
1935	1935–36: Ravel, *Alborada del gracioso* (twice) Debussy, *Ibéria*		
1936	1936–37: Ravel, *Rapsodie espagnole* Lalo, *Symphonie espagnole* (Manuel Quiroga, vln.) [Chávez, *Sinfonía de Antígona*] Falla, "Three Dances" from ***El sombrero de tres picos*** [Chávez, *Sinfonía índia*] Ravel, *Alborada del gracioso* Albéniz, ***Triana*** (the latter two as a pair, March 10, 12, Apr. 3, 4)	Ravel, *Rapsodie espagnole*	
1937	1937–38: Debussy, *Ibéria* (3 times) Goossens, "Overture" to *Don Juan de Mañara* Lalo, *Symphonie espagnole* (M. Piastró, vln.) Falla, "Three Dances" from ***El sombrero de tres picos*** (twice)	Ravel, *Rapsodie espagnole*	

Table 7.1. Con't.

Year	New York	Boston	Chicago
1938	Mar. 16, 17, 19: Falla, *Noches en los jardines de España*	Rimsky-Korsakoff, *Capriccio español* Ravel, *Rapsodie espagnole*	
1939	1939–40: Rimsky-Korsakoff, *Capriccio español* Ravel, *Bolero* Debussy, *Ibéria* (twice) Falla, "Three Dances" from *El sombrero de tres picos* (3 times)		
1940	1940–41: Rimsky-Korsakoff, *Capriccio español* Ravel, *Rapsodie espagnole* Lalo, *Symphonie espagnole* (Milstein, vln.)	Falla, "Three Dances" from *El sombrero de tres picos*	
1941	1941–42: Centennial season	Rimsky-Korsakoff, *Capriccio español*	
1942		Rimsky-Korsakoff, *Capriccio español*	
1943		Rimsky-Korsakoff, *Capriccio español*	
1944		Ravel, *Rapsodie espagnole* Albéniz, Three pieces from *Iberia* (arr. Arbós)	
1945		Rimsky-Korsakoff, *Capriccio español* Ravel, *Rapsodie espagnole* Lalo, *Symphonie espagnole*	
1945		Falla, *El amor brujo*	
1946		Falla, *El amor brujo* Falla, "Three Dances" from *El sombrero de tres picos* Falla, *Noches en los jardines de España*	
1949		Albéniz, *Iberia* (complete; arr. Arbós)	

Notes: Pieces by Spanish composers are in italic boldface. The "New York" column includes data for the Symphony Society of New York (NYSS), 1878–1928, and the Philharmonic Society of New York (the New York Philharmonic Orchestra), 1842–1942.
Sources: See note 112.

It is noteworthy that Arbós was invited to be guest conductor of the Boston orchestra for two seasons, whereas his more famous French colleague Maurice Ravel conducted it only twice in 1928. Two of Ravel's large-scale pieces in the "Spanish idiom," the *Alborada del gracioso* (U.S. premiere January 1 and 2, 1925) and the *Rapsodie espagnole* (New York, November 21, 1909), received their first U.S. performances by the Symphony Society of New York, the same organization that presented Arbós and that had performed the U.S. premiere of Joaquín Turina's highly successful *La procesión del Rocío* (1912), a nationalist symphonic poem drawing on Andalucian folk tunes, on November 13, 1919.[124] For his own concerts with the Symphony Society, Arbós included both Ravel works, along with Debussy's *Ibéria*, Granados's "Intermezzo" from *Goyescas*, Falla's *El amor brujo*, and the Ernesto Halffter *Sinfonietta*. These New York programs, and those Arbós put together for Boston the next season, join French works in the "Spanish idiom" with more contemporary works by Spanish composers.

In the material I have been able to collect about the Boston Symphony Orchestra, it is unclear whether Arbós was responsible for some landmark performances of more recent Spanish works, such as the U.S. premiere of Falla's *Concerto for Harpsichord, Flute, Oboe, Clarinet, Violin, Cello* (composed 1923–26) on December 31, 1926; the U.S. premiere of Falla's "Three Dances" from *The Three-Cornered Hat* on December 30, 1921; the unique appearance of Carlos Salzedo, harpist, as soloist in his own symphonic poem *Enchanted Isles* for harp and orchestra, February 16, 1923; and the world premiere of the Basque composer Raoul Laparra's *Un Dimanche Basque,* for orchestra and piano, on April 18, 1919, with the composer as piano soloist. Laparra, with whom Van Vechten corresponded, was living in the United States and had given a concert at Aeolian Hall in New York in April 1918 entitled "A Musical Journey Through Spain," in which he expressed "the vision of a French traveller."[125]

In general, the 1920s and 1930s seem to have been a sort of golden window of opportunity for Spanish music in the United States and for talented classical musicians from Europe, including visiting Spaniards.[126] The virtuoso violinist Joan Manén, from Barcelona, performed an old warhorse in the "Spanish idiom," the Lalo *Symphonie espagnole* (1875), with the New York Philharmonic under Josef Stransky's baton for the 1920–21 season, and another Spaniard, Manuel Quiroga, performed it with the New York Philharmonic in February 1937. The *Symphonie espagnole* was the great favorite among pieces in the Spanish idiom on U.S. concert programs in the first decades of the twentieth century, whether performed with Spanish or non-Spanish violinists. This French violin concerto in five movements in the Spanish idiom was composed originally for the Spanish violinist Pablo Sarasate, and Sarasate's performances in Paris brought Lalo his first important recognition as a composer. The virtuoso qualities of Spanish musicians who made a splash in the United States were generally attributed in part to a Spanish temperament, though at least two of these—the young cellist Pablo Casals and the pianist José Iturbi—did not specialize in Spanish music on their early U.S. tours. Casals was noted especially for his revivals of music by J. S. Bach, and Iturbi (who personified the Spanish musical artist for many Americans because of his appearances in Hollywood movies) played mostly Mozart and Beethoven on his many U.S. tours, which began in 1928.[127] During his U.S. tour of 1930 Iturbi gave seventy-seven concerts. In 1936 Iturbi was named principal conductor of the Rochester Philharmonic Orchestra.

Highly sensitive, romantic, rubato- and vibrato-filled virtuoso performances, and a strong identification with both Spanish repertory and the most Spanish and most popular of instruments, the guitar, made Andrés Segovia the best-known representative of Spain's musical culture, especially in the United States, where Segovia made his concert debut in 1928. Though his musical choices were to some extent aligned with early twentieth-century eclecticism (he cultivated earlier Spanish guitar music but also performed music by contemporary Spanish composers and expanded the instrument's repertory with transcriptions and arrangements of J. S. Bach and other baroque composers), Segovia's musical temperament and public personality were romantic, such that his presence in the United States tended to cement the image of the flashy, hopelessly nostalgic, sensual, romantically charged, and Spanish entertainer.

If Segovia had his place in U.S. concert life (and in the living rooms of music lovers, thanks to his many recordings, the first of which was issued in 1927), so did the colorful Spanish idiom. For the New York Philharmonic's concerts under the direction of Josef Stransky (a Czech) between 1911 and 1923, a stable handful of favorites by major French, German, and Slavic composers brought forth the Spanish idiom. The New York Philharmonic Orchestra's repertory in this period was representative of the prevailing musical taste, if a bit more difficult and varied than that of other U.S. orchestras. Stransky was a popular conductor, and these colorful, novel pieces were heard season after season in New York, thanks to his historically important broadening of the orchestra's repertory and deemphasis of the Austro-German monuments that previously had dominated the orchestra's offerings.[128]

Though the "familiar accusation that the gates of the concerts are too wide open to new music" was evidently heard by the music directors of the New York and Boston orchestras with some regularity, the Spanish pieces that were most smoothly received into the orchestral repertory (by Albéniz, Granados, Falla, and Turina) were those whose overt nationalism was heard as merely "folkloric" and wrapped in a harmonious consonance.[129] These were the pieces whose modernism resided in a striking rhythmic vitality that could be heard as lively but not jarring or barbaric (à la Stravinsky) to the tender ears of middle-class U.S. music lovers. In large part as well, the non-Spanish pieces in the "Spanish idiom," which U.S. audiences already enjoyed as lighter fare, had allowed this same public to develop an appreciation and appetite for a Spanish musical nationalism, even if it entered the concert halls not through the front door as confrontationally authentic modernism but through the side door as exotically flavored virtuoso novelty. One example is that Albéniz's lovely postromantic "Triana" from *Iberia,* in its orchestration by Arbós, was performed in December 1928 during a New York Philharmonic concert conducted by Walter Damrosch only a few days before the strikingly modern concerts of December 20–21, which included the world premiere of the Swiss-born immigrant Ernest Bloch's *America* and George Gershwin's *An American in Paris.*[130] Excerpts from Manuel de Falla's ballet score *El amor brujo* (composed 1914–15; concert version 1916) received their U.S. premiere April 15–17, 1922, with the Philadelphia Orchestra and were performed in New York only a few years later (the 1927–28 season) by the New York Philharmonic with Sophie Braslau (a contralto with the Metropolitan Opera). This singer also performed excerpts from *El amor brujo* with the New York Philharmonic for the 1933–34 season. Falla's *Nights in the Gardens of Spain* (1911–15) was performed in December 1926 and October 1927 by the New York Philharmonic, though on both occasions the piano soloist was E. Robert Schmitz and the piece was programmed for him by the principal conductor, Wilhelm Mengelberg. In March 1939 Falla's *Nights in the Gardens of Spain* was again performed by the New York Philharmonic, conducted by John Barbirolli with the pianist Arthur Rubinstein. The Falla pieces—excerpts from *El amor brujo* with Sophie Braslau, and *Nights in the Gardens of Spain* with virtuoso pianists—may have been chosen by the soloists in each case. The orchestral suite of "Three Dances" from Falla's ballet score *The Three-Cornered Hat* (*El sombrero de tres picos;* composed in 1918–19 but given its New York premiere by the Symphony Society of New York in December 1923) clearly became part of the regular repertory of the New York Philharmonic during the years in which Arturo Toscanini led the orchestra (1929–36), and it was presented by this orchestra in multiple performances in 1929, 1931, 1937, 1938, and 1940.

Special circumstances most likely led to the sudden increase in "Spanish" pieces in the New York Philharmonic's programs for the 1936–37 concert season. It is tempting to ask whether political sympathies were ignited in New York at the outbreak of the Spanish Civil War, because "Spain, as the battleground for [an] assortment of European political ideologies, became a focal point for the idealism of American liberals in general and the youth of the country in particular."[131] It appears more likely, however, that local artistic decisions in New York were responsible. During this season three guest "composer-conductors" from different countries directed the orchestra for two weeks each (Carlos Chávez [from Mexico], Igor Stravinsky, and Georges Enesco) in addition to the concerts directed by the two new principal resident conductors designated to share the season, Barbirolli and Artur Rodzinski. The French composer Maurice Ravel's "Spanish" pieces (*Rapsodie espagnole* and *Alborada del gracioso*) were clearly carried over from the two previous seasons—Toscanini's final ones with the orchestra. Lalo's *Symphonie espagnole,* op. 21, was programmed for the Spanish violinist Manuel Quiroga, and the two pieces by Chávez were recent and showcased this musician's presence as one of the special guest conductors.

The Chicago Symphony Orchestra (whose players had first been brought together as the Theodore Thomas Orchestra) attracted a few of the same soloists as the New York Philharmonic and performed a similar repertory, though it was not as well funded, gave many fewer concerts, and had a slightly lower professional profile (though the Chicago orchestra under Thomas was the first to play the music of Richard Strauss in the United States in the 1880s and 1890s).[132] In Chicago, as in New York, Boston, and Philadelphia, flashy pieces by non-Spanish composers brought the "Spanish idiom" to U.S. audiences for classical music. In its twentieth season (1910–11), for example, the Chicago orchestra conducted by Frederick Stock (the principal conductor and successor to Thomas) performed the Lalo, *Symphonie espagnole* (October 28–29, 1910), with violinist Jaroslav Kocian. For the opening of its thirty-second season, October 13–14, 1922, the orchestra performed Claude Debussy's *Ibéria* (1905–8) and later in the same month at the University of Chicago's Mandel Hall, the Chabrier orchestral rhapsody *España* (1883). Debussy's *Ibéria* was performed again by the Chicago Symphony April 25–26, 1924. The first performances of a Spanish orchestral composition by the Chicago Symphony Orchestra seem to have taken place on March 23 and 24, 1923, when Alfredo Casella, soloist and guest conductor with the Chicago Symphony, performed the Albéniz *Rapsodía española,* op. 70 (1887), in his arrangement for piano and orchestra.[133]

Spanish music had enjoyed a brief but certain vogue in the highest levels of U.S. concert life in the early twentieth century, especially in the 1920s and 1930s. The history of Spanish music as a subject for historical research in the United States has been conditioned to some extent by the presence, absence, and marketing of Spanish music in U.S. concert life, and the attitudes of U.S. musicians and musical patrons, more than by scholarly obscurantism or the lure of the historical unknown. The few who wrote about Spanish music in the first four decades of the twentieth century were attracted to their subject by the sound of the music, its lively exoticism and novelty, and the much-touted "Spanish idiom." This was true as well of the first complete history of Spanish music published in English—Gilbert Chase's *The Music of Spain* (1941).[134]

Chase was a noted and many-faceted contributor to U.S. musicology, but he was not a professional musicologist (from 1929 to 1961 he worked as a music critic, cultural consultant, bibliographer of the Latin American collection at the Library of Congress, broadcaster, administrator, and diplomat). He did not feel constrained by the questions that occupied others in the discipline, but neither did he place himself at its center. In the decades in which U.S. musicology was shaped as an academic area, Spanish music came to be associated with what we might call the softer, more American, more journalistic, and less documented side of musicology. Several aspects of the history of Spanish music in the United States to the 1940s resonate in important ways with attitudes toward Spanish music in Spain, but some of these seem remarkably similar to the problems that scholars of U.S. music struggled with in the same period. Isabel Pope, whose articles are in the traditional vein of documentary scholarship, had studied romance philology at Radcliffe and was a musicology student at Harvard when she began writing about early Spanish music. Charles Lummis and Eleanor Hague were collectors of folk songs, Arthur Farwell was a composer, and Carl Van Vechten and J. B. Trend were journalists (though Trend was more of a scholar and trained Hispanist than Van Vechten was). In the writings of the first Americans to take on Spanish music from a historical perspective, a sort of promotional criticism weighed more heavily than a strictly documented positivism or a theoretically driven analysis. All these writers described Spanish art music and art music in the Spanish idiom with the same adjectival passion and sense of mystery. And just as François-Auguste Gevaert heard the chords of sixteenth-century Spanish *vihuela* pieces call forth the "most mysterious" sounds of European music, U.S. scholars and listeners in the early twentieth century listened for echoes of an interesting and mythologized musical past different from the majority's European inheritance. They listened to Spanish music, from Juan del Encina and Miguel de Fuenllana to Granados, Turina, and de Falla, in much the same way as more recent listeners have heard salsa. What I am suggesting is akin to what Frances R. Aparicio has described: "Perceptions by Anglos of Latin musical culture in the United States reveal an eroticized reading, a sort of tropicalization, that is not limited to the field of music. . . . This primitivist othering relies on strategies of depicting Latinas/os as figures that embody emotions, sentiment ("heart"), and magic . . . thus continuing the discursive tradition of Anglo-constructed stereotypes and tropicalized representations of the regions and cultures south of the border."[135] Just as the romantically exotic elements in Spanish history attracted U.S. nineteenth-century historians to Spanish subjects, the lure of the musically picturesque and seductively audible exotic bewitched twentieth-century attitudes toward Spanish music.

Notes

1. Charles Hamm, *Music in the New World* (New York: W. W. Norton, 1983), 86–88.

2. For John Adams's disparaging opinion of the early musical life in the United States in 1780, see John H. Mueller, *The American Symphony Orchestra: A Social History of Musical Taste* (Bloomington: Indiana University Press, 1951), 17.

3. Hamm, *Music in the New World,* 92.

4. H. Wiley Hitchcock, *Music in the United States: A Historical Introduction,* 3d ed. (Englewood Cliffs, N.J.: Prentice Hall, 1988), 53–36.

5. Richard Crawford, *America's Musical Life: A History* (New York: W. W. Norton, 2001), 7–9.

6. Hitchcock, *Music in the United States,* 39.

7. British-style ballad opera is described in Hitchcock, *Music in the United States,* 34. The first opera performed in the Americas was *La púrpura de la rosa* (libretto by Pedro Calderón de la Barca, music by the Spanish composer Tomás de Torrejón y Velasco after Juan Hidalgo), performed in Lima in 1701 for the viceroy Melchor Portocarrero Laso de la Vega, count of Monclova, in honor of King Philip V's accession to the Spanish throne. It was revived in later years in Lima and Mexico City (see the introduction to *La púrpura de la rosa,* ed. Louise K. Stein (Madrid: Fundación Autor/Instituto Complutense de Ciencias Musicales, 1999). The first opera to be composed by an American-born composer was Manuel Zumaya's *Partenope,* which set an older libretto in Italian by Silvio Stampiglia and was performed May 1, 1711, in Mexico City on commission from the recently arrived viceroy of New Spain, the duke of Linares. From 1796 French operas were regularly performed in New Orleans. The first Italian operas heard in the United States were those by Rossini and Mozart presented by the Spaniard Manuel García's Italian opera company in its yearlong visit to New York in 1825–26. Manuel García was already a famous singer, as were his daughters, María Malibran and Pauline García Viardot. See Carmen de Reparáz, *María Malibran, 1808–1836* (Madrid: Ministerio de Educación y Ciencia, 1976); and James Radomski, *Manuel Garcia (1775–1832): Chronicle of the Life of a "Bel Canto" Tenor at the Dawn of Romanticism* (Oxford: Oxford University Press, 2000).

8. In this exchange between Franklin and the Infante Gabriel, interest in a rare and expensive musical instrument, known today as the glass harmonica, was the basis for an important diplomatic initiative. On December 30, 1776, Congress had decided to seek military alliance with France and Spain and to solicit their aid in the continued war against Great Britain. In January 1777 Franklin was appointed by Congress to serve as "commissioner" to the court of Carlos III of Spain, charged with establishing a "friendly and commercial connection between the subjects of his most catholic majesty the King of Spain and the people of these states" that would be "beneficial to both nations." Franklin was directed to secure a "true and sincere friendship and a firm, inviolable and universal peace for the defense, protection and safety of the navigation and mutual commerce of the subjects." Franklin recognized that he had been assigned this mission merely because he had briefly corresponded with the Infante, a dedicat-

ed musician and collector of musical instruments, and they had exchanged gifts. The original of Franklin's letter of December 12, 1775, is among the papers of the Infante Gabriel in the archive of the Palacio Real de Oriente in Madrid (Archivo del Infante don Gabriel, Secretaría, leg. 738), though it is not mentioned by the editors of Franklin's correspondence, who cite only the two extant copies. The relevant letters are transcribed in *The Papers of Benjamin Franklin,* ed. William B. Willcox, 35 vols. (New Haven, Conn.: Yale University Press, 1959–99) 22:61–63, 298–99. Concerning the Infante Gabriel and music, see Juan Martínez Cuesta and Beryl Kenyon Pascual, "El Infante Don Gabriel (1752–88), gran aficionado a la música," *Revista de musicología* 11 (1988): 767–806 and other references cited therein; and Celia López Chávez, "Benjamin Franklin, España y la diplomacia de una armónica," *Espacio, Tiempo y Forma,* ser. 4, 13 (2000): 319–37.

9. Charles Burney, *A General History of Music from the Earliest Ages to the Present Period,* ed. Frank Mercer, 2 vols. (1789; rpt., New York: Harcourt, Brace, 1935), 2:235–41; see also Kerry S. Grant, *Dr. Burney as Critic and Historian of Music* (Ann Arbor: UMI Research Press, 1983), 139.

10. As Judith Etzion has pointed out, Burney's list of musicians was partly drawn from earlier French and German writings, namely, Sébastian de Brossard's *Dictionnaire de musique* (Paris, 1703) and especially Johann Gottfried Walther's *Musikalisches Lexicon* (Leipzig, 1732); see Judith Etzion, "Spanish Music as Perceived in Western Music Historiography: A Case of the Black Legend?," *International Review of Aesthetics and Sociology of Music* 29 (1998): 100.

11. Grant, *Dr. Burney as Critic,* 305. Burney's *General History* was for sale in 1784 in Boston, as were his books about his musical travels in Europe; the singing master Andrew Law owned Burney's volumes and had purchased them in Boston in 1784. My thanks to Richard Crawford for pointing out this reference from Richard Crawford, *Andrew Law, American Psalmodist* (Evanston, Ill.: Northwestern University Press, 1968), 136. Beginning in 1820, issues of a musical periodical published in Boston, *The Euterpeiad; or, Musical Intelligencer,* edited by John R. Parker of the Franklin Music Warehouse, included "A Brief History of Music" that "continued for nearly two years, and which was unblushingly appropriated without acknowledgment from the voluminous pages of Dr. Burney," as noted in Harold Earle Johnson, *Musical Interludes in Boston, 1795–1830* (New York: Columbia University Press, 1943), 251.

12. Frederic V. Grunfeld noted that the Spanish guitar entered colonial America from the American Southwest but offered no documentation on this point (Grunfeld, *The Art and Times of the Guitar* [New York: Collier Books, 1974], 238 and 241). The term *Spanish guitar* might have been applied to several different instruments—the old five-course guitar whose vogue had taken over Europe and Latin America in the baroque era, the newer six-course guitar usually identified as a Spanish instrument, and the modern six-string guitar that became the instrument for the virtuoso romantic repertory of the nineteenth century (Paul Warren Cox, "Classic Guitar Technique and Its Evolution as Reflected in the Method Books, ca. 1770–1850" [Ph.D. diss., Indiana University, 1978], 6–27, 180–81).

13. According to Grunfeld, "colonial and Revolutionary America was well supplied with English-made guitars" (Grunfeld, *Art and Times of the Guitar,* 238). I acknowledge with gratitude the clarifications generously offered me about the guitar in the United States by the late Calvin Elliker, my colleague at the University of Michigan, and by James Tyler and Richard Crawford. Eighteenth-century references to the guitar in America are provided in Oscar George Theodore Sonneck, *A Bibliography of Early Secular American Music (18th Century),* revised and enlarged by William Treat Upton (Washington, D.C.: Library of Congress, Music Division, 1945).

14. John Tasker Howard, *Our American Music,* 4th ed. (New York: Thomas Y. Crowell, 1965), 65–68.

15. Grunfeld, *Art and Times of the Guitar,* 238–41.

16. Johnson, *Musical Interludes in Boston,* 292–95.

17. Ibid., 85.

18. Etzion, "Spanish Music," 111.

19. Grunfeld, *Art and Times of the Guitar,* 241.

20. Ibid., 238–41.

21. Crawford, *America's Musical Life,* 16–18, 435. John Donald Robb describes the Spanish and Mexican "tap roots" of this tradition, explaining that a number of the songs were composed in North America in the mid-nineteenth century, while others may be versions of songs originating in Spain as far back as the sixteenth century (Robb, *Hispanic Folk Music of New Mexico and the Southwest: A Self-Portrait of a People* [Norman: University of Oklahoma Press, 1980], 5–8). In *A Texas-Mexican Cancionero: Folksongs of the Lower Border,* which includes six Spanish ballads from "Colonial days," Américo Paredes has stated, "It is well to remember that, whatever the genetic makeup of the settlers who moved into the frontier provinces, what welded them together into one people were the Spanish language and the Spanish culture. . . . Another thing Spain gave us was her folksongs. When they came to the Rio Grande, our ancestors brought with them many songs of Spanish origin. . . . The songs were already Mexicanized, to be sure, though how much we cannot know" (Paredes, *A Texas-Mexican Cancionero* [Urbana: University of Illinois Press, 1976], 5).

22. Charles Lummis, "Flowers of Our Lost Romance," prefatory essay to *Spanish Songs of Old California,* 3d ed., collected and translated by Charles F. Lummis (Los Angeles: By the author, 1923), 3; Crawford quotes Lummis's remembrance that the songs of the "quiet Mexican herders" displayed a remarkable and natural "sense of time and rhythm" (Crawford, *America's Musical Life,* 437).

23. See John Koegel, "Mexican-American Music in Nineteenth-Century Southern California: The Lummis Wax Cylinder Collection of the Southeast Museum, Los Angeles" (Ph.D. diss., Claremont Graduate School, 1994).

24. Crawford, *America's Musical Life,* 441.

25. Eleanor Hague, *Spanish-American Folk-Songs,* Memoirs of the American Folklore Society 10 (1917; rpt., New York: Kraus Reprint Co., 1969), 21, 111.

26. Carl Van Vechten, "Notes to the Text," *The Music of Spain* (New York: Alfred E. Knopf, 1918), 170.

27. Crawford, *America's Musical Life,* 439–41.

28. Merle Armitage, foreword to *Spanish Folk Songs of the Southwest,* collected and transcribed by Mary R. Van Stone (1928; rpt., Fresno, Calif.: Academy Guild Press, 1963), 3–4.

29. Gilbert Chase, *America's Music* (New York: McGraw-Hill, 1955), 319.

30. Hitchcock, *Music in the United States,* 55–68.

31. Ibid., 91.

32. Ibid., 85–86.

33. Ibid., 85–87; Irving Lowens, "Gottschalk, Louis Moreau," *The New Grove Dictionary of Music and Musicians,* ed. Stanley Sadie, 20 vols. (London: Macmillan, 1980), 7:570–74.

34. "Verdad es que . . . ni nosotros podemos presentar obras ni tratados del siglo XV para demostrar nuestras encontradas opiniones" (quoted in Emilio Casares Rodicio, "Las relaciones musicales entre los Países Bajos y España vistas a través de los investigadores del siglo XIX," in *Musique des Pays-Bas Anciens, Musique Espagnole Ancienne, Actes du Colloque Musicologique International, Bruxelles, 28–29 X 1985,* ed. Paul Becquart and Henri Vanhulst [Louvain: Peeters, 1988], 28 [my translation]).

35. Etzion, "Spanish Music," 114. Ponz was the author of the eighteen-volume *Viage de España* (Madrid, 1776), and Viardot wrote *Sur l'histoire des institutions, de la littérature, du théâtre et des beaux-arts en Espagne* (Paris, 1835).

36. I refer here to Robert Eitner, *Bibliographie der Musik-Sammelwerke des XVI. und XVII. Jahrhunderts* (Berlin: L. Liepmannssohn, 1877) and *Biographisch-bibliographisches Quellen-Lexicon* (Leipzig: Breitkopf and Härtel, 1900–1904); August Wilhelm Ambros, *Geschichte der Musik* (Leipzig, 1862; facsimile, ed. Heinrich Reiman, Hildsheim: G. Olms, 1968); and François-Joseph Fétis, *Biographie universelle des musiciens et bibliographie générale de la musique,* 8 vols. (Bruxelles: Leroux, 1835–44).

37. Etzion, "Spanish Music," 115. Etzion gives an excellent survey of the coverage of Spain by eighteenth- and nineteenth-century European music historians (93–116).

38. François-Joseph Fétis, *Music Explained to the World; or, How to Understand Music and Enjoy Its Performance* (Boston: O. Ditson; New York: C. H. Ditson, 1800).

39. Gevaert received the Cruz de Isabel la Católica for his *Fantasía sobre motivos españoles,* which Emilio Casares has dubbed "one of the first pieces of European [musical] romanticism inspired by Spain." Casares has questioned whether Gevaert came to know Spanish music well during his travels there or whether he became yet another foreign visitor under the spell of Spain's romantic attraction (Casares, "Las relaciones musicales," 23).

40. François-Auguste Gevaert later modified this position. See his foreword to Guillermo Morphy, *Les Luthistes espagnols du XVIe siècle,* 2 vols. (Leipzig: Breitkopf and Härtel, 1902), 1:ix–xi, to the effect that the modern-sounding harmonies of the Spanish *vihuela* pieces opened the way to understanding the "most mysterious" of European music.

41. The following summary of the historiography of Spanish music is indebted to conversations I have had with my friend Professor Cristina Bordas and to the published

studies of a number of friends and colleagues, most notably, Jorge de Persia, "Distintas aproximaciones al estudio del hecho musical en España durante el siglo XIX," *Revista de musicología* 14 (1991): 307–23; Begoña Lolo, "El sentido de la historicidad en música: España versus Europa," *Anuario del Departamento de Historia y Teoría del Arte* (Madrid: Universidad Autónoma) 4 (1992): 359–65; and Emilio Ros-Fábregas, "Historiografía de la música en las catedrales españolas: Nacionalismo y positivismo en la investigación musicológica," *Codex XXI, revista de la comunicación musical* 1 (1998): 68–135.

42. Mariano Soriano Fuertes, *Historia de la música española desde la venida de los fenicios hasta el año de 1850*, 4 vols. (Madrid and Barcelone: Martín y Salazar, 1855–59).

43. A mostly reliable index to the Barbieri papers in the Biblioteca Nacional is Francisco Asenjo Barbieri, *Biografías y documentos sobre música y músicos Españoles (Legado Barbieri)*, ed. Emilio Casares, 2 vols. (Madrid: Fundación Banco Exterior, 1986). The first volume includes several important historiographical essays about Barbieri. Other major studies of Barbieri include John E. Henken, "Francisco Asenjo Barbieri and the Nineteenth-Century Revival in Spanish National Music" (Ph.D. diss., University of California at Los Angeles, 1987), and Emilio Casares, *Francisco Asenjo Barbieri: El hombre y el creador*, 2 vols. (Madrid: Instituto Complutense de Ciencias Musicales, 1994).

44. Francisco Asenjo Barbieri, ed., *Cancionero musical de los siglos XV y XVI* (Madrid: Tipografía de los Huérfanos, 1890; 2d. ed., Buenos Aires: Editorial Schapire, 1945).

45. On the reception of Barbieri's *Cancionero*, see Casares, "Las relaciones musicales," 22–24.

46. On this point the testimony of Adolfo Salazar seems particularly relevant. See Salazar's *La música de España desde el siglo XVI a Manuel de Falla* (Madrid: Espasa Calpe, 1953), 150–51.

47. Manuel de Falla's essay "Felipe Pedrell," *Revue musicale* (February 1923), was reprinted in Manuel de Falla, *Escritos sobre música y músicos*, ed. Federico Sopeña (Buenos Aires: Espasa-Calpe, 1950), 63–79, which has been translated into English by David Urman and J. M. Thomson, *On Music and Musicians* (London and Boston: Marion Boyars, 1979), 54–64.

48. Ros-Fábregas traces this negative perception of Spain to France in 1782 and describes the "defensive" attitude that it engendered in Spanish scholars (Ros-Fábregas, "Historiografía de la música," 70).

49. The quote is from Edward Hanslick's polemical concert review of Bretón's opera *Los amantes de Teruel,* published in the *Neue Freie Presse* (October 6, 1891), quoted and translated in Etzion, "Spanish Music," 93–94.

50. Grove is quoted in Van Vechten, *Music of Spain,* 20, from the proceedings of the thirty-fourth session of the London Musical Association (1907–8). The nationalist movement in England was roughly contemporary with that in Spain, and Sir George Grove was among the leaders in a revival of English music, a cause served directly by his *Dictionary of Music and Musicians;* on this point see Robert Stradling and Meirion Hughes, *The English Musical Renaissance, 1860–1940* (London: Routledge, 1993). They

note that "by the 1880s the Empire seemed to need English Music as much as it did the Royal Navy" (25).

51. W. S. Rockstro, "Schools of Composition," in *A Dictionary of Music and Musicians (A.D. 1450–1889) by Eminent Writers, English and Foreign*, ed. Sir George Grove, 4 vols. (London: MacMillan, 1890), 3:267–68.

52. Rafael Mitjana, "La musique en Espagne (Art religieux et art profane)," in *Encyclopédie de la musique et dictionnaire du conservatoire*, ed. Albert Lavignac and Lionel de la Laurencie (Paris: Libraire Delagrave, 1920), vol. 4.

53. The Spanish reads: "sacar a la música patria del marasmo en que se encontraba liberándola de la tiranía extranjera" (my translation from the introduction by Antonio Alvarez Cañibano to Rafael Mitjana, *La música en España* [Madrid: Centro de Documentación Musical/INAEM, 1993], ix).

54. Mitjana, *La música en España*, 3.

55. The principal editor of the *Encyclopédie*, Albert Lavignac, also published a book in English called *Music and Musicians*, ed. Henry Edward Krehbiel and trans. William Marchant (New York: Henry Holt, 1899). Although Lavignac had invited Mitjana to write for the *Encyclopédie* (see n.52), in *Music and Musicians* Spain is mentioned only as the home of the guitar and the workplace of the Italians Domenico Scarlatti and Carlo Broschi (Farinelli).

56. Anglés was head of the music section of the Biblioteca de Catalunya, of the musical activities of the Diputación Provincial de Barcelona, professor of music history at the Conservatorio del Liceo in Barcelona (from 1927), and professor of music history at the University of Barcelona (1933–36). From October 1943, the date of its founding, Anglés directed the Instituto Español de Musicología of the Consejo Superior de Investigaciones Científicas and in 1947 was called to Rome by papal appointment to head the Pontificio Istituto di Musica Sacra.

57. Anglés would have known Carl Engel, head of the music division of the Library of Congress in Washington, D.C., and later editor of the *Musical Quarterly* in New York, because they served together on the board of the International Musicological Society (IMS) in 1930; in subsequent years Anglés was among the presenters at IMS conferences who also included Vincent Duckles (University of California at Berkeley), Karl Geiringer (Hamilton College and then Boston University), Glen Haydon (University of North Carolina at Chapel Hill), Jan La Rue (Columbia University), Edward Lowinsky (Black Mountain College, Queens College, University of California at Berkeley, and then the University of Chicago), Bruno Nettl (University of Michigan, Wayne State University, and then the University of Illinois at Urbana-Champaign), Dragan Plamenac (University of Illinois at Urbana-Champaign), Gilbert Reaney (University of California at Los Angeles), Walter Rubsamen (University of California at Los Angeles), and Emanual Winternitz (Harvard University and Columbia University), for example. A number of scholars teaching at U.S. universities were among those who contributed to the Festschrift in honor of Anglés—Willi Apel (Indiana University), Daniel Devoto (Tufts University), Donald J. Grout (Cornell University), Nino Pirrotta (Harvard University), Dragan Plamenac, Isabel Pope (then a tutor at Radcliffe), Walter Rub-

samen, and Leo Schrade (Yale University). See *Miscelánea en homenaje a Monseñor Higinio Anglés*, ed. Miguel Querol, José María Llorens, and José Romeu Figueras, 2 vols. (Barcelona: CSIC, 1958–61).

58. Higini Anglés, "Die mehrstimmige Musik in Spanien vor dem XV. Jahrhundert," *Kongressbericht Beethovens Zentenarfeier* (Vienna, 1927): 158–63.

59. The single-minded pursuit of this agenda alienated a number of scholars, especially those outside Catalunya, and this had a chilling effect on the growth of musicology as a discipline in Spain during the Franco period.

60. On the history of the American Musicological Society, see Richard Crawford, *The American Musicological Society, 1934–1984: An Anniversary Essay* (Philadelphia: American Musicological Society, 1984).

61. From Charles Seeger, "Toward an Establishment of the Study of Musicology in America," an unpublished position paper that he wrote and circulated, quoted in Ann M. Pescatello, *Charles Seeger: A Life in American Music* (Pittsburgh: University of Pittsburgh Press, 1992), 55–56.

62. Pescatello, *Charles Seeger*, 55.

63. Ibid., 55–56. Seeger's early thought was influential, though he did not publish as a scholar until later on.

64. The romantic view of musical folklore had a small place in U.S. musical circles as well; among composers, thoughts about an American music based on American tunes, especially those associated with Native Americans, had been in the air since the last years of the nineteenth century. Chase described the American composer Edward MacDowell's conflicting views and MacDowell's use of Native American melodies in his *Indian Suite* of 1896 (Chase, *America's Music*, 354–64). Hitchcock described the folklorism of Arthur Farwell and others from about 1900 to about 1915 (*Music in the United States*, 155–59). When the Czech composer Antonín Dvořák arrived in the United States to become director of the National Institute of Music in New York (1892–95), he was welcomed as a champion of the cause of "American" music, because in some famous remarks to the press he also called for the use of American musical materials by U.S. composers. The special context for Dvořák's remarks and their misinterpretation through the years are the subject of Michael Beckerman, "The Master's Little Joke: Antonín Dvořák and the Mask of Nation," in *Dvořák and His World*, ed. Michael Beckerman (Princeton, N.J.: Princeton University Press, 1993), 134–54.

65. *Report of the International Society for Music Research, First Congress* (Liége, 1930). The Spanish scholars in attendance were Anglés, José Subirá, and Dom David Pujol; Carl Engel of the Library of Congress's music division represented the United States, as Oscar G. Sonneck had before him. I discuss John B. Trend, *The Music of Spanish History to 1600* (London: Oxford University Press, 1926), later in the chapter.

66. Jon Newsom, "Barbour, James Murray," *The New Grove Dictionary of Music and Musicians*, ed. Stanley Sadie (London: Macmillan, 1980), 2:144.

67. J. Murray Barbour's dissertation was later published as *Tuning and Temperament: A Historical Survey* (East Lansing, Mich.: Michigan State College Press, 1951) and is still required reading on this subject.

68. In 1909–11 Sonneck and Albert A. Stanley of the University of Michigan were setting up a North American section of the Internationale Musik-Gesellschaft, and these are the two Americans who, sometimes together with Mrs. Stanley, attended several international musicological meetings in Europe and England early in the century. Stanley was also an elected vice president of the 1911 congress in London. See *Report of the International Musical Society, Second Congress, Basel, 1906* (Leipzig: Breitkopf, 1907), and *Report of the Fourth Congress of the International Musical Society, London, 1911* (London: Novello, 1912).

69. According to Richard Crawford, Sonneck's scholarly ideal was "responsible scholarly truth, irrespective of subject matter," and he rejected the "intellectual complacency that gives exaggerated respect to received knowledge" (Crawford, "Sonneck and American Musical Historiography," in *Essays in Musicology: A Tribute to Alvin Johnson,* ed. Lewis Lockwood and Edward Roesner [N.p.: American Musicological Society, 1990], 279).

70. Adolfo Salazar's *Music in Our Time: Trends in Music since the Romantic Era* seems to have been a popular text in U.S. academe in its time, to judge by the many copies purchased and found today in the stacks of the Music Library at the University of Michigan (Salazar, *Music in Our Time,* trans. Isabel Pope [New York: W. W. Norton, 1946]).

71. Joseph Kerman, *Contemplating Music: Challenges to Musicology* (Cambridge, Mass.: Harvard University Press, 1985), 26. Kerman continued: "That the most coherent body of thought to develop should centre around Western music of the past was not a requirement, only the unavoidable consequence of academic history. Musicology —the history of Western art music—had thrived in the universities of German-speaking countries for more than fifty years before the war, and habits of mind formed at those times and in those places have been with us ever since" (26).

72. Ibid., 26.

73. Van Vechten notes: "There are no books in English devoted to a study of Spanish music, and few in any language, but what few exist take good care to relate at considerable length (some of them with frequent musical quotation) the state of music in Spain in the sixteenth, seventeenth, and eighteenth centuries, the golden period" (Van Vechten, *Music of Spain,* 30).

74. Edward Lueders, *Carl Van Vechten and the Twenties* (Albuquerque: University of New Mexico Press, 1955), 10–11; Bruce Kellner, *Carl Van Vechten and the Irreverent Decades* (Norman: University of Oklahoma Press, 1968), 20–34.

75. As Richard Crawford has pointed out, in 1909 Sonneck's diagnosis was that "music critics and journalists had amply met the public's desire for musical information. In Sonneck's words, there had been 'no demand for musicologists'" (Crawford, "Sonneck and American Musical Historiography," 275). Around 1930 Charles Seeger noted that "any serious discussion about music was carried on only in newspapers" (Pescatello, *Charles Seeger,* 120).

76. Carl Van Vechten, "Shall We Realize Wagner's Ideals?," *The Musical Quarterly* 2 (1916): 387–401. Van Vechten published a yearly essay in *The Musical Quarterly* from

1916 to 1921, as noted in Bruce Kellner, *A Bibliography of the Work of Carl Van Vechten* (Westport, Conn.: Greenwood, 1980), 108–12. A letter from Van Vechten to Sonneck about the 1916 article is included in *Letters of Carl Van Vechten,* ed. Bruce Kellner (New Haven, Conn.: Yale University Press, 1987), 16–17.

77. Lueders, *Carl Van Vechten and the Twenties,* 14.

78. Carl Van Vechten's "Igor Stravinsky: A New Composer" (August 6, 1915), in Van Vechten, *Music after the Great War* (New York: G. Schirmer, 1915), 88, covered all the composer's works to that date (see Lueders, *Carl Van Vechten and the Twenties,* 38). Van Vechten attended the first performance of *Le Sacre du printemps* in Paris in 1913 (Kellner, *Carl Van Vechten and the Irreverent Decades,* 73–75). Lueders notes the importance of Van Vechten's early dance criticism in New York (Lueders, *Carl Van Vechten and the Twenties,* 42–43), as does Paul Padgette in his introduction to *The Dance Writings of Carl Van Vechten* (New York: Dance Horizons, 1974), xii–xv.

79. Much of the correspondence between Van Vechten and Langston Hughes has been edited in Emily Bernard, ed., *Remember Me to Harlem* (New York: Knopf/Random House, 2001).

80. Kellner lists the subjects of many of the photographs, which are to be found today in numerous U.S. libraries and museums (Kellner, *Bibliography,* 184–216). The Carl Van Vechten Photographs Collections at the Library of Congress consists of 1,395 photographs by Van Vechten taken between 1932 and 1964; the photographs in this collection can be viewed at <http://memory.loc.gov./ammem/vvhtml/vvhome.html>.

81. Rosa Rolando (1897–1962), born Rosemonde Cowan, was an American dancer in the troupe of Isadora Duncan and performed "Rancho Mexicano" in 1924. She was married to the Mexican artist and scholar Miguel Covarrubias (1904–57). See Van Vechten's 1938 portrait of her in the Museo Virtual of the Library at the Universidad de las Américas, Puebla, Mexico, <http://biblio.pue.udlap.mx/udla/museo/rosa.html>. Some of Van Vechten's portraits of dancers are reproduced in *The Dance Photography of Carl Van Vechten,* selected and with an introduction by Paul Padgette (New York: Schirmer Books, 1981).

82. *Letters of Carl Van Vechten,* 27–28.

83. The book is actually a compilation of three essays; "Spain and Music" (1–88), dated New York, March 20, 1916, was first published in Carl Van Vechten's *Music and Bad Manners* (New York: Alfred A. Knopf, 1916); Van Vechten added copious notes to the 1918 reprinting.

84. Van Vechten, *Music of Spain,* 30.

85. Ibid., 77, 86.

86. Kellner, *Carl Van Vechten and the Irreverent Decades,* 114–15.

87. Ibid., 15–18.

88. Ibid., 74, 78.

89. Ibid., 99.

90. Ibid., 100.

91. Ibid., 38–39.

92. Ibid., 20–24.

93. Aaron Copland and Vivian Perlis, *Copland, 1900 through 1942* (New York: St. Martin's/Marek, 1984), 245–46; see also Crawford, *America's Musical Life*, 587.

94. Mueller, *American Symphony Orchestra*, 255.

95. Trend, *Music of Spanish History*.

96. Trend, preface to *Music of Spanish History*, ix.

97. Julián Ribera, *Music in Ancient Arabia and Spain*, trans. Eleanor Hague and Marion Leffingwell (London: Oxford University Press, and Stanford, Calif.: Stanford University Press, 1929); Eleanor Hague and Marion Leffingwell, foreword to Ribera, *Music in Ancient Arabia*, v.

98. See Gustave Reese, *Music in the Middle Ages* (New York: W. W. Norton, 1940); Manfred F. Bukofzer, *Studies in Medieval and Renaissance Music* (New York: W. W. Norton, 1950); Albert Seay, *Music in the Medieval World* (1965; rpt., Englewood Cliffs, N.J.: Prentice Hall, 1975); Richard H. Hoppin, *Medieval Music* (New York: W. W. Norton, 1978); Giulio Cattin, *Music in the Middle Ages*, trans. Steven Botterill, 2 vols. (Cambridge: Cambridge University Press, 1984); Jeremy Yudkin, *Music in Medieval Europe* (Englewood Cliffs, N.J.: Prentice Hall, 1989); David Fenwick Wilson, *Music of the Middle Ages: Style and Structure* (New York: Schirmer Books, 1990).

99. Alec Harman, *Medieval and Early Renaissance Music* (Fair Lawn, N.J.: Essential Books, 1958); Alec Harman and Anthony Milner, *Late Renaissance and Baroque Music* (London: Barrie and Rockliff, 1959), both from the series Man and His Music: The Story of Musical Experience in the West; Gustave Reese, *Music in the Renaissance* (New York: W. W. Norton, 1954).

100. See Howard M. Brown and Louise K. Stein, *Music in the Renaissance*, 2d ed. (Upper Saddle River, N.J.: Prentice Hall, 1999), 213–27.

101. Manfred Bukofzer, *Music in the Baroque Era* (New York: W. W. Norton, 1947); Edith Borroff, *The Music of the Baroque* (Dubuque, Iowa: Wm. C. Brown, 1970); Claude V. Palisca, *Baroque Music*, 3d ed. (Englewood Cliffs, N.J.: Prentice Hall, 1991). Several newer collections of essays include chapters on Spain. See Louise K. Stein, "Spain," in *The Early Baroque Era: From the Late 16th Century to the 1660s*, ed. Curtis Price, vol. 3 of Music and Society (London: Macmillan, 1993; and Englewood Cliffs, N.J.: Prentice Hall, 1994), 327–48; Stein, "The Iberian Peninsula," in *The Late Baroque Era: From the 1680s to 1740*, ed. George J. Buelow, vol. 4 of Music and Society (London: Macmillan, 1993; and Englewood Cliffs, N.J.: Prentice Hall, 1994), 411–34; and Stein, "The Spanish and Portuguese Heritage," in *Companion to Baroque Music*, ed. Julie Anne Sadie (London: J. M. Dent and Sons, 1990; New York: Schirmer Books, 1990), 327–47.

102. Theodore E. Hager, *Music of the Classical Period* (Dubuque, Iowa: Wm. C. Brown, 1969); Leonard G. Ratner, *Classical Music: Expression, Form, and Style* (New York: Schirmer Books, 1980); Julian Rushton, *Classical Music: A Concise History from Gluck to Beethoven* (London: Thames and Hudson, 1986); Reinhard G. Pauly, *Music in the Classic Period*, 3d ed. (Englewood Cliffs, N.J.: Prentice Hall, 1988); and Philip G. Downs, *Classical Music: The Era of Haydn, Mozart, and Beethoven* (New York: W. W. Norton, 1992).

103. Rey M. Longyear, *Nineteenth-Century Romanticism in Music* (Englewood Cliffs,

N.J.: Prentice Hall, 1969); Carl Dahlhaus, *Nineteenth-Century Music,* ed. Joseph Kerman, trans. J. Bradford Robinson (Berkeley: University of California Press, 1989); Leon Plantinga, *Romantic Music: A History of Musical Style in Nineteenth-Century Europe* (New York: W. W. Norton, 1984).

104. Alfred Einstein, *Music in the Romantic Era* (New York: W. W. Norton, 1947). The German edition appeared in 1950, followed by the Italian (1952), the French (1959), and the Polish (1965) translations.

105. Glenn Watkins, *Soundings: Music in the Twentieth Century* (New York: Schirmer Books, 1995), 422. Among the surveys that do not mention Spanish music are Nicolas Slonimsky, *Music since 1900,* 3d ed. (New York: Coleman-Ross, 1949); Howard Hartog, ed., *European Music in the Twentieth Century* (New York: Frederick A. Praeger, 1957); Peter S. Hansen, *An Introduction to Twentieth-Century Music,* 2d ed. (Boston: Allyn and Bacon, 1967); and Paul Griffiths, *Modern Music: A Concise History,* rev. ed. (London: Thames and Hudson, 1994).

106. Marion Bauer, *Twentieth-Century Music: How It Developed, How to Listen to It* (New York: G. P. Putnam's Sons, 1933); Eric Salzman, *Twentieth-Century Music: An Introduction* (Englewood Cliffs, N.J.: Prentice Hall, 1967).

107. William M. Austin, *Music in the Twentieth Century from Debussy through Stravinsky* (New York: W. W. Norton, 1966).

108. This is the case in Otto Deri, *Exploring Twentieth-Century Music* (New York: Holt, Rinehart, and Winston, 1968); William R. Martin and Julius Drossin, *Music of the Twentieth Century* (Englewood Cliffs, N.J.: Prentice Hall, 1980); and Robert P. Morgan, *Twentieth-Century Music: A History of Musical Style in Modern Europe and America* (New York: W. W. Norton, 1991).

109. Watkins, *Soundings,* 422–24.

110. I am indebted to Christopher Scheer, Timothy Freeze, Stephanie Heriger, Rebekah Nye, and Thomas Oram, all doctoral students at the University of Michigan, for their invaluable contributions to this section of this essay and for many helpful editorial suggestions.

111. The music critic Anthony Tommasini recently reasserted, "Though it is not polite to say so out loud, some of the best Spanish music was written by French composers" (Tommasini, "Spanish Music Out of France with Help from Canada," review, *New York Times,* October 24, 2000, "Living Arts" sec., p. B1. Manuel de Falla's essay "Claudio Debussy y España," published in the *Revue musicale* (December 1920), both acknowledged the indebtedness of some Spanish composers to Debussy and distinguished between what Falla and others viewed as the sterility of the old romantic Pedrellian "authenticity" of pieces based on folk materials and what Falla admired as a pure "evocation" of an idealized Andalucia by Debussy. Debussy, for example, adopted Andalucian guitar "effects" such that Falla wrote that "Debussy has taught the way to use them." See Falla, *Escritos sobre música,* 49–56; Manuel de Falla, *On Music and Musicians,* trans. David Urman and J. M. Thomson (London and Boston: Marion Boyars, 1979), 41–45.

112. I am most grateful to Rich Wandel, Associate Archivist for the New York Phil-

harmonic, for generously providing me with information from the historical archives of that institution. My information concerning orchestral repertories, conductors, and performances in the United States (see table 7.1) is drawn from Henry Edward Krehbiel, "Programmes of the Concerts of the Philharmonic Society, 1842–1892," in *The Philharmonic Society of New York: A Memorial* (New York: Novello, Ewer, 1892), 95–163; James Gibbons Huneker, "Compositions Performed by the Philharmonic Society of New York [1892–1917]," in *The Philharmonic Society of New York and Its Seventy-fifth Anniversary* (New York: Printed for the Society, 1917), 49–130; John Erskine, "List of Programs of Subscription Concerts [New York Philharmonic Orchestra]," in *The Philharmonic Society of New York: Its First Hundred Years* (New York: Macmillan, 1943), 61–168; Howard Shanet, *Philharmonic: A History of New York's Orchestra* (Garden City, N.Y.: Doubleday, 1975); Richard Aldrich, *Concert Life in New York, 1902–1923* (New York: G. P. Putnam's Sons, 1941); Mark Anthony DeWolfe Howe, *The Boston Symphony Orchestra, 1881–1931* (1914), revised and extended by John N. Burk (Boston: Houghton Mifflin, 1931; rpt., New York: Da Capo Press, 1978); Johnson, *Musical Interludes in Boston;* Harold Earle Johnson, *Symphony Hall, Boston* (Boston: Little, Brown and Co., 1950; rpt., New York: Da Capo Press, 1979); Philo Adams Otis, *The Chicago Symphony Orchestra: Its Organization, Growth, and Development, 1891–1924* (1924; rpt., Freeport, N.Y.: Books for Libraries Press, 1974); and Frances Anne Wister, *Twenty-five Years of the Philadelphia Orchestra, 1900–1925* (Philadelphia: Women's Committees for the Philadelphia Orchestra, 1925).

113. American Symphony Orchestra League, *Americanizing the American Orchestra* (Report of the National Task Force, June 1993) (Washington, D.C., 1993), 3.

114. Paul J. Di Maggio, "Cultural Entrepreneurship in Nineteenth-Century Boston," in *Nonprofit Enterprise in the Arts: Studies in Mission and Constraint* (New York: Oxford University Press, 1986), cited in American Symphony Orchestra League, *Americanizing the American Orchestra,* 3.

115. Pieces by Beethoven, Brahms, Liszt, Mendelssohn, Mozart, Schubert, Schumann, R. Strauss, Wagner, and Weber, with a lesser representation of French and Russian or Slavic composers, such as Berlioz, Chopin, Dvorak, Tchaikovshy, Rimsky-Korsakoff; later on, more pieces by modern French composers, such as Bizet, Debussy, Delius, and Massenet, were added, and the likes of Elgar, Grieg, and Smetana joined the orchestral repertory. Early music was less frequently performed, though some pieces by J. S. Bach, Handel, and Vivaldi were becoming favorites in the early twentieth century.

116. Ronald L. Davis, *A History of Music in American Life,* vol. 2: *The Gilded Years, 1865–1920* (Huntington, N.Y.: Robert Krieger, 1980), 22.

117. Krehbiel, *Philharmonic Society of New York,* 7.

118. As a performer, Sarasate himself had introduced the "Spanish idiom" during his time in Paris, just as the fashion for things Spanish began to take hold there in the 1870s; he was an icon of the romantic Spanish musician, as pointed out in Luis G. Iberni, *Pablo Sarasate* (Madrid: Instituto Complutense de Ciencias Musicales, 1994), 52–55.

119. On this point I am indebted to the unpublished work of Roland J. Vázquez, summarized in "Presenting the Spanish Orchestral Idiom: Enrique Fernández Arbós

in the United States," a paper presented at the Congress of the International Musico-logical Society, Madrid, April 1992. See also the study of Spanish nationalism in his dissertation, "The Quest for National Opera in Spain and the Re-Invention of the Zarzuela (1808–1849)" (Ph.D. diss., Cornell University, 1992).

120. Aldrich, *Concert Life in New York,* 495.

121. See Victor Espinós Molto, *El maestro Arbós* (Madrid: Espasa-Calpe, 1942); Arthur Jacobs, "Arbós, Enrique Fernández," in *The New Grove Dictionary of Music and Musicians,* ed. Stanley Sadie (London: Macmillan, 1980), 1:545–46.

122. Vázquez, "Presenting the Spanish Orchestral Idiom," and Jacobs, "Arbós."

123. Vázquez, "Presenting the Spanish Orchestral Idiom," 4.

124. Van Vechten deemed this piece worthy of a New York performance (Van Vechten, *Music of Spain,* 148).

125. Ibid., 152.

126. Is it merely coincidental that the popularity of Latin (Cuban) popular music, led by the rumba, increased in New York in the 1930s as well? "The demand for Latin music among a general New York audience was by this era [the late 1930s] so wide-spread that even clubs and hotel ballrooms without an explicitly Latin orientation were compelled to hire Cuban-style relief bands to alternate sets with their swing bands" (Ruth Glasser, *My Music Is My Flag: Puerto Rican Musicians and Their New York Communities, 1917–1940* [Berkeley: University of California Press, 1995], 122–23, quoted in Steven Loza, *Tito Puente and the Making of Latin Music* [Urbana: University of Illinois Press, 1999], 4). On the other hand, as my colleague Richard Crawford has noted (in private correspondence, March 16, 2001), "George Gershwin's *Cuban Overture* (1932), composed after a trip to Havana, and premiered at Lewisohn Stadium in the summer of 1932, has had a lot fewer performances than one might have predicted for a work by a figure so incandescently popular with audiences."

127. Reviews of Casals's earliest New York appearances do not attribute to him a particularly Spanish sound, however, but describe his playing of a Haydn cello concerto and Bach unaccompanied suites as full of "grace, delicacy and a truly musical feeling" (January 15, 1904) (Aldrich, *Concert Life in New York,* 56–57).

128. Shanet, *Philharmonic,* 222–33.

129. Howe, *Boston Symphony Orchestra,* 160.

130. "As a harmonist Mr. Bloch goes to the limit of modern procedure and writes much that is drastic and mordant discord . . . he is most extreme in his modernist tendencies" (Aldrich, *Concert Life in New York,* 543–44); thus a New York critic described Bloch's music following a concert generously devoted to his *Jewish Cycle* in May 1917.

131. Leta F. Miller, introductory essay to Lou Harrison, *Selected Keyboard and Chamber Music, 1937–1994,* ed. Leta F. Miller, Music of the United States, vol. 8 (Madison, Wis.: A-R Editions, 1998), xxii. Miller points out that the composer Lou Harrison and his associates in San Francisco were "caught up in the frenzy, raising emergency funds for the Republican forces." Sympathy for the Republican forces in the Spanish Civil War prompted Lou Harrison's *France 1917–Spain 1937* (for string quartet and two percussionists), inspired by the composer's despair over "Spain and its agony." Harrison's

"concern about Spain" was connected to his studies of early Spanish organ music and California mission music. Two "Sarabandes" and a "Passacaglia" were among the other pieces he worked on in 1937. The dance known as the baroque sarabande was derived from the *zarabanda,* and, likewise, the passacaglia form was an Italian and then pan-European derivation from the typical Hispanic *pasacalles* of the early seventeenth century. My thanks to my colleague Mark Clague, executive editor of *MUSA,* for bringing Lou Harrison's piece to my attention.

132. Mueller, *American Symphony Orchestra,* 101–12.

133. Otis, *Chicago Symphony Orchestra,* 373.

134. Gilbert Chase, *The Music of Spain* (New York: W. W. Norton, 1941).

135. Frances R. Aparicio, *Listening to Salsa: Gender, Latin Popular Music, and Puerto Rican Cultures* (Hanover, N.H.: Wesleyan University Press, 1998), 104–5.

Prescott's Paradigm: American Historical Scholarship and the Decline of Spain

Richard L. Kagan

I believe the Spanish subject will be more *new* than the Italian, more *interesting* to the majority of readers, more *useful* to me by opening another & more practical department of study, & *not* more *laborious,* in relation to the authorities to be consulted, and *not* more *difficult* to be discussed, with the lights already afforded me by judicious treatises on the most intricate parts of the subject, and with the allowance of the introductory year for my novitiate in a new walk of letters. The advantages of the Spanish topic, on the whole, overbalance the inconvenience of the requisite preliminary year.

    For these reasons, I subscribe to the history of Ferdinand and Isabel.[1]

With these words, entered into a memorandum on January 19, 1826, William Hickling Prescott—a wealthy New Englander with a taste for letters—inaugurated the writing of Spanish history in the United States. Equally important, Prescott's decision to investigate the achievements of the Catholic Monarchs represented a milestone within U.S. historical scholarship itself. Americans in the early nineteenth century read European history—primarily as interpreted by Edward Gibbon, David Hume, William Robertson, and Voltaire—but

---

An earlier version of this appendix first appeared in *American Historical Review* 101 (April 1996): 423–46. It is reprinted here, with stylistic changes, some factual corrections, and minor revisions, mainly of a bibliographical nature, for the convenience of readers of this collection.

no U.S. scholar had yet dared, as Prescott proposed, to utilize original documents in order to write something *new* about the history of any nation other than the United States. Not until the end of the nineteenth century did other U.S. historians, medievalists mostly, duplicate the kind of original synthesis envisioned by Prescott in 1826 and subsequently realized in his *History of the Reign of Ferdinand and Isabella,* published on Christmas Day 1837, a work still well worth reading today.

As a historian, Prescott (1796–1859) was not particularly innovative, either in terms of method, philosophy, or technique. Influenced primarily by Gibbon (whom he found nonetheless "circumloquacious" and disliked because of his "egotism" and "skepticism") and by Abbé Mably (whose rules of history he admired), Prescott sought to write history that was "romantic" yet also "useful," studded with what he called "general reflections" of a philosophical bent. Whether in his history of Ferdinand and Isabella or his later books on the conquests of Mexico (1843) and Peru (1847), Prescott attempted to incorporate insights gleaned from documents, contemporary chronicles, and other sources into what he described as "a continuous closely connected narrative" centering on "political intrigue."[2] Yet Prescott also wanted his books to be "very interesting" and accessible to a wide audience. In terms of his aims and method, therefore, Prescott resembled his contemporaries: George Bancroft, Francis Parkman, and other historians of the "romantic" school. Nevertheless, Prescott emerged, in the United States at least, as the Lycurgus of Spanish history and as the scholar who shaped both the character and direction of historical research in Spanish studies for well over a century. This essay examines the specific nature of Prescott's contribution and, more important, the extent to which his ideas about the juxtaposition of Spanish decadence and U.S. progress—summarily referred to here as "Prescott's paradigm"—still exert influence over Spanish historical scholarship, particularly of the early modern era, in the United States.

Prescott's Paradigm

To begin with, it is interesting that an individual of Prescott's background—Boston, Unitarian, money, Harvard—even contemplated a subject dealing with Spanish history.[3] No American had ever done so before, not even Thomas Jefferson, who otherwise collected Spanish books and encouraged study of "the language, manners, and situation" of both Spain and Portugal.[4] In general, early nineteenth-century America's impression of Spain was colored by the Black Legend, first popularized by Dutch and English Protestant writers in the sixteenth century. One variant of this legend, traceable to Bartolomé de Las

Casas's condemnation of Spanish atrocities in the New World, described Spaniards as barbaric bigots with an insatiable lust for gold. Another variant of the legend, rooted in the early seventeenth-century treatises of Spanish *arbitristas* (economic projectors), among them writers such as Pedro Fernández de Navarrete, portrayed Spanish society as one sunk in the depths of decline: a nation that wasted the silver it had mined in the Indies on monasteries and religious wars without bothering to invest it productively in commerce.[5]

To a large extent young America's antipathy toward Spain owed much to the British—to the Scottish historian John Campbell (1708–75), who painted a rather negative portrait of "Old Spain" in his *Concise History of the Spanish America* (1741) as well as in other works;[6] to Adam Smith, whose *Wealth of Nations* (1776) highlighted Spain's failure to develop economically; and to William Robertson (1721–93), whose *History of America* (1777) commented at length about the Spanish indifference to agriculture and commerce and the extent to which "the enormous and expensive fabric of their ecclesiastical establishment . . . greatly retarded the progress of population and industry."[7] American authors repeated these observations, adding several of their own. Jedidiah Morse's *American Universal Geography* (1793), a popular school text, taught several generations of young Americans that Spaniards (and Portuguese) were not only "bigotted Catholics" subject to "despotic monarchy" but lazy, indolent people prone to "the practice of every vice."[8] Other textbooks depicted Spaniards as "a poor, lazy, idle, dirty, ignorant race of almost semisavages," and literary journals of the period regularly published essays critical of both Spain and its people.[9] Typical were the derogatory remarks about Spanish intellectual achievement included in the essay "Trait of Spanish Character" that appeared in the *North American Review* in 1817: "As a nation, the Spaniards are at present a full century behind every other nation in Europe in the arts of life, the refinements of society, and enlightened views of civil polity; and almost a millenium, in modes of education, and intellectual culture. It may be questioned whether they have taken a step in the right road of learning since the days of the Cid."[10]

Beginning in the 1820s, writers of the romantic school helped temper this negative image. Washington Irving (1783–1859) and Henry Wadsworth Longfellow (1807–82), although critical of Spain and its institutions, were favorably disposed to the Spaniards and their culture. For these writers, all of whom fastened on the more traditional aspects of Spain's rural economy, the country was "picturesque" because it was both exotic and backward—a quintessential Other, still medieval, still subject to Moorish and other "oriental" influences. On a visit to Madrid and Seville in 1828, for example, Longfellow remarked, "There is so little change in the Spanish character, that you find everything as it is said to have been two hundred years ago."[11] Irving, on the other hand, who had been invited to Spain in 1826 in order to translate certain Columbus documents that had recently come to light, offered an orientalist interpretation of the Spanish character. With reference to Madrid's inhabitants, he observed that "these people preserve the Arab look and manner." Irving's first glimpse of Andalucía elicited an equally fanciful comment: "country like a historic map—full of history and romance, where the Moors and Christians have fought."[12]

Young Prescott's view of Spain must have been somewhat similar. Although he never visited the country, Prescott regarded it as one whose people had suffered from the evil effects of both monarchical absolutism and Roman Catholicism. This also was his view of Portugal. In 1815, only twenty and just out of Harvard, Prescott stopped off in the Azores en route to London in order to seek treatment for an ailment that had deprived him of much of his sight. A brief visit sparked the following comment: "Whatever opinion I had formed of the Portuguese, I could have no idea of the debasement which our capacities may suffer when crampt by arbitrary government and Papal superstition."[13]

Under the circumstances it seems somewhat odd that Prescott, who was determined to follow a literary career, opted to write about Spain. He entertained other alternatives: a "history of the revolution of Ancient Rome which converted the republic into the Empire"; a "biographical sketch of eminent geniuses, with criticisms on their productions and on the character of their ages"; a study of Italian literature during the Renaissance. By December 1825, however, only a year or so after he started reading Spanish history and literature, the Spain of Ferdinand and Isabella attracted him more and more: "I shall probably select [Spain], as less difficult than [Rome], & as more novel and entertaining than the [biographies]."[14] In addition, Spain offered a connection with America's origins, a linkage that was already apparent to Irving and that led to his highly romanticized but enormously successful biography of Christopher Columbus, first published in 1828. Prescott, more of a historian than Irving, also understood that Spain afforded numerous opportunities for philosophical reflection. He summarized the many advantages—as well as the possibilities—of such an inquiry in a memo to himself in early January 1826. These included "a retrospective picture of the constitutions of Castile & Aragon; of the Moorish dynasty—the causes of its decay & dissolution? Then I have the Inquisition, with its bloody persecutions,—the conquest of Granada a brilliant passage,—the exploits of the 'Great Captain' in Italy, a proper character for romance as well as history,—the discovery of a new world, my own country—the new policy of the monarch towards the overgrown aristocracy &c &c."[15]

Here, in short, were all the elements an "entertaining" and "interesting" narrative required: battles against Moors; the exploits of courageous captains; the discovery of continents and oceans. Prescott was clearly, as David Levin has argued, a romantic.[16] Yet as this list suggests, Prescott knew his Livy, his Tacitus and Polybius as well, and in keeping with the work of Gibbon, Abbé Raynal, Robertson, and other "philosophical" historians, he sought to determine the forces that destined certain societies for greatness, others to decadence and decay. With respect to his Spanish project he noted these particular concerns in a short memo of 1828: "How many of the seeds of the subsequent decay of this great empire are to be fairly imparted to the constitutions of Ferdinand and Isabel? Could not a skilful contrast show that they are mainly imputable to the defective policy of the succeeding monarchs?" (that is, the Habsburgs).[17]

What is not immediately apparent in these notes, but what was evidently paramount in Prescott's mind was the comparison between the relative fortunes of the United States and Spain. Toying with the prospect of writing a history of the United States, Prescott recurrently reflected upon the factors that were helping to make his country great. So when Prescott decided in January 1826 to write about the Spain of Ferdinand and Isabella, he was also writing about the young United States. In both countries Prescott detected the enlightened leadership, the sound government, national will, and the dynamism necessary for monumental achievement. Prescott in fact was undoubtedly thinking of the United States when, in a review of Irving's *Conquest of Granada*, he used the following language to describe late fifteenth-century Spain: "It was the season of hope and youthful enterprise, when the nation seemed to be renewing its ancient energies, and to prepare like a giant to run its course."[18]

Yet for all his pro-Spanish sympathies, Prescott could not escape the Protestant prejudices of his age. He understood that Spain had two deep-seated weaknesses from which the United States was exempt. One was Catholicism, cruelly manifested in the Inquisition that his avowed heroes, Ferdinand and Isabella, the Catholic Monarchs, had helped to create.[19] His memo book reads: "The reign of Ferdinand and Isabel will thus form an epoch lying between the anarchy of the proceeding period and the despotism & extravagant schemes of the succeeding, during which epoch the nation attained its highest degree of real prosperity; although the seeds of its most degrading vice, religious bigotry, were then implanted. (Were they not before?)."[20] Spain's other fatal flaw was royal absolutism, the inherent defects of which were manifested less by the Catholic Monarchs than by their Habsburg successors, most notably, Philip II (1556–98), whose biography Prescott published in 1855. For Prescott, a staunch proponent of liberty, the "tranquility that naturally flows from a free and well-conducted government," and the "spirit of independence" embodied by the United States, Philip II was evil incarnate: "[he] ruled . . . with an authority more absolute than that possessed by any European prince since the day of the Ceasars [*sic*]." Prescott, moreover, faulted Philip for having "nurtured schemes of mad ambition" that undermined the dynamism and energy that Ferdinand and Isabella brought to Spain, forcing the nation into "a state of paralytic torpor" that contributed, directly and inevitably, to its economic and political decline. Even more reprehensible was Philip's narrow brand of Catholicism, a religion that "admitted no compromise" and led the monarch to embrace persecution, and its handmaiden, the Inquisition, as his principle weapon.[21] Firm in his belief that progress required liberty in the guise of democratic institutions, freedom of worship and of expression, and laissez-faire economics, Prescott blamed Philip for having denied Spain the opportunity to join the modern world.

For Prescott, then, an unhealthy combination of political despotism and religious bigotry set Spain and the United States on two fundamentally different paths. The United States, as a republic, enjoyed the energy, enthusiasm, and the "bold commercial spirit" that liberty engendered—the qualities nations required for lasting success. In Prescott's view medieval Spain had exhibited most of these qualities in the guise of "free institutions," "liberal and equitable forms of government," "independence of character," "lofty enthusiasm," and "patriotism." However, in the course of the sixteenth century the Habsburg monarchy, aided by the Inquisition, conspired to crush Spain's ancient "liberties," creating a huge gulf between America and the nation that had helped to discover it. In the United States liberty ensured both individual enterprise and national prosperity. In Spain its absence created economic backwardness, intellectual stagnation, political weakness, and moral decay, each compounded by the sloth and corruption that the riches of empire brought in its wake.[22] In the Middle Ages, Spaniards were energetic, hard working, their future still bright. But by the end of the sixteenth century all this had changed, and Prescott offered a particularly gloomy assessment of the country's future near the end of *Philip II*:

> Folded under the dark wing of the Inquisition, Spain was shut out from the light which in the sixteenth century broke over the rest of Europe, stimulating nations to greater enterprise in every department of knowledge. The genius of the people was rebuked, and their spirit quenched, under the malign influence of an eye that never slumbered, of an unseen arm ever raised to strike. How could there be freedom of thought, where there was no freedom of utterance? Or freedom of utterance, where it was dangerous to say too little as to say too much. Freedom cannot go along with fear. Every way the Spanish mind was in fetters.[23]

What I call "Prescott's paradigm" is an understanding of Spain as the antithesis of the United States. Most of the elements contained in this paradigm—anti-Catholicism, critcism of absolutism, support for commerce and individual liberty—were to be found in the work of other writers, but Prescott bundled them into a single package that offered a means of approaching Spanish history through the lens of that of U.S. history. Just as Prescott cherished the notion of "American exceptionalism," the idea that his own country possessed a unique history that destined it for greatness, Spain was equally exceptional but seen from the inverted perspective of a nation separated from the European, that is, Protestant, mainstream, and consequently bereft of the progress and prosperity that flowed in its wake. Earlier New England writers, Cotton Mather and Samuel Sewall among them, had also espoused a negative view of Spain, but Prescott was the first to adopt a truly comparative perspective, setting the trajectory of the two nations side by side. Medieval Spain provided Prescott—and presumably other Americans who shared his Whiggish political views—an example of a society in which individual liberties had been productively channelled into nation building, a heroic enterprise that offered ready comparison with America's colonial era and, for Prescott at least, one that may also have served as a refuge from the dangerous populist tendencies that Jacksonian democracy had unleashed.[24] But Spain's principal attraction was that its history, especially in the Habsburg era—the period that Prescott regarded as its nadir—represented everything that his America was not. America was the future—republican, enterprising, rational; while Spain—monarchical, indolent, fanatic—represented the past. As it developed, however, Prescott's paradigm was less a clear model of analysis than a series of assumptions and presuppositions about the inherent backwardness of Spanish culture and the progressiveness and superiority of the United States. Yet this particular formulation, especially when combined with the pervasive belief in national character engendered by the rise of nineteenth-century nationalism, managed to exert a powerful influence on the way succeeding generations of U.S. scholars thought and wrote about Spain.[25]

Nineteenth-Century U.S. Hispanism

Prescott's juxtaposition of the United States (the new) and Spain (the old) undoubtedly counted among the many reasons why *Ferdinand and Isabella* sold so well. Prescott himself could hardly believe the book's success, and at one point, shortly after the publication of his *Conquest of Mexico* in 1843, he candidly admitted to a Spanish friend that "my countrymen . . . seem to me more in love with Spanish history than the Spanish themselves."[26] The old adage that opposites attract may also explain why other nineteenth-century U.S. scholars found themselves drawn to Spain. Romanticism, as noted earlier, provided an additional lure. George Ticknor (1791–1871), Harvard's first professor of modern languages, visited Spain in May 1818, only to find it woefully backward—"Imagine a country so deserted and desolate, and with so little travelling and communication, as to have no taverns"—and lacking in both "cultivation and refinement," an absence he attributed to "the long, *long* oppression of tyranny and inquisition." On the other hand, Ticknor found the common people both natural and graceful. Even their "resting positions," he wrote, were "picturesque."[27] Harvard's third professor of modern languages, James Russell Lowell, held an equally romantic view of Spain and its people. Writing in 1878, he admitted to a friend that "you can't imagine how far I am away from the world here—I mean the modern world. Spain is as primitive in some ways as the books of Moses and as oriental." As for the people, Lowell echoed Irving when he wrote that "they are still orientals to a degree one has to live among them to believe. . . . They don't care about the same things that we are fools to believe in [ledgers]." This opinion led Lowell to conclude that hard-working Americans preferred the economic benefits associated with the "mill-pond," while Spaniards preferred the peaceful pleasures derived from the "brook."[28]

Lowell's letters from Spain never mentioned those aspects of Spanish society—railroads, industry, commerce—that smacked of modernity. The Spain that he and other U.S. scholars wanted to see was the Spain of the Middle Ages, the sole era in which, as Prescott described it, Spaniards enjoyed the benefits of liberty. Medievalism of this sort pervaded most nineteenth-century U.S. scholarship about Spain, initially manifesting itself in the *History of Spanish Literature* (1849).[29] Ticknor's was the first critical survey of a European literature ever written by a U.S. scholar.[30] It was also replete with Prescottian language, freely employing such romanticized terms as "enthusiasm," "spirit and activity," "vigor and promise" to describe the temper of Spain's Middle Ages. For Ticknor such qualities made for great literature, and he probably had Sir Walter Scott in mind when he presented the popular ballads and chronicles of the period as Spain's greatest literary accomplishments, its true Golden Age. And Ticknor, like Prescott before him, understood that Spain's early cultural florescence was doomed to decay. In his words, "that generous and manly spirit which is the breadth of intellectual life of any people was stifled and restrained"—by the corrosive forces of courtly life, by corrupt and despotic government, by the Inquisition. From his perspective glimmers of Spain's "old spirit" briefly survived in early seventeenth-century theater, but even the stage soon succumbed to the forces that crushed Spain's "heroic temperament." The work of Miguel de Cervantes Saavedra, Francisco de Quevedo, and Pedro Calderón de la Barca notwithstanding, Ticknor's seventeenth-century was more iron than gold, an era in which "life . . . was evidently passing out of the whole Spanish character."[31]

William H. Prescott died in 1867, but his paradigm lived on. It lay at the core of John Lothrop Motley's *The Rise of the Dutch Republic* (1856), an immensely popular work that presented the Spain of Philip II as the enemy of democracy, the nation opposed to the (liberal) forces shaping the modern world. Motley (1814–77), another wealthy Bostonian, was close to Prescott and was both helped and influenced by his older friend. He also shared Prescott's presuppositions. Motley vilified aristocrats ("extravagant and dissipated"), elevated both commoners and commerce ("the mother of freedom") to lofty rank, and presented Spaniards as the personification of religious intolerance and hate. Motley thus found it relatively easy to describe the principal shortcomings of his villain, Philip II:

> He [Philip] was entirely a Spaniard. The Burgundian and Austrian elements of his blood seem to have evaporated, and his veins were filled alone with the ancient ardour, which in heroic centuries had animated the Gothic champions of Spain. The fierce enthusiasm for the Cross, which in the long internal warfare against the Crescent had been the romantic and distinguishing feature of the national character, had degenerated into bigotry. That which had been a nation's glory now made the monarch's shame. . . . Philip was to be the latest and most perfect incarnation of all this traditional enthusiasm, this perpetual hate.[32]

Philip's foil, and the hero of Motley's narrative, was the Dutch leader, William of Orange, an individual whose "political genius," "eloquence," and patriotism practically made him an American, a figure comparable to George Washington.[33] It follows that the United Provinces appeared in the pages of Motley's history as a miniature United States. Just as Washington had led his people in their struggle for freedom against England, William led the Dutch in their battle for liberty—and thus the future—against the forces of the past embodied in the Spaniard and epitomized in the person of Philip II.

If Motley's *Rise of the Dutch Republic* strengthened the negative Spanish stereotype inherent in Prescott's paradigm, the next and indeed last generation of America's gentlemen-historians inscribed it in stone. Their ideas about Spanish backwardness and decadence came to the fore in various books and essays published at the moment of the Spanish-American War of 1898, a short but decisive conflict that simultaneously ended Spain's imperial era while initiating that of the United States. Many of these publications presented Spain's defeat as inevitable, the foreordained outcome of three centuries of decline and decay.[34] The most nuanced, and, in a way, most Prescottian explanation for Spain's defeat came from Henry Charles Lea (1825–1909), the Philadelphia businessman turned church historian who developed a special interest in the corrosive effects of "clericalism" upon humanity. Already known for his scholarly *History of the Inquisition of the Middle Ages* (1887–88), Lea became interested in Spanish history largely to determine what he described as "the profound modification wrought in the Spanish character by the Inquisition."[35] He published a preliminary book on the subject in 1890 and in 1898 was already preparing what later became his monumental four-volume *History of the Inquisition of Spain* (1906–7) when asked by the editor of the *Atlantic Monthly* to offer his interpretation of the reasons underlying Spain's defeat in its war with the United States. Lea seized the opportunity to convey to a wide audience his ideas concerning the detrimental effects of the Inquisition on Spanish society.[36]

Lea's essay, "The Decadence of Spain," published in July 1898, began on a distinctly triumphal note, attributing Spain's defeat to a national character distinguished by a "blind and impenetrable pride" and a "spirit of conservatism which rejected all innovation in a world of incessant change." Spaniards, he wrote, were incapable of adapting to "modern industrialism." Nor could Lea resist the opportunity to criticize the Catholic Church. Whatever the defects in Spain's "national trait," "clericalism" served only to make them worse as it ignited a "ferocious spirit of intolerance" that rendered the Spaniards "unfit" for self-government, led to the expulsion of the Jews, helped to create the Spanish Inquisition, and eventually "benumbed the intellectual development of the people." Lea, moreover, knew exactly where such misfortunes would lead. "While the rest of the civilized world was bounding forward in a career of progress, while science and the useful arts were daily adding to the conquests of man over the forces of nature, and rival nations were growing in wealth and power, the Inquisition condemned Spain to stagnation." Finally, to add yet another familiar scapegoat to the story of Spanish decadence and defeat, Lea concluded with a ringing attack on Habsburg absolutism and the extent to which "ineffective governance" prevented the nation from developing the "liberal institutions" necessary to lead it into the modern world. "There was," he wrote, "no national political life, no training in citizenship, no forces to counterbalance the follies and prejudices of the king and his favorites."[37]

At the dawn of the twentieth century, therefore, political events seemingly confirmed Prescott's contention that Spain and America inhabited different worlds. Most scholars accepted this premise; so did the popular press. Even Archer M. Huntington (1870–1955), founder of New York's Hispanic Society of America in New York (1908), benefactor of the Hispanic Division of the Library of Congress, and a connoisseur otherwise interested in promoting Spanish art and culture, accepted 'Spain' and 'modernity' as antithetical concepts. Like Irving, Huntington's Spain was romanticized. "In Spain," he wrote, "fanaticism is natural, chivalry a necessity."[38] Yet Huntington resembled Prescott to the extent that he took seriously the general trajectory of Spanish history, especially the reasons for what he perceived as the nation's failure to modernize along Western lines. Prescott's influence, for example, may be detected in the list of the ingredients Huntington concocted to explain Spanish decadence: "Pride, a weak monarch, a dissolute court, religious intolerance, all these are admirable starting points from which to prove a nation's decline." To this master recipe Huntington added one, albeit vital, ingredient: "Spain lacks the trading spirit . . . the great primitive developing agency," the very absence of which condemned Spain to centuries of isolation and decay.[39] To escape this era, Huntington, like Prescott and Ticknor before him, took refuge in Spain's Middle Ages, especially in that of El Cid, a heroic figure whose *Poema* he endeavored to translate. It follows that the art of medieval Spain figured as the centerpiece of the museum Huntington outfitted in New York. For similar reasons, the first American historians of Spanish art—Charles Caffin, Georgiana Goddard King, A. Kingsley Porter, Chandler Post, and John Kenneth Conant—also displayed a distinct preference for the Middle Ages. An exception was Charles B. Curtis, who in 1883 had published a catalog of paintings by Diego de Velázquez y Silva and Bartolomé Esteban Murillo. But Curtis viewed Spain's seventeenth century in wholly romantic terms, claiming that upon first visiting Madrid "I found myself carried in a day to the middle of the seventeenth century. I discovered a country that had preserved almost unchanged their habits, customs, and traditions of a long-buried age."[40] In comparison, Chandler Post, Harvard's hard-headed historian of Spanish art, attributed Spain's artistic achievements in the seventeenth century to that "rare artist" (probably Velázquez) with a "rugged, weird, and titanic spirit," one able to free himself from the grave Spanish temperament and the strictures of the Catholic Church.[41]

The Paradigm and the Professors

The professionalization of American history, starting in the 1890s, did relatively little to alter the basic presuppositions about Spanish culture and politics that Prescott and his immediate followers set forth. Admittedly, the university-based historians endeavored to strip away some of the more romantic and overtly anti-Catholic components of Prescott's ideas about Spain, but the topic of Spanish decline, coupled to the notion that Spanish character was some-how defective, or at least incompatible with modernity, remained paramount, so much so that it left little room for alternate approaches to the Spanish past.

Foremost among the first generation of professional scholars dealing with Spain was the great Harvard historian Roger B. Merriman (1876–1945). Togeth-er with Charles Homer Haskins, his medievalist colleague, Merriman in 1903–4 introduced Harvard's history curriculum to the study of *Kulturgeschichte,* a reform that allowed for the discussion of historical issues and problems only tangentially related to what had previously been the focus of European histo-ry at Harvard: the origins of American institutions. Interestingly, one of the first undergraduates to benefit from this reform was Samuel Eliot Morison, who, in 1908, long before he developed an interest in Columbus, wrote an es-say, "The Expedition of Cádiz, 1596," which analyzed the count of Essex's dar-ing raid on the Spanish port city. The topic, for an American historian at least, was original, and clearly one that reflected Merriman's influence. On the oth-er hand, the young Morison simply repeated old stereotypes when he conclud-ed that "The demoralization of Spain's society, culture and art was both the cause and effect of Spain's military defeat."[42]

Spanish decline was also implicit in Merriman's work. His four-volume *Rise of the Spanish Empire in the Old World and the New* (1918–34) began as a series of lectures in 1903, and when the first volume appeared Merriman dedicated it, pointedly, to Prescott. Merriman, however, dealt with decline by ignoring it, admitting at the outset of his book that his narrative would end with Phil-ip II and leave "decline and fall" to others. It was a pleasure, he wrote, "to emphasize the other side of the coin." Accordingly, Merriman devoted his study to a detailed analysis of the internal structures that contributed to Castile's imperial expansion. Yet decline hovered over the book like a rain cloud, and even Merriman, despite his initial promise, felt compelled to dis-cuss the topic at the end of his final volume. There he offered a sophisticated multicausal analysis that attributed Spanish decline to a series of cultural and political factors, among them, the monarchy's refusal to exchange the old idea of imperial preponderance for "national individuality," and what he called "the transfer of energy and genius from conquest and war to literature and art."[43] Significantly, Merriman's list of factors contributing to Spanish decline did not include any reference to Lea's "clericalism" nor reference to any particular flaw in the Spanish national character.

But Merriman was ahead of his time. Other American historians who wrote about Spain did so well within the familiar confines of Prescott's paradigm. The inaugural 1893 issue of the *Journal of Political Economy,* for example, con-tained an article by Bernard Moses, an economic historian from the University of California, that attributed Spanish decline to such factors as indolence, idleness, and the nation's excess of churches.[44] Similarly, Sarah Simons's essay on "Social Decadence," published in the 1901 issue of the *Annals of the American Academy of Political and Social Science,* utilized Spain (along with traditional China) as the model of what she defined as "a society which is not capable of maintaining a former level of excellence in social products." Simons, more sociologist than historian, was not herself a Hispanist, but she had evidently read Prescott and had no qualms about blaming the church for Spain's deterioration from "an active, enterprising, independent people to the inert, servile race we know today." As she explained it, "The mind of the Spaniard did not want to improve; they were satisfied with their inheritance; they were and still are unable to doubt; and this is the fault of the church."[45]

Simon's anti-Spanish bias was palpable, but her reading of Spain and its people differed only in degree from that of other professional scholars, including some of the first North American historians to specialize in the history of Latin America. References to the "dead hand" of the church and the "vanity" of the Spanish people figure prominently in Clarence H. Haring's important *Trade and Navigation between Spain and the Indies in the time of the Hapsburgs* (1918). That same year, the first issue of *Hispanic American Historical Review* appeared with an article on "The Institutional Background of Spanish American History." Its author, Charles H. Cunningham, attributed Spanish decline to "the individual inefficiency of the Spaniard from a mercantile point of view."[46]

Prescott's paradigm carried equal weight for the first economic historians to write about Spain, most of whom did little more than to quantify what they already understood: Spain's seventeenth-century decline. Julius Klein's classic account of the Mesta (1920), the Spanish sheepherders' guild, was a case history of the evils of state intervention in economic affairs. Klein, who studied with Merriman at Harvard, was interested in the economic foundations of newly organized states and studied the Mesta in order to measure the role of a specific raw material—in this case, wool—in nation building. Klein offered a clear, documented exposition of the Mesta's history, yet his assumptions about the relationship between economic and political phenomena, especially his notion that state intervention in the economy was incompatible with free trade, had a Prescottian ring. Klein was certain, for example, that royal support for the Mesta sparked Spanish regionalism, undermined the "unifying spirit" the nation possessed during the fifteenth century, and thus contributed to "the general decay of the country" in later times. Like Prescott, moreover, Klein pointedly portrayed the seventeenth century as one of "dismal depression and sordid melancholy" in order to draw attention to the adverse effects arising from the "autocratic government" of Philip II and the "feeble incompetence of his successors."[47]

The ideas embodied in Prescott's paradigm were equally important for the work of Earl J. Hamilton, arguably one of the most influential economic historians of the 1930s and a scholar whose research on Spanish prices of the sixteenth and seventeenth century is still useful today. Hamilton originally conceived his *American Treasure and the Price Revolution in Spain, 1501–1650* (1934) as an effort to analyze the transformative powers of precious metals, a problem which drew him to the question of whether the influx of silver bullion from the Americas had created greater upheavals in Spain than in other parts of Europe. By the time of publication, however, Hamilton added a new issue: the extent to which bullion contributed to "Spanish economic decadence" and whether this decadence was "provincial or national in character." Hamilton, meticulous in his scholarship, pointed out that most "liberal" historians exaggerated Spanish decadence in order "to place absolutism, the Inquisition, the persecution of minorities, and the Moorish expulsions in the worst light." As he saw it, both the Germans and the French had grossly and purposefully overestimated the extent of Spain's seventeenth-century decline in order to glorify their own country's achievements.[48] Hamilton was right, and in this respect he ranks as one of the first scholars to examine Spain's history comparatively and to examine the presuppositions underlying its "decline." Nevertheless, his study suggests that he was also determined to marshal the statistical evidence necessary to prove what he described—unproblematically—as Spain's "economic decadence." In a subsequent article, "The Decline of Spain" (1938), Hamilton repeated his assertion that economic causes were the primary reasons for Spain's political decline, yet his conception of decline remained equally unproblematic and the list of factors he presented to account for this phenomenon had a definite Prescottian ring: "the dead hand of the church," a deterioration in the character of the Spanish monarchs, poor administration, and so forth.[49]

Spain Is Different

In the decades immediately following the Spanish Civil War, Prescott's paradigm enjoyed continued vitality. If anything, General Franco's victory in 1939 gave it renewed life by reaffirming existing ideas about the endemic backwardness of Spanish culture and political life. Hemingway's *For Whom the Bell Tolls* (1940) had romanticized ordinary Spaniards by depicting them as heroes struggling for political freedom, but the prevailing image of Franco's Spain was that of a nation openly hostile to the democratic values that the United States and its allies fought to defend in World War II. John B. Crow, whose *Spain: The Root and the Flower* (1963) was widely read in classes on Spanish literature and civilization, neatly summarized American postwar attitudes toward Spain with a pithy quotation borrowed from the English author J. B. Trend: "What was lost in the [civil] war was not merely a government, but a whole modern culture."[50]

In this era American colleges and universities were investing heavily in "Western Civilization," "area studies" (especially on Latin America), as well as the specialized study of individual national histories, particularly those of nations determined either to be of strategic importance for the United States or those considered to have made significant contributions to the emergence of Western democratic institutions and ideas. Prescott's paradigm, however, recently invigorated by the antipathy of most American scholars toward Franco, effectively curtailed America's investment in Spanish history. One early indicator of this indifference was Harvard's failure to appoint a scholar in Spanish history to succeed Merriman, who had died in 1945. Another was the Prescottian portrayal of Spain's "gloomy fanaticism" and "lack of vitality" in books published in William L. Langer's influential series *The Rise of Modern Europe*, the first volumes of which appeared in 1951 and 1952.[51] During this era, when Spain was practically a pariah, shunned by most of the Western democracies, one of the few U.S. scholars who seriously engaged its history was John E. Longhurst (University of New Mexico). But Longhurst's books on the Inquisition's persecution of Spanish Erasmians and Lutherans were partially inspired by McCarthyism and served only to reinforce old notions about the ingrained repressiveness of Spanish society.[52]

So pervasive were these ideas that by the 1960s the U.S. historical establishment virtually decided to ignore Spain, employing the persistence of Spanish fascism, together with Spaniards' own explanations of their nation's alleged "difference," as convenient excuses. With few notable exceptions—the University of California at Berkeley, UCLA, and the University of Virginia, where Julian Bishko taught the history of Spain's Middle Ages—instruction in Spanish history (as opposed to Spanish literature and civilization) languished, creating a situation that not only limited opportunities for students to enter the field but assured the survival of Prescottian stereotypes.[53]

Meanwhile, the scholarly contributions of that handful of Americans who continued to work in the area did little, if anything, to alter the paradigm Prescott had set into place. What little original scholarship there was focused either on the twentieth century, highlighting the Spanish Civil War and the nation's failure to develop stable democratic institutions, or the eighteenth century and the somewhat abortive experiment of the Spanish Bourbons with

Enlightenment.[54] Research on the sixteenth and seventeenth centuries remained equally sparse, restricted either to diplomatic history or traditional
Black Legend themes, such as the Inquisition's persecution of Protestants. Of
particular influence was Garrett Mattingly's best-selling study, *The Armada*
(1959), which—echoing Prescott—presented Elizabethan England as the
champion of freedom, a latter-day David destined to triumph over the tyrannical Goliath: Philip II of Spain.[55]

Much U.S. scholarship on Spanish topics during the postwar era fell under
the influence of Spanish philosophy, especially that of Miguel de Unamuno
(1846–1936) and José Ortega y Gasset (1883–1955), both of whom, like Prescott
before them, isolated Spain by portraying it as a nation whose history did not
bear comparison with that of other European states. Spanish literary scholars
in the United States were especially susceptible to this particular variant of
Spanish exceptionalism, particularly followers of the brilliant Spanish émigré
Américo Castro (1885–1976), whose books taught that Spaniards were consti-
tutionally different from other Europeans, owing to their particular admix-
ture of Christian, Jewish, and Moorish blood and the particular set of ethnic
and religious problems that this mixed heritage had engendered. Castro also
cultivated a particular interest in Spain's *converso* population, and under his
influence this persecuted minority of former Jews served as the simulacrum
for Spanish religious intolerance and hate. *Conversos* consequently attracted
inordinate attention as the historians and literary scholars who studied them
not only diminished the extent to which they successfully assimilated into
Spanish society but also the negative effects that resulted from their persecution by the Spanish Inquisition.[56] Ideally, the study of the challenges confront-
ing the *conversos* might have been connected with those of Europe's other ethnic and religious minorities, yet what was described as the "*converso* problem"
was customarily presented as solely a Spanish problem and therefore yet another reason why Spain was inherently unique.

The first break from this particular pattern occurred late in the 1960s as a
number of scholars, united in their doubts about the utility of national character as a causal factor in Spanish history, employed other means to examine
the nation's past. Influenced by the emergent *Annales* school of history, these
scholars—and I include myself among them—through detailed archival investigation and methods borrowed from the social sciences, endeavored to
create a Spain that was at once more vital and more varied than the Prescottian paradigm allowed. Nevertheless, the topics selected, many of which still
touched on issues connected to Spain's intellectual stagnation or economic
decline, did little to alter the prevailing image of Spain as a country whose
contribution to Western history did not merit serious scholarly investigation.[57]

A Paradigmatic Shift?

At present, signs of a shift in the paradigm that Prescott formulated are somewhat mixed. On the one hand, there are some positive signs, including increases
in the number of scholars associated with Spanish history and the continuing availability of financial support for both publication and research on topics relating directly to Spain.[58] On the other, academic positions in Spanish
history are still relatively few, although there is the likelihood of more as North
America's Hispanic population looks beyond its more immediate linkages with
Spanish America to the culture and history of Spain itself. Whatever the future, the field is starting to attract new adherents from increasingly diverse
educational and ethnic backgrounds, a phenomenon that augurs well for a
more pluralistic and, ultimately, a less Prescottian approach to the study of the
Spanish past.

One current approach may be characterized as a shift away from Spanish
exceptionalism and its concomitant emphasis upon decline as an intrinsical-
ly "Spanish" phenomenon. Such an approach began with Hamilton, but it was
Merriman's *Six Contemporaneous Revolutions* (1937) that offered the first comparative analysis of the political history of seventeenth-century Spain, largely
in an effort to determine the extent to which the revolts that rocked Europe's
monarchies in the 1640s belonged to an international movement, possibly even
a conspiracy. At the time Merriman was interested in drawing parallels between
these revolts and the spread of European fascism, but over the decades his study
had the effect of reattaching Spanish history to European history. This particular movement gained momentum in the 1960s, owing primarily to the work
of the influential English scholar John H. Elliott, who, having rejected the
notion that an immutable national character rendered the Spanish incapable
of innovation and change, interpreted the erosion of Habsburg power in the
1640s as part of the "general crisis of the seventeenth century."[59] Elliott's comparative approach to Spanish history won wide acceptance in France and England and—somewhat more slowly—in Spain itself. It also attracted adherents in the United States, itself a sign of movement in the Prescottian paradigm
as well as one signal of a fundamental change in the way U.S. scholars thought
and wrote about Spain.

One thing is certain: old orientations and presuppositions are definitely under attack. In Spanish art history, for example, the medievalism of the early part
of the century is giving way to emphasis on the art of more modern periods,
including that of the era generally associated with Spanish decline. This change
in focus is accompanied by a willingness to reexamine some of the fundamental premises associated with Spanish seventeenth-century art. Early in the cen-

tury Chandler Post argued for Spanish artistic exceptionalism. No country, he believed, was "less responsive to foreign influences than Spain."[60] Yet recent work on a wide range of topics—individual artists, architecture, palace decoration, artistic genres such as still life—suggests that Spain was anything but isolated from the main currents of European art.[61] Jonathan Brown, moreover, has written extensively about the art patronage and collecting of Philip IV (1621–65), emphasizing the extent to which this monarch's preference for painting not only created the largest—and most envied—art collection in seventeenth-century Europe but also served to make painting, as opposed to sculpture and tapestries, the most respected of all the arts.[62] In this perspective, paintings that Prescott might have used as evidence for the decadence of Spain's monarchs are being refigured as markers of the nation's cultural vitality and intellectual interchange, two qualities that it supposedly lacked.

Another sign of shift in the paradigm is a willingness to challenge the old teleology of Spanish economic backwardness and decline. David Ringrose, for example, has recently achieved this by disaggregating the Spanish economy into various "urban networks" and reevaluating its performance (upward) in the eighteenth and nineteenth century through the use of data that previously escaped attention. His findings are by no means definitive, but they do suggest that the Spanish economy was far more modern—and changing—than earlier historians of the Spanish economy, Hamilton included, would have ever allowed.[63]

The old teleology is also suffering at the hands of scholars less interested in the ups and downs of the Spanish empire than in exploring the internal character of Spanish society and culture.[64] The monolithic "Spain" that Prescott and other historians presented is currently being dismantled as scholars examine it microhistorically, divide it into regions, examine peripheries rather than centers, and peer into the minutiae of everyday life.[65] Furthermore, Prescott's stereotype of the Spaniard as the cruel conquistador and the indolent priest is gradually giving to way to a more varied picture of individuals of vastly different stripes—of a Catalan artisan coping with the rigors of plague, a young Castilian girl who dreamed of a better life, university-educated clergymen struggling to educate their parishioners in the rudiments of the faith, Basque shipbuilders diligently attempting to make a profit in difficult times, olive-growing nobles determined to introduce commercial agriculture into southern Spain, and courtiers who, together with other European office seekers, made the promotion of their family and their friends a primary concern.[66] Even more pronounced is the growing tendency to temper Prescott's image of omnipotent Habsburg absolutism with that of a monarchy whose power was circumscribed by numerous constitutional and juridical checks.[67]

Today's historians of Spain can therefore be likened to iconoclasts, bent on breaking the old images that had formed the Spain envisioned by their fore-bears and, in some cases, their own teachers as well. One young historian, partly on the basis of new evidence gleaned from the Spanish state archives in Siman-cas, is suggesting that Juana la Loca (1479–1555)—the "mad" queen from whom the feeblemindedness of the later Habsburgs allegedly derived—may not have been nearly as deranged as Prescott had assumed.[68] Similarly, recent work on Pedro Ciruelo, a humanist attached to the University of Alcalá de Henares, is challenging the traditional notion that the Inquisition and state censorship successfully crushed all that was innovative and vital in sixteenth-century Spanish thought.[69] Meanwhile, another scholar—a Canadian, in this instance —has transformed the bullfight—once emblematic of Spanish cruelty, and for the romantics, of the Spanish picturesque—into a symbol of Spanish commer-cial enterprise as he documents the way in which nineteenth-century promot-ers of the corrida transformed what had been a popular festival into a com-mercialized, professionalized, mass-market spectator phenomenon.[70] But perhaps the most significant shift in Prescott's paradigm involves the study of the role of religion in Spanish history. Of particular interest here is the work of scholars who have used the trial records of the Inquisition not, as Lea would have done, to emphasize the institution's cruelty but rather as a vast histori-cal data base containing materials that can be used to explore a culture far more complex and far more heterodox than previously imagined.[71] In addition, what Prescott, Lea, Hamilton, and others derided as the fanaticism and superstition of Spanish Catholicism is being converted into a vital, constituent force that drew its energy from village society and provided the peasantry with ways of managing the difficulties of everyday life.[72]

Yet, for all these signs of a shift in the paradigm, old perceptions die hard. Inherited notions of Spanish exceptionalism, for example, help to explain why so many historians in the United States still write and teach European history as if the Continent, as Dumas suggested, actually stopped at the Pyrenees. Habits of a similar sort may also be responsible for the tendency of U.S. scholars who actually write Spanish history to employ what John Elliott has described as an "excessively 'internalist' approach" to their subject.[73] Too fre-quently, it seems, Spain remains something of an aberration, a nation inher-ently different from the rest of Europe, albeit a Europe that is generally (and erroneously) equated with either England or France. With respect to absolut-ism, for example, a recent study rightly highlighted the political fragmenta-tion that resulted in Castile from the Habsburg's "sale of towns" but did so without reference either to central Europe or even to neighboring Portugal where the local, institutional, and corporate checks on Leviathan were just as important as those in Castile.[74] This "excessively 'internalist' approach" applies equally well to other questions—discrimination toward women and religious minorities, ethnic and linguistic differences, regional rivalries—all of which are still conceived as if rooted to what Prescott would have called Spain's national "spirit," what Lea described as its national "trait," or what is now described as "*españolismo*," Spanishness.[75] Otherwise, it is difficult to understand why a new and fascinating study of Spanish funereal customs would attribute, albeit obliquely, Spain's economic decline in the seventeenth century to the excessive investment in masses arising from the Spaniards' alleged—and supposedly ongoing—fascination with death.[76]

The personal stakes involved in Spain's presentation in exceptional terms are none too clear. Yet for many historians, and possibly many other Americans as well, Spain remains a nation whose leaders only recently declared it hostile to the political and religious pluralism championed by the United States. Spain, therefore, still remains something of an Other, a nation synonymous with the ominous figure of Torquemada (as in Mel Brooks's 1981 film *The History of the World, Part I*) and connected, inextricably perhaps, to Columbus, to Cortés, and to the other conquistadors now credited with the extermination of the civilizations as well as the ecology of the New World, as in Kirkpatrick Sale's *The Conquest of Paradise* (1991) and other publications occasioned by the quincentenary of 1992. In fact, it turns out that many books and celebrations associated with this anniversary did little more than spark a revival of Black Legend themes, thus making it even easier for Americans, even those with little of the anticlericalism evinced by Prescott and Lea, to distance themselves from both Spain and its history. In part, this distancing can be attributed to lack of mass emigration from Spain to the United States, in part to Americans' inability to associate Spain with anything except the pathetic figure of Don Quixote tilting at windmills or the more picturesque elements of its culture—bullfighting, castles, flamenco, gypsies, and the like.[77] Racism too plays a role here, as few Americans truly understand the difference between Spaniards—known traditionally in Latin America as *gachupines* or *peninsulares*—and the Latinos in search of citizenship in the United States. It is no accident, therefore, that the best-selling Spanish olive oil in the United States is marketed under the assumed Italian name of *Pompeian*. Put simply, a gap still separates the two societies, reinforcing (mutual) misunderstanding and increasing the temptation on the part of all Americans to view Spaniards through a Prescottian lens.

Yet something has definitely changed since Prescott first published *Ferdinand and Isabella* more than 150 years ago. In the nineteenth century U.S. historians regarded Spain as their opposite. They looked back to its seventeenth century as the exemplum of everything that America was not: backward, enervated, a society in decline. Few scholars understood—or cared to understand—that "decline" was a relative rather than an absolute concept. Even fewer compared Spanish accomplishments, economic and otherwise, to those of nations other than Great Britain, France, Germany, or the United States. Fortunately, such rigid thinking is increasingly a thing of the past, and the changeover is accompanied by the understanding that imperial power is rarely long lasting. Increasingly popular, therefore, is the view that Spain's American empire—with a life span of more than three centuries—needs to be examined in terms of the factors that contributed to its longevity instead of those that contributed to its decay. Even so, the image of Spanish decline remains tempting, and even in our own day, in the guise of Paul Kennedy's best-selling *The Rise and Fall of the Great Powers* (1987), seventeenth-century Spain, though still at arm's length, has acquired new meaning. Prescott's Protestant bias is absent; so too are references to Spaniards' instinctive abhorrence for trade. What remains is the portrait of a mismanaged kingdom top heavy with military expenditures, and through this image Kennedy literally transforms a society that Prescott conceived as the antithesis of the United States into a specter of what an overextended America might soon become.[78]

Viva Prescott!

A final anecdote, trivial perhaps, will serve to illustrate that the topic of Spanish decline retains much of the popularity that Prescott described in 1843. Not long ago, during a routine medical examination in Baltimore, my physician, upon learning about my interest in Spain's history, asked me for a quick summary of what I considered the reasons for the nation's decline as a great power. The question, he avowed, was one he had long considered but one to which he had never received a satisfactory answer. As a historian I tried to explain decline as a relative phenomenon, briefly alluding to Kennedy's book, the seventeenth century's general crisis; I even asked him to consider carefully what he meant by the term *decline* itself. The exam was soon over, my shirt buttoned up, but my measured response to the query was clearly inadequate. My doctor's view of Spain is surely different from Prescott's, yet, without saying so directly, what he wanted was an answer with at least one of the elements that Prescott would have assigned to Spanish decline: the rise of the Inquisition, the expulsion of the Jews, the defeat of the Spanish Armada, the leadership qualities of the Habsburg monarchs, possibly even Spanishness itself. Generalizations are risky, but the incident does seem to suggest that Spanish history possesses a popular appeal far greater than most universities and colleges are likely to admit. More important, it serves as a reminder that the identity of the United States may still depend on national histories that are both conceived and constructed as antithetical to its own.

Notes

1. *The Literary Memoranda of William Hickling Prescott,* ed. C. Harvey Gardiner, 2 vols. (Norman: University of Oklahoma Press, 1961), 1:68.

2. Ibid., 1:51, 66, 97. These memoranda are invaluable for understanding Prescott's methodology.

3. For his biography see George Ticknor, *The Life of William Hickling Prescott* (Boston: Ticknor and Fields, 1864); Stanley T. Williams, *The Spanish Background of American Literature* (New Haven, Conn.: Yale University Press, 1955), 2:78–121; and, most recently, C. Harvey Gardiner, *William Hickling Prescott: A Biography* (Austin: University of Texas Press, 1969). Also useful is the *Hispanic American Historical Review* 100 (1959), which contains a brief biography ("William Hickling Prescott: The Man and His Work") by R. A. Humphreys and other articles celebrating Prescott's achievement.

4. Thomas Jefferson to John Rutledge, July 18, 1788, Paris, cited in Edward Dumbauld, *Thomas Jefferson American Tourist* (Norman: University of Oklahoma Press, 1946), 148. Jefferson's Spanish books are cataloged in *Thomas Jefferson's Library: A Catalog with Entries in His Own Order,* ed. James Gilreath and Douglas L. Wilson (Washington, D.C.: Library of Congress, 1969). For the teaching of Spanish in the colonial era, see J. R. Spell, "Early Interest in Spanish in New England (1815–1835)," *Hispania* 29 (1946): 326–51.

5. The term *Black Legend* was coined by the Spanish scholar Julián Juderías in *La leyenda negra: Estudios acerca del concepto de España en el extranjero* (Madrid: Tip. de la Revista de Archivos, Bibliotecas, y Museos, 1914). The most recent survey of Black Legend history is Ricardo García Carcel, *La leyenda negra: Historia y opinion* (Madrid: Alianza Editorial, 1992). English titles on the subject include Charles Gibson, ed., *The Black Legend: Anti-Spanish Attitudes in the Old World and the New* (New York: Knopf, 1971); William S. Maltby, *The Black Legend in England: The Development of Anti-Spanish Sentiment, 1558–1660* (Durham, N.C.: Duke University Press, 1971); and Philip W. Powell, *Tree of Hate* (New York: Basic Books, 1971). For the *arbitristas* see J. H. Elliott, "Self-Perception and Decline in Early Seventeenth-Century Spain," in his *Spain and Its World, 1500–1700* (New Haven, Conn.: Yale University Press, 1989), 241–61.

6. John Campbell also wrote about Spain in *The Present State of Europe* (London: Longman and C. Hitch, 1753), 304–56, as well as in volumes 20–22 of *The Modern Part of the Universal History,* 44 vols. (London: J. Batley et al., 1759–66), which Prescott read in 1827–28 (see *Literary Memoranda of Prescott,* 1:88, 94).

7. William Robertson, *History of America,* 7th ed. (London: Printed for A. Strathern et al., 1796), bk. 8, p. 245. Prescott, who first read this book in 1827, noted that "*Robertson's* extensive subject is necessarily deffient in connection," but he praised the au-

thor for his "sagacious reflections," "clear & vigorous diction," and for his "interesting, philosophical, and elegant narrative" (*Literary Memoranda of Prescott*, 1:82–83).

8. Jedidiah Morse, *The American Universal Geography*, 3d ed., 2 vols. (Boston: Isaiah Thomas and Ebenezer T. Andrews, 1796), 2:397; Morse, *The American Universal Geography*, 6th ed., 2 vols. (Boston: I. Thomas and E. T. Andrews, 1812), 2:349. See also the entries for Spain in Morse's *Geography Made Easy*, 5th ed. (Boston: Isaiah Thomas and Ebenezer T. Andrews, 1796).

9. Quoted in Marie Leonore Fell, *The Foundations of Nativism in American Textbooks, 1783–1860* (Washington, D.C.: Catholic University of America Press, 1941), 37. See also Francis Fitzgerald, *America Revisited: History Schoolbooks in the Twentieth Century* (Boston: Little, Brown, 1972), 49.

10. "Trait of Spanish Character," *North American Review* 5 (1817): 54.

11. *The Letters of Henry Wadsworth Longfellow*, ed. Andrew Hilen, 6 vols. (Cambridge, Mass.: Belknap Press of Harvard University Press, 1966), 1:122. In 1833 Longfellow, who taught literature at Bowdoin College, published an essay, "Spanish Language and Literature," in the *North American Review* 36 (1836): 316–34. Longfellow was subsequently professor of modern languages at Harvard from 1834 to 1855. For his interests in Spanish literature see Iris L. Whitman, *Longfellow and Spain* (New York: Instituto de las Españas en los Estados Unidos, 1917), and Williams, *Spanish Background*, 2:152–79. For the various meanings attached to the term *Oriental*, see Edward Said, *Orientalism* (New York: Pantheon, 1978).

12. *The Complete Works of Washington Irving*, ed. Wayne R. Kime and Andrew B. Meyers (Boston: Twayne, 1984), vol. 4: *Journals and Notebooks*, 140. Irving had been invited to Madrid by Alexander Hill Everett, the U.S. consul, to translate the first volume of Manuel Fernández de Navarrete, *Colección de los viajes y descubrimientos que hicieron por mar los españoles desde el fin del siglo XV*, 5 vols. (Madrid: Imprenta Real, 1825–37).

13. *The Papers of William Hickling Prescott*, ed. C. Harvey Gardiner (Urbana: University of Illinois Press, 1964), 8.

14. *Literary Memoranda of Prescott*, 1:65.

15. Ibid., 1:66.

16. David Levin, *History as Romantic Art: Bancroft, Prescott, Motley, and Parkman* (Stanford, Calif.: Stanford University Press, 1959).

17. *Literary Memoranda of Prescott*, 1:97.

18. William H. Prescott, *Biographical and Critical Miscellanies* (New York: Kelmscott Society, 1845), 118. His review of Irving first appeared in 1829. Prescott resented Irving's intrusion into a subject he regarded as his own, once confiding to a friend that Irving "helped himself to two of the biggest and fattest slices" in the Catholic Monarchs' reign. See Prescott to Jarold Sparks, February 1, 1841, in *The Correspondence of William Hickling Prescott, 1833–1847*, ed. Roger Wolcott (Boston: Houghton Mifflin, 1925), 204.

19. Prescott's view of the Inquisition was undoubtedly influenced by Juan Antonio Llorente, *A Critical History of the Inquisition of Spain* (New York: G. C. Morgan, 1826).

The book, originally published in French, *Histoire critique de l'inquistion d'espagne* (Paris: Treuttel et Würtz, 1817–18), was first mentioned by Prescott in 1826. See *Literary Memoranda of Prescott,* 1:74, 96.

20. *Literary Memoranda of Prescott,* 1:140.

21. William H. Prescott, *History of the Reign of Philip II of Spain,* 3 vols. (Boston: Phillips, Sampson, 1855), 1:3, 145, 554. Many of Great Britain's nineteenth-century Hispanists held similar views of Spain, the Inquisition in particular. See, for example, Richard Ford, *A Hand-Book for Travellers in Spain and Readers at Home,* ed. Ian Robertson (1845; rpt., Carbondale: Southern Illinois University Press, 1966), 1:418–21. The history of British Hispanism, along with the American, remains to be written, although the latter may be approached through Williams, *Spanish Background.*

22. Prescott's negative view of empire, derived in part from Adam Smith, helps to explain his determined opposition to the Mexican War and the annexation of Texas. See, for example, Prescott to George Sumner, April 1, 1847, where he refers critically to "our mad ambition for conquest" (*Correspondence of Prescott,* 627). See also the letter to Sumner cited in note 24.

23. Prescott, *History of the Reign of Philip II,* 2:446.

24. For Prescott's political views see Gardiner, *William Hickling Prescott,* 95, 166–68. That history offered Prescott a refuge from domestic politics became patently clear in 1846, when in the midst of writing *History of the Conquest of Peru* and with specific reference to the Mexican War, Prescott wrote the following to George Sumner: "I am sick of our domestic troubles. . . . I take refuge from them in Peruvian hills, where the devildoms I read of—black enough—have at least no reference to ourselves" (May 15, 1846, in *Correspondence of Prescott,* 597).

25. For the myth of national character, with particular reference to Spain, see Julio Caro Baroja, *El mito del caracter nacional* (Madrid: Seminarios y Ediciones, 1970).

26. Prescott to Pascual de Gayangos, December 21, 1843, in *Correspondence of Prescott,* 428. Prescott's *Conquest of Mexico,* first translated into Spanish in 1846, was also a commercial success in Spain. However, the book's reception there, its influence on subsequent Spanish historiography, and its particular appeal among Spanish *liberales* sympathetic to Prescott's anticlericalism and hostility to absolutism awaits detailed study.

27. George Ticknor, *Life, Letters, and Journals of George Ticknor* (Boston: James R. Osgood, 1876), 198–99.

28. James Russell Lowell to Thomas Hughs, November 17, 1879, and Lowell to W. D. Howells, May 2, 1879, both in *Letters of James Russell Lowell,* ed. Charles Eliot Norton (New York: Harper and Bros., 1893), 2:235, 241. Lowell was professor of modern languages at Harvard from 1855 until 1877, when he was named minister to Spain. For his life see Martin Duberman, *James Russell Lowell* (Cambridge, Mass.: Houghton Mifflin, 1966). Lowell's friend Henry Adams regarded Spain as equally out of date after he visited the country in 1879. See *The Letters of Henry Adams,* ed. J. C. Levenson, 6 vols. (Cambridge, Mass.: Belknap Press of Harvard University Press, 1982), 2:379–83. Fran-

cis Parkman had a similar reaction during his visit in 1887. See *Letters of Francis Parkman*, ed. Wilbur R. Jacobs, 2 vols. (Norman: University of Oklahoma Press, 1960), 2:200.

29. On nineteenth-century medievalism in the United States, see T. J. Jackson Lears, *No Place of Grace: Ante-Modernism and the Transformation of American Culture, 1889–1920* (New York: Pantheon, 1981), 141–81; John Fraser, *America and the Patterns of Chivalry* (Cambridge: Cambridge University Press, 1982); and Robin Fleming, "Picturesque History and the Medieval in Nineteenth-Century America," *American Historical Review* 100 (October 1995): 1061–94.

30. Ticknor's literary achievement is summarized in Williams, *Spanish Background*, 46–77. See also Thomas J. Hart Jr., "George Ticknor's *History of Spanish Literature: The New England Background*," *Publications of the Modern Language Association,* March 1954, pp. 76–88. Note that the first comprehensive survey of French literature by U.S. scholars was William A. Nitze and E. Preston Duncan, *A History of French Literature* (New York: Henry Holt, 1922).

31. George Ticknor, *History of Spanish Literature,* 6th ed. (New York: Gordian Press, 1965), 413, 417, 433. In comparison, Friedrich Bouterwek's *History of Spanish Literature,* published initially (in German) between 1805 and 1817 (first English edition, 3 vols., London: David Bogue, 1847), noted that Spain's literary "spirit" survived until 1665 when it finally succumbed to a "vicious system of government" (3:254).

32. John Lothrop Motley, *Rise of the Dutch Republic* (London: Oxford University Press, 1906), vol. 1, pt. 1, 132.

33. Ibid., vol. 2, pt. 6, 449, 454.

34. This literature is best approached through Williams, *Spanish Background*, 1:113–17, and Powell, *Tree of Hate,* 122–25.

35. Henry Charles Lea to W. E. H. Lecky, April 9, 1888, quoted in E. S. Bradley, *Henry Charles Lea* (Philadelphia: University of Pennsylvania Press, 1931), 328.

36. Lea by this date had also published several scholarly articles on Spanish history, including "The First Castilian Inquisitor," which appeared in the premier issue of the *American Historical Review* 1 (1896): 46–50.

37. Henry Charles Lea, "The Decadence of Spain," *Atlantic Monthly* 82 (1898): 36–46. Lea's subsequent book on the Inquisition reaffirmed his belief in the negative effects of the Holy Office upon Spanish society. See Lea, *A History of the Inquisition of Spain,* 4 vols. (New York: Macmillan, 1906–7), esp. 4:438, 472–513. For Lea's scholarship in general see Bradley, *Henry Charles Lea;* Williams, *Spanish Background,* 1:153–57; and Edwards Peters, "Henry Charles Lea and the 'Abode of Monsters,'" in *The Spanish Inquisition and the Inquisitorial Mind,* ed. Angel Alcalá (Boulder, Colo.: Atlantic Research and Publications, 1987), 577–608.

38. Archer M. Huntington, *A Note-Book in Northern Spain* (New York: G. P. Putnam's Sons, 1898), 2.

39. Huntington, *Note-Book in Northern Spain,* 2, 7.

40. Charles B. Curtis, *Velázquez and Murillo: A Descriptive and Historical Catalogue . . .* (New York: J. W. Bouton, 1883), 1.

41. Chandler Post, *A History of Spanish Painting,* 14 vols. (Cambridge, Mass.: Harvard University Press, 1930–66), 1:10. This work was preceded by E. W. Washburn, *The Spanish Masters* (New York: G. P. Putnam's Sons, 1884); Charles H. Caffin, *The Story of Spanish Painting* (New York: Century, 1910); Georgiana Goddard King, *The Way of Saint James,* 3 vols. (New York: G. P. Putnam's Sons, 1920); John Kenneth Conant, *The Early Architectural History of the Cathedral of Santiago de Compostela* (Cambridge, Mass.: Harvard University Press, 1926); and A. Kingsley Porter, *Spanish Romanesque Sculpture* (Florence: Pantheon, 1928).

42. Cited in Gregory M. Pfitzer, *Samuel Eliot Morison's Historical World* (Boston: Northeastern University Press, 1991), 24.

43. Roger B. Merriman, *The Rise of the Spanish Empire in the Old World and the New,* 4 vols. (New York: Macmillan, 1918–34), 4:678.

44. Bernard Moses, "The Economic Condition of Spain in the Sixteenth Century," *Journal of Political Economy* 1 (1893): 513–94.

45. Sarah E. Simons, "Social Decadence," *Annals of the Academy of Political and Social Science* 18 (1901): 251–79.

46. Clarence H. Haring, *Trade and Navigation between Spain and the Indies in the Time of Hapsburgs* (Cambridge, Mass.: Harvard University Press, 1918), 131, 179; Charles H. Cunningham, "The Institutional Background of Spanish Economic History," *Hispanic American Historical Review* 1 (1918): 24. More balanced assessments of Spain's colonial achievement came from the Yale professor Edward G. Bourne, *Spain in America* (New York: Harper, 1906), and the University of California at Berkeley's Herbert E. Bolton, "The Mission in Spanish-American Colonies," *American Historical Review* 23 (1917): 42–61. Bolton's article, a response by a historian of the American West to the Turner thesis on the role of the frontier in American history, actually referred to "Spain's frontiering genius." The image of Spain in twentieth-century U.S. scholarship on colonial Latin America awaits detailed study.

47. Julius Klein, *The Mesta: A Study in Spanish Economic History, 1273–1836* (Cambridge, Mass.: Harvard University Press, 1920), 244, 352. Klein in a later publication repeated his contention that the reign of Ferdinand and Isabella marked the beginning of a "long and sordid chronicle of decay and of royal exploitation." See Klein's "Medieval Spanish Guilds," in *Facts and Factors in Economic History* (New York: A. M. Kelley, 1932), 187. For a new, less-critical look at the Mesta, see Carla Rahn Phillips and William D. Phillips Jr., *Spain's Golden Fleece: Wool Production and the Wool Trade from the Middle Ages to the Nineteenth Century* (Baltimore: Johns Hopkins University Press, 1997).

48. Earl J. Hamilton, *American Treasure and the Price Revolution in Spain, 1501–1650* (Cambridge, Mass.: Harvard University Press, 1934), 303.

49. Earl J. Hamilton, "The Decline of Spain," *Economic History Review* 8 (1935): 168–79.

50. John Crow, *Spain: The Root and the Flower* (1963; rpt., Berkeley, Calif.: University of California Press, 1985), 340. Crow, a specialist in Spanish literature, had been educated in pre-Franco Spain.

51. The volumes referred to are John B. Wolf, *The Emergence of the Great Powers, 1685–*

1715 (New York: Harper, 1951), 123, and Carl J. Friedrich, *The Age of the Baroque, 1610–1660* (New York: Harper, 1952), 226.

52. The first of John E. Longhurst's books were *Erasmus and the Spanish Inquisition: The Case of Juan de Valdés* (Albuquerque: University of New Mexico Press, 1950), and *Luther and the Spanish Inquisition: The Case of Diego de Uceda, 1528–29* (Albuquerque: University of New Mexico Press, 1953).

53. My own experiences reinforce the point. In 1964, when I first considered studying the history of Habsburg Spain, opportunities to do so in the United States were extremely limited, as few research universities had specialists in Spanish history. Notable exceptions were Joan Connelly Ullman (University of Washington) and Stanley Payne (UCLA; he moved to Wisconsin in 1968), both of whom worked primarily in the twentieth century. Early modernists associated directly with Spain were Richard Herr (University of California at Berkeley), author of *The Eighteenth-Century Revolution in Spain* (Princeton, N.J.: Princeton University Press, 1958); Charles H. Carter (Tulane University), a diplomatic historian whose *The Secret Diplomacy of the Habsburgs, 1598–1625* (New York: Columbia University Press, 1964) had only just appeared; and Ruth Pike, then assistant professor at Hunter College and still writing her *Enterprise and Adventure: The Genoese in Seville and the Opening of the New World* (Ithaca, N.Y.: Cornell University Press, 1966). In order to pursue my studies I found my way to Cambridge University in England where I completed my doctoral dissertation in 1968 under the direction of John H. Elliott.

54. Noteworthy U.S. contributions to twentieth-century Spanish history included Stanley G. Payne, *Falange: A History of Spanish Fascism* (Stanford, Calif.: Stanford University Press, 1961), as well as his *Politics and the Military in Modern Spain* (Stanford, Calif.: Stanford University Press, 1967); Gabriel Jackson, *The Spanish Republic and the Civil War, 1931–1939* (Princeton, N.J.: Princeton University Press, 1965); and Joan Connelly Ullman, *The Tragic Week: A Study of Anti-Clericalism in Spain, 1875–1912* (Cambridge, Mass.: Harvard University Press, 1967). Interest in the eighteenth century increased following the 1958 publication of Richard Herr's important book *The Eighteenth-Century Revolution in Spain.*

55. Garrett Mattingly, *The Armada* (Boston: Houghton Mifflin, 1959), 401. Note that in his other books, notably *Renaissance Diplomacy* (London: Cape, 1955), Mattingly lauded the many innovations introduced by the Spain of Ferdinand and Isabella. The first major postwar publication on medieval Spain by a U.S. scholar was Robert I. Burns, *The Crusader Kingdom of Valencia: Reconstruction on a Thirteenth-Century Frontier,* 2 vols. (Cambridge, Mass.: Harvard University Press, 1967).

56. Many of Castro's ideas about Spanish culture may be found in his influential study *The Structure of Spanish History,* trans. Edmund King (Princeton, N.J.: Princeton University Press, 1954), a book that elicited considerable criticism. See especially Eugenio Asensio, *La España imaginada de Américo Castro* (Barcelona: Ediciones el Albir, 1976).

57. Representative titles include Ruth Pike's book on the role of the Genoese in the Atlantic economy (see note 53) and its companion piece, *Aristocrats and Traders: Sevillian Society in the Sixteenth Century* (Ithaca, N.Y.: Cornell University Press, 1972); David

R. Ringrose, *Transportation and Economic Stagnation in Spain, 1750–1850* (Durham, N.C.: Duke University Press, 1970); and my *Students and Society in Early Modern Spain* (Baltimore: Johns Hopkins University Press, 1974).

58. The Society for Spanish and Portuguese History held its first annual meeting in 1969 and currently possesses more than 400 members, of whom approximately 300 are from the United States. Such a figure is dwarfed by that of the French Historical Society, with a membership of almost 2,000. As for funding, the Program for Cultural Cooperation between the Spanish Ministry of Culture and United States Universities, which was founded in 1983 at a base in Minneapolis, offers inducements for the study of Spanish history in the form of publication subsidies and grants for travel and research. For a decade the program worked in conjunction with the U.S.-Spanish Joint Committee for Cultural and Educational Exchange, an agency connected with the Council for the International Exchange of Scholars, but the joint committee is now defunct.

59. Of crucial importance was John H. Elliott's essay, "The Decline of Spain," *Past and Present* 20 (1961): 52–75, now reprinted in Elliott, *Spain and Its World*, 217–40.

60. Post, *History of Spanish Painting*, 1:23.

61. Representative titles include Jonathan Brown, *Images and Ideas in Seventeenth-Century Spanish Art* (Princeton, N.J.: Princeton University Press, 1978) and his *Velázquez: Painter and Courtier* (New Haven, Conn.: Yale University Press, 1986); Jonathan Brown and John H. Elliott, *A Palace for a King: The Buen Retiro and the Court of Philip IV* (New Haven, Conn.: Yale University Press, 1980); William B. Jordan and Peter Cherry, *Spanish Still Life from Velázquez to Goya* (London: National Gallery Publications/ Yale University Press, 1995); and Cathy Wilkinson-Zerner, *Juan de Herrera: Architect to Philip II of Spain* (New Haven, Conn.: Yale University Press, 1993).

62. Jonathan Brown, *Kings and Connoisseurs* (New Haven, Conn.: Yale University Press, 1995).

63. David R. Ringrose, *Patterns, Events, and Preconceptions: Revisiting the Structures of Spanish History, 1700–1900* (Cambridge: Cambridge University Press, 1995). David Sven Reher employed a similar methodology in his *Town and Country in Pre-Industrial Spain* (Cambridge: Cambridge University Press, 1992).

64. Representative titles include Ida Altman, *Emigrants and Society: Extremadura and America in the Sixteenth Century* (Berkeley: University of California Press, 1989); Jodi Bilinkoff, *The Avila of Santa Teresa: Religious Reform in a Sixteenth-Century City* (Ithaca, N.Y.: Cornell University Press, 1989); Carla Rahn Phillips, *Ciudad Real, 1500–1700: Growth, Crisis, and Readjustment in the Spanish Economy* (Cambridge, Mass.: Harvard University Press, 1979); and David Vassberg, *Land and Society in Golden Age Castile* (Cambridge: Cambridge University Press, 1984).

65. The Catalan periphery has proved especially attractive in view of the many differences between this part of the peninsula and Castile, the region that Prescott and indeed most U.S. historians have identified with Spain. Catalonia is the focus of James S. Amelang's *Honored Citizens of Barcelona: Patrician Culture and Class Relations* (Princeton, N.J.: Princeton University Press, 1986) and Peter Sahlins's *Boundaries: The Making of France and Spain in the Pyrenees* (Berkeley: University of California Press, 1989).

66. I allude here to James S. Amelang, *Journal of the Plague Year: The Diary of the Barcelona Tanner Miquel Parets, 1651* (New York: Oxford University Press, 1991); Richard L. Kagan, *Lucrecia's Dreams: Politics and Prophecy in Sixteenth-Century Spain* (Berkeley: University of California Press, 1990); Sara T. Nalle, *God in la Mancha: Religious Reform and the People of Cuenca, 1500–1650* (Baltimore: Johns Hopkins University Press, 1992); Carla Rahn Phillips, *Six Galleons for the King of Spain: Imperial Defense in the Early Seventeenth Century* (Baltimore: Johns Hopkins University Press, 1986); and James Boyden, *The Courtier and the King: Ruy Gómez de Silva, Philip II, and the Court of Spain* (Berkeley: University of California Press, 1995).

67. Helen Nader examines the checks limiting the exercise of monarchical power in Castile in *Liberty in Absolutist Spain: The Habsburg Sale of Towns, 1516–1700* (Baltimore: Johns Hopkins University Press, 1991). I expect that the formulation of the Habsburg monarchy as more limited than absolute will soon establish itself as a new orthodoxy. Such ideas are also manifest in such recent publications as Ruth Mackay's *The Limits of Royal Authority: Resistance and Obedience in Seventeenth-Century Castile* (Cambridge: Cambridge University Press, 1999) and Antonio Feros's *Kingship and Favoritism in the Spain of Philip III, 1598–1621* (Cambridge: Cambridge University Press, 2000).

68. Bethany Aram, "Joanna 'the Mad's' Signature: The Problem of Invoking Royal Authority, 1505–1507," *Sixteenth-Century Journal* 29 (1998): 331–58.

69. See Lu Ann Homza, *Religious Authority in the Spanish Renaissance* (Baltimore: Johns Hopkins University Press, 2000).

70. Adrian Shubert, *Death and Money in the Afternoon: A History of the Spanish Bullfight* (New York: Oxford University Press, 1999).

71. Among a recent avalanche of revisionist works on the Inquisition, notable studies by U.S. authors include Stephen Haliczer's *Inquisition and Society in the Kingdom of Valencia* (Berkeley: University of California Press, 1990), and E. William Monter's *Frontiers of Heresy: The Spanish Inquisition from the Basque Lands to Sicily* (Cambridge: Cambridge University Press, 1990).

72. See William Christian Jr., *Local Religion in Sixteenth-Century Spain* (Princeton, N.J.: Princeton University Press, 1981) and its companion study, *Apparitions in Late Medieval and Renaissance Spain* (Princeton, N.J.: Princeton University Press, 1981). Both employ an anthropological approach to Spanish Catholicism, emphasizing its local character and functional importance. See also Sara T. Nalle, *Mad for God: Bartolomé Sánchez, the Secret Messiah of Cardenete* (Charlottesville: University Press of Virginia, 2001).

73. Elliott, *Spain and Its World*, 69.

74. I refer to Nader, *Liberty in Absolutist Spain* (see note 67), which, its lack of a comparative focus notwithstanding, is an important and provocative book. James Amelang has offered similar criticism in his review of this and other recent books (primarily by U.S. authors) on various aspects of early modern Spain. See *Journal of Modern History* 65 (June 1993): 357–74.

75. Crow, *Spain: The Root and the Flower*, 9.

76. Such ideas are expressed in the introduction and conclusion of Carlos Eire's *From

Madrid to Purgatory: The Art and Craft of Dying in Sixteenth-Century Spain (Cambridge: Cambridge University Press, 1995).

77. These stereotypes may be found in James Michener's *Iberia* (New York: Random House, 1968), but they are by no means unique to the United States. Encouraged in part to foment tourism in the 1960s by the Spanish Ministry of Tourism, they can also be found in Bartolomé Bennassar's *L'homme espagnol* (Paris: Hachette, 1975); English translation, *The Spanish Character* (Berkeley: University of California Press, 1979).

78. For Kennedy's discussion of Spanish decline, see Paul Kennedy, *The Decline of the Great Powers* (New York: Random House, 1987), 31–55.

Contributors

Rolena Adorno is a professor of Latin American literature at Yale University. She is the author of *Guaman Poma: Writing and Resistance in Colonial Peru* (1986, 2000) and (with Patrick Charles Pautz) of *Alvar Núñez de Cabeza de Vaca: His Account, His Life, and the Expedition of Pánfilo de Narváez* (1999) and the editor (with Kenneth J. Andrien) of *Transatlantic Encounters: Europeans and Andeans in the Sixteenth Century* (1991).

Jonathan Brown is the Caroline and Milton Petrie Professor of Fine Arts at New York University. His many publications include *Velázquez: Painter and Courtier* (1986), *The Golden Age of Painting in Spain* (1991), *Kings and Connoisseurs: Collecting Art in Seventeenth-Century Europe* (1995), and (with Carmen Garrido) *Velázquez: The Technique of Genius* (1998).

Mitchell Codding has served as director of The Hispanic Society of America in New York since 1995. He is the coeditor of *Maps, Charts, Globes: Five Centuries of Exploration* (1992), *Facsimiles from an Illuminated Hebrew Bible of the Fifteenth Century at The Hispanic Society of America* (1993), and *Coastal Charts of the Americas and West Africa from the School of Luis Teixeira, circa 1585* (1993).

James D. Fernández is an associate professor in the Department of Spanish and Portuguese at New York University and the director of its King Juan Carlos I of Spain Center. He is the author of *Apology to Apostrophe: Autobiography and the Rhetoric of Self-Representation in Spain* (1992) as well as numerous articles on nineteenth- and twentieth-century Spanish literature.

Thomas R. Hart Jr. is a professor emeritus of comparative literature and romance languages at the University of Oregon and editor emeritus of *Comparative Literature*. His books include *Cervantes and Ariosto: Renewing Fiction* (1989) and *Cervantes' Exemplary Fictions: A Study of the Novelas Ejemplares* (1994).

Richard L. Kagan is a professor of history and romance languages and literatures at Johns Hopkins University. He is the author of *Students and Society in Early Modern Spain* (1974), *Lawsuits and Litigants in Castile, 1500–1700* (1981), *Lucrecia's Dreams: Politics and Prophecy in Sixteenth-Century Spain* (1990), and *Urban Images of the Hispanic World, 1493–1793* (2000) and the editor of *Spanish Cities of the Golden Age* (1989) and (with Geoffrey Parker) *Spain, Europe, and the Atlantic World* (1995).

Janice Mann is chair of the Department of Art and Art History at Bucknell University. Her main research interests are the architecture and sculpture of eleventh-century Spain and the historiography of that field. Among her publications in the area of historiography is "Romantic Identity, Nationalism, and the Understanding of the Advent of Romanesque Art in Christian Spain" in *Gesta*. She is writing a book on Arthur Kingsley Porter and the American discovery of medieval art.

Louise K. Stein is a professor of musicology at the University of Michigan at Ann Arbor. A specialist in the history of Spanish music of the Renaissance and baroque periods, her publications include *Songs of Mortals, Dialogues of the Gods: Music and Theatre in Seventeenth-Century Spain* (1993) and (with Howard M. Brown) *Music in the Renaissance* (1999). She also served as a collaborator on the 1999 critical performing edition of *La púrpura de la rosa*, the first opera produced in the New World (Lima, 1701).

Index

Index

Index

Index

Index

Index

Index

Hispanisms

The University of Illinois Press
is a founding member of the
Association of American University Presses.

Composed in 10.5/13 Adobe Minion
with Minion display
by Jim Proefrock
at the University of Illinois Press
Manufactured by Thomson-Shore, Inc.

University of Illinois Press
1325 South Oak Street
Champaign, IL 61820-6903
www.press.uillinois.edu